THE STATE OF THE WORLD'S CHILDREN
1986

Oxford University Press, Walton Street,
Oxford OX2 6DP
London Glasgow New York Toronto Delhi Bombay Calcutta Madras Karachi Kuala Lumpur Singapore Hong Kong Tokyo Nairobi Dar es Salaam Cape Town Melbourne Auckland and associates in Beirut Berlin Ibadan Mexico City Nicosia

Oxford is a trade mark of Oxford University Press
Published in the United States by Oxford University Press, New York

British Library Cataloguing in Publication Data
The state of the world's children.
1. Children—Care and hygiene
613' 0432 RJ101
ISBN 0–19–828537–X cloth
ISBN 0–19–828536–1 ✓ paperback

ISSN 0265–718X

Library of Congress Cataloging in Publication Data
The state of the world's children—Oxford
New York: Oxford University Press for UNICEF v.:ill.; 20cm. Annual. Began publication in 1980.
1. Children—Developing countries—Periodicals. 2. Children—Care and hygiene—Developing countries—Periodicals. I. UNICEF.
HQ 792.2.S73 83–647550 362.7'1'091724

UNICEF, 866 U.N. Plaza, New York, N.Y. 10017 U.S.A.
UNICEF, Palais des Nations, CH. 1211
Geneva 10, Switzerland.

Cover and design: Miller, Craig and Cocking, Woodstock, U.K.
Charts and tables: Stephen Hawkins, Oxford Illustrators, Oxford, U.K.
Typesetting and Printing: Burgess & Son (Abingdon) Ltd, U.K.

Edited and produced for UNICEF and Oxford University Press by P & L Adamson, Benson, Oxfordshire, U.K.

THE STATE
OF THE WORLD'S
CHILDREN
1986

James P. Grant
Executive Director of the
United Nations Children's Fund
(UNICEF)

PUBLISHED FOR UNICEF

Oxford University Press

CONTENTS

I THE STATE OF THE WORLD'S CHILDREN 1986

**Immunization
leads the way**

Demand for vaccines has trebled in the last two years and many nations are moving within striking distance of immunizing the vast majority of their young children by the UN target date of 1990. New strategies for mobilizing all organized resources and all possible channels of communication are enabling immunization programmes to reach a much greater proportion of a nation's families. Meanwhile, progress in promoting oral rehydration therapy means that the lives of well over a million children have been saved – in the last twelve months – by the recent spread of two of the least expensive of all child protection methods.

**Reaching
all children**

ORT and immunization are therefore leading the way towards a revolution in child survival and development – made possible by a range of low-cost methods including growth checking, improved weaning, the promotion of breast-feeding, and the prevention of vitamin A deficiency. But the potential of this new knowledge can only be realized if ways and means can be found to put it at the disposal of all parents. This is the 'social breakthrough' which many countries are also now making.

**The benefits
for women**

Applying low-cost ways of protecting the lives of children depends, in the main, on the women of the developing world – most of whom already have too long a working day. But most of the basic child survival strategies would also result in considerable savings of money, time, and energy for mothers – and so help to bring about improvements in the lives and health of women.

**The self-health
potential**

Because it depends on parents as front-line health workers, the move towards a child survival revolution is part of a wider shift in the concept of health care. In both industrialized and developing worlds, the next generation of advances in human health will come about not through more medical technology but through ordinary people knowing more and doing more about their own and their families' health. This process is basic to primary health care, but its potential should not be used as an excuse for governments to abrogate responsibility for essential services and for the social and economic causes of ill health.

**Children and
world development**

The physical and mental development of children is intimately related to the social and economic development of nations. Today's children must not be made to bear the burden of difficult economic times. Broadly applicable and low-cost methods of enabling parents to improve child health are now available. With present knowledge, and with international support, it is therefore possible to achieve, in the next few years, one of the greatest goals which mankind has ever set for itself – basic protection for the lives and normal development of all its children.

II LIFELINES

Extracts and summaries from recent research and writing on cost-effective strategies for protecting the lives and normal development of the world's children

III STATISTICS

Economic and social statistics on the nations of the world, with particular reference to children's well-being.

PANELS

TEXT FIGURES

PREFACE

The range of issues which could legitimately be included under the title *The State of the World's Children* is clearly wider than the focus of this year's report.

In particular, the effects of economic recession continue to reverberate through the world's poorest communities as increasing unemployment and falling real wages bear down most heavily on those who spend the highest percentage of their income on necessities – the poor. At the same time, government cut-backs on such vulnerable items of expenditure as health clinics and food subsidies also leave exposed those who are most dependent on such services – again the poor. As a result, progress for children is being slowed down in some nations and thrown into reverse in others.

Last year a special UNICEF study – *The Impact of World Recession on Children* – detailed the process by which the heaviest burden of economic recession is in most cases passed on to those who are least able to sustain it. This year, evidence of the continuing impact of that process on the lives of the poorest children is continuing to come in (see, for example, Figs. 21 and 22 in the main text of this report).

Most immediately, this crisis for the poorest is surfacing in sub-Saharan Africa where, as all the world has witnessed, the failure of development – and of the rains – has pushed hundreds of thousands of families to the margins of survival and beyond. Because of the diversity and complexity of this crisis, UNICEF has this year published a separate report on the problems now facing the poorest communities, and particularly the children, of Africa.

Such problems have been exacerbated rather than caused by immediate pressures such as recession and drought. Even in years of normal rainfall, many millions of children are growing up deprived of what most people reading this page would consider to be basic necessities of life – adequate food, clean water, safe sanitation, basic education, and competent health care.

But faced with a myriad diverse problems, and an almost hopeless shortage of resources for dealing with them, those charged with the responsibility of trying to bring about practical improvements in the lives of children have no choice but to make some decisions about priorities.

The problems of poverty are infinitely complex. The causes, as is well known, are political, economic, social, historical, geographical, agricultural... But what is required now is not a more refined and sophisticated analysis of poverty but more practical and effective ways of empowering people to liberate themselves from it.

To achieve that means identifying practical starting-points. For the problem is less likely to succumb to a complete and comprehensive set of solutions which have to be realized all at once than to a structured series of achievable goals which, while being important in themselves, also help to lead the way, step by achievable step, towards more comprehensive long-term progress.

To find such beginnings, it is vital to pool the accumulated knowledge of a generation of development efforts and to use this past experience to sharpen the attack on present problems.

In the process, many of those most closely involved are coming to the conclusion that we are now faced not only with great difficulties but also with a very great opportunity. For it is clear that there are now several low-cost and potentially very powerful ways of protecting the lives and the normal development of many millions of children in ways which are politically and financially feasible even in such difficult economic times. The coincidence of technical and social advances which has created this opportunity is relatively new, and its potential is therefore vastly underexploited.

That is why this year's State of the World's Children report focuses on a limited number of achievable aims such as universal immunization, the spread of oral rehydration therapy (ORT), and the low-cost prevention of malnutrition – aims which are relevant to the needs of children now as well as to longer-term goals.

In this context, the reasons for selecting these particular priorities may be simply explained:-

◯ Taken together, vaccine-preventable infections, diarrhoeal disease, and poor nutritional health, constitute by far the most important problem in any objective consideration of the 'state of the world's children'. Common to almost all developing countries, they account for the great majority of the 15 million infant and child deaths in the world each year and are the principal cause of both physical and mental disability.

◯ The technology and the knowledge to solve these problems are now available at a cost which most nations and most families could afford even in hard economic times – especially with a modicum of international support.

○ Most important of all, the techniques and knowledge involved are cheap and simple enough for parents and communities to be principal participants. In other words, it is now possible to recruit literally hundreds of millions of effective health workers with the highest possible motivation for the protection of children's lives and growth.

○ Most low-income countries have, in recent years, built up the channels of communication and organization which now make it possible to reach, inform, and support the vast majority of families in applying today's knowledge. This is the 'social advance' which, combined with recent advances in knowledge creates a new potential.

Only by involving millions of people in knowing more and demanding more and doing more about their own and their families' health can low-cost technical solutions such as ORT and immunization fulfil that potential. But precisely for that reason, the promotion of these basic health actions can also be an important contribution towards participation in more comprehensive primary health care strategies. For as this year's report shows, working towards a vital and immediate goal such as immunization for all children offers an almost unparalleled opportunity for popular, professional, and political mobilization of a kind and on a scale which is relevant to almost any other kind of progress against poverty, ill health, and underdevelopment.

For all of these reasons, this report focuses on this new opportunity – and on those specific and concrete measures which can contribute to long-term solutions at the same time as doing something on a very significant scale – *for children in need today*.

As the panels interspersed throughout this year's report show, these strategies are constantly being refined by reality. For although techniques such as immunization represent common solutions to common problems, the more difficult task of mobilizing a society to actually bring about the immunization of all its children is a task which is inevitably specific to each country and each culture.

The important common factor is therefore not the technique but the approach. There are important goals which can be achieved for children now. There are ways in which every one of us can help to advance those goals. And in doing the possible today, we take one more step towards achieving the impossible tomorrow.

Within Human Reach~
a future for Africa's children

This special UNICEF report documents the range of problems behind the decline of living standards in Africa and describes the practical steps which can and are being taken to confront the crisis. The major argument of the report is that the neglect of the 'human dimension' is a major cause of Africa's present problems and that solutions will depend on finding ways to liberate and enhance the contribution which individual men and women make to the development of the continent.

The report is available in English and French, free of charge, from UNICEF Headquarters (866 UN Plaza, New York, NY 10017, USA), from UNICEF Headquarters for Europe (Palais des Nations, CH-1211 Geneva 10, Switzerland), from national and regional UNICEF offices, and from National Committees for UNICEF.

I

THE STATE OF THE WORLD'S CHILDREN 1986

James P. Grant

Immunization leads the way

Reaching all children

The benefits for women

The self-health potential

Children and world development

Infant Mortality Rate

The infant mortality rate (IMR) is the number of deaths before the age of one year – per 1,000 live births.

Figures given for the infant mortality rates of particular countries, in both the text and statistical tables of this report, are estimates prepared by the United Nations Population Division on an internationally comparable basis, using various sources. In some cases, these may differ from national estimates.

Most national IMR figures are collected every five or ten years as part of the national census and do not yet reflect the impact of any of the recent campaigns and child survival programmes mentioned in the text.

Immunization leads the way

Despite the continuing crisis in Africa,* there is dramatic progress to report this year on the struggle to improve the lives and the health of many millions of the world's children.

In the last eighteen months, several nations have doubled and trebled their levels of immunization against the vaccine-preventable diseases which were killing almost 4 million children a year and leaving another 4 million permanently disabled. Throughout 1985, world-wide demand for vaccines has been running at approximately three times its 1983 level[1] and the annual number of child deaths being prevented by vaccines is now estimated to be approaching one million a year (Fig. 1).

With the continuing and rapid uptake of oral rehydration therapy (ORT),** the new figures mean that the lives of well over one million children have been saved – in the last twelve months – by the recent spread of two of the least expensive of all child protection techniques.

Immunization for all by 1990

This sudden acceleration in immunization coverage has been made possible, in large part, by new strategies for reaching a much greater pro-

portion of a nation's parents than are normally touched by modern health services. Together with improved vaccine technologies and the training of many thousands of immunization teams in the 1980s, these new outreach strategies now offer a new chance to bring immunization to the vast majority of the world's children within the next few years.

Acting on this information, the Secretary-General of the United Nations has taken the unprecedented step of writing to the presidents or prime ministers of all 159 member states, drawing their attention to this new potential and asking for their personal support for the goal of immunization for all the world's children by the year 1990 (Fig. 2).***

Several nations are already moving to within striking distance of that goal. As against an average of less than 5% immunization coverage for the children of the developing world only a few years ago, coverage rates against some or all of the vaccine-preventable diseases have recently been pushed to 60%, 70% or even 80% in Pakistan and Turkey, in El Salvador and the Dominican Republic, in Bolivia and Brazil, in Colombia and Nicaragua, in Burkina Faso and Lesotho, in Saudi Arabia and Zimbabwe, and in parts of India and China.

---

* UNICEF has this year published a special report on the continuing crisis facing the children of Africa (see box in preface for details).

** Oral rehydration therapy (ORT) is a simple technique for preventing and treating the diarrhoeal dehydration which claims the lives of approximately 4 million children each year and is the leading cause of child death in the developing world

(see Lifelines: ORT). UNICEF estimates that the spread of the technique is already saving over 500,000 children's lives each year.

*** The target of providing immunization for all children by 1990 was adopted by the World Health Assembly in 1977 and is one of the key elements of the World Health Organization's overall goal of 'Health for All by the year 2000'.

Immunization: a new surge forward

1

Examples from the last eighteen months of achievements and commitments in the struggle towards the immunization of all children by 1990:-

○ In **India**, Prime Minister Rajiv Gandhi has announced this year that immunizing every child born in India is to be the 'living memorial' to the memory of his mother, the late Indira Gandhi. When that monument is built (target date 1990), it will save the lives of over 1 million Indian children each year. To date, districts in Delhi and Karnataka have used new approaches to raise their immunization rates from less than 20% to more than 80% in little more than a year.

○ In **China**, the last eighteen months have seen immunization rates lifted from 40% to 90% in parts of five provinces with a total population of 90 million – and the President has this year announced that this achievement will be extended to reach 85% immunization coverage (against six major diseases) in *all provinces* of China by the end of 1988.

○ In **El Salvador** this year, three separate days of cease-fire were observed by both sides in the civil war so that two-thirds of the nation's 400,000 unimmunized young children could be protected against five major infectious diseases on three National Vaccination Days. Bringing the first Vaccination Day to an end on 3 February 1985, El Salvador's President Duarte announced: "*We have had a day of peace, a day of life, a day of hope*" (see panel 4).

○ In **Turkey** two months ago (September 1985), the President launched the first of three ten-day campaigns to immunize 80% of the nation's young children against five of the major vaccine-preventable diseases by the end of the year. In the first eight days of the first round (11 to 18 September 1985), at least 3 million children were vaccinated (see panel 3).

○ In the **Dominican Republic**, where national immunization days have already vaccinated almost 95% of children against polio and measles, full immunization against five of the major diseases of childhood is expected to be achieved by the middle of 1986. (see panel 7).

○ In **Brazil**, the largest immunization campaigns ever held have virtually eliminated poliomyelitis by immunizing 20 million children on each of two National Vaccination Days every year for the last five years. In 1984, measles and DPT vaccines were added and nation-wide coverage has now risen to over 60% with a target of 95% for 1985. To reach that target will mean immunizing more than 25 million children against five of the major vaccine-preventable diseases (see panel 10).

○ In **Colombia**, following the successful 1984 campaign which reached almost 800,000 children and raised the nation's immunization rates to more than 75% for five of the vaccine-preventable diseases, President Belisario Betancur has announced that: "*We are going to keep immunizing our children until there are no more cases of vaccine-preventable diseases*" (see panel 5).

○ In **Ecuador**, the first phase of a national vaccination campaign went into action on 26, 27 and 28 October (1985) with the aim of immunizing 80% of the nation's under-ones (and 95% of those aged one to five) against the six major vaccine-preventable diseases.

○ In **Bolivia** this year, immunization rates have been pushed to over 70% for polio and to 85% for diphtheria, whooping cough, and tetanus (see panel 8).

○ In **Pakistan**, the percentage of children under five fully immunized against the major diseases has risen from less than 5% in the early 1980s to approximately 65% today (with coverage rates of 80% in the Punjab but considerably lower in areas like Baluchistan). According to the World Health Organization: "*the lives of more than 170,000 infants will be saved yearly ... as a result of the stepped up immunization campaign now under way in Pakistan*". (see panel 11).

(Continued in next panel)

In all, approximately 40 nations with approximately two-thirds of the developing world's children are rapidly accelerating their vaccination programmes and now have a realistic chance of immunizing almost all their young children by the year 1990.

Immunization and oral rehydration therapy (ORT) are therefore beginning to lead the way towards the revolution in child survival which has been the main theme of this report for the last three years.

It is a revolution made possible by new knowledge about how parents themselves might take action to protect the lives and normal development of their children against some of the worst effects of the poverty into which they are born.

It is a revolution based on a small number of relatively simple and inexpensive methods which are now known to exert powerful leverage on child health – methods like ORT and immunization, breast-feeding and improved weaning, maintaining vitamin A levels and checking weight gain, avoiding low birth-weights and leaving longer intervals between births.

It is a revolution which could reduce child deaths and child malnutrition by half, in many nations of the world, over the next seven or eight years.

It is a revolution which could help to reduce births as well as deaths and so contribute to the slowing down of population growth (see panel 25).

It is a revolution which is already beginning in several of the nations whose commitment and achievements are briefly summarized in the panels on the left-hand pages of this year's report.

Above all, it is a revolution which depends largely on the commitment of a nation's leadership and on the mobilization of a nation's organized resources in order to break present knowledge and techniques out of the medical chest and put them into the hands of many millions of parents.

Recent achievements in extending immunization coverage from less than 20% to more than 80% of a nation's children therefore have a double importance for the 'state of the world's children'. Not only have these sharply accelerated immunization programmes saved tens of thousands of lives and prevented tens of thousands of disabilities, they have also pioneered new ways of *taking known solutions to basic health problems and putting them at the disposal of the majority of those who need them.*

And it is precisely this task – the task of making available on a massive scale *what is already known* – which could now help to bring about a

Fig. 1 Estimated annual numbers of deaths and prevented deaths from vaccine-preventable diseases (children under 5)

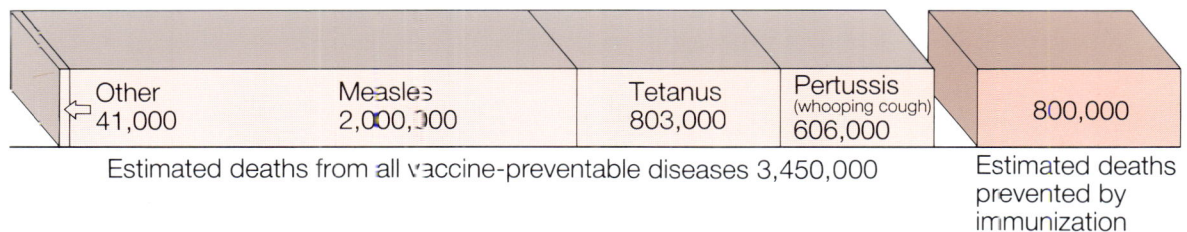

Other 41,000	Measles 2,000,000	Tetanus 803,000	Pertussis (whooping cough) 606,000	800,000

Estimated deaths from all vaccine-preventable diseases 3,450,000

Estimated deaths prevented by immunization

Note: The above estimates are calculated from data relating to years between 1981 and 1984.

This year, substantially improved data on the numbers of vaccine-preventable deaths have been published by the World Health Organization. Previously, the figure of approximately 5 million a year has been most commonly used – based on estimates made by WHO in the mid-1970s. The improved and updated data (applying to the year 1983), based on a narrower definition which admits only those deaths directly attributable to specific vaccine-preventable diseases, shows that

immunization coverage has increased to the point where vaccines are preventing approximately 800,000 deaths each year. As a result of these changes, WHO now estimates that vaccine-preventable diseases kill a total of 3,450,000 children each year in the developing world. The new figure does not include China, where generally well-nourished child populations and improved levels of vaccine coverage probably mean that deaths from vaccine-preventable diseases are proportionally less than in most developing nations.

Source : Report of the Expanded Programme on Immunization, Global Advisory Group Meeting, Copenhagen, November 1985.

Immunization: a new surge forward (cont.)

2

○ In **Sri Lanka**, where an expanded programme of immunization has already reached well over half the nation's children, the President and Prime Minister have launched a new drive (6 September 1985) and committed the government to universal immunization before the end of 1986 (see panel 18).

○ In **Viet Nam**, the national immunization programme is being accelerated to reach an extra 573,000 children in the last three months of 1985 (in addition to the 353,000 children reached each year by regular immunization programmes), so taking the national coverage rate to nearly 70% for the first time.

○ In **Nigeria**, a campaign has begun (October 1984) to repeat, nation-wide, the successful trials in Ondo state where coverage was raised from less than 10% to more than 80% in less than twelve months. Initial results from the capital cities of all 19 states of Nigeria show that eight to ten times as many children are being vaccinated each month as were reached in the the corresponding months of 1984 (see panel 17).

○ In **Tanzania**, immunization coverage has been pushed to 56% for polio, 82% for measles, and 54% for tuberculosis.

○ In the **Sudan**, Africa's largest country, 200,000 children in the capital city of Khartoum have been immunized this autumn (1985) and the Minister of Health has announced that "*the Khartoum campaign marks the beginning of a campaign to reach 90% of Sudan's children by 1990*". On present plans, 80% of Sudan's children will be immunized against the biggest killer – measles – by March 1986.

○ In **Ethiopia**, the Minister of Health has launched (13 February 1985) a campaign to immunize every child in Addis Ababa against the main vaccine-preventable diseases and every pregnant woman against tetanus. By September 1985, over 50% of the city's children had already been reached (see panel 15).

○ In **Somalia**, a presidential directive (9 June 1985) has requested all regions to prepare for immunization drives to repeat the successes in the cities of Hargeisa and Mogadishu where more than 80% of children under two have been immunized this year (see panel 14).

○ In **Syria**, nurses and students working in their vacations have succeeded in lifting immunization coverage from 13% to 63% in the Ragga area – one of the most remote and inaccessible governorates in the country.

○ In **Burkina Faso**, a presidential decision of 19 September 1984 led to the mounting of operation 'Vaccination Commando' in which Committees for the Defence of the Revolution throughout the country brought almost 65% of the nation's children to be immunized with the 'single-shot' vaccines against measles, meningitis, and yellow fever. The usual epidemics, in which thousands of children die and tens of thousands of children fall seriously ill, have thereby been prevented – giving the health services a breathing-space in which to build towards a system of regular immunizations for all children against the major vaccine-preventable diseases (see panel 6).

○ In **Suriname**, immunization coverage has risen to over 80% after the proclamation of the National Vaccination Act which now requires that all children under the age of one be immunized against diphtheria, whooping cough, tetanus and polio.

○ In the Gulf, **Oman** has reached an immunization level of 70% by means of campaigns in July and October 1985. The United Arab Emirates has now reached 80% coverage of its children. And Saudi Arabia has moved its immunization rates from 33% in 1980 to 75% in 1984.

○ In Kabul, **Afghanistan**, this year, immunization rates among the capital city's children have been pushed from less than 20% to more than 80% against all six vaccine-preventable diseases.

revolution in child survival and protect the normal growth and development of many millions of today's children and tomorrow's citizens. For in an often unjust world, a major improvement in the protection afforded to the children of the poor is unlikely to come about through any steep rise in incomes for the poorest third of the human family for at least the next ten or fifteen years. Protecting lives and health, during that time, will therefore continue to depend, for the most part, on the kind of care which families and communities are able to provide. And it is in that setting that recent breakthroughs assume such importance. For it is now possible for families themselves to quite

drastically increase their children's chances of survival and normal growth – if the ways and means can be found to put that knowledge at the disposal of the majority.

In the process, large numbers of parents are also becoming involved in putting flesh and blood on the bones of the primary health care idea. By knowing more and demanding more and doing more about such basic health strategies as immunization and ORT, large numbers of people are finding a practical starting-point from which to progress, step by achievable step, towards the larger goal of more comprehensive primary health

Fig. 2 Immunizing all children by 1990: progress achieved and progress required

The target of universal child immunization by 1990 was adopted by the World Health Assembly in 1977 and is one of the key elements in the World Health Organization's overall goal of 'Health for All by the year 2000'.

The lighter tints show the actual rate of progress (1970–83) in immunizing children (under one year) in the developing world. The heavier tint indicates the required rates of progress (1983–90) if the target of universal immunization is to be met by 1990. 1983 is the latest year for which international data is available.

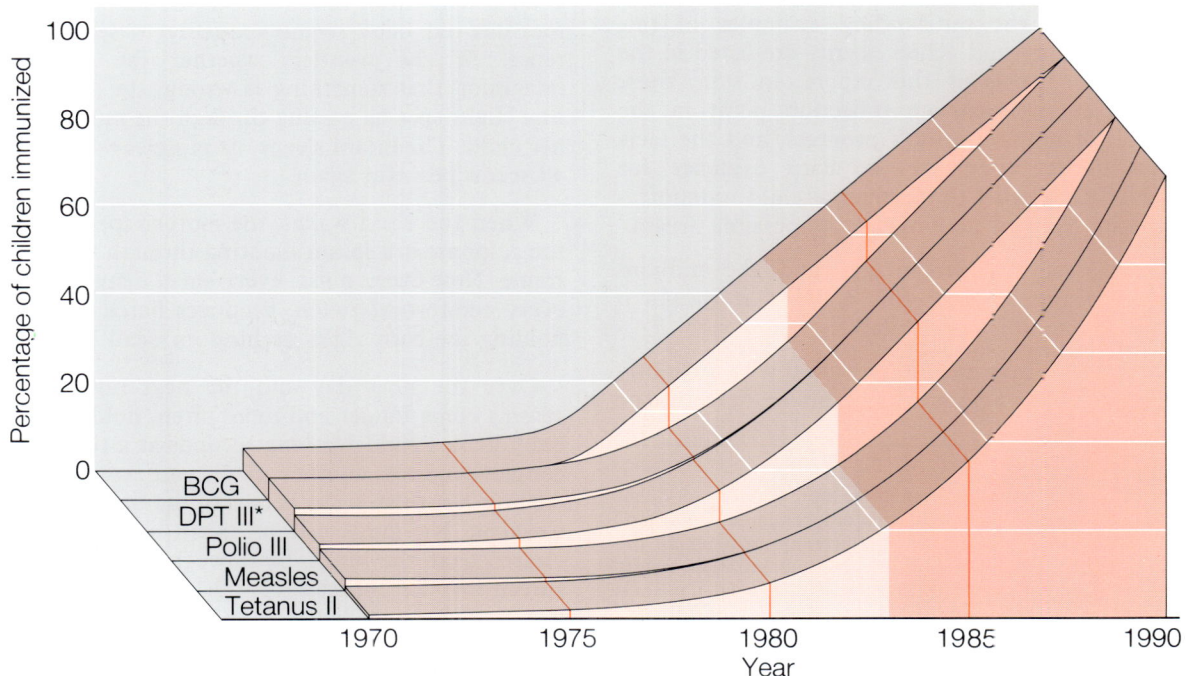

Note: To promote universal immunization, the World Health Organization (WHO) launched its Expanded Programme on Immunization (EPI) in 1974.
* Numerals indicate the number of vaccinations required for immunization.
Source: Report of the Expanded Programme on Immunization, Global Advisory Group Meeting, Copenhagen, November 1985.

DPT = Diphtheria, Pertussis (whooping cough), Tetanus. Tetanus II: Two tetanus injections are required in pregnancy to protect against tetanus of the newborn which accounts for the vast majority of infant tetanus deaths in the developing world. Tetanus II coverage therefore applies to pregnant women.

care and a greater degree of control over their own and their families' health.

This year's *State of the World's Children* report therefore turns first to an account of this upsurge in immunization rates, of how they are being achieved, and of what lessons they might hold for putting other basic child protection techniques at the disposal of the majority of parents.

The meaning of immunization

Immunization coverage today ranges between 20% and 40% of the developing world's children (Fig. 4) – despite the theoretical availability of vaccines to a much greater proportion of their populations. But in the last eighteen months to two years, several nations have effectively committed themselves to immunization coverage of a different order of magnitude.

Some of the outstanding examples of this commitment – and achievement – are listed in the first two panels of this report. In sum, these examples represent an inflection point in the graph of immunization's progress, and the facts and figures cited are the hard evidence for UNICEF's belief that universal child immunization by 1990* is no longer an impossible dream.

But lest the percentages and the millions become meaningless, this is what it means if immunization is not available:-

At first it may mean that a child who is slightly malnourished begins to lose his or her appetite

and feel the beginnings of a small fever. After a day or two, the fever is higher, appetite is gone, coughing begins, and a vivid florid rash is appearing on the skin as if from nowhere. As the days pass, the diarrhoea begins, the skin dries, and the rash spreads until the eyes also become infected and inflamed. By the second week, the rash has begun to peel, leaving open raw sores on the skin, and by now the coughing is persistent and prolonged and the diarrhoea is unremitting. No food is being taken, and water, salts, and nutrients are draining from the weakened body. Dehydrated to the point where the thirst is unbearable and racked by coughing fits which are becoming too weak to clear the lungs but too strong for the muscles of the small heart, the lights of the body begin to go out.

In this way, measles killed 2 million children in 1985.

Or it may mean that a mother notices that her four-day-old baby seems suddenly to feel more tense. As she wonders whether she is only imagining that something is wrong, she sees the first slight spasms passing through the muscles of her child. The infant sleeps, its muscles relax, and all seems peaceful again.

When the child wakes, the mother speaks and the response is a spasm shooting through the tiny frame. Now every noise, every small disturbance, every comforting touch, produces fierce spasms, holding the baby rigid, arching its small back.

Over the next day and the next night, the spasms come longer and more often, holding the baby locked rigid for long seconds at a time. All contact produces another spasm and even breast-feeding has to stop. In between, the baby visibly weakens. No fluids can be taken in, no mucus cleared from the lungs. By now, the spasms have spread to the muscles of the mouth and the mother is looking down on an agonized grin.

Another night and day and the spasms are making impossible demands on the baby's heart. Now the whole body is being held rigid, the tiny fists clenched, the face fixed in grimace, the back arched, the stomach locked like iron, the small chest clamped down against all breathing. For thirty slow seconds the small body is locked in this

---

* In practice no country, even in the industrialized world, has ever achieved 100% immunization of its children. 'Universal' immunization is therefore best interpreted as implying the ideal that no child should be denied immunization against tuberculosis, diphtheria, pertussis (whooping cough), tetanus, poliomyelitis, and measles. It is, however, generally agreed that when immunization coverage reaches a figure of 80% or more then disease transmission patterns are so severely disrupted as to provide a degree of protection even for the remaining children who have not been immunized (providing that the majority of the unimmunized population are not concentrated into areas where overall coverage consequently remains low).

It is also important that children are immunized during the first year of life and that levels of immunization are sustained so that each new generation is protected.

vice, then slowly relaxes, muscles twitching as they loosen their grip and the spasms recede.

A gentle, comforting touch and immediately a total body spasm locks the child rigid all over again, as if it were repelled by its mother's love.

In this way, tetanus killed almost a million infants in 1985.

Or it means that a child, in any ordinary village or neighbourhood, begins to sniffle or cough with what seems like the beginnings of another ordinary cold. Over the next week, very slowly and almost unnoticed, the cough becomes deeper and more persistent. Suddenly, it is no longer ordinary. The coughing now is so rapid-firing, a stuttering engine pumping air from the lungs, that there is no time to take any inward breath as more and more air is hammered out until there is none at all left to fuel another cough and the child slumps forward, chest collapsed. Slowly, with a shudder, the child breathes in, relaxes the tension, and sits up again with sweating skin and frightened eyes.

At the next fit, the parents too are growing frightened as the child's face darkens and the coughing goes on and on until it seems that an inward breath will never be taken. Now, the whole body of the child is geared to the task of

expelling air until, at the end, the child finally inhales uncontrollably, swallowing coughed-up mucus from the bronchial tree and choking from the vomit drawn into the lungs. With every fit now comes more vomiting as the muscles of the stomach contract with the coughing and force everything, food, drink, milk, back through the throat and nose – only to be inhaled chokingly as that inward breath is finally taken.

Weakened by vomiting and coughing, struggling to breathe through lungs blocked by mucus

Fig. 3 Percentage of pregnant women immunized against tetanus

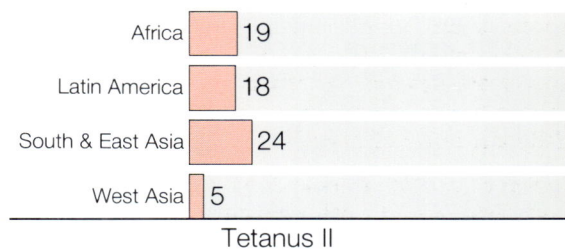

Africa	19
Latin America	18
South & East Asia	24
West Asia	5

Tetanus II

Note: Two tetanus injections are required in pregnancy to protect against tetanus of the newborn which accounts for the vast majority of infant tetanus deaths in the developing world.

Source: WHO (39 countries), UNICEF field offices (31 countries). Population Division of the United Nations (for population data).

Fig. 4 Percentage of children immunized in the first year of life

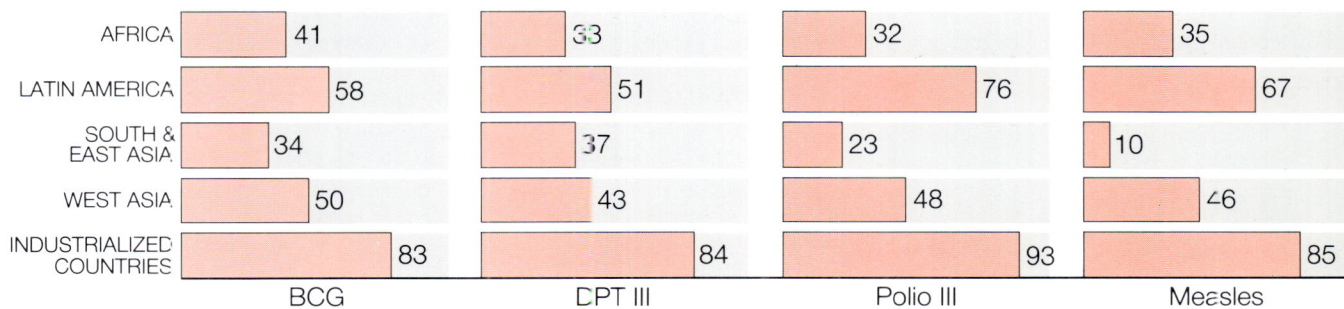

	BCG	DPT III	Polio III	Measles
AFRICA	41	33	32	35
LATIN AMERICA	58	51	76	67
SOUTH & EAST ASIA	34	37	23	10
WEST ASIA	50	43	48	46
INDUSTRIALIZED COUNTRIES	83	84	93	85

Note: The difference between the above percentages and the figures published in a similar table in last year's State of the World's Children report are accounted for by changes in the classification of countries by region and by recent improvements in data collection which have yielded more reliable and up to date figures for immunization coverage.

Source: WHO (67 countries), UNICEF field offices (52 countries). Population Division of the United Nations (for population data).

West Asia = Asia west of Iran
South & East Asia = rest of Asia (except China which is not included in this table).

DPT = Diphtheria, Pertussis (whooping cough), and Tetanus. In some countries DPT and polio are given in two doses only. In countries where measles vaccination is given after the age of 12 months, the figure used is the percentage coverage of 1 to 5 year olds.

Turkey: to immunize 5 million

3

"*Through this campaign, the high infant mortality rate in this country will drop,*" promised Turkish President Kenan Evren during a 11 September ceremony at which he immunized the first two infants in the country's nation-wide immunization drive. In three ten-day periods, the nation aims to immunize more than 80% of its 5 million under-fives against the diseases which are now killing more than 500 Turkish children every week.

From the same platform, Prime Minister Turgut Ozal announced that the campaign was "*the most important programme started by this government*". As he spoke, the valis (governors) of all of Turkey's 67 provinces were launching the campaign nation-wide by immunizing children in each provincial capital.

Immediately after the launch in Ankara, government ministers and deputy ministers from Egypt, Pakistan, the Sudan, and Syria met with President Evren to discuss immunizing all the children of their five nations before the end of this decade. Meanwhile, across Turkey itself, 35 million doses of vaccine had arrived at the 45,000 immunization stations and all 536 *kaymakams* (local district heads) were also immunizing children.

Over the next eight days (with 70% of the vaccination stations having reported in as this account goes to press), a total of 3.2 million children were vaccinated – two-thirds of the nation's under-fives.

If such progress can be sustained in the second and third rounds (October and November 1985) then Turkey will be on course for universal immunization by the end of 1986 – well ahead of the 1990 target date.

After briefings at UNICEF headquarters in New York, the Centers for Disease Control in Atlanta, and a visit to see Colombia's immunization campaign in action, a high-level Turkish government team returned to Ankara in April 1985 to make the key decisions for the campaign. The most important of those decisions was to attempt the mobilization of all the nation's resources to increase both the availability of, and *the demand for*, immunization.

The result, this September, was an unprecedented national effort headed by the Ministry of Health. For the first time ever, all 67 valis met together in Ankara – to be briefed on the leadership roles expected of them. The Turkish armed forces put their vehicles and communications facilities at the campaign's disposal. Turkish television gave the equivalent of $10 million in airtime and reached 30 million homes. National radio broadcast eight to ten immunization reminders a day and an average of six articles a day appeared in the press.

A total of 5,000 Rotarians from over 60 clubs – plus many members of the Turkish Red Crescent societies – volunteered their time and their cars. The national meat and fish company provided refrigerated long-distance trucks for transporting vaccines. A private company paid for 5 million 'passports to health' containing a child immunization record, a growth chart, and advice on basic child health care.

In the months leading up to September, imams and muhtars in 40,000 villages and neighbourhoods, helped by primary school teachers and their pupils, made sure that every household knew about the campaign. And as the date for the first round neared, sermons on immunization were preached in 54,000 mosques.

Achieving and sustaining full immunization is seen in Turkey as an important practical contribution towards the building of primary health care and the long-term development of the country. For as Health Minister Mehmet Aydin commented at the outset of the campaign:-

"*The time has come to take immediate action in the reduction of child mortality and the protection of child health, so as to entrust Turkey to a dynamic generation with better physical and spiritual health.*"

and food, the child begins another fit, uncontrollable coughing pumping the air unremittingly from the lungs, finally forcing the chest to collapse, slumping the child forward until the fit ends and the house is suddenly silent. Only this time, the child does not breathe in.

In this way, whooping cough killed more than half a million children in 1985.

The cost of protection against all this is approximately $5 per child. The cost of immunizing all children, and saving more than 3 million children from dying in this way, is approximately $500 million per year* – slightly less than the cost of three advanced fighter planes.

The two breakthroughs

Based on information available as of mid-1985, those countries accelerating their immunization programmes towards the 1990 goal include:- Argentina, Bangladesh, Bhutan, Bolivia, Botswana, Brazil, Burkina Faso, Chile, China, Colombia, Democratic Yemen, the Dominican Republic, Ecuador, Egypt, El Salvador, Ethiopia, Haiti, India, Indonesia, Iraq, Jordan, Lesotho, Nicaragua, Nigeria, Pakistan, Peru, Panama, Rwanda, Saudi Arabia, Senegal, Somalia, Sri Lanka, the Sudan, Suriname, Syria, Tanzania, Trinidad and Tobago, Turkey, the United Arab Emirates, Uruguay, Viet Nam, Yemen, and Zimbabwe.

This sudden surge of progress, a surge which will bring many nations within striking distance of universal immunization, is happening in the mid-1980s because of two different breakthroughs.

The first is a 'supply breakthrough' brought about by more heat-stable vaccines, by more reliable 'cold chains', by continuing research and training, by the installing of more equipment and supplies, and by the growing numbers of health workers trained in the management and organization of immunization programmes.[2] In the 1980s, there has been solid progress on all these fronts. The latest freeze-dried measles vaccines, for example, remain potent for up to three weeks even in tropical temperatures.[3] Cold chains of refrigeration – based on kerosene, bottled gas, electricity, solar energy, or ice boxes – are now in place in most nations. Most important of all, many thousands of immunization teams have been trained and fielded since the WHO launched the Expanded Programme on Immunization (EPI) in 1974. To date, almost 17,000 people from over 100 nations have been trained on courses sponsored by WHO and UNICEF and many times more have been trained by governments themselves. China alone, for example, has drawn on EPI programmes to train over 100,000 health workers in immunization management.[4]

But the second and equally important advance is the 'demand breakthrough' by which some thirty or forty nations are now mobilizing, on a massive scale, to make immunization available in practice and not just in theory. And it is political commitment to new ways of reaching out to inform and support the *majority of parents* which now offers new hope for putting into practice other child protection strategies on a scale which is commensurate with the problem.

To bring vaccination to people, to inform many tens of millions of parents of the when and the where and the why of immunization, and to get many more millions of children to the right place at the right time on several separate occasions each year, is a massive organizational and communications task which usually far exceeds the capacity and the experience of over-stretched medical services. In most developing nations, those medical services reach only about 20% or 25% of the people and are inevitably more concerned with meeting demand than creating it.

For all these reasons, comprehensive immunization coverage has risen only slowly, often reaching only one in five of a nation's children, even when vaccination services have been theoretically available to the majority for many years.[5]

Clearly, something extra is needed, some new dynamic, some new way of forcefully taking the

---

* Although more resources are needed if the goal of universal immunization by 1990 is to be met, finance is by no means the only restraint. If universal immunization is to be achieved and sustained, then it is also essential to find ways of overcoming the problems of management, training, supervision, education of the public, and organization of permanent immunization programmes.

El Salvador: children – a zone of peace

4

Salvadorian government and rebel soldiers briefly stopped shooting each other in 1985 while the nation confronted a common foe – the diseases which kill some 20,000 small children a year and maim many thousands more.

Three perilous day-long pauses in the fighting – so frail that edgy officials shied away from calling them cease-fires or truces – enabled some quarter of a million children under five to be vaccinated against polio, diphtheria, tetanus, measles and whooping cough.

The 'days of tranquillity' – agreed to by government and guerrilla leaders with the help of leading Roman Catholic prelates – almost fell apart on at least two occasions.

Hours before the opening of the second national immunization day, on Sunday 3 March, with 20,000 health workers and volunteers poised in more than 2,000 vaccination centres across the country, what officials euphemistically called a 'military incident' threatened an eruption of fighting that could have spilled over into the first day of the campaign and scared off many parents and children. Prompt intervention by representatives of the Roman Catholic Church prevented a collapse of the *de facto* truce.

Though the totals fell short of the target of vaccinating 80% of El Salvador's 400,000 unimmunized children under five, in round figures 217,000 children were reached on 3 February, 262,000 on 3 March and 241,000 on the last day.

But achieving the complete immunization of almost two-thirds of its children was rightly hailed as a remarkable achievement in a nation at war with itself.

"*This reconciliation for progress and the common good announced loudly El Salvador's commitment to a positive future and has been an inspiration to the rest of the world,*" United Nations Secretary-General Javier Pérez de Cuéllar said in a letter to President Napoleon Duarte of El Salvador.

The war was but one obstacle. With 58% of the rural population illiterate, even making parents aware of the immunization campaign was a major task.

House-to-house visits by 3,100 health workers to locate and inform parents increased between the first and second vaccination days and were largely credited for the increased number of children turning up to be immunized on 3 March.

Posters and printed handbills announced the dates for vaccination and even lottery tickets carried the campaign emblem and the slogan "*prevenir es … vacunar*" – to vaccinate is to prevent. Other publicity included air drops of leaflets in remote areas. More conventionally, newspapers, magazines, radio and television stations carried many thousands of advertisements placed by government and by private businesses as well as feature articles and news stories on the campaign itself.

Each Sunday, during the weeks leading up to the vaccination days, the Church carried the message to the people from the pulpit, telling parents it was their duty to protect their children from disease.

The areas controlled by guerrillas received special treatment, with health workers from the International Committee of the Red Cross operating the vaccination posts. Posters advertised the vaccination days in those districts – but without giving the dates, because rebel authorities wished to avoid giving the impression of being dictated to by the government.

At one point, guerrillas abducted two doctors and took them to an unmanned health centre, where several parents and children waited to be vaccinated. The vaccines administered, the two physicians were returned to their homes.

world's most powerful public health technology off the pedestal of its vast potential and putting it to everyday work in a million villages and neighbourhoods.

Something special is needed. And something special is what the nations who are now moving towards full immunization have begun to pioneer in the mid-1980s:-

Social mobilization

Brazil's National Vaccination Days, for example, have mobilized no less than 400,000 volunteers – from all sections of society – to support the health services in manning over 90,000 vaccination posts and bringing immunization within walking distance of almost every family. At the same time, the country's mass media have made sure that virtually every parent in the country is well-informed about the time, place, and importance of the immunization days themselves. On television and radio, 30-second immunization 'advertisements' have been broadcast twenty times a day. In the mass-circulation newspapers, pages of editorial have been devoted to the campaign for weeks in advance. On walls and in windows throughout the land, tens of millions of posters have kept the message in front of the public. On bank statements, electricity bills, and lottery tickets, the reminder has gone out that every child should be immunized. In supermarkets and football stadiums, the public address systems have announced the same message. And in 10,000 parishes, Catholic priests and the Church's 14,000 health workers have talked with millions of parents about vaccinating their children (see panel 10).

In India, the immunization of more than 80% of the young children in districts of Delhi and Karnataka has been achieved not just through the passive availability of vaccines, but through the active involvement of entire communities. To bring vaccination within the reach of all parents, immunization posts were set up in temples and schools and polling booths. To let parents know about the importance of vaccination, messages were carried by radio and newspapers, by poster and car sticker, by banner and procession, by song

and play, by cinema and loudspeaker, by school-teacher and village leader, by members of parliament and panchayat, by Rotary clubs and women's organizations, by Hindu and Methodist leaders, by youth movements and family planning associations, and by the hundreds of village volunteers who travelled house to house to make sure that all parents were aware of the need to vaccinate and to remind them of the time and place.

In Pakistan, 7,000 vaccinators and 15,000 traditional birth attendants have been trained and the number of immunization posts has been increased by 50% in the last eighteen months alone (Fig. 5 and panel 11).

In Nigeria, the pushing of the immunization rate in the test area of Owo from 9% to over 80% within twelve months – an achievement now being attempted in every state – was made possible by the support of the community leaders, the schoolteachers, the traditional chiefs, the mass

Fig. 5 Percentage of infants fully immunized, Pakistan, 1980–1987

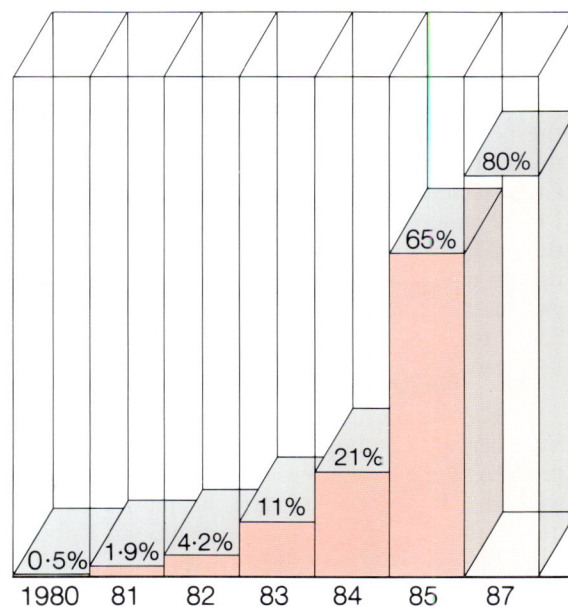

Sources: WHO, Report of the Expanded Programme on Immunization, Global Advisory Group Meeting, Alexandria, October 1984. (1985 figure from UNICEF, Islamabad).

media, the Muslim leaders and imams, the Catholic bishops and priests, the international agencies and the local organizations (see panel 17).

In Colombia, the full immunization of 75% of all under-fours has been achieved by one of the most significant recent examples of mass participation in public health. Watched by observers from Haiti, El Salvador, Burkina Faso, and Ecuador, 10,000 immunization posts were set up across the nation – in health clinics, schools, civic centres, market-places and parks. To inform the nation's parents, almost all major newspapers and almost all radio and television stations promoted the campaign to a point where it was virtually impossible for anyone to be unaware of where and when and why children had to be taken for vaccination. To publicize and organize the three National Vaccination Days, 200,000 teachers made announcements in schools, over 2,000 priests preached immunization from pulpits in every parish, over 120,000 volunteers, plus the police and the armed forces, helped with the logistics of the campaign, and approximately 13,000 volunteers from the Colombian Red Cross assisted the health services with the actual vaccination of over three-quarters of a million children (see panel 5).

In El Salvador this year, the immunization of over a quarter of a million children was made possible by the government and the guerrillas, by the health services and the Catholic Church, by the Rotarians and the Boy Scouts, by the Red Cross societies and the international agencies, by 14,000 announcements on radio and television, by the 5,000 'promoters' who went house to house to inform parents of the campaign, and by the 20,000 vaccination-team members who manned over 2,000 temporary health posts across the nation (see panel 4).

In Kabul, Afghanistan, thousands of children have been immunized in mosques this year as the mullahs and the community leaders have joined with the health services and the mass media to quadruple the immunization rate among Kabul's children.

In Turkey, this year's campaign to immunize over 80% of the nation's children has involved not just the health services but the President and Prime Minister, several cabinet ministers, the Association of Paediatricians, and many different departments of both provincial and national government. The country's 220,000 primary school teachers began work three weeks early to help in the preparations for the campaign. The religious leaders (muftus and imams) delivered sermons in support of the immunization programme from 54,000 mosques. The military provided transport and fuel, the government's meat and fish warehouses provided cold storage for vaccines, and students at Hacettepe University took on the national surveys to evaluate vaccination coverage both before and after the campaign. In total, $10 million's worth of television and radio time has been donated to publicize the campaign (see panel 3).

In the Americas, the Director of the Pan American Health Organization (PAHO) has announced plans for a "*massive final five-year effort to achieve the eradication of polio from the Americas*".* In the words of PAHO's Director-General, Dr. Carlyle Guerra de Macedo, this can be achieved not by the health services acting alone but by "*tapping the voluntary organizations in every country, inviting the participation of the mass media, mobilizing individual families and communities ... and promoting a nation-wide effort in every country, dedicated to a common strategy, committed to a common goal ... for the time has come for us to say that it is unacceptable for any child in the Americas to suffer from polio*".[6]

The health services have provided the technology and the medical expertise for all these achievements. But that technology and know-how has been made available to 80% instead of 20% of the people because it has been fitted to the engine of social mobilization and geared to working through a whole range of organized resources with a 'social reach' going far beyond the usual outreach of the health services themselves. In this

---

* Almost all governments and international organizations involved – including WHO (of which the Pan American Health Organization is part), and UNICEF – share the view that polio immunization should be promoted not as an isolated venture but as a leading edge of progress towards the immunization of all children, by 1990, against all of the major vaccine-preventable diseases included under the EPI.

way, in nation after nation, it is proving possible to inform and involve the majority of parents and to help both create and meet a much louder demand for the immunization of children.

Immunization and primary health care

These extraordinary efforts are of course attended by a turbulence of concerns about their sustainability, about the complacency they may temporarily induce, and about their place in advancing the broader goal of more comprehensive and permanent primary health care services.

Sustainability is a legitimate worry. A change of government or of a key minister, a falling-off of interest by the media, a failure to educate new parents about the importance of immunization – any and all of these can mean a dwindling away of coverage rates and the sudden return of tetanus, measles, whooping cough, or polio.

Another worry is that the boosting of immunization coverage to two or three times its previous level will be considered achievement enough. If that happens, then the idea of immunization for all will not be carried right through to the point where it reaches those who are the hardest of all to reach, those who belong to the very poorest 30% of society, those whose lack of money and time and information and confidence means that they are usually left in the margins of a nation's life, those whose children are most in need of that degree of protection against poverty which immunization can provide.

A third question mark over mass immunization asks whether such campaigns are merely a substitute for the more patient and less spectacular work of building comprehensive and permanent structures of primary health care.

In answer to these concerns, experience to date suggests that the cause of primary health care can in fact be significantly advanced through the involvement of health professionals in a major achievement for national development, through the pioneering of ways and means to bring a basic piece of health technology within reach of the majority, through the setting up of the necessary outreach structures, and through the involvement of the majority of the public in knowing more and

doing more about their own and their families' health. It is for this reason that immunization programmes can serve both as an end and as a means of primary health care, achieving both immediate protection against specific diseases and the involvement of whole societies in the wider and longer-term cause of health promotion.

Such concerns deserve sustained attention. But after twenty years of vaccine availability, the denial of its protection to two-thirds of the developing world's children demands that something new must now be tried.

It would of course be preferable if there were enough fuel and roads and refrigerators and clinics and schools and health workers so that every parent knew all about immunization, lived within easy reach of permanent immunization services, received computerized reminders in the mail, and brought his or her children to be vaccinated at exactly the right time for each individual child. But that is to say nothing more than that it would be preferable if developing countries were not developing countries. And the sentence that *universal immunization must await economic development and the coming of a permanent health clinic to every village* is simply a sentence of unnecessary death and disability for many millions of today's children and for even more millions of those who are still to be born.

If immunization remains at today's levels then polio, to take just one example, will paralyse for life approximately 2.5 million children over the next ten years (Fig. 1). In addition to the personal suffering, the process of economic development itself will thereby be deprived of the contribution of most of those children and of most of those upon whom they become and remain dependent. When a cheap and simple technology to prevent polio is already in our hands, it is therefore neither humane nor economic to allow the disease to continue crippling over a quarter of a million children a year.

In the case of measles, the figures become unthinkable. At present levels of immunization coverage, a total of at least 20 million children are condemned to die over the next ten years from a disease which can be prevented by a single injection (Fig. 1).

Colombia: a child survival plan

5

Extracts from the speech delivered by President Belisario Betancur, on national television, on the launching of the Plan for Child Survival and Development in Colombia on 19 December 1984

We are proud to be the vanguard of programmes and actions recommended by UNICEF in its report on *The State of the World's Children* and by the World Health Organization in its plan for Health for All by the year 2000...

We have embarked on a significant change in our approach to health education and the promotion of new technologies. We have begun to mobilize all services and all sectors of the community behind actions such as the recent national vaccination campaign which, you will recall, has had an international echo.

Nevertheless, I know that we still need deeper and more aggressive action. Every year in Colombia, 60,000 children under five still die from eminently preventable causes. They die from diarrhoea, respiratory infections, problems during delivery, and malnutrition...

The most elementary human principles prevent us from allowing this situation to continue.

Therefore today we are committing ourselves before the entire world: we are committing ourselves to preventing, during the next five years, the deaths of 60,000 children every year. To achieve this, we are going to put all the resources of our nation, under the leadership of the Ministry of Health, behind a Plan for Child Survival.

This plan will be the most spectacular advance in Colombia's health for many years...

We are going to reach each house, each one of our 3.6 million children under five years of age.

We are going to reach them in order to work with them, and with their families, towards implement-

ing simple actions of proven effectiveness in the protection of children's health.

We are going to distribute oral rehydration salts to all corners of Colombia so that no children die from diarrhoea.

We are going to keep immunizing our children until there are no more cases of vaccine-preventable disease.

We are going to give food supplements to our children, to babies under two, and to pregnant women in nutritional danger. And we are going to provide adequate treatment to children suffering from acute respiratory infections.

But above all we are going to make an even greater effort with all the mass media, with the participation of all of you, and of the entire community, to educate fathers and mothers so that they acquire simple knowledge and simple methods for guaranteeing the health and life of their children.

To do this, we will draw up plans involving all health personnel and young people... But we are also seeking the participation of the religious community, the military, the police, the Red Cross, the voluntary organizations, the trade unions, the community action boards, the co-operatives – in other words, everybody in our nation, with the invaluable support of the World Health Organization and UNICEF.

Let us recall that in dramatic and crucial moments in the history of mankind, many countries have called upon all the human resources of their nation, and especially their youth. Unfortunately, they have usually called upon them for the purposes of war. Today, Colombia has decided to call upon all the resources and capacities of our nation not to go to war, but on the contrary, to carry out the noble task of saving the lives of thousands and thousands of Colombian children.

There is no valid reason for further delay. And there is no pre-ordained reason why the developing nations should tread the same path to full immunization as was beaten by the industrialized world a generation ago. For like many of the other powerful low-cost basic health strategies available to the developing world today, immunization could become a contributing cause rather than an eventual consequence of economic growth and comprehensive health care. It is clear that there is a long-term connection between the mental and physical development of children and the social and economic development of their nations. And basic steps towards protecting the lives and health and normal growth of the young are therefore a slowly maturing but exceptionally high-yielding investment in economic development itself.

There are also shorter-term economic benefits. In the industrialized world, the immediate economic gains from immunization programmes have by now almost been forgotten. But to take the United States as an example, the present cost of vaccination programmes against three of the common infectious diseases comes out at $96 million a year. Without this programme, the cost to society of dealing with those three diseases (for hospital treatment and rehabilitation) would be at least $1,400 million a year – meaning that approximately $14 is saved for every $1 invested in the vaccination programme.[7] Similarly, the United States is now saving $500 million a year on measles treatment – for an outlay of only $50 million a year on preventing measles by immunization programmes.[8] According to Dr. William Foege, former Director of the United States Centers for Disease Control and now head of the international Task Force on Child Survival:*
"*The return on such an investment in the developing*

world, where morbidity and mortality for measles are higher, would be even greater... a preliminary analysis of vaccine programmes in the Ivory Coast, for example, suggests the benefit to cost ratio may well exceed 20:1".[9]

New technologies

So far, it has been convenient to discuss the technology of immunization and the strategies for making it more widely available as two separate components. In practice, of course, technological changes can have a significant effect on both supply and demand.

And today, vaccine technology has moved on to the point where a nation's ability to reach high levels of immunization coverage has become significantly *less* dependent on its level of overall economic development.

It has been commonplace for some years, for example, for two drops of oral polio vaccine to be administered by village health workers. But recent trials in Central and South America have shown that children can also be injected with vaccine – against DPT and measles – using disposable syringes in the hands of community volunteers with a few hours well-thought-out training (see panel 7). And as this report goes to press, trials are beginning in Guatemala with the 'Ezeject' system of vaccination in which both vaccine and needle come packed together in a single-shot disposable plastic syringe. As yet, there has been no complete evaluation of this method and the syringe-needle-vaccine package is not in commercial production.**

But in the last few years, more conventional kinds of disposable syringe have demonstrated their power to extend the outreach of immunization's arm in settings as different as Pakistan, El Salvador, Brazil, and the Dominican Republic.

---

* The Task Force for Child Survival was formed at a high-level meeting in Bellagio, Italy, in 1984, to assist selected countries in increasing and sustaining immunization coverage, to identify research needs in the field of immunization, and to mobilize resources for immunization programmes. The Task Force was established by, and reports to five agencies concerned with child health: WHO, UNICEF, the World Bank, the United Nations Development Programme (UNDP), and the Rockefeller Foundation. The Bellagio group held its second major meeting, 'Bellagio II', at Cartagena, Colombia, in October 1985.

** Specific training is required to use the 'Ezeject' method of vaccination. An evaluation of the field trials now under way among a group of 2,000 children in Guatemala should be available by early 1986. Pioneering trials with the 'Ezeject' system were conducted in the United States and Costa Rica during 1976 and 1977, but there is a need for further field evaluation.

Burkina Faso: a vaccination commando

6

In one three-week period, starting on 25 November 1984, Burkina Faso has vaccinated over a million of its children against measles, yellow fever and meningitis. In the whole of 1981, the health services had immunized only 25,000 of the country's half a million children under two.

No expert would have considered Burkina Faso, formerly Upper Volta, a likely candidate for such an achievement. Desperately poor, beset by fifteen years of drought, it has one of the highest infant mortality rates in the world – 150 deaths per 1,000 live births. Less than half of the largely rural population lives within reach of a health centre. Over a third of young children are chronically malnourished, leaving them easy prey to the epidemics which sweep the country during the dry season from February to June. The death rate in meningitis outbreaks averages 11%. Measles causes half of all deaths of children between one and four, and in a bad year the tally can go as high as 43,000 cases.

These problems inspired the country's new government to 'Vaccination Commando' – a massive catch-up immunization drive designed to give the health services a respite from the epidemic season, and a breathing-space in which to plan for expanding their regular vaccination coverage.

To spur people's awareness of the value of immunization, Vaccination Commando tackled the diseases best known as killers in Burkina Faso. Vaccines were chosen that are both easy to give and require only one shot for full protection.

On 19 September the Council of Ministers set the date. The National Vaccination Committee, headed by the Director of Public Health, marshalled support from the ministries of education, information, agriculture and defence, and from the vaccination committees set up in every province, district, village and town. UNICEF, the Red Cross and other international agencies, together with other governments, notably China and the Republic of Korea, supplied technical assistance.

The Committees for the Defence of the Revolution (CDRs) – political volunteer groups active in every village, town and work-place – took on the most crucial task of all: mobilizing their communities.

As 25 November neared, CDR members went door to door explaining the benefits of vaccination to parents. They put up posters in schools, bars, and public places all over the country. Roadside billboards announced the campaign; plays about immunization were performed in the villages. The national radio service issued communiqués in all the local languages, urging attendance and broadcasting results as they came in.

When the vaccination posts opened up for business, they were besieged. In some villages the line of parents and children stretched for kilometres, patiently waiting through the day. Families came over the border from neighbouring countries, alerted by their relatives in Burkina Faso. Children came who were over age, under age, and already immunized. Many vaccination posts had to request extra vaccine because far more children turned up than expected: families have been on the move in Burkina Faso, as in all the countries of the drought-stricken Sahel.

The result: in a population of just under 7 million, 62% of children under fifteen are immunized against yellow fever and 64% against meningitis, while the number of under-sixes protected against measles has leapt from 7% to 60%.

Whether this level of coverage can be sustained in the face of all the country's difficulties remains to be seen. But Vaccination Commando has made an impressive beginning. The alliances have been forged to make children's health the concern of everyone. Parents are more aware of what their children gain from vaccination. And Burkina Faso has drawn up plans for introducing primary health care to all its 30 provinces, and immunizing all its under-fives by 1990.

In particular, the use of disposable syringes in the hands of community volunteers on certain set days or weeks of the year is opening up broad new paths to the immunization of all children:-

○ Because the syringe is disposed of rather than sterilized for reuse, vaccination programmes can be freed from the weight of time and energy required to boil syringes for 20 minutes before reuse (at the same time as reducing the possibility of disease transmission via multiple use of the same needle).

○ Because community volunteers can be taught to use the syringe, immunization programmes can escape from the strait-jacket of the doctor's white coat (fully qualified doctors can play a supervisory role in such programmes, rather than being personally involved in giving each and every injection).

○ Because village vaccinators receive supplies on just two occasions a year and use them within days of their arrival, immunization programmes could be cut free from the cold chains of refrigeration.

○ And because this method could be used to immunize such a high proportion of children all at one time, it might mean that the transmission of the infectious diseases was so severely interrupted that a degree of protection would be provided even to those who were not reached by the vaccination itself.

Technological developments of this kind are therefore making it more possible for other organized sections of society, far greater in their outreach than the health services themselves, to become involved in extending immunization to all a nation's children.

But making universal immunization possible by no means makes it inevitable. And to convert this new potential for universal immunization into the actual vaccination of all children, an act of galvanizing political will – by a nation's leaders – is the catalyst which is so desperately needed. As the Secretary-General said this September (1985) in his report to the General Assembly on the occasion of the fortieth anniversary of the United Nations:-

"The great endeavour to bring immunization to all children in the world by 1990 now seems capable of realization if there is a will to make the final effort."

In the last year and a half, some outstanding examples of that 'will' have been seen in several nations of the developing world. They have been examples set by heads of state and government ministries, by health service administrators and primary health care workers, by doctors and nurses, by local government officials and civil servants, by the women's organizations and the youth movements, by the representatives of international agencies and of voluntary organizations, by journalists and broadcasters, by priests and imams, by teachers and students, by the Red Cross and the Rotarians, by the private sector and the trade unions, and by many millions of parents.

In most if not all cases, the mobilization of a society's resources on such a scale and behind such a cause has been made possible by the decision of a nation's political leaders to put their own personal and political commitment, and their government's financial and organizational resources, behind the effort to immunize the vast majority of the nation's children. In El Salvador and the Dominican Republic, in Colombia and Brazil, in Turkey and Sri Lanka, in Burkina Faso and the Sudan, success so far has been made possible by a nation's leadership deciding on a goal which it could see was both dramatically important and realistically achievable.

The industrialized world

In the industrialized world, the commitment to world-wide immunization has so far, and with a few honourable exceptions, been modest. An exception large enough to demand acknowledgement is the $100 million allocated this year by the government of Italy as a special contribution towards *"saving the lives of one million children"*.[10]

Overall, the developing countries themselves are providing over 80% of the resources for their vaccination programmes.[11]

Meanwhile the total amount of aid being provided by the governments of the industrialized nations for all health services in the developing

Dominican Republic: reaching every home

7

The greatest single threat to hopes of achieving a revolution in child health is the difficulty of reaching the very poorest of the developing world's children.

The difficulty stems from the fact that poorer people have less information and confidence, less status and access, and less time and money. And what makes it doubly important is the fact that health problems such as diarrhoeal disease or measles are both more common and more severe among the poorer sections of any society.

This fundamental problem gives special significance to what is now being achieved – and planned – in the Dominican Republic.

Other countries have attempted to immunize greater numbers of the poor by setting up temporary immunization posts closer to people's homes. But the Dominican Republic is going all the way – carrying vaccination right into the home of every single family.

In 1983, the Ministry of Health's new system went into action for the first time as 20,000 volunteers gave oral polio vaccine to children under five. One of those 'volunteers' was the President of the Dominican Republic – who set the example by himself immunizing 27 children in his own neighbourhood. Some 95% of the nation's children have been fully protected against polio ever since, and no new cases have been reported for over two years.

Following the Health Minister's step-by-step plan, the system went into action again in October 1985 – this time to take on the more difficult task of vaccinating all the nation's children against measles. In many nations, only qualified doctors or nurses are allowed to use syringes and needles to give injections. But in the Dominican Republic, pioneering methods have reduced the training to only four well-thought-out hours. An audio-visual teaching package – field tested, revised, and tested again by the Ministry of Health – conveys the exact information a volunteer needs to inject a

child safely against measles. This rigid training course has been followed by all 20,000 volunteers, working in small groups under the supervision of specially trained personnel. During the training, volunteers practised actual immunization by giving each other an injection of vitamin B12. During the campaign itself, disposable syringes were used to obviate the difficulties of sterilizing equipment.

At the end of 1985 the volunteer force is due to immunize all women of child-bearing age against tetanus, so also protecting the new-born babies of the future. At the same time, all children under two are due to be given the first of the three injections against diphtheria, whooping cough, and tetanus.

Provided the current schedules are met, the Dominican Republic will have immunized the vast majority of its under-fives against the main killer diseases of childhood by mid-1986 – three and a half years ahead of the international target date.

By instituting national vaccination days (with vaccines sent out just in advance from a central cold storage depot), the programme has solved the problem of maintaining year-round refrigeration at every health clinic. By training thousands of volunteers, the programme has solved the problem of not having enough doctors or paramedics. By visiting every home, the programme has solved the problem of reaching the poorest. By building the staff and funding for national vaccination days into the Ministry of Health's own budget (including provision for the regular training of replacement volunteers), the programme has tackled the problem of sustainability.

To support these efforts, the government in August 1985 launched a National Programme for Mothers and Children, with the emphasis on improving their well-being in poor rural and slum areas. The plans include family planning services, pre-natal care and midwife training, along with advice on breast-feeding, growth monitoring, and oral rehydration to forestall diarrhoeal dehydration.

world is only about $4,000 million a year[12] – the equivalent of about two days' military spending (Fig. 19). And of that $4 billion, only about 20% goes to all mother and child health services, including immunization.[13]

By contrast, many private groups in the industrialized nations are heavily and generously involved in contributing towards the goal of immunization for all children by 1990. To mention another particularly outstanding example, the one million members of Rotary International have committed themselves to paying for all the vaccine required in any polio campaign in any developing country over the five years from now until the year 1990. The total cost of Rotary International's 'Polio 1990' campaign could be in the region of $120 million; the total benefit could be the prevention of more than 1 million cases of paralytic poliomyelitis.[14] In many industrialized countries, national committees for UNICEF and other non-governmental organizations are also working to help raise funds – and awareness – to support the goal of immunization for all the world's children by 1990.

There are perhaps two main reasons why the governments of the industrialized world might wish to consider a much greater level of support in order to help realize this new potential for universal immunization.

The first, and most important, is that the immunization of all children remains one of the greatest of all humanitarian goals.

The second is that it would also result in very significant economic gains for the industrialized nations themselves.

Evidence for this is to be found in the annals of the international campaign to eradicate smallpox:-

In 1967, smallpox killed an estimated 2 million people. In 1977, the last case of smallpox was recorded in Somalia. The cost of the eradication campaign was approximately $24 million a year, of which about one-third came from the industrialized nations and two-thirds came from the developing countries themselves.[15] For the duration of the programme, the United States contributed a total of $32 million (in 1970 dollars).[16] Since then, the United States government has been able to discontinue smallpox vaccination and dismantle its elaborate quarantine and surveillance systems – which were costing approximately $120 million a year in today's terms.[17] In other words, the eradication of a major disease has meant that the United States is now saving *every few months* more than the total amount it invested in the eradication programme itself.

As we have already mentioned, the United States is today spending approximately $50 million a year on vaccination and routine surveillance against measles and will continue to do so for as long as measles is at large in the world. A successful eradication programme would therefore save the United States $50 million a year – every year from now on.

The humanitarian case for immunizing all children is beyond all question. The technology for immunizing all children is readily available. The cost of immunizing all children would be repaid many times over for both industrialized and developing nations. And the all-important organizational and communications capacity for reaching out to create and meet the demand for immunizing all children, has been shown to be within the power of those nations with the will and commitment to do it.

In the process, important strides could be made towards primary health care for all and new ways could be opened up for putting other pieces of vital health knowledge and other low-cost technologies at the disposal of the majority of the people.

The next chapter of this report discusses some of those other low-cost techniques and looks at what can be learned from experiences so far in the attempt to put them at the disposal of the majority. And as with immunization, the solution does not rest solely in the techniques themselves, but rather resides in the will and the capacity of nations – and their leaders – for reaching out to inform and support parents in using those techniques to take more control over their own and their families' health.

If that can be achieved, and if in the process health care can come to be seen not only as passive recipiente of services when sick but as active and informed involvement in the daily process of staying well, then the technologies and the knowledge now available are cheap enough and manageable enough for parents themselves to bring about a revolution in child health and cut by at least half the rate of malnutrition, infection, and death among the children of the developing world.

Reaching all children

Parents cannot make their own vaccines. But there is a product which parents can make, which they can give to their own children, and which is just as important for protecting their lives and their health.

That product is oral rehydration solution. It can be made with one of the 200 million sachets of oral rehydration salts which were mass-produced in the developing world last year (Fig. 6). Or it can be made at home using either salt and sugar solutions or traditional remedies such as rice conjees or carrot soups.[1] Either way, such a solution can effectively prevent or treat the diarrhoeal dehydration which is still killing approximately 4 million children each year.*

The technical details of ORT are set out in Part II of this report (see Lifelines: ORT). But such a breakthrough bears restating in all its simplicity:-

There is now an incredibly cheap, simple, safe, and effective method by which parents themselves, however poor, can protect the lives and growth of their children against one of the most common causes of child malnutrition and child death in the modern world.

At present, only about 20% of the world's families know enough about ORT to be able to use it. But it is already estimated to be saving the lives of more than half a million children a year.

Together with rising immunization coverage, the spread of ORT therefore holds out the promise of a drastic reduction in child deaths and child malnutrition over the next few years. But as with immunization, realizing this enormous potential now depends not on the scientific breakthrough itself but on finding the equivalent 'social breakthrough' which can put ORT at the disposal of many millions of parents.**

---

* In the first instance, ORT means continuing to give a child food and fluids during any episode of diarrhoea. To replace the essential fluids and salts, oral rehydration solutions can be administered by the parents in the child's own home – using either a 10 cent sachet of oral rehydration salts; or a home-made solution of salt, sugar (or rice powder), and water (in the right proportions); or a version of one of the effective traditional remedies such as rice conjees or carrot soups. Approximately 10% of all cases will need more specialized treatment (such as the sachet of WHO/UNICEF formula oral rehydration salts, or even intravenous therapy). But in all cases, the risk and severity of dehydration is reduced, and the effectiveness of more specialized treatments is increased, by the early administration of oral rehydration in the home.

** The United States Agency for International Development (USAID), under its Administrator Peter McPherson, has made a major commitment to the promotion of oral rehydration therapy in the developing world and is contributing substantially to several of the major ORT programmes mentioned in this year's report (see panel 9). The UNDP has also played a significant role in the development and refinement of oral rehydration therapy, through its long-term support of the International Centre for Diarrhoeal Disease Research in Bangladesh (ICDDR,B), through its programmes of which ORT promotion is now a part, and through its co-sponsorship (with WHO, UNICEF and USAID) of the International Conferences on Oral Rehydration Therapy. The second Conference is convening in Washington D.C. as this report goes to press and will again bring together, from many different nations, experts and practitioners who are directly involved in the task of promoting ORT. Another United Nations agency, the Fund for Population Activities (UNFPA) has also made an important contribution to the work of the ICDDR,B and, in particular, has funded research which has demonstrated that reductions in child deaths through simple measures like ORT, when linked to effective family planning programmes, lead to both improved survival rates and a decline in population growth (see panel 25).

Basic protection and vitamin A

ORT and immunization therefore stand in the front line of a revolution in child survival. But they do not stand alone.

Over the last three years, the *State of the World's Children* report has brought together research and experience from around the world to show that several such basic breakthroughs have now been made. Taken together, they could enable most parents in poor communities to protect the lives and normal growth of their children.

Specifically, previous years' reports have demonstrated that knowledge about breast-feeding, improved weaning, and regular monitoring of children's growth could, along with immunization and ORT, save the lives of at least half the 40,000 children who are now dying each day in the developing world.

It has been found, for example, that babies in poor communities who are bottle-fed are two or three times more likely to die in infancy than babies who are breast-fed (Fig. 12). Reversing the trend towards the use of artificial infant formulas (Fig. 7) could therefore save the lives – and protect the normal growth – of hundreds of thousands of infants in the developing world (see panel 23 and Lifelines: breast-feeding).

It is also now thought that regular growth checking, along with changes in the timing and method of weaning, could reduce by half the incidence and severity of malnutrition among the poor world's children (see Lifelines: growth monitoring).

This year, another potential breakthrough must be added to the list. The findings from a major child health study in Indonesia appear to have confirmed a long-held suspicion that a lack of vitamin A in the child's diet, long known to be a cause of xerophthalmia (drying of the eyes) and eventual blindness, is also an important determinant of a child's overall health. Page 22 illustrates the remarkable finding that the incidence of both respiratory and diarrhoeal infections (the two most common causes of illness and death among children of the developing world) is closely associated with the degree of vitamin A deficiency.[2]

At first, it was believed that this association could be explained by the idea that the lack of vitamin A was probably only an indicator of the more general malnutrition which is well known to predispose a child to illness. But further analysis has suggested that otherwise well-nourished children who lack vitamin A are more prone to both diarrhoeal and respiratory illnesses than are poorly nourished children who happen to have adequate levels of vitamin A.[3]

In the one major test of the practical significance of these findings, it appears that distribution of the standard UNICEF vitamin A capsule every six months has succeeded in reducing child death rates (in the age group one to three years) by approximately 30% among a population of over 15,000 children in Indonesia.[4]

Fig. 6 Global supply of oral rehydration salts (WHO/UNICEF formula)

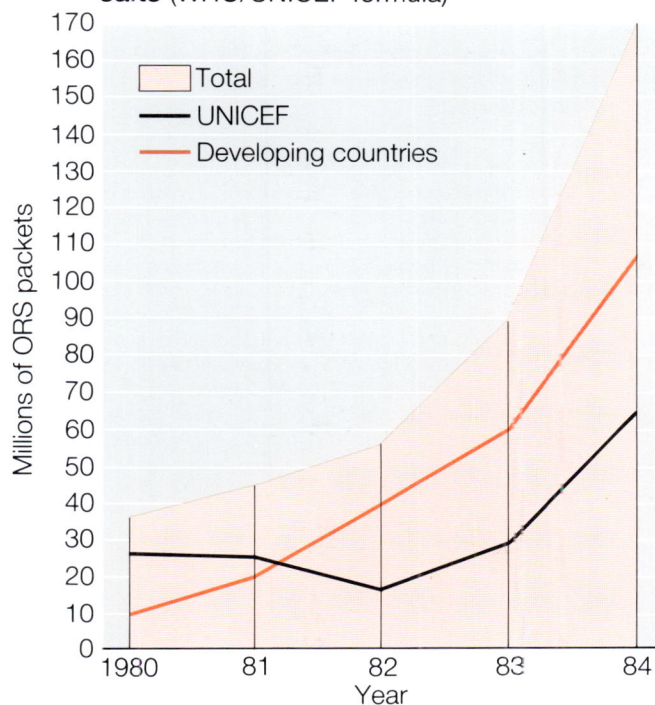

Note : Figures exclude commercial production. In addition to the above figures, an estimated 10 million packets are supplied by other international and bilateral aid agencies.

Source : UNICEF

THE VITAMIN A STORY

Although it has long been known that approximately 250,000 children are blinded every year by xerophthalmia brought on by severe vitamin A deficiency, only one large-scale field study in recent years has looked at the relationship between the lack of vitamin A and overall child health. For an 18 month period, 4,000 Indonesian children, aged 1 to 5, were given health checks every three months. Health records from a total of over 20,000 three-month 'child intervals' were therefore assembled. The differences in the health records of children with and without vitamin A deficiency (as measured by the degree and kind of eyesight problems) were then analysed. The results are shown in chart A.

As the chart shows, the child death rate almost triples with each increase in the degree of vitamin A deficiency.

The records were then re-examined to try to analyse *why* death rates were so much higher among those with vitamin A deficiency. As an obvious starting point, the study looked at the incidence of diarrhoeal disease and respiratory infections — two of the main causes of child deaths in the developing world. The findings are presented in chart B.

Again, the chart shows that children with vitamin A deficiency are many times more likely to contract diarrhoeal disease and respiratory infections.

But there is an obvious doubt to be raised about these findings. Is vitamin A deficiency an important factor in its own right? Or just an indicator of the more general malnutrition which is well-known to be associated with higher rates of child illness?

To find out, the records of the children in the study were divided into two groups — those who were adequately nourished and those who were undernourished. The differences can be seen in chart C.

Generally malnourished children were indeed more prone to infection than those who were adequately nourished. But as chart C shows, *a generally well-nourished child with vitamin A deficiency is at greater risk of infection than is a generally malnourished child without vitamin A deficiency — suggesting that the level of vitamin A is a more important determinant of risk to the child than is the child's overall nutritional status.*

The next step was to try to find out whether these findings could be put to practical use — in other words would the distribution of vitamin A capsules to children result in significantly fewer illnesses and deaths?

Choosing an area where the government of Indonesia was steadily expanding its vitamin A distribution, a new study was launched to look at the health of 30,000 children, half of whom were already receiving the standard UNICEF Vitamin A capsule once every six months and half of whom had not yet been reached by any extra vitamin A supplement. Chart D shows the results.

All children were examined at the beginning of the study and then again one year later (after those receiving supplements had received two doses of vitamin A).

As chart D shows, the distribution of vitamin A reduced overall child death rates by over one-third among children over the age of one year.

The overall conclusions of this study have been summed up by its principal investigator, Dr. Alfred Sommer:-

''The significance of these findings is obvious, at least for countries like Indonesia. We know that five to ten million children develop mild xerophthalmia, hence vitamin A deficiency, every year. Given these figures, and the increased risk of death among children with mild, and probably even with subclinical vitamin A deficiency, it may account for as much as 20-30% of all preschool-age deaths in developing countries.*

''. . . Increasing vitamin A intake may therefore be the most practical effective means for improving child survival in the developing world.''

---

* ''As striking as these results are, they may, in fact, underestimate the potential impact of vitamin A supplementation in this population. The highest risk groups, children with xerophthalmia at the baseline examination, were treated and dropped from the study; coverage was extremely high because a special mechanism was in place, but was still considerably less than 100%. Data suggests those who needed the vitamin A capsule were the least likely to have received it. Therefore universal coverage might have produced an even greater impact. This area did not have an excessive rate of vitamin A deficiency, one barely meeting the WHO criteria for a significant public health problem, and therefore the impact should not be greater than would be expected in most developing countries with vitamin A deficiency. The control group was not purely isolated: children with xerophthalmia who presented to the clinic received treatment, and an outreach program provided vitamin A to neighbours because of the known clustering effect of vitamin A deficiency. If there had not been such an outreach program, the difference in mortality rates might have been even greater. Finally, we do not yet know the duration of protection provided by a single 200,000 IU capsule. While we assume it will prevent blindness for a six month period, blood studies suggest it only maintains vitamin A levels within the normal range for 8 to 12 weeks. Further analysis of the data may indicate that most of the impact occurred after vitamin A supplementation, with a waning of the impact, as vitamin A levels fell, over time.''

Chart A Mortality rates in relation to eyesight status, (indicator of vitamin A status)

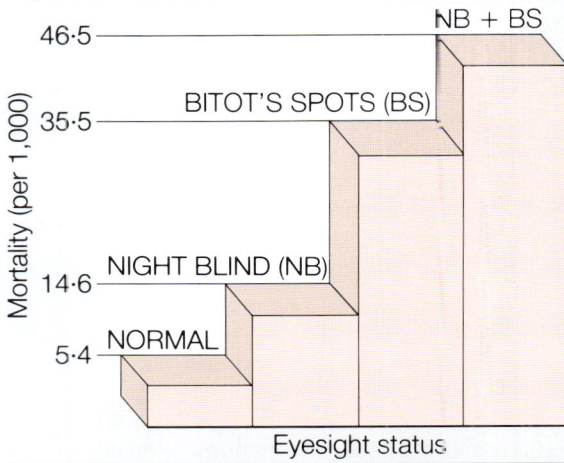

Mortality (per 1,000)

46·5 — NB + BS
35·5 — BITOT'S SPOTS (BS)
14·6 — NIGHT BLIND (NB)
5·4 — NORMAL

Eyesight status

Chart B Incidence of diarrhoeal and respiratory disease among children with and without xerophthalmia, (by age)

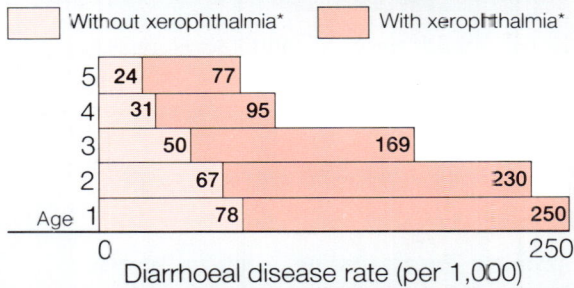

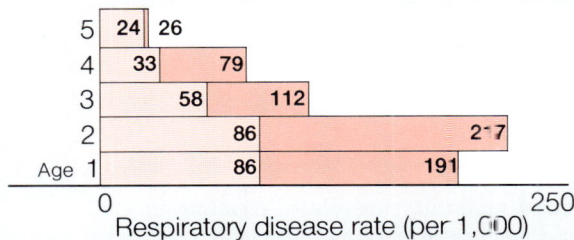

Without xerophthalmia*   With xerophthalmia*

Diarrhoeal disease rate (per 1,000)

Age	Without	With
5	24	77
4	31	95
3	50	169
2	67	230
1	78	250

0 — 250

Respiratory disease rate (per 1,000)

Age	Without	With
5	24	26
4	33	79
3	58	112
2	86	217
1	86	191

0 — 250

*Without xerophthalmia = Children with normal eyes at both the start and end of the 3 month observational interval.
With xerophthalmia = Children with mild xerophthalmia (night blindness and/or Bitot's spots) at both the start and end of the interval.

Chart C Incidence of diarrhoeal and respiratory disease among adequately nourished and undernourished children with and without xerophthalmia, (by age)

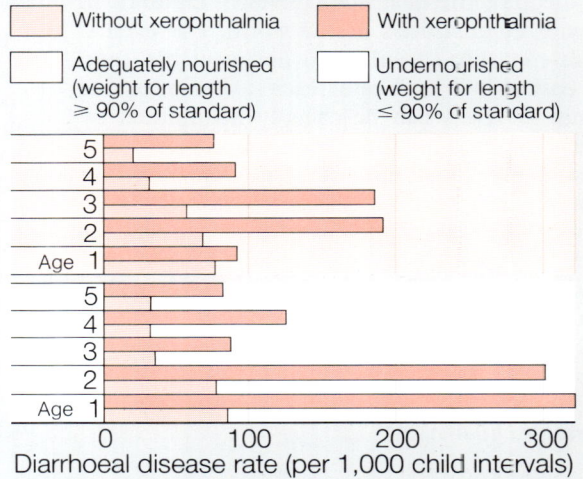

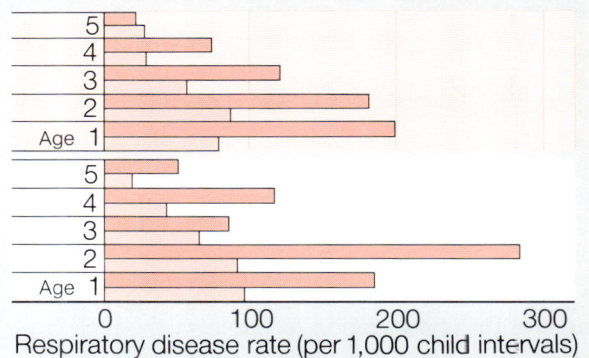

Without xerophthalmia   With xerophthalmia

Adequately nourished (weight for length ≥ 90% of standard)   Undernourished (weight for length ≤ 90% of standard)

Diarrhoeal disease rate (per 1,000 child intervals)
0 — 100 — 200 — 300

Age 5 4 3 2 1 (adequately nourished)
Age 5 4 3 2 1 (undernourished)

Respiratory disease rate (per 1,000 child intervals)
0 — 100 — 200 — 300

Age 5 4 3 2 1
Age 5 4 3 2 1

Chart D Age-specific mortality, (preliminary results)

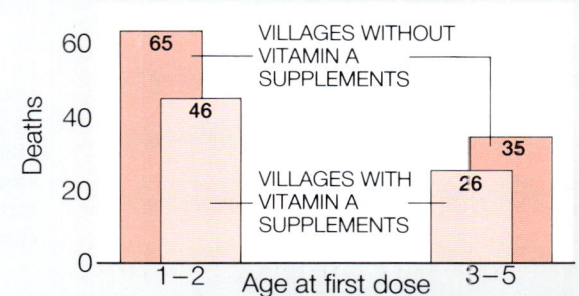

Deaths

VILLAGES WITHOUT VITAMIN A SUPPLEMENTS
VILLAGES WITH VITAMIN A SUPPLEMENTS

1–2: 65, 46
3–5: 35, 26

60 — 40 — 20 — 0

Age at first dose

23

Should these findings be confirmed, then the maintenance of an adequate level of vitamin A will join the range of low-cost, parent-based ways of protecting the health and lives of children in the poor communities of the world. For even if the six-monthly capsules are not available (and they cost only 2 or 3 cents each), then adequate vitamin A levels can be cheaply maintained by parents themselves – *if* they are empowered with the knowledge that vitamin A is vital for their children's health and if they know that it can be provided by the dark-green leafy vegetables which are among the commonest and cheapest foods in almost all regions of the developing world.* Or as the Executive Director of Helen Keller International has expressed it: *"vitamin A is a simple, low-cost intervention that can save the sight and the lives of millions of the world's most vulnerable children".***[5]

Action on the 'children's revolution'

Together, these advances in basic child health protection add up to a potential revolution for the developing world's children. And it is a revolution which could serve as a starting-point for building up more comprehensive basic health systems and so help to promote the kind of healthier, more productive, and more confident communities which are the power and the purpose behind the progress of development itself.

But as with immunization technology, the real potential of knowledge breakthroughs about ORT, about infant-feeding methods, or about vitamin A levels, resides not only in the efficacy of the techniques themselves but in the fact that they can be put into practice by parents. Most of the new techniques are cheap and simple enough to become part of a mother's normal way of bringing up and caring for her children. And this means that the benefits of this knowledge could be made available to all children and not just to the few who have access to sophisticated medical facilities.

But by the same token, the challenge of the child survival revolution has now become the challenge of finding ways and means to mobilize much more far-reaching forces than just the health facilities in order to reach out to inform and support the vast majority of parents in using this new knowledge to bring that revolution about.

This year, several nations have mobilized their societies to double and treble the percentage of children who are reached by immunization services. But some nations have also been demonstrating that the strategy of mobilizing all possible organizations and channels of communication can also be used to put other low-cost methods of child protection at the disposal of the majority of all parents. Some examples:-

The Americas

In Brazil, child survival and development programmes are being launched not only by the Ministry of Health but by three different government ministries in co-operation with the Catholic Church, the mass media, the Brazilian Assistance League, and the 18,000-strong Brazilian Association of Paediatricians.

To promote breast-feeding, and to reverse Brazil's long-standing trend towards artificial infant formulas, more than 50,000 health workers have been trained to inform and support mothers with present knowledge. At the same time, the mass media have devoted $1 million in air-time to the task of promoting the facts to the general public. In the state medical colleges, the value of breast-feeding is now a compulsory subject. And in all state maternity hospitals, 'rooming-in' and encouraging breast-feeding from birth is now standard practice.[6] Internationally, the UNFPA has allocated $15 million in support of this campaign.

Growth monitoring is also being adopted as standard practice in all maternal and child health clinics and a new Brazilian growth chart is now being tested.

---

* Other vegetables, such as carrots, and fruits such as papaya and mango, also contain the carotene from which the body can derive significant quantities of vitamin A.

** Among the earliest responses to the new finding is the announcement by the USAID that it will make available a total of $8 million for vitamin A programmes over the next three years.

Oral rehydration therapy, backed by the free distribution of over 10 million sachets a year, has now spread to the point where at least 5 million cases of diarrhoeal illness in Brazilian children have been treated with the new therapy in the last twelve months.

To increase the outreach of the child survival campaign in the desperately poor north-east, the National Council of Brazilian Bishops has decided that its 'Pastorate of the Child' programme will reach 1 million of the poorest children by the end of 1985. Pilot campaigns in the southern town of Florestopolis – including immunization, growth monitoring, oral rehydration therapy, and child spacing – have sharply reduced infant and child deaths and the programme is now being extended to 20 other cities.[7] In all, the outreach capacity of Brazil's Catholic Church includes not only its 5,000 parish priests but 14,000 health workers, 1,200 Catholic hospitals, 120 Catholic radio stations, 23 newspapers, 35 magazines, a major publishing house, and over 3,000 bulletins and newsletters. "*This formidable potential*," reports *UNICEF's office in Brasilia, "is now being mobilized in order to bring child survival strategies to the north-east*" (see panel 10).

In Central America, UNICEF and the Pan American Health Organization have this year signed an agreement to support national child survival plans in Belize, Costa Rica, El Salvador, Guatemala, Honduras, Nicaragua, and Panama. All of the region's governments plan to 'go national' with ORT and to push their immunization rates above the 80% mark before 1990 as part of an effort to halve the region's infant mortality rate and save the lives of approximately 90,000 children each year.

In Nicaragua, UNICEF has agreed to provide 1.5 million sachets of oral rehydration salts per year – for distribution through the country's tens of thousands of *brigadistas* (health volunteers) as well as through commercial pharmacies, corner shops, market-traders, and the 356 oral rehydration units which have been set up across the country over the last three years. At the moment, an estimated 58% of all cases of childhood diarrhoea in Nicaragua are being treated with ORT. Other child protection strategies are now being put at parents' disposal via the three People's Health Days which mobilize 20,000 volunteers each year. Since 1982, for example, not a single case of polio has been reported (panel 12).

In Haiti, over 80% of parents in the slums of Port-au-Prince – and 30% in the rural areas – have now begun to use ORT. Sachets of the salts have been distributed through thousands of small commercial outlets and demand has been created by promoting the ORT idea through newspaper and radio advertisements. To reinforce the impersonal message of the media, one day's training in ORT has been given to all organized groups who are in regular contact with a wide public – the schoolteachers, the health workers, the agricultural extension workers, the traditional healers, and over 15,000 members of the Boy Scouts (panel 19).

In Colombia, the President has announced a National Plan for Child Survival and Development "*to prevent the deaths of 60,000 children every year*". Backing up the professional health services, the plan will involve the Catholic Church, the mass media, the Red Cross, the voluntary organizations, the co-operatives, the police, the army, and some of the 120,000 community volunteers who have been involved in the recent immunization campaigns. "*We are going to reach each house, each one of our 3.6 million children under five years*

Fig. 7 Decline in breast-feeding, São Paulo, Brazil, 1974–1980

Percentage of infants breast-fed for six months or more.

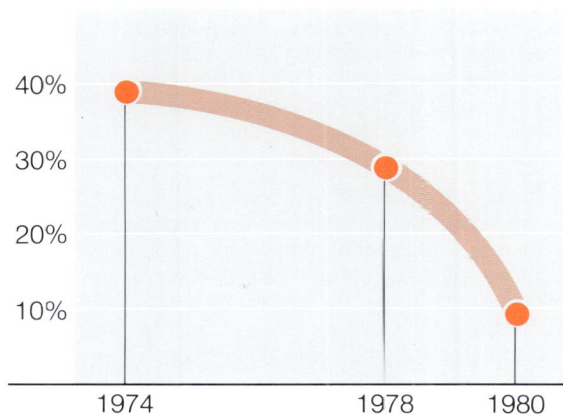

Source: International Union of Nutrition Scientists, Ad Hoc Task Force on Rethinking Infant Nutrition Policies, March, 1982.

Bolivia: reducing child deaths

8

Despite considerable economic difficulties, the government of Bolivia has been carrying out a programme to reduce its infant death rates by 50% over the next five years, using low-cost techniques such as expanded immunization and oral rehydration therapy.

The problem was clearly too big for the health services to tackle alone. The regular immunization programme, for example, was reaching less than a quarter of Bolivia's children, despite being theoretically available to all. So in February 1983 the Minister of Health decided to enlist the help of the country's other organized resources – the schools, the churches, the mass media, the workers' unions and the farmers' unions – in order to reach more families and support them in improving their own and their children's health. 'People's health committees', each headed by a volunteer 'people's health representative', were set up throughout Bolivia.

The first test came with the anti-polio campaign of late 1983 and early 1984. Every possible resource was employed to increase the availability of immunization and to inform parents of its importance. The result was that three shots of oral polio vaccine reached 70% of children in Bolivia's rural areas and 90% of the children in towns and cities.

A few months later, on 8 April 1984, the machinery went into action again to immunize the nation's children against measles – and again, over half a million children were vaccinated.

In 1985 a similar assault was launched on diphtheria, pertussis (whooping cough) and tetanus, using DPT 'triple vaccine'. Newspapers, television stations and some 80 radio stations alerted parents to the coming vaccination days. The people's health representatives visited every house to inform all parents that vaccination was available and essential. In the city of Santa Cruz, a special message from the Bishop, urging parents to take their children to be immunized, was read out in every church of the city during Sunday mass.

Two days before the launch date of 10 March, Bolivia's national trade union called a general strike; 10,000 demonstrators poured into the capital, La Paz, and road-blocks went up on main highways throughout the country. But with the union's support, the vaccination campaign went ahead unhindered. In total, 15,000 health workers, mostly volunteers, manned 5,000 vaccination posts and vaccinated 215,237 children – 85% of Bolivia's children under three. In previous years, triple vaccine had reached only 10% of under-threes.

Another major killer of Bolivia's children – diarrhoeal dehydration – is being tackled by setting up oral rehydration units, both to supply oral rehydration salts and to teach parents when and how to use them to forestall dehydration. So far 5,000 units, most of them managed by the people's health representatives, have been established. To create the demand and to teach the public how to use the salts, all possible communication channels have been used – from church services to radio and television 'advertisements', from street dramas to wall murals.

In a further move to safeguard children's well-being, all state maternity hospitals have adopted the policy of 'rooming-in' new-born babies with their mothers to encourage breast-feeding. The government is also iodizing table salt to counter iodine deficiency, since 65% of Bolivian schoolchildren suffer from goitre. And messages on child survival are now part of the curriculum of rural primary schools and colleges.

The Ministry of Health's programme has already saved thousands of children's lives and put basic elements of health care at the disposal of three or four times as many children as in previous years. If this programme can be sustained, it will bring a revolution in child survival to the country which still has the highest infant and child death rates in South America.

of age," said President Betancur at the launching of the campaign; "*and we are going to work with all families towards implementing simple actions of proven effectiveness in the protection of children's health*" (see panel 5).

In Honduras, deaths from diarrhoeal dehydration are reported to be falling after a one-year campaign to market ORT via television and radio. With mass-media messages backed up by 1,200 health workers making home visits, over 90% of Honduran women now know about the new remedy for diarrhoeal illness and almost 50% have begun using Litrosol – the local brand name for oral rehydration salts.

In Ecuador, a national plan has been launched to put four of the most basic strategies of child survival (growth checking, oral rehydration therapy, breast-feeding and improved weaning, and immunization) into practice on a national scale. The Ministries of Education, Defence, and Social Welfare, as well as the Ministry of Health, are involved and the plan is being supported by the mass media, the National Association of Medical Schools, and the National Council of Bishops. The same basic child health strategies are being introduced into the curriculum of all primary and secondary schools and volunteer university students are taking a house-to-house inventory of all young children in preparation for the national vaccination programme.

In Venezuela, 600,000 children are now receiving growth monitoring charts which also carry advice on breast-feeding, immunization, and ORT.

In Bolivia, where over 100,000 children have been dying each year from diarrhoeal dehydration, over 5,000 oral rehydration units have now been set up – 70% of them community-based – and over 2 million sachets of oral rehydration salts have been distributed. To promote breast-feeding, state maternity hospitals have changed to policies of 'rooming-in', television and radio are making the facts known to the public, and a national code is being drawn up to prevent the marketing of artificial infant formulas direct to the public (see panel 23). In support of these policies, the basic messages of the 'child survival and development revolution' have been introduced into the 'health

and home-making' curriculum of all the country's rural primary schools (see panel 8).

Asia

In India, where the Prime Minister's commitment has opened the way for a nation-wide campaign to immunize all children over the next five years, other child protection strategies are already going into action via the Integrated Child Development Services (ICDS) and the Urban Basic Services schemes – huge outreach projects, which, in the case of the ICDS alone, are now providing basic care to 10 million of India's poorest children.

In some areas, the results of the ICDS are already evident in lower rates of malnutrition, falling rates of low birth-weight, higher levels of immunization coverage, and fewer child deaths. Sample studies in 15 states have shown that 85% of malnourished children gain weight through the ICDS scheme and the Chairman of the ICDS Technical Committee estimates that almost 100,000 children's lives have already been saved.[8] The primary participants in the ICDS are the poor. And over the next five years, the scheme is scheduled to reach 60% of the children living in India's poor communities.

Broadening the base of this progress, India's massive drinking water programmes have now reached more than 200,000 villages and are beginning to have an effect on reducing infection.

In Bangladesh, the government's own National Oral Rehydration Programme is distributing over 17 million sachets of oral rehydration salts each year and the mass media are helping to create the demand by carrying the ORT message into millions of homes.

Meanwhile the Bangladesh Rural Advancement Committee (a non-governmental organization) has trained and fielded almost 1,000 ORT workers who have so far visited over 5 million mothers and 15,800 schools to give practical demonstrations of why, when and how to use

Egypt: leading the world on ORT

9

Egypt has passed the half-way point in its five-year campaign to promote oral rehydration therapy (ORT) and save the lives of the 80,000 and more children who now die each year from diarrhoeal dehydration. Results so far show that child death rates have been cut by approximately 30% in the test governorate of Alexandria.

Using what was learned in Alexandria, the project is now going nation-wide. As of mid-1985, over 4,000 clinics throughout Egypt have started oral rehydration centres to administer ORT and to teach mothers how to use the new therapy. Ahead of schedule, the programme is already beginning to have an impact on the infant death rate nation-wide. ''*By the end of this project*,'' says a member of the campaign team in Cairo, ''*we fully expect to achieve a 25% reduction in overall mortality among Egyptian children.*''

For ten years, ORT has been an officially recommended treatment in Egypt. But the salts were only available on prescription and there was little promotion to the public. So probably fewer than 1% of Egyptian parents were using the cheap life-saving breakthrough which could enable them to fight the single biggest threat to their children's lives and health.

But in January 1983, after six years of careful preparatory work and trials, the Egyptian government became one of the first in the world to pick up the ORT weapon on a national scale and declare war on the disease which is responsible for half of all child deaths in Egypt. With the help of a grant of $26 million from the United States Agency for International Development, the Ministry of Health launched the National Diarrhoeal Disease Control Programme under a high-powered secretariat with a total budget of more than $50 million.

Specially arranged lectures, workshops, articles in medical journals, and courses at a dozen universities – plus the setting up of over 100 ORT training units – educated large numbers of Egyptian doctors and nurses about the new treatment.

To capture the next generation of health professionals, ORT courses have been introduced onto the curricula of all medical colleges, teaching hospitals, and nursing schools.

The larger goal is to enable mothers themselves to prevent dehydration and to protect the child's nutritional health by the early use of ORT, by continuing to give plenty of food and fluids, and especially by continuing breast-feeding, during episodes of diarrhoea. In the Alexandria trials, television commercials for ORT had been broadcast every night for a month at peak viewing times. By the end of the month, most mothers knew about ORT and 36% had already begun using it. Now the television campaign is being broadcast nationally and the ORT symbol is reported to be the most widely recognized advertisement in Egypt.

To meet the demand, all pharmacists stock sachets of ORT. A 30% profit margin for the shopkeeper – plus free ORT measuring cups which can be sold to customers – is helping to compensate for profits lost on sales of anti-diarrhoeal drugs (which are more expensive and in most cases totally ineffective). National production of the sachets themselves is now running at 80 million a year.

When the National Diarrhoeal Disease Control Programme comes to an end in 1987, ORT should be a normal part of the nation's health system and of the people's own health behaviour. In the meantime, President Mubarak has announced his government's intention to seize the next great opportunity for protecting the lives and the growth of the nation's children – accelerating the country's immunization programme against the infectious diseases which now kill more than 50,000 Egyptian children each year and leave a similar number disabled. The target will be met before 1990 and, if at all possible, by September 1987 – the thirty-fifth anniversary of the Egyptian revolution.

home-made oral rehydration solutions (see panel 16). In Dhaka, the 1,000 urban volunteers who distribute 4,000 sachets of oral rehydration salts each week are also now distributing vitamin A capsules and bringing present knowledge on diarrhoeal disease control and improved weaning and feeding methods to the poorest areas of the city.

In Thailand, more than half of the nation's 3.3 million under-threes are now regularly growth-checked and more than half of the nation's parents have begun to use ORT to treat diarrhoeal illness (see panel 21).

In Indonesia, child survival strategies are being introduced, via the Family Nutrition Improvement Programme, into two-thirds of the country's 67,000 villages. A few days' training has been given to 400,000 volunteer nutrition *kaders* who are now able to advise parents on basic health and infant feeding and refer more difficult cases to one of over 5,000 clinics. By 1990, the aim is to involve virtually all Indonesian mothers in the regular checking of their children's growth (panel 13).

In the Philippines, approximately 70% of moth-

ers now know about ORT and an estimated 25% have begun using the new therapy.

In Pakistan, 1,300 doctors and 4,500 paramedics have been trained in ORT and an annual supply of 22 million sachets of oral rehydration salts is being promoted to the public via television, newspapers, posters, meetings of community leaders, and by the training of 5,000 traditional birth attendants each year (see panel 11).

In Kabul, Afghanistan, a campaign has already begun to halve the city's infant mortality rate by 1990 through basic child survival strategies. Approximately 100,000 children now have growth charts, immunization rates have begun to rise sharply, and an initial 1 million sachets of oral rehydration salts have been made available through health posts, day-care centres, local government offices, commercial pharmacies, literacy centres, kindergartens, and the city's youth and women's organizations. To reach the public with the message of ORT, over 100 television 'advertisements' have been broadcast, radio has carried the information up to twenty times a day, and 300,000 leaflets and posters have gone up on walls and in windows throughout the capital city.

Backed by the authority of 250 paediatricians, health workers are carrying child survival messages into the poorest homes of Kabul, over 4,000 teachers are now introducing 'child protection' lessons into the city's schools, and most water and sanitation programmes are also being used to promote both ORT and immunization.

Africa

In Egypt, death rates from diarrhoeal disease have been halved by ORT in a large pilot campaign which has now been extended to the whole nation (Fig. 8). Approximately 8,000 doctors have been retrained and, as of mid-1985, 4,000 clinics had started to use ORT against the diarrhoeal dehydration which kills more than 80,000 Egyptian children each year. To promote *demand*, television commercials for ORT have been broadcast nightly and all doctors are being asked to recommend the new therapy. To meet the demand, 80 million sachets of salts a year are now being locally produced and made available

Fig. 8 Impact of ORT on infant deaths, Alexandria, Egypt, 1980–1984

Overall infant deaths (all causes) during the summer 'diarrhoea season' in Alexandria Governorate, Egypt, 1980–84. Figures in parentheses indicate the rate per thousand in age group.

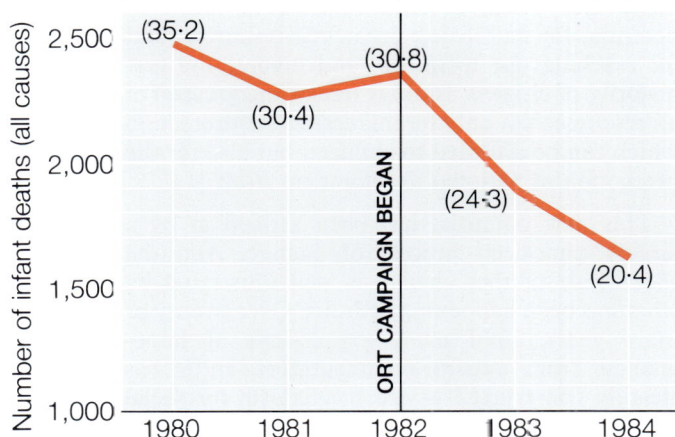

Source: Diarrhoeal Control Newsletter, National Control of Diarrhoeal Diseases Project, Egypt, 1984.

both from health posts and from thousands of commercial pharmacies.

In late 1981, only 5% of Alexandria's mothers knew about ORT and only about 1% had ever used it. Today, 90% know of ORT and 50% have used it (see panel 9).

Following the successful launch of the ORT programme, President Mubarak has this year made the commitment to universal immunization by or before 1990. At present, more than 50,000 Egyptian children are dying each year from vaccine-preventable diseases.

In Djibouti, the Council of Ministers has approved a plan to halve the country's infant mortality by 1990 and has launched a National Child Survival Plan, to be co-ordinated by a central committee including several government ministers and representatives from the mass media and the national women's organizations.

In Ethiopia, where the effort to relieve the dramatic suffering of the countryside has been the focus of world-wide attention, a quieter effort is also being mounted to try to cope with the everyday crisis facing many of the children of Addis Ababa. Last year, the Ministry of Health and city council set themselves the challenge of reducing the capital city's infant mortality rate from 136 per 1,000 in 1985 to less than 50 per 1,000 by 1990. Supported by the Ministry of Health and UNICEF, the Addis child survival campaign is now going into action through the city's 284 city dwellers' associations or *kebeles*. Volunteers from each *kebele*, trained and supervised by a qualified community health and development agent, are promoting ORT, organizing immunization, and helping mothers to monitor the progress of their children on the newly-designed Amharic growth chart (see panel 15).

In Somalia, a month of radio broadcasts, newspaper articles, TV programmes, loudspeaker announcements, and community meetings have prepared the ground for over 2,500 volunteers, drawn from political parties and women's organizations, to visit 150,000 homes in the capital city of Mogadishu – registering children and urging their parents to bring them to the vaccination centres.

In the Sudan, basic child survival strategies are proving their sharpened relevance in the midst of drought and famine. Through the emergency operations, and through the large-scale water supply programmes, ORT and immunization are combating the diarrhoeal and other diseases to which overcrowded refugee camps and emergency feeding centres are particularly vulnerable. So far, close to 6 million sachets of oral rehydration salts have been distributed during 1985 and hundreds of community health workers have been trained in their use (Fig. 9). Reports UNICEF's office in Khartoum: "*All who have used the salts – including the previously sceptical – say that their effect is remarkable.*" For both ORT and the present immunization drive, demand is being promoted by every means from media blitzes to travelling troupes of nomad players.

The social breakthrough

Not all of these ambitious programmes will succeed. And some of the difficulties which face them will be discussed in the next chapter. But an extraordinary beginning has been made. And in all of these cases, it is clear that the 'social breakthrough' in ways and means of reaching out to the *majority* of parents is just as important as any scientific breakthrough in knowledge about child health.

Steadily over the last ten or twenty years, many nations have levered themselves into a position to make that 'social breakthrough'. And this new potential for mobilizing organized resources, and for reaching out to inform and involve the vast majority of citizens, is today one of the greatest of all resources not only for increasing the protection which can be afforded to children but also for the promotion of national development itself.

This new potential has been arrived at by a largely unnoticed process of change. And the sheer scale of that change is well illustrated by what has been happening in India. Over twenty or more years, amid many expressions of hopelessness from outside commentators, India has steadily constructed a vast mechanism for social development which is now capable of touching the lives of the vast majority of the nation's 670 million people.

Each of the country's 5,100 'development blocks' now has an organized structure with the capacity to begin reaching out to inform and involve communities in development activities. All of those development blocks now have at least one primary health centre and an average of more than ten subcentres. To staff these health centres over 300,000 doctors and 300,000 paramedics have been trained. And over the next five years the number of 'health guides' is scheduled to double to 600,000 – one for every village in India. And now, under the ICDS scheme, an additional 5,000 *anganwadi* workers and 2,500 supervisors are being trained every year to help bring basic services to all of India's families.[9]

At the same time, tens of thousands of schools have been built and hundreds of thousands of teachers have been trained – putting a primary school within one kilometre of 90% of India's children. As a result, 80% of the nation's children now start school, and literacy – bringing with it a vastly increased capacity for the communication of new knowledge – is steadily rising.[10]

Nor have the mass media been standing still. Today, the nation has at least 20,000 newspapers, including over 1,000 dailies, and radio services now reach more than 90% of the nation.[11] And unthinkable as it might have seemed only a decade ago, it is now estimated that television will be within reach of as many as three-quarters of India's people before the end of the decade.

Not least among these increases in resources for development is the growth of the more than 12,000 national and international voluntary organizations which are now operating in India, often in the very poorest communities.

These are staggering achievements – with equivalents in many other nations. And since, in most cases, the health services themselves are a necessary but still not sufficient resource for reaching the majority, a full inventory of these 'outreach resources' will need to be taken if present knowledge about low-cost child protection is to be placed at the disposal of all families.

Resources for outreach

Perhaps the most underused of all those resources is the formal education system itself. Over the last twenty years, the developing nations as a whole have more than doubled the proportion of their children who are enrolled in school. And today, at least 80% of all children are enrolling in formal education for at least a few years.

By contrast, only about 20% of the developing world's children have any regular contact with formal health services. In Indonesia, for example, there are 5,000 primary health centres with one doctor each as opposed to 100,000 schools with an average of six teachers each.[12]

In other words, the school system is one of the most important channels of communication with the vast majority of today's and tomorrow's parents. By the most elementary definition of education as a preparation for life, present knowledge about basic child protection techniques is surely worth its place in the world's schools. And the example of Thailand, where child survival and development lessons are now being introduced onto the formal curriculum of 6.3 million schoolchildren, is surely one worthy of being followed by other nations.[13]

Fig. 9 Changes in treatment for diarrhoeal disease, Sudan, 1980–1982

Change in the percentage of diarrhoeal cases treated with oral rehydration therapy after ORT training workshops for health workers, 1980–82 (summary of all health stations).

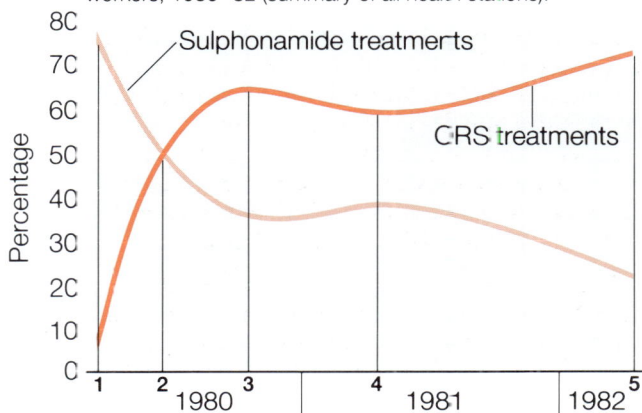

1 Before introduction of ORT (March 1980)
2 During cholera epidemic (June 1980)
3 One month after training workshops (October 1980)
4 Seven months after training workshops (April 1981)
5 Nineteen months after training workshops (April 1982)

Source: Tropical Doctor, October 1984.

Brazil: vaccinating 20 million

10

Brazil's national programme for mothers and children, launched in October 1984 in the wake of a successful breast-feeding campaign, combines all the child survival measures discussed in *The State of the World's Children* report:-

○ The regular weighing of children to monitor their growth spearheads the programme; the first health workers began their training in October 1984, in 10 of Brazil's 23 states, and a national growth chart is being tested.

○ To counter the 80,000 child deaths a year from diarrhoeal dehydration, Brazil is now manufacturing oral rehydration salts for free national distribution and for export to neighbouring states. An estimated 5 million cases of diarrhoea in Brazilian children were treated by oral rehydration therapy in 1985.

○ To reverse the drift towards bottle-feeding, 50,000 health personnel have been trained to promote breast-feeding. The 'rooming-in' of new-born babies with their mothers, to encourage breast-feeding, is now mandatory in all government-backed hospitals.

○ Until Brazil introduced vaccination days in 1980, some 2,000 children were paralysed by polio each year. Today the toll is less than 40. Six years on, the National Vaccination Days are an established complement to the regular health services. In 1984 other vaccines were added to the roster: protection of children under one against measles has risen from 58% in 1978 to 80%, and protection against diphtheria, whooping cough and tetanus from 39% in 1980 to 67%. And since June 1985, all children turning up on vaccination day have been fully registered and vaccination cards given to their mothers.

On each of the two yearly vaccination days more than 20 million children under five have been vaccinated against polio. Women's groups, schools, church groups and the armed forces have all participated; newspapers, radio and television, loudspeaker systems and even lottery tickets carry the call to vaccination all over the country. Brazil can now draw on 400,000 experienced volunteers – including teachers, firemen, and police – to man 90,000 vaccination posts across a territory larger than Western Europe.

In a parallel move to safeguard children's well-being, Brazil launched a national breast-feeding campaign, in 1981, which is now part of the mother and child programme. Posters extolling breast-feeding were distributed nation-wide; nearly $1 million worth of radio and television time was donated for breast-feeding 'commercials'; the paediatricians' association, 18,000 strong, actively promotes the campaign; and Brazil's medical schools now include breast-feeding in their curriculum. In the city of Recife, to cite one example, the proportion of children breast-fed at three months has doubled.

The Catholic Church has been a major ally in these efforts. Its 370 bishops and 5,000 priests, along with 14,000 monks and nuns working in clinics and hospitals, backed by newspapers, magazines and 120 radio stations, make it a powerful presence in Brazilian daily life. In 1985 the National Conference of Brazilian Bishops established a 'Pastorate of the Child' to disseminate child survival measures. The Pastorate is expanding this year to tackle an ambitious goal – reaching a million children under six in the impoverished north-east, where infant mortality is running at twice the national rate.

On 28 August 1985, the government also launched a major new initiative for child survival. Encouraged by two pilot projects in urban slums, one of which brought infant deaths down from 76 to 20 per 1,000 live births, the President has launched a national 'Child First' programme, to be put into action by the Brazilian Assistance Legion with funding of $150 million for the first year. Starting in January 1986 in poor urban areas of the north-east, the programme will focus on low-cost ways to improve children's chances of survival.

A second major resource for reaching a majority of all parents is obviously the mass media itself. With a total of 8,000 radio stations transmitting into almost every home, television reaching 50% to 60% of the people in most urban areas, and rising literacy bringing in its wake a rising newspaper readership, the developing world's electronic and printed mass media now have the potential to reach and inform the vast majority of the people in almost all countries.

Usually, the mass media are a necessary but not sufficient source of new information about something as fundamental as family health. If the mother is to make a change in some aspect of child care, then she will need to hear about it, and be convinced of it, from several respected sources. The basic message may be first heard or read about on the radio or in the newspaper, but it may need to be reinforced by the health worker or doctor, sanctioned by a religious or political leader, or approved by her peer group or parents-in-law.

Nonetheless, it has recently been the mass media which have put such subjects as immunization, ORT, and breast-feeding onto the national agenda – and onto the family agenda – in countries like Pakistan, Turkey, Colombia, Brazil, Honduras, Egypt, and the Gambia.

In other countries, the communications resources of organized religion – of the priests and the Catholic Church in Brazil, Colombia and El Salvador, of the imams and Muslim leaders in Indonesia, Oman, and the Philippines, and of the Buddhist priests in the villages of Burma and Sri Lanka – have also helped to bring new knowledge about child protection to many millions of parents, and from a most trusted source.

Next come the resources of the private voluntary organizations. Ranging from a *mahila mandal* women's organization with 200 members in a village of India to a Rotary International with a million members and 21,000 clubs in 159 nations, the non-governmental organizations have been a part of the action in almost every case of child survival campaigns which have reached out to the vast majority of a nation's parents.

To fight diarrhoeal disease, the Red Cross has launched its world-wide 'Child Alive' campaign with the very specific intention of "*preventing child deaths by extending the correct use of oral rehydration therapy*".[14]

Fig. 10 Developing countries producing oral rehydration salts

WHO REGION	COUNTRY
AFRICA	BURKINA FASO* BURUNDI ETHIOPIA KENYA MOZAMBICUE ZAIRE
AMERICAS	ARGENTINA BRAZIL COLOMBIA COSTA RICA DOMINICAN REPUBLIC EL SALVADOR HAITI HONDURAS MEXICO PARAGUAY PERU VENEZUELA
EASTERN MEDITERRANEAN	AFGHANISTAN EGYPT GAZA STRIP IRAN (ISLAMIC REPUBLIC OF) IRAQ PAKISTAN SYRIAN ARAB REPUBLIC TUNISIA
EUROPE	MOROCCO TURKEY
SOUTH-EAST ASIA	BANGLADESH* BURMA INDIA INDONESIA NEPAL MONGOLIA* SRI LANKA THAILAND
WESTERN PACIFIC	CHINA* DEM. KAMPUCHEA* MALAYSIA PHILIPPINES REPUBLIC OF KOREA

*Indicates a cottage industry approach
Note: Countries in colour are those which are self-sufficient in ORS production
Source: *World Health Organization, WHO/CDD/85.1?, Geneva 1984.*

Pakistan: saving 100,000 lives

11

In June 1985, Pakistan's health planners drew up the balance sheet for the country's three-year Accelerated Health Programme, launched in 1982 to tackle Pakistan's high infant mortality rate of 120 deaths per 1,000 live births.

○ Vaccine-preventable disease: 80% of the budget has been allocated to an all-out effort to immunize every child against the six diseases which kill a quarter of a million Pakistani children every year. Every province has organized mass vaccination drives, which draw on specially trained workers, mass-media campaigns, and every available resource to motivate communities. By June 1985 over 3,000 vaccination posts, motivation teams, and mobile vaccination units were in operation throughout the country.

The graph on page 11 shows the results. In 1982 barely 5% of under-fives were immunized; by mid-1985, 65% were vaccinated, which means that more than 100,000 lives are already being saved every year, and 3 million illnesses prevented. The government is confident that 75% of children will be protected by the end of the year. In the Punjab, where 55% of Pakistan's people live, coverage has already passed the 80% mark. Correspondingly, coverage in areas such as Baluchistan is below average and insufficient to promote 'herd immunity'.

To back up the immunization services, Pakistan is now one of the first developing countries to become self-sufficient in measles vaccine, thanks to a production plant opened in 1984 and financed by the efforts of His Royal Highness Prince Talal of Saudi Arabia.

○ Diarrhoeal dehydration: the second element of the accelerated programme is oral rehydration therapy, to forestall the diarrhoeal dehydration which kills nearly 300,000 Pakistani children every year. And here the record is not so impressive. Production of oral rehydration salts has been stepped up, from 1 million to 22 million sachets a year. But the programme has been less successful in creating demand than in increasing supply. Many doctors have yet to adopt the therapy; many pharmacists prefer to sell more lucrative – and ineffective – drugs; and there is as yet no great breakthrough in putting this life-saving technique at the disposal of the vast majority of Pakistan's parents. Today perhaps only 10% of Pakistan's parents use oral rehydration therapy – despite the fact that diarrhoeal dehydration remains the number one killer of Pakistani children.

In an effort to turn the tide, the Pakistan Paediatric Association has lobbied successfully for some anti-diarrhoeal drugs to be taken off the official drug register, and the Ministry of Health has launched a media campaign, directed at doctors as well as parents, to increase the demand for oral rehydration. Television advertisements are being broadcast at prime time to educate parents about oral rehydration and other low-cost measures that can save their children's lives.

○ Training traditional birth attendants: the third element is the training of traditional birth attendants (TBAs). For the majority of Pakistan's mothers, TBAs are the maternal and child health services. They deliver 80% of babies in rural areas and their level of knowledge – about pregnancy, safe delivery, hygiene, and infant care – is a key determinant of maternal and child health through the nation.

The aim is to train 50,000 TBAs so that every village and slum in Pakistan will have at least one TBA able to deliver babies safely and offer sound advice on health care. So far, 15,000 have received three months' training and have returned to their communities.

With the balance sheet looking so healthy, Pakistan is extending the Accelerated Health Programme for another three-year term. If the second term can match the achievements of the first, Pakistan will have dramatically improved its children's chances of survival and of healthy growth and development.

On the immunization front, Rotary International's Polio 1990 initiative and the Save the Children Fund's Stop Polio campaign are helping government health services to fight the paralytic polio which is still disabling *5,000 children a week* in the developing world. And as part of their world-wide Child Alive programme, national Red Cross societies have been heavily involved in the success of the recent immunization campaigns in the Americas – fielding more than 13,000 volunteer vaccinators for the Colombian campaign alone.

For the promotion of knowledge about vitamin A, Helen Keller International (HKI) is now launching a $6 million Child Survival Plan to *"make a dramatic impact on child survival by preventing and treating widespread vitamin A deficiency in countries where children are at grave risk of blindness and child mortality"*.[15] At the same time, HKI has also moved 5 million doses of vitamin A into the camps of Ethiopia and the Sudan where it is not untypical for 10% of children to have advanced symptoms of vitamin A deficiency and where many are irreversibly blind.[15]

In the industrialized world there are now over 3,000 voluntary organizations sending an estimated $1,500 million a year to their counterpart organizations in the developing world. And in the developing nations themselves, uncounted thousands of organizations – an estimated 6,000 in Bangladesh, for example – are working with the people of the poorest villages and neighbourhoods where children are most at risk.

In each nation, local knowledge and creativity will usually be able to pick out other ways and means of reaching out to particular groups of parents. In Brazil, for example, child survival is now one of the 'badges' which can be earned by the nation's 10 million Boy Scouts. In Colombia, the government has decided to boost its National Plan for Child Survival and Development by creating a force of 180,000 'health guards' through a law which obliges all fourth-year high-school students to be trained in child survival knowledge and to serve at least 100 hours a year in the community. In Nepal, an attempt is being made to take advantage of a contraceptive distribution system in order to promote sachets of oral rehydration salts through the same 5,000 retail outlets. In Indonesia, it was the structures set up to promote family planning, and the 10,000 family planning workers already in place across the country, which made possible the subsequent launch of the Family Nutrition Improvement Programme (see panel 13). In the Middle East, it is the national women's organizations (in Oman and the United Arab Emirates) and the women's unions (in Iraq, Syria, and Democratic Yemen) who have begun to take a particular interest in the promotion of immunization and ORT. In Nigeria, it has been the traditional chiefs who have helped immunization campaigns to reach much larger numbers of parents. In Honduras, local mayors or alcaldes have lent their authority to the messages about ORT going out on the radio stations. In India, villagers who have been trained to maintain village hand-pumps are now also being trained to promote ORT along with the clean water supplies. In Brazil, the traditional healers or rezadeiras are also promoting ORT. In Bombay, schoolchildren have both prepared the lists of all under-ones in the community and helped to inform their parents of the times and places for immunization. In Haiti, over 2,000 ordinary homes which are also small shops for everyday provisions like batteries and soft drinks are now selling sachets of oral rehydration salts as well.

Primary health workers

When formal health services reach only a minority of the population, it is only by mobilizing all of these resources that present knowledge about family health can be broken out of its medical show-case and put into the hands of millions of families.

But experience has shown that all of these new ideas about health are put into practice more quickly and more surely if there is a health worker, even one with only a few weeks' or months' training, who actually lives in the community and who is there at the time the mother most immediately needs the advice about how to use the new oral rehydration therapy, about going for an injection in pregnancy, about whether to take a child for a third immunization, about continuing to breast-feed or about when to begin weaning. If such a person is part of, and available to, the community, whether it be an anganwadi worker in India or a *promotora de salud* in Colombia, then all other messages from all other sources are more likely to take root.

At the moment, there is still a long way to go before every village and neighbourhood has access to modern knowledge of family health methods via some kind of resident trained health worker.

In most developing countries, three-quarters or more of the health budget is still devoted to expensive hospital and doctor-based care for less than 20% of the population.[17] In most countries, primary health care is still something to be tacked on to the existing health services – if there is anything left in the budget when the hospitals and the urban-based curative services have been paid for. In most countries, there are still too few primary health care workers with too little training and supervision and with not nearly enough support from referral services. But despite all this, progress has been made in the last few years.

Almost all developing nations have now adopted primary health care as official policy. In some, that commitment is so far only rhetorical. In others, there has already been a significant rise in the numbers of paramedics and community health workers:-

In China there are over 2 million 'barefoot doctors' at work in the community. In India, as has already been mentioned, there are now over 300,000 health guides at work and there will soon be 600,000 in villages throughout the country.[18] But these, the two most populous nations of the world, are not the only examples of large-scale training of paramedical staff.

In Burma, 26,258 community health workers and 8,700 auxiliary workers have been posted and the plan is now to put one community health worker in each of Burma's 65,000 villages.

In Thailand, 43,000 village health workers and over 419,000 'health communicators' have been trained to bring basic health messages to families in over 90% of all villages. In total, Thailand now has more than 7,000 health centres, each staffed by a trained midwife and a health sanitarian (see panel 21).[19]

In Pakistan, tens of thousands of traditional birth attendants are being trained in basic mother and child protection strategies (see panel 11).

In the Republic of Korea, community health practitioners are now available to over 80% of all rural people.

In Bangladesh, there are now 23,000 trained midwives and 30,000 more are scheduled to be trained by 1990.

In Nepal, there are now almost 2,000 auxiliary health workers, with either one or two years' basic training, working in 800 rural health posts.

In Tanzania, 90% of the population now lives within 10 kilometres of a health post (and over 70% within 5 kilometres).

In Niger, 13,000 community health workers have been trained to serve almost 4,000 villages.

And in three-quarters of all the developing countries, there are now some kind of training programmes for the traditional birth attendants (see panel 11) who are relied upon by the majority of the world's mothers for help and advice in matters of bearing and caring for children.[20]

In summary, the techniques and the knowledge for a revolution in child survival are now available. The capacity to inform and support parents in bringing that revolution about – and beginning to put primary health care into practice – is also in place in most nations of the world. The only catalyst needed to compound these two elements into a practical improvement in the lives of the world's children is therefore the political will and commitment to do it.

In several nations, nations where that political will and commitment have already been demonstrated, it is already clear that there is going to be a steep fall in the rate of child malnutrition and child deaths over the next few years.

But in all countries, there are important difficulties to be acknowledged.

The benefits for women

The greatest of those difficulties is the fact that the majority of the developing world's women have too large a share of responsibility for family well-being and too small a share in the decisions which affect it.

For whether we are talking about breast-feeding or weaning, oral rehydration therapy or immunization, regular growth checking or frequent handwashing, it is obvious that the mother stands at the centre of the child survival revolution.

Acquiring and applying present knowledge about child health therefore makes great demands on the mother. But as this chapter will summarize, strategies for protecting the lives of children are also among the most important strategies for improving the lives of women. Inasmuch as they save considerable amounts of money, they effectively increase a woman's income. Inasmuch as they prevent illness and disability, they liberate a woman's time and energy. Inasmuch as they save lives, they help to liberate women from the trap of too-frequent pregnancy (see panel 25). Inasmuch as they empower a woman to protect her own and her children's health by her own actions, they increase a woman's ability and confidence to take more control over her own life.

On 26 July this year, at a World Conference in Nairobi, the United Nations Decade for Women formally drew to an end. And although it is not possible here to examine the whole fabric of issues which has been woven during the Decade, it is useful to follow those strands which lead directly to the quality of children's lives and to the capacity of mothers to bring about improvements:-

First of all, the Decade has dispelled forever the idea that 'farmer' is a masculine noun. Survey after survey has shown that women often work more hours per day and more days per year in the fields than their menfolk (Fig. 11) and that they are directly responsible for producing more than half of all the food grown in the developing world.[1] In West Africa, for example, women do 70% to 80% of all agricultural work and produce 40% to 50% of all staple food crops.[2]

Then, after spending up to six or seven hours a day planting, weeding, hoeing, threshing and gleaning, the woman returns home to the tasks of pounding and winnowing, grinding and boiling, drying and storing, carrying and marketing, cooking and serving.

After feeding the men and seeing that the children have eaten, she herself eats a small proportion of the food she has grown. Then she turns to the tasks of washing the pots, cleaning the house, sweeping the compound, bathing the infants, mending the clothes, laying out the bedding, feeding the animals, tending the kitchen garden, going to the market, fetching the firewood, carrying the water, and looking after the elderly, the sick ... and the children.

In other words, women put in approximately twice as many hours of work as men.

At the same time, the Decade for Women has also brought out the fact that many millions of the world's women are permanently in poor health. To take one indicative example: almost half of the women in the developing world are anaemic – and among pregnant women that figure rises closer to 60% (see Lifelines: iron, iodine and vitamin A).[3]

The cause is not usually a specific illness. It is rather the general 'maternal depletion' caused by too much work and too little food combined with too many pregnancies too close together.

From girlhood to womanhood, the females of many societies are fed last and least.* Malnutrition in girls is much more common than among boys and the fact that, on average, an American woman weighs approximately 25% more than an Indian woman is to be explained not by race but by food.[4]

Frequent pregnancy sharpens the problem. Poor growth in her own childhood may have left the mother less able to withstand the heavy

---

* *"The cumulative result of poverty, under-nutrition and neglect which girls suffer right from birth is reflected in their poor adult body size, which in turn influences high maternal mortality, low birthweight and poor nutritional status of their infants. The relative neglect of the female child is evident from the greater prevalence of growth retardation even in infancy among girls than in boys...".[6]*

Nicaragua:
child deaths down 30%

12

In the 1960s and 1970s Nicaragua had one of the highest levels of infant mortality in Latin America. Diarrhoea was the chief killer of infants and children, followed by respiratory infections, tetanus, measles, malaria and whooping cough.

After the change of government in 1979, Nicaragua's health and social security systems were reorganized to begin building a comprehensive primary health care system. In four years, the number of health posts and health centres was trebled, and over 80% of the population now has access to free primary health care.

Limited resources have meant searching for low-cost, high-impact, community-based ways of protecting the health of mothers and young children. So health activities have centred around child growth monitoring, diarrhoeal disease control, promoting breast-feeding and appropriate weaning, immunization, family food supplements and the care of pregnant and lactating women.

But improving health care is not equated only with the expansion of government services. Health is also seen as the responsibility of organized people's groups. 'People's health councils' enable trade unions, neighbourhood organizations, and associations of young people and women to take an active role in carrying out health programmes.

Building on the experience of the national literacy crusade in 1980, a series of People's Health Days (*jornadas populares de salud*) was launched in 1981. Co-ordinated by the people's health councils, the health days have become the leading edge of campaigns against malaria, dengue fever, polio and measles. In 1981, the malaria and dengue campaigns involved 1.9 million people (70% of the population) and 70,000 volunteer health workers, or brigadistas. Every year, on three week-ends between January and June, the anti-polio and measles campaigns regularly mobilize around 20,000 *brigadistas*.

Improved water supplies and sanitation have reduced the incidence of diarrhoea among young children, and deaths from dehydration have been cut by setting up 356 oral rehydration units in health centres and health posts. Nurses at the units teach mothers how to mix and administer oral rehydration salts, and also educate them in preventing diarrhoea through continued breast-feeding and better hygiene in the home. The salts are now due to become widely available from *brigadistas* and through outlets such as small shops and market-traders. To meet the expected demand, UNICEF is supplying 1.5 million packets of oral rehydration salts a year.

Mass communications play a key role in the health campaigns. Neighbourhood organizations produce their own posters, leaflets and notices, and announce forthcoming health days with loudspeakers mounted on cars.

Nicaragua's programme has already yielded results. Since oral rehydration therapy was introduced in 1980, the death rate among children with diarrhoea in hospitals has fallen by 42%, and diarrhoea has fallen from the first to the fifth cause of child death. Immunization rates rival those of some developed countries. In 1984, according to UNICEF estimates, 97% of infants were protected against tuberculosis, 60% against measles and 76% against polio. No polio case has been registered since 1981. Immunization against diphtheria, whooping cough and tetanus is increasing, but only 33% of infants were fully protected in 1984. Neonatal tetanus is still prevalent, but a nation-wide campaign begun in 1983 aims to vaccinate all women of child-bearing age.

Although some important issues still remain to be tackled, Nicaragua's focus on the priority health problems of women and children is having a measurable national impact. Between 1978 and 1983 the overall infant mortality rate fell by one-third, from 121 to 80 per 1,000 live births – one of the most dramatic improvements in child survival in the developing world.

nutritional burdens of pregnancy and breast-feeding.[5] A pregnancy every eighteen months with nothing in between but hard work, frequent illness, and poor food, gradually depletes the mother's body of protein and calories, health and energy. And if the late stages of pregnancy also happen to coincide with the season of heaviest work in the fields, then the mother-to-be may even fail to gain any weight at all as her pregnancy advances.[7]

The net result is that the mother's time and energy – the most valuable of all resources for improving child health – are eroded by both the poverty and the injustice of her circumstances.

Inevitably, short cuts have to be taken merely to reach the end of the day.

To save time and firewood, the mother may cook food less frequently and in larger quantities – storing it for longer in unhygienic surroundings and at tropical temperatures.

To allow a long day's earnings in the fields or plantations, an infant may be left with an eight-year-old brother or sister for the whole day.

To save a trip back from the fields or the market, a young child may be fed only twice a day, at adult mealtimes, instead of the four or five smaller meals which a young child's small stomach needs.

To save firewood, water may go unboiled. And to save an hour's trip to the well, the family's hands may not always be washed after using the latrine or before preparing the food.

To save time in cooking, the mother may cut down on protein-rich foods like pulses which usually take longer to prepare.

To save making special weaning foods, children may be weaned on a porridge made from the same food as is given to the adults – even though children need more calorie-dense foods to avoid becoming malnourished.

To save coming home every few hours, the mother may only breast-feed her infant two or three times a day – even though this may lead to less milk and the premature ending of breast-feeding. Or she may decide that using artificial infant formula in a bottle is worth the expense as it means that somebody else – a sister or a grandmother – can feed the child and allow the mother to carry on working.

To save time and energy in the fields, she may switch to less demanding food crops like cassava instead of maize or rice, not knowing of the nutritional losses this will bring to her children.

To make sure that the staple crop is planted or harvested, she may neglect the kitchen garden, even though it is the source of the vegetables, beans, or fruits which provide the minerals, the oils, the vitamin A, which are essential ingredients of the young child's diet.

Fig. 11 Male and female shares of agricultural tasks and training, Africa

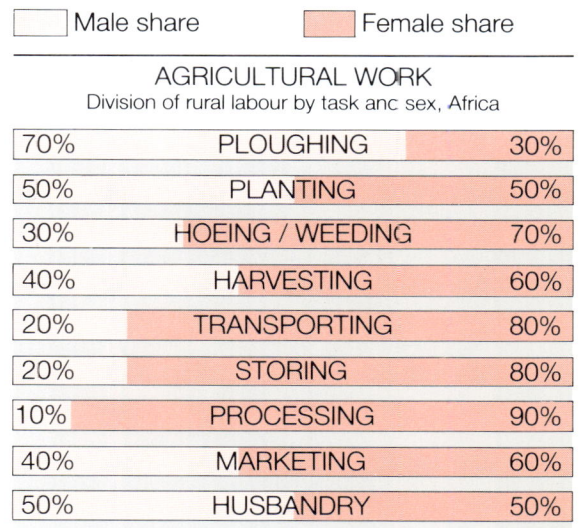

Male share		Female share

AGRICULTURAL WORK
Division of rural labour by task and sex, Africa

Male	Task	Female
70%	PLOUGHING	30%
50%	PLANTING	50%
30%	HOEING / WEEDING	70%
40%	HARVESTING	60%
20%	TRANSPORTING	80%
20%	STORING	80%
10%	PROCESSING	90%
40%	MARKETING	60%
50%	HUSBANDRY	50%

Source: Economic Commission for Africa, 1975.

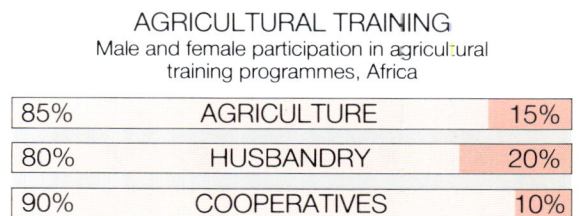

AGRICULTURAL TRAINING
Male and female participation in agricultural training programmes, Africa

Male	Programme	Female
85%	AGRICULTURE	15%
80%	HUSBANDRY	20%
90%	COOPERATIVES	10%

Source: International Children's Centre, "Children in the Tropics", Issue No 146, Paris, 1983.

Indonesia: one million health workers

13

In over 40,000 of Indonesia's 67,000 villages, trained village volunteers, or *kaders*, are working to help their community protect its children's health. One result is that 5 million Indonesian mothers are now regularly weighing their children and checking up on their growth.

The *kaders* are chosen by their communities for brief training and usually serve 10 to 15 households. Their duties include helping mothers to weigh under-fives every month; providing advice on nutrition; distributing food supplements to malnourished children; supplying vitamin A, iron supplements and oral rehydration salts; promoting family planning and issuing contraceptives; and mobilizing villagers for immunization.

Close to one million *kaders* are now in place, in a country with 160 million people. A quarter of a million of them work with the family planning programme. Some 400,000 work with the Family Nutrition Improvement Programme. Three-quarters of a million work with Indonesia's family welfare movement as well. Many *kaders* work with two or more of these different programmes.

The idea of village volunteers is not new to Indonesia. The age-old tradition of *gotong-royong*, or mutual self-help, puts great value on voluntary work for the community, and played an important role in spreading the message of the 'Green Revolution' which so dramatically raised Indonesia's rice yields in the 1970s. Largely because of this voluntary tradition, the basic services provided by nutrition *kaders* cost only $2 per child per year.

A 1983 study reviewed the effectiveness of nutrition *kaders* in seven villages in Bali, Java and Sumatra with a total population of 16,000. The researchers found that:-

○ 89% of under-fives regularly attended the monthly weighing sessions.

○ 85% of mothers believed in maintaining or increasing their food intake during pregnancy – a practice running counter to traditional beliefs.

○ 75% of mothers breast-fed for two years or more.

○ Almost 90% of mothers added vegetables and more energy-rich food to their child's diet before the age of a year.

○ 51% of children had been immunized against tuberculosis and 57% had had two shots against diphtheria, whooping cough and tetanus.

○ 65% of mothers knew about oral rehydration to prevent diarrhoeal dehydration; 57% could mix the pre-packaged oral rehydration salts and 47% knew the ingredients for making a salt and sugar mix at home.

Such figures have yet to be reached on a national scale. Improved child nutrition has been hard to document; children in need of referral have slipped through the net; and *kaders* have sometimes fallen short in the time-consuming task of counselling mothers about health and nutrition. A quarter of the 400,000 nutrition *kaders* have moved or dropped out.

Nation-wide only 50% of children who could come for regular weighing actually do so, and those who stay away may well be those most in need – a problem common to most programmes aiming at universal coverage.

Even so, the figure of 50% compares well with the 10% of under-fives attending health clinics. And the perplexing variety of services *kaders* provide are now being brought together in the *posyandu* – the 'one-stop' health post, where the monthly weighing session also supplies the setting for health, immunization and family planning services.

Another million *kaders* are due to be trained by the end of the decade, and Indonesia looks set to achieve its stated goals for 1989: lowering its infant mortality rate to 70 deaths per 1,000 live births, raising immunization levels to a minimum of 65%, and extending the Family Nutrition Improvement Programme to every village in the country.

To save losing a day's work in the fields during harvest time, she may decide that one immunization is enough.

To save an hour's walk to the clinic when she is pregnant, and possibly two hours queueing in the sun when she gets there, she may decide not to bother with another pre-natal check or a second tetanus injection. And to save yet another trip with an eight-month-old baby to carry, she may decide not to bother weighing the child that month.

To have more help with all of this, a woman may decide that she needs more daughters – and that she needs them at home, not in school.[8]

Saving time, money, and energy

All of these demands on the time and energy and health of women help to explain, if not to solve, one of the most intransigent of all development's problems – the problem of 'reaching the poorest'.

For although it is among the poorest 25% or 30% of a nation's people that the problems of malnutrition and ill health are concentrated, it is also in this group that women have the least time and energy, the least information and confidence, to become involved in acquiring and applying new knowledge or taking advantage of available services.

The problem is one which runs like a fault line through most development efforts in most nations. For whether we are talking about methods of improving the productivity of the land or methods of improving the growth and development of children, it is the poor, those whose need is greatest, who have the least surplus of resources – of money, time, energy, health, knowledge and confidence – to invest in improvements. That is the catch-22 of poverty. And it means that the problem is perpetuated through a cycle of poor nutrition, poor health, poor performance at school and at work, poor productivity, low income, no surplus money or effort to invest in improvement, leading to continued poverty, continued poor nutrition ... and so the cycle goes on.

Protecting the normal physical and mental development of children is clearly essential if that cycle is ever to be broken. Today, because of new knowledge and new outreach capacity, that protection can be provided to the majority of the poor world's children at a cost which is within the capacity of most of the poor world's families. But for all the other kinds of support which will be necessary to bring this about, the critical health worker at the centre of the child survival revolution is still the child's mother.

Does the fact that so many women are so overworked mean that there is no realistic hope of new knowledge and new techniques being acquired and applied? Or can the major low-cost ways now available for protecting child health also allow mothers themselves to save both time and money and conserve their own health and strength?

Answering that question means looking at some of the practical and everyday aspects of the techniques themselves:-

Breast-feeding, although taking a considerable amount of the mother's time, can save the $200 to $300 a year which is the average cost, in a developing country, of bottle-feeding a baby on artificial infant formulas.[9] A family living on the official minimum wage in Mexico, for example, would need to spend 25% of its food budget on milk formula to provide enough for just one infant.[10] In Africa, the proportionate costs are even higher – and even an employed person, say a hospital cleaner or a government clerk, would have to spend over 30% of his or her monthly salary to buy enough milk powder for a two-month-old infant.[11]

In addition, breast-feeding usually delays the return of menstruation and offers the mother a considerable degree of protection against the stresses of another pregnancy following too close upon the last. On average, the post-natal period of infertility lasts for 3 months for a woman who does not breast-feed at all and for 13 months for a woman who breast-feeds for 18 months.[12] And although not a totally reliable method of contraception from the individual woman's point of view, it is still the case that, on average, each additional month of breast-feeding can give the mother an additional month of protection against pregnancy.[13]

Not least, breast-feeding can halve the number of illnesses – particularly diarrhoeal and respiratory infections – which a child has to be nursed through in its first year of life (Figs. 12 and 15).

Oral rehydration therapy also offers savings of both money and time. For of all the childhood diseases which a mother has to cope with, diarrhoea is the most frequent. Each episode usually lasts four or five days and there may be as many as six or more episodes a year. And in the one study on the subject so far, it has been found that the average length of diarrhoeal illness was reduced from just under five days to approximately two and a half days in homes where ORT was used.[14] The result is not only a reduction of nursing and worrying time, but also less bathing of children and less washing of soiled clothes.

Once a mother has the confidence to use ORT in her own home, being certain that it is the best possible therapy, then the time, travelling expenses and treatment costs of clinic and hospital visits can usually be saved. In most developing nations today, diarrhoeal disease and respiratory infections are the two most common reasons for visits to pharmacies, health clinics, and hospitals. In some countries, families are now spending up to 10% of their income on anti-diarrhoeal drugs which are of no value.* The early use of oral rehydration in the home will normally mean that dehydration will not set in and a clinic visit will not be necessary. But even if the diarrhoea persists and dehydration begins, a child who has been treated at home with an oral rehydration solution will arrive at a clinic in better condition and can be given the necessary treatment (with WHO/UNICEF-formula oral rehydration salts or, in more extreme cases, intravenous therapy) in less time and at less expense and with greater certainty of success.

---

* The import and sale of anti-diarrhoeal drugs has recently been banned in Jordan and the Sudan and, in Syria, the government subsidies for such products have been withdrawn.

Immunization would take out at least two or three major, worrying illnesses which a child would otherwise have to be nursed through. It would also prevent at least half of the childhood disabilities, especially paralytic polio and blindness, which have a serious effect on the life of the mother as well as on the development of the child. With full immunization, for example, the chances of a child becoming disabled are reduced by approximately 30%.

Similarly, low-cost action to fortify diets with vitamin A, iodine, or iron may be essential for protecting the normal development of young children in certain areas of the world (see panel 22). And the time taken to include these minerals and vitamins in the diet – or to collect capsules from a clinic – can also protect the mother from the consequences of a child's disablement. Vitamin A supplements, or the inclusion of more green vegetables in the child's meals, could save the eyesight of the quarter of a million children who now go blind each year from vitamin A deficiency. But the same action could also save the mothers of those children from the agony of watching their children's eyes slowly cloud over and from the lifelong extra work of bringing up a sightless child. In other areas, going for iodine injections or buying iodized salt is necessary to protect both the foetus from brain damage and the mother from the consequences of giving birth to a permanently retarded baby.

Growth monitoring will normally mean a visit to a clinic or a village weighing centre once a month. But it too can repay with interest the time invested. The main aim of regular growth monitoring is to bring the mother into regular contact with basic advice and help on child health and to give that mother early warning of any faltering in her child's growth. And at that early stage, relatively cheap and simple action can be taken to stop the child from slipping into the cycle of malnutrition and frequent illness – a cycle which takes such a toll both on the child's growth and on the mother's time and energy.

Those demands on a woman's time caused by the sheer frequency of child illnesses are hard to imagine from the perspective of the industrialized world. In very poor countries, children may be ill for 30% to 50% of their young lives. According to one survey in Bangladesh, for example, the average child has one illness or another for 75% of all the days of its life.[15] Such figures mean that a mother, with perhaps three or four children to look after, is permanently coping with the illness of at least one child. And not only does this take time, it also costs money. Many families in the developing world spend over 10% of their income on health – in travelling expenses to clinics, in costs of medicines, and in fees to doctors or traditional healers. In a country like Malawi, for example, it has been calculated that one-third of the nation's total expenditure on health is spent by families themselves.[16] Or in Honduras, where the average family sustains about thirty illnesses a year, the direct cost to the family is approximately $7.50 per illness or a total of over $200 a year – half of which goes on drugs.[17] So the financial costs of illness, as well as the costs in the mother's time, energy, and worry, are proportionately much higher than in the industrialized nations.

Fig. 12 Relative rates of infection by feeding method

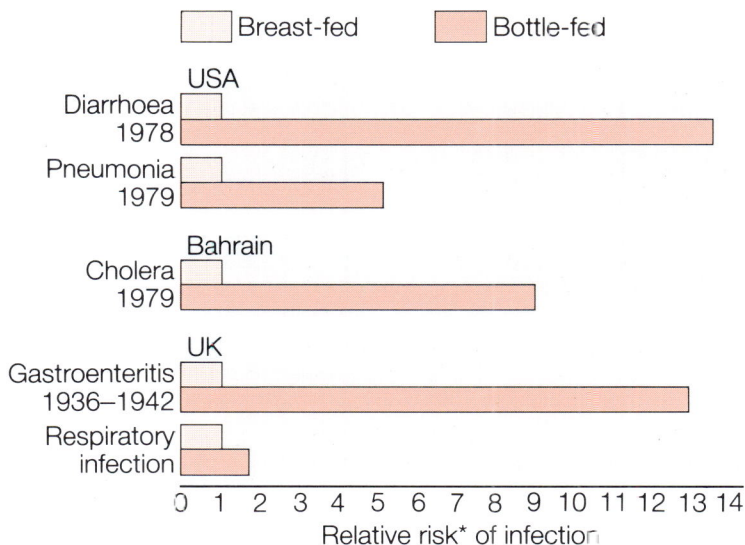

Breast-fed   Bottle-fed

USA
Diarrhoea
1978
Pneumonia
1979

Bahrain
Cholera
1979

UK
Gastroenteritis
1936–1942
Respiratory
infection

0 1 2 3 4 5 6 7 8 9 10 11 12 13 14
Relative risk* of infection

*Relative risk is the number of cases appearing in 100 bottle-fed babies divided by the number of cases in 100 breast-fed babies from the same socio-economic environment over the same time period.

Source: Journal of Tropical Pediatrics vol. 8, No. 4, August 1982.

Growth checking, as a focal point of child health protection, could bring together present knowledge both about the prevention of illness and about the special weaning and feeding needs of the young child. The result could be at least a 50% reduction in the days spent in illness during a child's earliest years.

The 'three Fs'

In previous years' reports, child survival and well-being has also been shown to be closely related to the 'three Fs' of family spacing, food supplements, and female education. All of these exert powerful upward leverage on a child's chances of survival and normal growth. But all of them also exert powerful upward leverage on the well-being of women themselves:-

Family spacing. Leaving at least two years between one pregnancy and the next can reduce the risk of an infant's death by 50% or more (Fig. 14). But it is also one of the most important ways, perhaps the most important way, of maintaining the health of those whose bodies are depleted by the heavy nutritional stresses of almost continuous pregnancy, child-bearing, and breast-feeding. In most developing countries, 'maternal causes' are the leading cause of death for women between the ages of 25 and 35.[18] In other words, more than a thousand young mothers are now dying every day – and many of those 'maternal deaths' are the result of too many births too close together.

Female education. The education of the mother has been found to be perhaps the most important social determinant of a child's chances of survival – even allowing for differences in economic class (see Lifelines: female education).[19] But it too is a powerful force for improving the lives of mothers themselves.

Even with only four or five years of schooling in which to achieve basic literacy, a woman stands a very much higher chance of acquiring the knowledge and the confidence to plan and space her pregnancies, to make use of available health services, to discover and apply new knowledge, to work outside the home and earn a higher income, and to participate in the family and community decisions which affect her life.

Somalia:
protection in emergencies

14

The basic strategies now available for bringing about a revolution in child survival are nowhere more relevant than in Africa, where the present crisis is exacerbating the basic health problems faced by children in all poor communities. An example from Somalia:-

During April and May 1985 an epidemic of cholera, the swiftest and most lethal of diarrhoeal diseases, swept through an encampment of 45,000 Ethiopian refugees at Gannet in north-west Somalia, killing 1,300 people, many of them women and children. In the neighbouring town of Hargeisa only 33 people died – thanks to Hargeisa's primary health care programme and the health workers who were immunizing children against the main killer diseases of childhood.

Hargeisa, with a registered population of some 120,000, is the capital of one of ten regions where primary health care services are being established. But even though immunization was available, only 15% of Hargeisa's children were fully vaccinated. As the possibility of famine loomed in late 1984, along with the risk of measles deaths in children weakened by malnutrition, the decision was made to vaccinate Hargeisa's children as quickly as possible.

The first round of vaccinations was set for January 1985. To complement Hargeisa's regular vaccinators, student nurses were trained; vaccine supplies were ordered in, local officials were briefed, and the leaders of *tabellas* (units of 50 families) registered all the children under five in their *tabella*. Radio programmes, jingles, loud-speakers and stickers advertised the campaign. During that first round, all of Hargeisa's 15,000 under-fives were vaccinated against measles and received their first doses for polio, diphtheria, whooping cough and tetanus.

The second round was about to start when cholera broke out at Gannet and threatened the town. Already trained in oral rehydration therapy

for diarrhoea, the primary health care personnel worked day and night alongside the townspeople to treat victims and contain the epidemic. The outbreak was stemmed before it could claim more than 33 lives.

A measles outbreak followed the cholera. In Gannet 365 children died. In Hargeisa no child died.

Encouraged by these results, the government adopted a more ambitious goal – immunizing the 65,000 children of the capital city of Mogadishu, where the regular vaccination services were reaching only 11%. The first step was a pilot campaign in early 1985, in a poor neighbourhood where fewer than 3% of children under two were fully vaccinated; in three months the rate had risen to 45%.

The first round of the city-wide campaign was launched on 3 July after a month of intensive preparations involving over 2,000 political and community workers, 500 other volunteers, and 500 student vaccinators. Community meetings were organized, training courses set up, and radio talks, spots and jingles broadcast every day. Press articles, television programmes, loudspeaker announcements, leaflets, banners and car bumper-stickers publicized immunization. Volunteers visited some 150,000 homes to register children under five and urge parents to take them to one of the city's 62 vaccination centres, 50 of them opened specially for the week-long campaign. More than 55,000 children – 86.5% of the children who had been registered – were brought to the centres, and over 17,000 women received tetanus shots.

When Hargeisa and Mogadishu have completed their vaccination programmes, about a fifth of Somalia's children will be protected. The presidential directive which established the Mogadishu campaign requested all other regions of the country to run similar immunization campaigns, so that all the country's children will be protected.

Food supplements. A relatively small amount of extra food each day, for at-risk pregnant women, has been shown to reduce the incidence of low birth-weight which is "*universally and in all population groups, the single most important determinant of the chances of the new-born to survive and to experience healthy growth and development*".[20] Similarly, extra food for breast-feeding women can mean more successful and longer lactation.[21]

But as well as being a key child survival strategy, extra food is obviously just as vital for maintaining the nutritional health of the mother herself. In the industrialized world, an average woman gains approximately 12 kilos in weight during her pregnancy[22] – much of which is accounted for by the fat stores and the energy reserves needed for child-bearing and breast-feeding. Many of the developing world's women – women with too much hard work to do and too little good food to eat – gain only 6 kilos or less in pregnancy and therefore do not build up any adequate reserves.[23] But the baby will still be born and will still breast-feed – at the inevitable cost of depleting the mother's own nutritional health.

Support for women

Applying present knowledge about protecting the lives and the normal development of children could therefore be the kind of investment which would yield returns in time, money, health, and energy for women in poor communities. But to take full advantage of this opportunity, women in most poor communities will need more support – from their own societies, from the international community, and above all from men.

They need basic technologies to save time and energy in the growing, processing, cooking and storing of food – including improved agricultural tools and machinery, grinding mills for grain, more fuel-efficient stoves and utensils, easier methods of collecting and conserving water, and less back-breaking ways of getting food from the fields to the market.

They need the kind of development programmes which do not discriminate against them by enlisting their labour in cash-cropping to improve men's incomes from land which women have traditionally used for 'minor crops' to improve and vary the family diet. For during the Decade for Women, a series of surveys has shown that the commercialization of economies in the name of development has frequently resulted in a further transfer of power from women to men.[24] Most women, for example, used to have some degree of control over what was done with the available land and the food that was grown on it, whereas men have almost total control over what is done with the income from cash crops.[25] And the evidence is that women devote a significantly higher proportion of the income at their disposal to the feeding of children.[26]

Next, women need credit and training (Fig. 11) in order to buy and to use the fertilizers, pesticides, irrigation equipment, and other technologies which could increase their productivity – and their investable surplus – as the principal producers of food. And over the last few years, the 80,000 landless women of the Grameen Bank project in Bangladesh have disproved the idea that poor women are also a poor credit risk. Loaned a total of $11 million, the Grameen Bank women have invested it so successfully in income-earning opportunities that their community repayment record has remained at 100%.[27]

In many areas of the world, women also need land reform to ensure that they are not forced to grow food on ever smaller and more marginal lands before finally having to pack up and leave for the nearest city where they must get what work they can while struggling to bring up their children in overcrowded slums.

From employers in the cities, women need not only a decent day's pay for a decent day's work but also civilized provision for child care, breast-feeding, and maternity leaves. And in the countryside, they need a living wage for day-labour instead of rates which are so much lower than men's that, to take an example from Tamil Nadu, women can find employment for 310 days of the year whereas men can only work for 190.[28]

From the health services, they need more conveniently located and better organized clinics so that the average waiting time is less than the 2 hours 42 minutes which was recorded in a recent survey in West Africa.[29] And they need immuniza-

Ethiopia:
the silent emergency

15

1985 has been the testing-period for the programme launched a year ago by Ethiopia's Ministry of Health and the city council of Addis Ababa to cut the city's infant mortality by two-thirds, to less than 50 deaths per 1,000 live births by 1990.

While the stark images of drought and hunger in the Ethiopian countryside have become familiar the world over, the quieter emergency facing the children of the country's capital has gone unheralded. Yet some 12,000 children have been dying every year in Addis Ababa – drought or no drought – from the same diseases which have brought death to the relief camps in the north.

The basic methods being used to save lives in the city's poorer quarters are therefore the same techniques which have saved so many lives in the camps – immunization against the diseases which can decimate children in crowded conditions, oral rehydration to prevent dehydration from diarrhoea, and regular growth monitoring to help prevent children from slipping into the downward spiral of malnutrition and infection.

So far, 1,062 volunteer health promoters have been recruited, supervised by 128 community health and development agents with two months' training: all necessary vaccines have been imported, 150,000 sachets of oral rehydration salts have been distributed, and a national growth chart has been designed. At the same time, the city was also tackling the harder task – informing and supporting all parents in taking new action for their children's health.

The 284 city-dwellers' associations (*kebeles*) spearhead the effort. All of the city's 1.5 million inhabitants are *kebele* members, and many also belong to mass organizations.

In each *kebele* teams of six volunteers from the mass organizations, backed by the health promoters, are encouraging parents to have their children immunized and teaching mothers how to prepare the oral rehydration salts available free from *kebele* co-operative stores.

The press, radio and television issue frequent messages on child survival, and all *kebeles* receive leaflets and posters, their impact reinforced by the literacy campaign which in five years has drastically reduced illiteracy, especially among women.

With the support system in place, on 13 February 1985 the Minister of Health launched an eight-month campaign in Addis Ababa to immunize every child under two against the six main killer diseases of childhood, and every pregnant woman against tetanus – 89,000 under-twos and 36,000 women in all. At the time, only 25% of under-twos and only 6% of pregnant women were immunized.

Five vaccination teams have moved steadily from one *kebele* to the next, preceded by a week-long publicity campaign. The area is flooded with posters and flyers; health promoters and volunteers go door to door urging attendance at the vaccination session. Members of the women's and youth associations visit every household, registering children and pregnant women so the health services can follow up on non-attenders. On the eve of vaccination day a loudspeaker van tours the kebele, broadcasting the call to vaccination.

The turn-out has been consistently high. In the first three weeks alone, over 7,500 women and children received their first vaccinations in 58 *kebeles*. By the end of September, over 50% of the city's children were immunized.

To reinforce the programme, the city's sanitation and regular health services are being upgraded, and supplementary feeding centres are planned for children whose growth chart shows them to be malnourished. The government now plans to extend the programme to other towns and regions, so that more of Ethiopia's children will be shielded from the worst that the future may bring.

tion days which are not set during the weeks of heaviest agricultural work or at times of the year when poor women have to travel to seek day-labour in factory or plantation.

From the legislators, they need new laws to oblige fathers to help support their children in rapidly modernizing urban areas where traditional structures of obligation and responsibility may no longer be enforced by any kind of sanction.

From the educators, they need policies which encourage more girls to enrol in school and which allow of some flexibility to take into account the seasonal labour responsibility of so many girls in rural areas.[30]

From their national economic orders, and from international economic arrangements, women need not only investment and credit and training but also a fair return for their labours. From the coffee plantations of the Americas to the tea estates of Asia, women work too hard for too long and for too little. To cite one example among a million possible examples, the women workers of Asia's largest textile factory, a subsidiary of an American company, are paid 50 cents per day, rising to 55 cents per day after six years' service (1983 figures). With overtime, those women can earn as much as $16 a month, which is not enough to meet the basic needs of themselves and their families. Each of those women turns out more than one hundred pairs of gloves a day – gloves which are eventually sold in the United States for more than 400 times that woman's daily wage.[31]

There is no justice in this. And although it is sometimes said that economic relationships are not the business of organizations like UNICEF, the day-to-day work of such organizations is constantly bringing them up against the fact that the principal cause of ill health and poor nutrition among the children of such women is that their mothers are overworked and underpaid by the system of economic relationships which now prevails both between and within nations.

A fairer deal in the family

Finally, women need a fairer deal within their own families. In the distribution of food and resources and work, women fare badly in most societies of the world – rich or poor. But in poor societies, it is this unequal load which also deprives so many women of both the time and the energy and the education to improve their own and their children's lives. And the words of Amartya Sen, although written specifically to and for his own society, go to the heart of the matter in countries other than India:-

"Deep-seated inequities persist by making allies out of the deprived – making them a party to the persistence of deprivation. The over-worked family servant, the exploited share-cropper, the debt burdened peasant losing his land to the money lender, have all been traditionally groomed to play these respective roles, and their traditionally unquestioning acceptance of these roles plays an important part in the continuation of these inequities. A sense of legitimacy and order, and one of naturalness, make the inequities entrenched and hard to dislodge.

"While this perception problem is present in the context of very many different types of inequities, it is especially important in the case of within-family distribution. The family is typically seen – with good reasons – as an area of affection, of love, of sacrifice for one another, and no family can work very well without these characteristics. This general element of good sense in the selflessness of family members becomes hopelessly mixed up with the extraction of unequal and unusual sacrifices from women, producing an enormous inequity in the position of women in traditional Indian society. The traditional family is a great compound of warmth, on the one hand, and exploitation, on the other...

"In the field of within-family distribution, the perception of the problem is a crucial part of the problem itself. Non-perception of the deep inequalities that exist reflects the depth of these inequalities as well as serving to sustain them. Role education of boys and girls trains them implicitly for the inequalities of the respective positions.

"It is worth mentioning in this context that the sex inequalities in sustenance and life emerge very clearly in Indian society. It has been observed that girls between the ages of 1 and 5 have a significantly higher mortality rate than boys. The differences in food consumption become particularly sharp in distress situations... There is also much evidence that

the female children receive much less medical attention than the corresponding male children do. Inequalities in the distribution of food within the family fit into this general pattern of relative deprivation.

"The perspective of battles may be very far from the way conflicts of interest in the use of scarce food and other facilities are perceived within the family. But that – if the foregoing analysis is correct – is part of the problem itself, and the first step in changing the objective situation is to make the subjective perception come closer to the observed reality. The placing of women, including little girls, in the position of persistent losers in these battles can be challenged and ultimately countered only by departing from the implicit acceptance of the losing role of the women. A low-key and clinically academic discussion of the problem of intra-family distribution is not quite adequate. We can do with a bit more rage, a bit more passion, a bit more anger." [32]

The self-health potential

If parents can be empowered with new knowledge about child protection – and supported from all sides in the task of putting that knowledge into practice – then it is now possible to halve the rate of child malnutrition and child death in the developing world at a relatively low cost and within a relatively short space of time.

But this extraordinary potential will not be realized if the task is seen simply as the teaching of a new set of techniques or the delivery of a new set of services. Far more fundamentally, the child survival revolution is part of the creation of a new ethic of health care itself.

In recent times, and in almost all societies, even those in which modern medical services are not available to all, health care has come to be thought of only as the curing of illness by medical professionals in hospitals or clinics. In other words, health has become something to be actively delivered by experts and passively received by the laity.

Under such a definition of health care, the present potential for a revolution in child survival and development cannot be realized – whatever the technical breakthroughs at its disposal.

One obvious reason is that modern medical services are not regularly available to the majority of the developing world's families. But an equally important factor is that doctors and hospitals, even if they were available, cannot create anything like as strong a wall of basic protection around a growing child as can be provided by the informed actions of the child's own parents in the child's own home.

Almost all of the most powerful methods now available for protecting children's lives and growth are based on knowledge, decisions, and actions by *parents*:-

Whether a woman will have a little more rest and a little more food in pregnancy; whether she will go for at least one pre-natal check and an anti-tetanus injection; whether her infant will be breast-fed and for how long; when she will begin weaning and with what mix of foods; how and how often to prepare a child's food; whether to pay particular attention to feeding a child during and after an illness; whether to make up and use an oral rehydration solution during episodes of diarrhoea; whether to check the child's weight-gain regularly; whether to take a child on three separate occasions to be immunized; and whether or when to have another child – these are all decisions which have far more effect on whether a child lives or dies, whether a child grows normally or is stunted, than anything a doctor or a hospital can do. And whatever the other influences at play, they are all decisions which are taken and acted on by the family itself.

Dependence on professional medical services is therefore not the child's first line of defence against poor health and poor growth. And only if families and communities come to see themselves as the active promoters of health, and only if parents can again come to see themselves as the most important of all front-line health workers, will present knowledge bring its benefits to the majority of the world's children.

In that sense, the child survival revolution is part of a much wider shift in thinking about health care. World-wide, it is now becoming clear that the next generation of advances in human health will come not via more dependence on medical services but via the return of primary responsibility for health to the individual, the family, and the community.

For the child survival revolution, this change, a change in the conventional wisdom about what constitutes health care and who is to be primarily responsible for providing it, is much more important than any specific breakthrough in knowledge or technique. And it is a change which is now just beginning to become evident in both industrialized and developing nations.

In the industrialized world, many medical professionals see the decades ahead as an *"era in which professional health care providers will play a lessening role in the lives of people while individuals learn increasingly to acquire, develop, and serve as the repository of, information, skills, and community-based resources and supports enabling them to participate more fully in promoting their own health."*[1]

In the developing world, with its quite different circumstances, several governments are also now pioneering the idea that present knowledge, combined with present communications capacity, can open up the way to much higher standards of health. And it can do so by drastically increasing the power of families themselves to promote their own physical well-being.

That is why *"education concerning prevailing health problems and the methods of preventing and controlling them"* was listed first among eight basic principles which emerged from the International Conference on Primary Health Care held at Alma

Ata in the Soviet Union during 1978.[2] And that is why a WHO expert committee, drawn from professors of medicine and directors of health services in both industrialized and developing nations, has recently reported:-

"The attitude that health care is someone else's responsibility is linked to the fact that, in the past, health professionals have taken away from the people their decision-making power with regard to health. Therefore an effort must now be made to give them back their confidence and to help them develop their skills in making the right choices".[3]

The returning of primary responsibility for health to the individual and the family is therefore coming to be seen as a more likely avenue to better health in both rich and poor worlds. This report therefore turns now to look at both the potential and the danger inherent in the idea of 'self-health' – a potential and a danger which can most clearly be seen in what is now beginning to happen in the industrialized world itself.

More health at less cost

In the economically advanced nations, it is the soaring cost of health services which has begun to cast a lengthening shadow of doubt about whether more and more medical technology is really the best way forward for human health. Today in the United States, for example, the health industry is the nation's biggest employer, biggest spender, and biggest growth point – costing the nation almost $400,000 million a year, or more than $1,500 per year for every man, woman, and child.[4]

If this colossal expenditure – 25 times as much as in the early 1960s – were rapidly making the United States a healthier nation, then perhaps such a cost would be acceptable. But as one American health educator has written:-

"What is so disturbing about the high cost of medical care is that despite the largesse we have so eagerly conferred on the development of biomedical research and technology since the 1940s, that investment has largely failed to produce (or at least it is widely thought by the public and many policy-makers to have failed to produce) a return in the

Bangladesh: visiting 5 million homes

16

Oral rehydration worker Krishna Mondul was on her way to the culminating point of another successful household visit when Afia Begum, the woman she thought she had convinced, ran out of the house and away into the village of Shialora.

Mondul, 23, herself village born and bred and a veteran of 10,000 such visits, knew what the problem was. Alone and without the reassurance of her menfolk, Afia Begum had lost her tenuous confidence in the purpose of Krishna's visit. In that moment of crisis, the simple mixing of a pinch of salt with a hand-scoop of molasses and a half litre of water – to treat diarrhoeal dehydration – somehow took on a sinister aspect, and Afia Begum fled.

Not an everyday event but representative of the delicate challenge underlying one of the world's largest and most sustained efforts to put a medical advance into the hands of mothers. It is now five years since the Bangladesh Rural Advancement Committee (BRAC) began to work house to house in Bangladesh. By the end of 1985, their village teams will have visited 5 million of the roughly 16 million households in the country and by the end of the decade, three-quarters of them.

Hard-working young women like Krishna Mondul are the backbone of the effort, teaching mothers in 30 minutes why and how to treat diarrhoea with household salt and molasses. Tight monitoring later tests mothers on overall understanding and on how accurately they can mix the solution (the oral rehydration workers are remunerated accordingly).

The effort itself has learned from experience as the village teams (some 1,000 men and women by late 1985) fed back the lessons from the accumulation of individual encounters, some 150,000 a month.

Most important among these lessons was the realization that getting most people to actually use the rehydration solution would take more than mothers and more than one visit.

To really work, the campaign had to involve the whole community, not just in advocacy and demonstration but in discussion, debate and – wherever possible – treatment. Visits to individual households had to be reinforced by meetings with men, particularly community opinion-leaders. In 10% of districts, special teams stay for six months to tackle public health issues, to teach the importance of breast-milk colostrum in the first days of life and proper weaning after the first four months, and to engage the health care 'establishment' (doctors, traditional healers and midwives) – including training women from the community as health educators and promoters. Special efforts are made to involve schoolchildren and teachers.

At first many are sceptical. Why come all the way to see them with nothing more substantial than information? BRAC is pragmatic: if it were not so important, why would they and the government invest so much time and money? "*We are all poor,*" BRAC workers tell their clients. "*This is a way of saving not just money for medicines but maybe even a child's life.*"

Krishna Mondul knows the link between fear and ignorance and dependence. She went back to Afia Begum, calmed her fears and finished training her to mix the oral rehydration solution. "*I knew that without the practical part, the theory I had given her would be meaningless,*" she said. "*Knowing the practical mixing for herself, she would not need to call anyone else for help; she could even teach others.*"

form of a reduction in morbidity and mortality that can be considered proportionate to our investment. This failure of costly, high-technology disease treatment has, in turn, focused recent interest on promoting health and preventing disease in order to reduce the costly burden of premature death and disability".[5]

Looking at alternative approaches, the same writer concludes: *"central to most of these alternatives is the return of primary responsibility for health to the individual, the family, and the community".*

A similar concern is also mounting on the other side of the Atlantic. This year, for example, Dr. Jurg Sommer of Basle University Teaching Hospital in Switzerland has written:-

"... a review of the literature reveals little evidence that further investments in medical services in developed countries will lead to any marked reductions in overall mortality and morbidity rates. The per capita expenditures for health care among Western nations vary by more than 200% but most of their health indices vary by less than 5% and there is little correlation between the two. Once a reasonable minimum of medical care has been provided, factors other than medical care – diet, life-style, heredity, environment – appear to have a much larger effect on health and longevity than does more medical care. Yet Switzerland is currently investing an additional 1.5 billion Swiss francs every year in medical care."[6]

Faced with the evidence of rising costs and diminishing returns from increasing dependence on medical services, the industrialized world is beginning to experiment with the opportunity for 'more health at less cost'. In the Soviet Union, for example, a $500 million mass-media campaign has just been launched to educate the public in healthier behaviour – concentrating on better diets, less alcohol, more exercise, and regular physical check-ups. And in New York City, the Department of Health has announced an attempt to cut the city's infant mortality rate by 20% before the end of 1988 – mainly by means of a mass-media public education campaign and a preventive programme to try to reduce the incidence of low birth-weight among the poorest of New York's mothers.[7]

With the possible exception of the Scandinavians, the governments of the industrialized nations are not yet going into action on a scale which matches this opportunity. The United Kingdom and the United States, for example, are still devoting much less than 2% of government health spending to the prevention of disease and the promotion of health.

Yet the economic sense of the new approach is reflected in the more immediate response of the business world. In recent years, at least 50,000 American corporations have started some kind of active programme to inform and support their employees in taking better care of their own health.[8] One company's programme to provide the time and facilities for employees to take regular exercise has resulted in 36% lower health care costs. Another company's 'wellness' programme found that those with 'unhealthy life-styles' were 86% more likely to be off work on any given day. Another found a 26% reduction in high blood pressure among employees after a company started an employee 'Live for Life' programme. In several such programmes, the health costs of employees who do not smoke have been found to be 30% to 50% lower.★[9]

Blaming the victim

The early results of these new approaches confirm their potential. Changes in eating habits in the United States, to take just one example, have already helped to reduce deaths from heart disease by approximately one-third.[10] And it is now thought possible that a change towards healthier life-styles could push average life expectancy in the industrialized world to well over 80 years for both men and women – something that doubling and trebling today's vast expenditures on medical services could not hope to do. According to the Centers for Disease Control in the

---

★ Whether in a country or a company, poor health is poor economics. Illness loses American corporations over 400 million working days a year – and costs approximately $40,000 million. In addition, actual spending on the health of employees is becoming a major factor in production costs: $500 of the purchase price of every General Motors car, for example, is now allocated to medical costs for General Motors' employees.

United States, for example, the average American male can achieve an 11-year increase in life expectancy by four basic self-health actions – not smoking, drinking only in moderation, taking regular exercise, and eating wisely in both quantity and quality.

Excitement about the present potential for preventive and promotive 'self-health care' in the industrialized world is therefore justifiable.

But every silver lining has its cloud. And in this case the cloud is that putting all the emphasis on life-styles and individual responsibility for health could also be used as a way of taking the emphasis away from the political, social, and economic causes of ill health which are largely beyond the control of the individual but which profoundly influence the individual's life-style.

In all societies, the one element of life-style which is likely to make most difference to a family's health is a family's wealth (Fig. 13). In rural Bangladesh, the infant mortality rate is twice as high among the families of those who own no land. In Manhattan, the infant mortality rate is twice as high among families who live north of 125th Street. In 19th-century Europe, the infant mortality rate in the slums was around 200 deaths per 1,000 babies: in the royal families of 19th-century Europe, the infant mortality rate was about 12 deaths per 1,000 babies – almost as low as in the most medically advanced country in the world today.[11]

So if the drive for better health is to take the road of changes in the life-style of the individual, then it must confront the fact that many of the industrialized world's families are living unhealthy life-styles primarily because they are poor. And at that point, it becomes obvious that employment policies, housing policies, and basic government services must also be part of any policy which seeks to improve health by changing the circumstances under which individuals live their lives. In the United States, for example, it would be a perversion of the great potential for 'self-health' to ignore the conclusion of this year's report to the New York Community Service Society, which pointed out that the number of children living in poverty was probably *"well over the 40 percent mark"*.

Similarly, the attempt to prevent illness by educating the public in the direction of better health habits cannot ignore commercial forces which may help to shape or reinforce behaviour conducive to poorer health. Stopping smoking, for example, may do more for an individual's health than any amount of complex medical technology: but is it entirely fair to place all the responsibility on the individual in a society which spends over 100 times as much on advertising tobacco as it does on educating the public about its dangers?[12]

Without doubt, informed action by individuals and families in taking primary responsibility for their own health now offers far more opportunity for advances in human health than further spending on, and advances in, curative medical technologies. But that does not mean that responsibility can be abrogated by those governmental or commercial forces whose actions help to shape the circumstances of the individual and the family. Or as Dr. John Allegrante, Director of the Center for Health Promotion at Columbia University, has put it:-

Fig. 13 Ownership of land and daily intake of food, Maharashtra, India, 1982

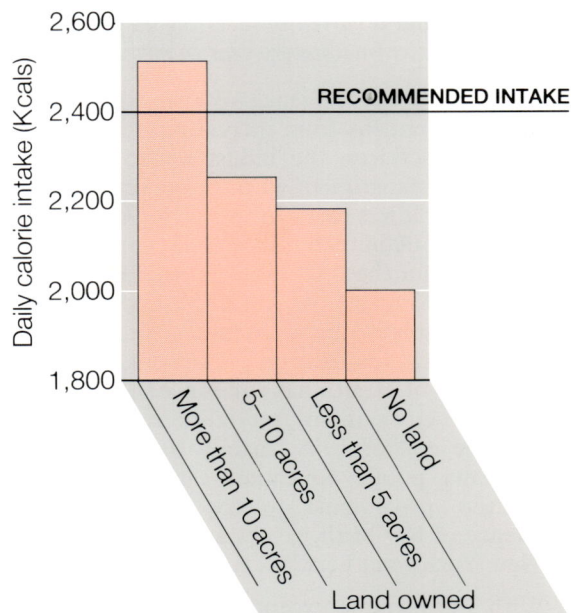

Source: National Institute of Nutrition, Hyderabad, India, 1982.

"...many of our recent efforts in the implementation of national policy in health promotion and disease prevention have been efforts that have abrogated our moral responsibility to provide the social and economic supports for necessary organizational and environmental changes. So, while we may have been thinking that our national health policy and our own local efforts at promoting health by teaching that individuals ought to do more for themselves, by themselves, may be more humane, cost-effective, and socially acceptable than more costly technologies like medical care or coercive means like punitive legislation that compels change, I am left only to argue that government must not abandon the role it has played in regulating the marketplace and subsidizing social conditions that facilitate or support behaviors thought to be conducive to health. This is, I believe, the single most important moral issue facing those of us who use health education as a technology in our attempts to prevent disease.' [13]

The responsibility of governments

In the developing world, the need and the potential for individuals and communities to take more control over their own health is even greater. External medical services are very much less available. Levels of family health are generally much lower. And many of the most basic problems are more susceptible to action by families and parents than by doctors and hospitals.

In particular, present knowledge, and present capacity to communicate that knowledge, add up to the possibility of a quite drastic improvement in the capacity of poor families to protect the lives and normal growth of their children.

But as in the industrialized world, this opportunity is shadowed by the danger that 'families doing more' might be interpreted as 'governments doing less'. For among the basic elements of 'lifestyle' in the poor world which contribute to poor health are the lack of clean water, safe sanitation, decent housing, basic education, land reforms, adequate incomes. And the prevention of ill health is therefore a responsibility not just of individuals and families but of governments and the international community.

In other words, there is all the difference in the world between a policy which uses the vast potential for 'self-health' as an excuse to pass on the responsibility for poverty and sickness to the poor and the sick, and a policy which uses all the resources of a nation to inform and support the majority of its people in the task of improving their own health by their own actions.

Families need the support of new knowledge about low-cost ways of protecting life and growth and health. But they also need the support of community health workers to reinforce that knowledge and to act as a channel for referring more complicated illnesses to more specialized services. And from governments and the international community, they need the support of development programmes which set the provision of basic services – water, sanitation, education, housing, land, jobs – at the centre of their sights and not at the periphery of their vision.

With this kind of support, informed action by families could now be a beginning not just of a rise in the level of health but of a rise in a community's consciousness and confidence that it can take more control over its own circumstances by its own actions. And that is a process which is both a means and an end of development itself.

Self-health in poor communities

'Self-health' is therefore an idea which poor communities are to be supported in rather than abandoned to. But this does not alter the fact that the majority of the world's poor families will remain poor for some time to come. And protecting the growing minds and bodies of young children from the worst effects of that poverty is essential to the breaking of the cycle by which poverty itself is perpetuated. This report therefore turns now to a more detailed look at the potential of present knowledge for empowering and supporting parents themselves to protect the lives and normal growth of their children.

What are the poor world's equivalents of the facts about heart disease, stroke, cancer, diet, smoking, exercise, cholesterol levels, blood pressure – facts which are now permeating public consciousness in the industrialized world? What

Nigeria:
going nation-wide

Between August 1983 and August 1984, immunization of children under two leapt from 9% to 83% in the Owo area of Ondo state, Nigeria, with little rise in costs. In October 1984 Nigeria's head of state pledged free vaccine to every state adopting the new approach. By August 1985, all of Nigeria's 19 states had taken up the challenge in 38 local government areas, which house a sixth of the country's 7 million children under two.

To take only measles, easily the principal killer of Nigerian children, the cases reported at a major hospital in Owo had fallen by 93% in August 1985. Experts from the Centers for Disease Control, USA, estimate that the immunization drive in Owo has forestalled 10,000 cases of measles, prevented over 300 deaths and saved at least 150 children from blindness, deafness or other disabilities.

The Owo approach ensures that vaccines are available and that parents are aware of the benefits of vaccination. Since power supply for refrigerating vaccine is unreliable in outlying areas, vaccines are moved swiftly in and out from a central depot in styrofoam cold boxes, which can keep vaccines at the right temperature for over a week. To make it easier for parents to bring their children for vaccination, temporary vaccination posts are set up in market-places, schools, mosques, churches and village halls. And to ensure that parents understand the need for vaccination, the community leaders, traditional chiefs, religious leaders and schoolteachers are called on to add their authority and backing to the posters, flyers, radio messages, songs, house-to-house visits and loudspeaker vans which publicize the vaccination sessions.

The cost: between $4 and $5 for each child completing the five visits needed for full protection against the main killer diseases of childhood.

Early returns in 1985 showed that the new approach was already increasing the numbers of vaccinations eightfold and tenfold compared with 1984. The cold boxes are now moving out into neighbouring areas. In two years' time, they are due to reach every village in the country.

Given Nigeria's steep falls in oil revenue and heavy debt, most states have established 'partners in health' committees to draw on every available resource. Rotary International is supplying polio vaccine for five years; Rotary clubs, the Paediatrics Association of Nigeria, the National Association of Nurses and Midwives, and the National Council of Women's Societies are all lending their support.

The enthusiasm for vaccination has proved easier to generate than to sustain. Even in Owo the coverage for measles, the last shot in the series, had slumped to 50% in May 1985, raising the threat of an epidemic before year's end. So Owo again became a testing-ground. Community education efforts were intensified, and mothers whose children complete the course now receive a 'good mother' certificate. By August, measles immunization in Owo had climbed back to 75%.

The drive to make vaccination available to every child in Nigeria has gone hand in hand with the promotion of oral rehydration, to prevent the diarrhoeal dehydration which currently kills 500 of the country's children every day. The first demonstration unit for oral rehydration opened its doors at Massey Street Children's Hospital, Lagos, on 5 February 1985. In its first six months the unit treated 2,000 children, and only three children died, compared with the 1984 average of 19 deaths a month. The hospital also saved over $40,000 on the costs of intravenous rehydration. All of the nation's states have now set up similar units, to promote oral rehydration to health workers and public alike, and at least one unit is planned for each of Nigeria's 304 local government areas in 1986.

are the corresponding breakthroughs in knowledge which can help families to prevent or treat the major causes of death and illness among the developing world's children – the respiratory infections, the diarrhoeal illnesses, the communicable diseases, the poor nutritional health?

The problems and possible solutions vary from community to community, country to country. But there is a core of basic low-cost 'self-health' actions which have almost universal relevance and which depend far more on parents than on doctors. And *together*, they are powerful enough to reduce by as much as *half* the incidence of malnutrition, illness, and early death, among the children of the developing world.

Strategies which are already going into action around the world, such as ORT and accelerated immunization, have already been touched upon. Others, which could be equally important, are not yet widely enough known.

For those readers who are not professionally involved in health care, it may therefore be useful to summarize those strategies – and the relationship between them.

And as the only true importance of such knowledge rests in it being put at the disposal of parents, this brief account makes no apology for stripping that knowledge of its medical vocabulary:-

Action in pregnancy

A child's nutritional health begins not at birth but at conception (and can be significantly affected by the nutritional well-being of the mother during her own childhood and adolescence). The first vital actions for protecting children are therefore to be taken before and during pregnancy. And present knowledge suggests three basic actions which many poor families might be able to take – if they had the necessary information and support:-

○ It is now known that becoming pregnant again soon after giving birth roughly doubles the risk to the life and health of both mother and children.[14] To protect both, there should be a

space of at least two or three years between one birth and the next (Fig. 14).

○ It is also known that too little food and too much hard physical work in pregnancy are seriously damaging to a woman's health – and seriously increase the risk that a baby will not grow properly inside the womb. If the result is that the baby's weight at birth is less than normal (i.e. lower than 2,500 grammes), then the risk of death in infancy is roughly doubled.[15] Even a handful of extra food each day of the pregnancy, and a half-hour's extra rest, can make a significant difference.[16]

○ It is also known that immunizing the mother against tetanus in pregnancy automatically immunizes the unborn child. If a community knows the importance of ensuring that a pregnant woman receives two anti-tetanus injections, and if basic health services are within reach, then approximately 800,000 infant lives a year can be saved.[17] If immunization against tetanus is just not possible, then the presence of a trained person at the birth – someone who knows the importance of clean hands, a clean delivery sheet, and the hygienic cutting and dressing of the umbilical cord – is almost as effective in protecting the child against the disease.[18]

Breast-feeding

For the first few months of a child's life, the best possible protection which any mother can provide for the baby's normal health and growth is exclusive breast-feeding (Fig. 12).

It is now known that breast-milk contains at least six anti-infective agents against some of the most common illnesses of infancy.[19] It is also the most nutritious and hygienic food which any baby can be given.

Bottle-feeding, by contrast, frequently means that a baby is fed on a less nutritious artificial formula which may well be over-diluted with unclean water in an unsterile bottle.[20]

In other words, breast-feeding mitigates the risks of poverty and poor hygiene while bottle-feeding exacerbates those risks (Fig. 15). And in dozens of surveys in poor communities, it has now

Sri Lanka: reaching the poorest

18

Sri Lanka ranks alongside China in showing that a country need not be rich to increase its children's chances of survival. Despite an average capita income of little more than $300 a year, Sri Lanka has brought its infant mortality below 40 deaths per 1,000 live births; 86% of the population is literate, and on average, 65% of one-year-olds are fully immunized. In September 1985 Sri Lanka took up the challenge of bringing immunization to the remaining third of its children – the hardest to reach – within a year.

Long-standing commitments to free education, free medical care and food subsidies for those in need lie at the heart of Sri Lanka's achievements over the years. Even so, an estimated quarter of all babies are born underweight, with the attendant risks of sickness and death, while some 45% of Sri Lanka's 2 million children under five are malnourished to some degree. Diarrhoea kills over 2,000 Sri Lankan children a year and undermines the nutritional status of many thousands more.

○ Since 1978, when Sri Lanka launched its expanded immunization programme, the incidence of polio and whooping cough has gone down by 65% and the incidence of diphtheria and neonatal tetanus by 90%. Over its one-year term, the new accelerated programme is designed to lay a permanent base for full vaccination of all the country's children well before 1990.

○ The national diarrhoea control programme, which reached more than a third of the population by the end of 1984 and was due to achieve national coverage by the end of 1985, stresses traditional remedies available in even the poorest homes, such as rice congee (gruel), to prevent dehydration before it starts. The government manufactures oral rehydration salts for children who need further treatment. Previously obtainable only from midwives and health centres, the salts are now available from pharmacies and general practitioners as well, and from early 1986 on will be sold by more than 10,000 retail outlets.

○ Sri Lanka has used the growth monitoring technique since 1975 to identify malnourished children for supplementary feeding. A new growth chart for mothers to keep at home was tried out in 1984 and is now being introduced nationally.

○ To counter the drift towards bottle-feeding in urban areas, where 25% of working mothers stop breast-feeding before three months, the government enforces a recent law banning the advertising of breast-milk substitutes. Maternity leave for working mothers has been doubled to three months to encourage breast-feeding.

Volunteers play a key role in Sri Lanka's attempts to achieve universal coverage. More than 10,000 young health volunteers assist midwives in their villages and some 4,000 staff of the Sarvodaya Shramadana village development movement are working towards child survival in 3,000 villages. Many of Sri Lanka's 19,000 Buddhist priests are also promoting child well-being. The Saukyadana medical volunteer movement, Sri Lanka Red Cross, Boy Scouts and Girl Guides, Lions clubs and Rotary clubs are all actively involved.

To raise parents' awareness of ways to improve their children's chances of survival and healthy development, the national broadcasting network gives free air-time; newspapers and magazines run regular features; private companies print child survival messages on pay slips, carrier bags, envelopes and exercise books. And in September 1985, the Indian and Sri Lankan national cricket teams agreed to have the message ''Immunize your child today'' painted in metre-high white letters on the pitch used for the Test Match – and watched by a television audience of tens of millions in both Sri Lanka and neighbouring India.

The effect of these measures will eventually be revealed by a new system for monitoring child survival and development. Taking a national sample of over 15,000 pregnant women, the system will follow their progress – and that of their children – for the next five years.

been shown that bottle-fed babies are as much as *two or three times* more likely to die in infancy than babies who are exclusively breast-fed for the first few months of life.[21]

Applying this knowledge can bring the majority of children in poor communities to the age of five or six months in good nutritional health. So far, the infant has been at least partly insulated from poverty by the womb and the breast.

But for millions of the poor world's children, it is now that the trouble begins. For now the child begins to come into increasing contact with the environment of poverty – a poverty which begins to gnaw at normal health and growth. It is at this point that the terrible 'growth gap' begins to open up between the smooth upward progress of children in affluent communities and the sudden weight losses, frequent illnesses, and faltering growth of children who grow up in poorer communities.

It is also at this point that one of the least understood and most important of all low-cost child protection strategies could begin to play its vital part. And because it can serve as a means and an aim and a measure of almost all the other low-cost actions which parents might take to protect their children in these vital, vulnerable years of growth, the strategy of *regular growth checking* deserves a more detailed consideration.

Protecting growth

The most insidious aspect of child malnutrition is that most mothers do not know that there is anything wrong.[22] And the very fact that the development of malnutrition is invisible – even to paediatricians and even to parents – is one of the main reasons for its prevalence and severity.

In most cases, no-one ever notices the lack of adequate weight gain, and the child simply lives

Fig. 14 Infant deaths by birth interval, uneducated mothers, 25 countries

Infant death rates for those born after short (less than 2 years) and long (2–6 years) birth intervals. To minimise social and economic differences, the following figures apply only to mothers with no formal education.

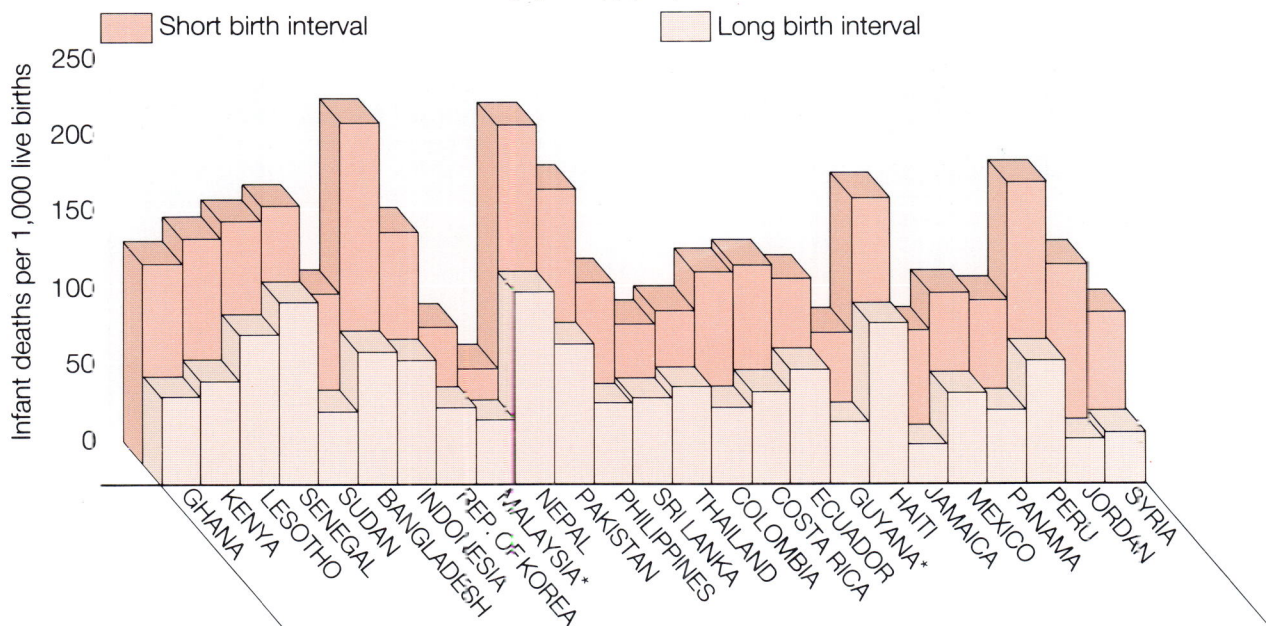

*Women with 1–3 years education used because too few with no education

Source: Population Reports, Series J, number 27, May–June 1984.

Haiti:
ORT reaches the majority

In less than a year, a campaign to promote oral rehydration therapy has succeeded in putting this scientific breakthrough into the hands of the majority of parents in one of the least likely of settings – the Caribbean island of Haiti.

Haiti has long been one of the poorest and least healthy countries in the Western hemisphere, with an infant mortality rate of 128 deaths per 1,000 live births and an average life expectancy of only 53 years. The annual health budget – about $3.50 per head – fell far short of the needs, so in 1982 Haiti's health planners shifted their approach: they would attack one problem at a time. Diarrhoea stood out as the largest killer, accounting for half of all deaths of infants and children; and a low-cost solution was available.

Oral rehydration therapy (ORT), the best and cheapest way to forestall diarrhoeal dehydration, was known in Haiti but rarely used. Between 1980 and 1982 Dr. Jean Pape and his colleagues at Haiti's State University Hospital had used ORT to reduce diarrhoea mortality in the children's wards from 35% to under 1%; but this dramatic confirmation of the value of ORT received more recognition outside Haiti than at home.

In late 1982 the tide turned. The Minister of Health called upon his staff and all other branches of government to help make ORT available to everyone in Haiti. Nine months later, in July 1983, the national ORT programme was launched.

During the following year over 6,000 health and other personnel were trained in how to use ORT and how to teach others to use it. Serum Oral, the locally manufactured brand of oral rehydration salts, was advertised on radio and television nation-wide; half a million flyers were posted on walls and given to schoolchildren. Starter supplies of Serum Oral were issued free to the more than 2,000 shops, stalls and roadside stands willing to sell it. Rehydration corners were set up in 250 public health clinics and some 200 private clinics to demonstrate Serum Oral to the public. Popular jingles were broadcast up to twelve times a day on the radio, making Serum Oral a household word.

Within a year, country-wide surveys found that more than three-quarters of mothers knew about Serum Oral, and a third had used it for their child's most recent diarrhoea episode.

In the slums of the capital, Port-au-Prince, a survey in April 1985 found that over 90% of mothers knew about Serum Oral; 49% had learned of it from radio or television and 39% from health centres. Even more important, 80% had used it for their child's latest diarrhoea episode and planned to continue using it, in spite of the fact that nearly half of them were paying more than the official price of 75 centimes a packet (15 US cents).

Admissions for diarrhoea to Port-au-Prince city hospital, once more than 5,000 patients a year, have dropped to less than half. Over two-thirds of the children coming in have already started oral rehydration at home, so that even in severe cases the medical care is more effective and the death rate has plummeted.

Public enthusiasm for ORT has grown so strong that the country's educators have altered the thrust of the national literacy campaign; it now concentrates on health messages as the surest way to attract greater interest and participation, especially from women.

The work continues to take ORT into the remotest mountain areas of Haiti. Meanwhile, Haiti's planners are now turning their sights to the next goal – using schoolchildren, radio, television and every possible means of communication to raise Haiti's level of child immunization from less than 10% to 50% within a year.

on with poor growth and frequent illnesses. In a minority of cases, the problem of malnutrition does eventually become visible – but by that point growth is already seriously affected and the task of putting the child back on course has become very much more difficult and very much more expensive.[23]

Prevention is usually possible if parents understand the importance of growth and can somehow measure it, see it, and take action to maintain it. And if any faltering in growth could somehow be seen at a much earlier stage, then there are now several relatively simple and relatively low-cost actions which poor parents can take to keep the child on course and prevent serious malnutrition from settling in. And therein lies the importance of regular monthly weighing.

The details of the growth monitoring process are brought together in Part II of this report (see Lifelines: growth monitoring). But the essence of the idea is that regular monthly weight gain is the best single indicator of any child's normal growth and that the process of regularly recording that weight gain, or the lack of it, is an essential technological aid to the mother in doing what she is trying to do anyway – bring up a healthy, well-nourished child in very difficult circumstances.

Simple as it may seem, the growth checking idea is beset by unanswered questions – questions about the right kinds of growth charts and weighing scales to use, about how the regular weighing of all young children is best promoted and organized, about whether graphing growth is too alien a concept for mothers who may well be illiterate, and above all about how to inform and involve millions of mothers in the process.[24]

But the stakes are high. For there is reason to believe that if parents could be involved in and informed by the regular growth checking of their children, then child malnutrition could be reduced by as much as half in the poor communities of the developing world.

The heart of the matter is the informed involvement of the mother. For the mother's participation in regular growth checking means

Fig. 15 Diarrhoeal illness by feeding method and income, Dar-es-Salaam

Percentage of families reporting infant diarrhoea in the three months prior to the survey.

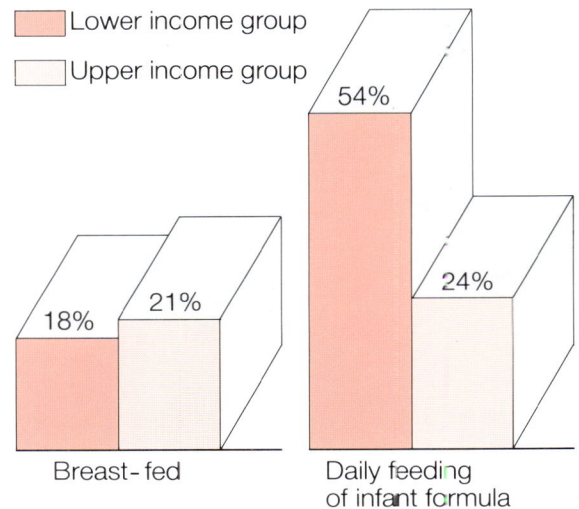

Lower income group
Upper income group

54%
24%
18%
21%

Breast-fed

Daily feeding of infant formula

Source: International Union of Nutrition Scientists, Ad Hoc Task Force on Rethinking Infant Nutrition Policies, March, 1982.

that the normal development of the child, or the lack of it, can be made visible to the one person who cares most and can do most to make sure that the child grows and develops normally.

But in itself, growth checking neither feeds children nor protects them from disease. Therefore its only true value resides in what *action* parents take as a result of getting much more timely and precise information about the nutritional status of their children.

The detailed actions which any particular parent can take are, of course, prescribed by local circumstance. But recent advances in knowledge have shown that there are certain kinds of low-cost action which most parents could take to provide basic protection for *growth*.

That knowledge can broadly be divided into knowledge about the special nutritional needs of the young child and knowledge about reducing the frequency and severity of illness:-

India:
towards a polio-free Madras

20

As India prepares to attempt the immunization of all its children by 1990, smaller-scale programmes are yielding valuable experience of how to involve all organized resources in reaching out to the poorest groups. This year, one such campaign has also succeeded in controlling one major disease in one major city.

This year the city of Madras made an unprecedented attempt to contain polio by immunizing the vast majority of its children. Without this extraordinary effort, as many as 1,000 of the city's children would have been permanently crippled by polio in the next twelve months alone.

What became known as the 'Madras momentum' started in 1984 as a collaboration between the state government of Tamil Nadu and Project Impact – a coalition of organizations working to prevent disability.

After two pilot campaigns in slum areas, a city-wide programme was mapped out for early 1985. The first task was to stock up on oral polio vaccine. With help from Indian businesses, Rotary International and the United Kingdom Save the Children Fund, the state ministry of health accumulated the necessary 600,000 doses during the early months of the year. To keep the vaccine cool until it was needed, three private companies volunteered their refrigerated storage space.

But as the pilot campaigns had shown, organizing the supply of immunization is often an easier task than organizing the demand. The next step was to inform all Madras parents of the three vaccination days and their importance.

First the slum-dwellers' own community leaders were asked for their advice and help. Volunteers were recruited and the plans drawn up to visit each of the city's 1 million homes. On average, there was one vaccine centre for every five streets.

Among the volunteer organizers were schoolchildren, teachers, university and medical college students, local officials, child care workers, mem-

bers of the Lions and Rotary clubs, and members of the general public. Touring films on polio were shown to thousands of slum-dwellers. The national radio and television networks ran advertisements, documentaries and panel programmes. Fleets of motor-driven rickshaws with megaphones toured the narrow streets announcing the vaccination days. A million handbills went up throughout the city. And on the streets, traditional puppet shows dramatized the war between polio and vaccine.

The Madras business community supplied ingenuity as well as cash to back up the campaign. Employees received notices in their pay packets stressing the importance of immunization, asking them to spread the message to friends and neighbours, and appealing for donations: the results were pinned up on company notice-boards. Immunization stickers were placed on telephone handsets in hundreds of small hotels and restaurants, which also offered their refrigerators for local storage of vaccine on immunization days. A vaccination 'advertisement' was rubber-stamped on outgoing mail in hundreds of commercial offices.

Between May and July, the majority of the city's children were immunized against polio, despite some falling-off in attendance. Even so, 94% of the city's children received the first dose, 88% the second, and 72% the third – a coverage level that may be high enough to interrupt the transmission pattern of the disease and so protect even those who were not immunized.

Successful as it was, the Madras initiative raises the questions of how to sustain such initiatives year by year and how to reach children under one, the most vulnerable group. The campaign also tackled only one of the six vaccine-preventable diseases that strike at children's well-being. But as the project newsletter Moksha comments, ''The creation, on a mass scale, of public awareness of the importance of immunization will further strengthen the existing expanded programme of immunization.''

Improving diets

One of the most common reasons for the faltering of a young child's growth is that the introduction of other foods, in addition to breast-milk, begins too late.

After about five months, breast-milk alone is no longer sufficient and other foods must be added if the child is not to become malnourished. Yet in many parts of the world, other foods are not introduced until the child is well into the second six months of life and, for many, a whole year goes by before any other food is taken. In rural India, for example, an estimated 40% of all infants are still being exclusively breast-fed at the age of one year.[25]

Fig. 16 Energy content of children's diets, rich and poor nations

The graph shows the amount, by weight, of the food which must be eaten each day to satisfy the energy requirements of growing children – at different ages. In the developing world, a diet including a staple plus some vegetables and some oil increases the energy density of a child's food to almost the same level as that of a child in the industrialized world.

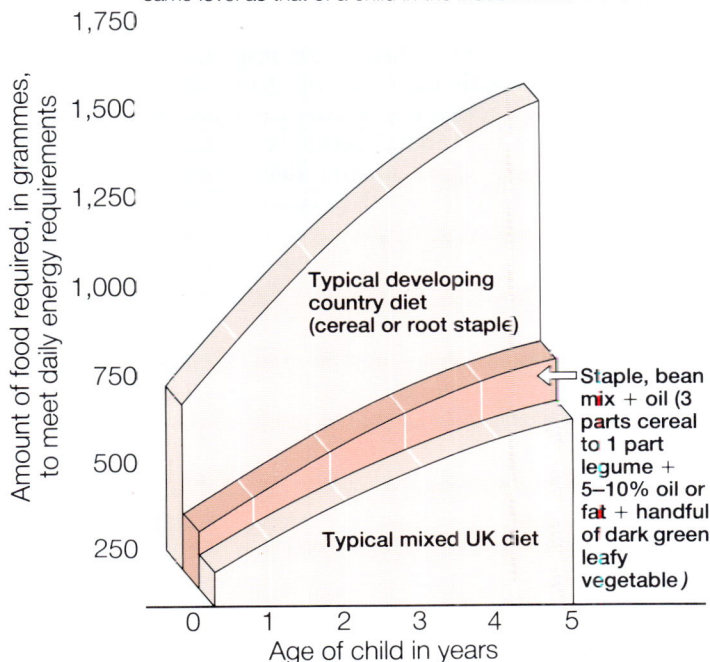

Source: Adapted from: Dietary fats and oils in human nutrition. Food and Agricultural Organization of the United Nations, Rome, 1977.

At the other extreme, the introduction of other foods at too early an age steeply and unnecessarily increases the risk of diarrhoeal and other infections.

Present knowledge about when to begin weaning could therefore help mothers avoid one of the major causes of faltering growth.

Just as important is the question of how a child should be weaned:-

In a poor community, the attempt to wean a child on nothing but the same staple food as adults is likely to lead directly to malnutrition. For a child's small stomach cannot take enough of the bulky, low-energy foods which are the staple diet of the poor (Fig. 16). The child may well eat enough to satisfy its hunger and be said to have 'eaten a good meal'. But it will not have eaten enough to meet its energy requirements for normal health and growth.[26]

The staple foods of the poor, unlike those of the rich, therefore carry a built-in danger of child malnutrition (Fig. 16). To counter that danger, a child has to be fed at more frequent intervals with more energy-dense foods. In practice, that means mixing fats and oils, and peeled and mashed vegetables, into the child's weaning food. And it also means continuing with one of the most energy-dense foods of all – breast-milk (Fig. 17).

Finally, there is the recent breakthrough in knowledge about the importance of vitamin A (see page 22). In practice, that breakthrough means that a daily handful of the cheapest dark-green leafy vegetables can help both to protect the child's eyesight and to reduce the number of diarrhoeal and respiratory infections which a child sustains.

Empowering parents with this vital knowledge about the special nutritional needs of the weanling child – in terms which parents can understand and act on – could therefore reduce malnutrition and help to maintain growth.

But in almost all cases, the oils, fats, and even cheap vegetables will mean at least a little more expense. The very poorest families will therefore not be able to make these small but vital improvements to their children's diet. And for such families, only the struggle for social justice and economic improvement can improve their children's chances of normal development.

But it is now known that a significant percentage of the world's malnourished children live in homes where there *is* enough food to provide an adequate diet for a young child. In a recent nation-wide survey in Indonesia, for example, no discernible difference was found in the amount or kind of food available in the homes of children who were malnourished and the homes of those who were not.[27]

In this circumstance, present knowledge about when and how to wean a young child could reduce both the incidence and the severity of child malnutrition – *if* that knowledge were to be made widely available.

But diet is not all. What the child's body does with the food that is eaten is just as important as food itself. And in recent years, evidence has been accumulating behind the idea that a poor intake of food may not be the only or even the main cause of child malnutrition.

Reducing illnesses

One of the most important of all recent advances in knowledge about child health is the realization that frequent infection is as important a cause of malnutrition as the lack of food itself.[28]

To fight an illness, a child's body requires extra energy. But illness usually means a loss of appetite – so the body receives less energy, not more. Usually, the illness itself also means that less of the food that is eaten is absorbed and available for growth. And if the illness involves diarrhoea, then nutrients are also drained out from the body. At the same time, the reaction of most parents (often encouraged by doctors) is to withhold food and drink. In all of these ways, the child's nutritional stock may be severely and frequently depleted by illness. The result can be malnutrition and poor growth – *even if adequate food is available in the home.*[29]

Many detailed studies have now demonstrated this causal relationship between illness and mal-

nutrition, and research in Asia has suggested that diarrhoeal disease alone is responsible for between 25% and 75% of growth faltering among the children of poor families.[30]

The real problem is therefore not either malnutrition or infection but both – as malnutrition itself predisposes the child to some infections which lead to further nutritional depletion. Or as Hossein Ghassemi has written: "*Poor diet and infection have synergistic effects in precipitating malnutrition among children, and by the same rule, simultaneous control of infection and improvements in a child's diet would have a synergistic result in improving its chances of survival*".[31]

While doing what is now possible to improve diets, and especially weaning diets, what then are the low-cost actions which parents can take to reduce illness?

Protection against diarrhoeal illness

The most common of all childhood illnesses is diarrhoeal disease. In very poor communities, for example, a child may contract a diarrhoeal infection perhaps six or more times a year – with each episode lasting for several days. If the response of the parents is to withhold food and drink, then diarrhoea may mean that a growing child is losing rather than absorbing nourishment for a total of up to 40 days in the year. And that alone is enough to cause normal growth to falter.[32] That is why many nutritionists now believe that diarrhoeal infection is one of the major causes of childhood malnutrition in the developing world today.[33]

So what can parents in poor communities now do to ward off this, the greatest threat of all to both the lives and the normal growth of their children?

More frequent handwashing with soap and water, and more hygienic ways of preparing and storing food, are the two main ways in which parents can help to prevent diarrhoeal disease – if they have adequate supplies of soap, water, fuel, and time.[34]

But for the most part, prevention depends on improved incomes and living conditions, safer sanitation and water supply, and a general rise in the level of health education.* In other words, prevention is related to basic changes in public health which are, in turn, closely related to the overall level of economic development. And to leave the control of diarrhoeal disease to the gradual and fitful process of economic growth means leaving 4 million young children to die each year – and many millions more to live on in malnutrition – until well into the next century.

There is now no excuse for allowing that to happen. For the discovery of oral rehydration therapy, touched upon at the beginning of this report, means that there is now a cheap and simple method by which all parents – rich or poor – can protect their children from the worst effects of diarrhoeal disease.

In previous years, this report has documented the fact that parents themselves can make and use oral rehydration solutions and help to save the lives of most of the 4 million children who now die each year from diarrhoeal dehydration.

But ORT has a less spectacular side to its nature. Even for those children whose lives are not directly threatened by dehydration, ORT could become one of the most incisive of tools for cutting into the cycle of infection and malnutrition which now holds back their growth.

The first and most basic element of ORT has nothing to do with technology or special formulas or foil-wrapped sachets. It has to do with informing parents that it is important to persist in giving a child food and fluids during an episode of diarrhoea.**

Continuing to feed, and especially to breast-feed, is therefore the beginning of ORT. It helps to prevent dehydration. It helps to prevent the

---

* Vaccines are not yet available (see Lifelines: ORT), although immunization can prevent the large number of serious cases of diarrhoea which are precipitated by measles.

** In some cases, informing parents of this 'discovery' will merely mean confirming what they or their parents once knew. For the starchy gruels, rice conjees, and carrot soups which were the traditional response to diarrhoea in many parts of the developing world are highly effective forms of 'first-response' ORT.

Fig. 17 Breast-feeding and calorie intake in the second year of life

Percentage and source of calories in the second year of life, Uganda.

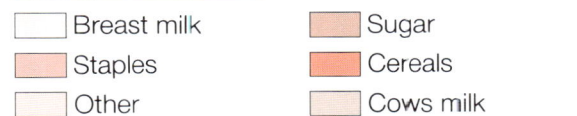

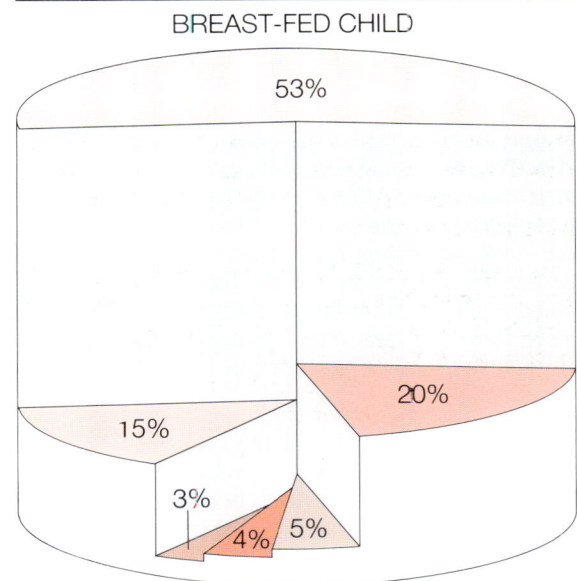

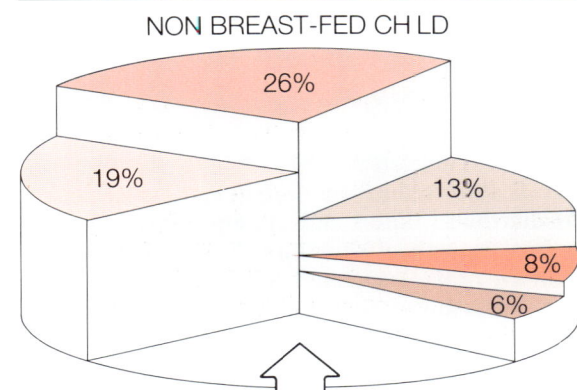

Legend:
- Breast milk
- Staples
- Other
- Sugar
- Cereals
- Cows milk

BREAST-FED CHILD

53% — 20% — 15% — 3% — 4% — 5%

NON BREAST-FED CHILD

26% — 19% — 13% — 8% — 6%

28% CALORIE DEFICIT IF CHILD IS NOT BREAST-FED IN 2nd YEAR OF LIFE – DESPITE INCREASING OTHER FOODS BY 60%

Source: Rutishauser, I. H. E., "Growth of the pre-school child in West Mengo district, Uganda". The East African Literature Bureau, Nairobi, 1975.

beginning of diarrhoeal malnutrition. And it helps to reduce the severity and duration of the illness itself.

But because diarrhoeal infections do reduce the body's capacity to absorb fluids and nutrients, the threat of dehydration is still present. The second stage of ORT is therefore the making up of a special oral rehydration solution which should be given to the child to drink in quantities sufficient to replace the amount of fluid lost during the diarrhoea.

Such an oral rehydration solution can be made up in the home using eight teaspoonsfuls of sugar to one of salt in a litre of water (or by making up effective traditional remedies such as carrot soups or rice conjees). Alternatively, parents can use the pre-packed sachets of oral rehydration salts which are now becoming available in most countries. Either way, the secret of the formula is that the glucose allows the body to absorb up to 25 times more fluid and salts than is normally the case in a child suffering from a diarrhoeal infection.[35]

In a relatively small percentage of cases, the diarrhoea will persist and the child will become very obviously ill. In such circumstances, if at all possible, the parent should seek the advice of a health worker and the pre-packed oral rehydration salts, made up to the exact WHO/UNICEF formula, should preferably be used.*[36]

If this simple procedure is followed, then literally millions of children who are now dying each year would recover as a direct result of the treatment given by their own parents in their own homes.

Just as important, this same procedure can significantly reduce the nutritional losses caused by diarrhoeal illness and so help to maintain the normal growth of the child. Recent research in Turkey, India, Iran, the Gambia, and the Philippines has shown that the median difference in weight gain between children who were treated with ORT and those who were not was almost 70 grammes per month (Fig. 18).

ORT is therefore one of the cheapest and most effective ways in which parents themselves can reduce the impact of illness on a child's growth. And by helping to maintain nutritional well-being, the new therapy also helps to maintain resistance against other infections. In other words it can be a force for converting the downward spiral into an upward spiral. And the same can be said for the next basic method by which parents can help to defend their children's growth against the threat of illness.

Vaccine-preventable illnesses

The massive increase in immunization coverage discussed earlier in this report can, of course, prevent several of the most serious childhood illnesses. But in this context of growth, it assumes even greater importance.

Vaccine-preventable illnesses like measles or whooping cough, as well as threatening a child's life, also have a heavy nutritional impact.[37] Therefore immunization against these specific diseases is also a partial 'immunization' against malnutrition. It is likely, for example, that many more children die of malnutrition and illness in the few months following an attack of measles than are killed by the measles itself.[38] And the reason is that measles has led to nutritional losses, growth faltering, lowered resistance, more diarrhoeal or respiratory infections, further weight losses and so on until this whirlpool of infection and nutritional depletion sucks the child down below the level of nutritional health at which life itself can be sustained.

Immunization itself can therefore also help to throw the 'downward synergism' of poor nutrition and frequent ill health into an 'upward synergism' of normal growth and fewer infections.

Respiratory infections

ORT and immunization can shield a child from more than half of the illnesses which strike at life and growth in the earliest years. But that still leaves unchecked the majority of the respiratory infections – infections like influenza, sinusitis,

---

* In an even smaller percentage of cases, intravenous rehydration therapy may still be necessary.

Fig. 18 Effect of ORT on weight gain in children with diarrhoea

Legend: ☐ Weight gain in group without ORT ▬ Weight gain in group with ORT

Country & period of follow up	Age of children	Mean weight gain per month (grammes)		
TURKEY 16 months	<1 year	246	283	(37)
	1–3 years	169	213	(54)
	3–5 years	159	209	(50)
TURKEY 3 months	Malnourished			
	<6 months	367	667	(300)
	7–12 months	33	183	(150)
	13–24 months	67	134	(67)
	25–72 months	150	150	(0)
	Well nourished			
	<6 months	417	500	(83)
	7–12 months	25	230	(205)
	13–24 months	83	217	(134)
	25–72 months	125	167	(42)
GAMBIA 3 months		40	107	(67)
INDIA 24 months	Malnourished children only	111	133	(22)
IRAN 6 months	1 episode			
	3–11 months	300	428	(128)
	12–23 months	237	282	(45)
	24–35 months	217	295	(78)
	>1 episode			
	3–11 months	272	340	(68)
	12–13 months	210	280	(70)
	24–35 months	175	253	(78)
PHILIPPINES 7 months	<1 year	159*	257*	(98)
	1–5 years	105	242	(137)
PHILIPPINES 5 months	<1 year	194*	244*	(50)
	1–5 years	608	647	(41)

Note: Figures in parentheses indicate the difference in monthly weight gain between the two groups
*Data recalculated in grammes from percentiles

Source: Norbert Hirschhorn, "Oral rehydration therapy: the program and the promise", paper prepared for UNICEF, May 1985.

tonsillitis, laryngitis, pneumonia, otitis media – which underlie the deaths of more than 2 million children a year and undermine the growth of many millions more.[39]

Because young lungs are not fully developed, all children are more vulnerable to respiratory disease. And a child who is weakened by frequent illness and poor nutritional health is more vulnerable still. A child who contracts bronchitis or pneumonia in the developing world is therefore more than 50 times more likely to die from it than is a child in Europe or North America.[40]

For those who survive, growth is often set back. In a severe case of bronchitis or pneumonia, for example, a child may lose as much as 12% of the protein from his or her body.[41] Weakened in this way, the child is then more susceptible to further infection and further malnutrition. To keep the child away from the edge of that steepening slope, basic protection against the main respiratory infections is therefore also necessary. And here too, there are actions which parents and families themselves can take.

First of all, breast-feeding offers a considerable degree of immunity against respiratory infections in the first year of life.[42] Secondly, immunization offers protection against four of the worst offenders – tuberculosis, diphtheria, whooping cough, and the respiratory complications which often wait on measles.

But if respiratory disease does strike, then there are also two vital pieces of knowledge by which a family can protect a child from the worst effects:-

○ As with diarrhoeal infections, parents need to know that continued feeding – and especially breast-feeding – is a vital part of the management of respiratory infections. The child needs both extra foods and extra fluids. And if its appetite is gone, then frequent and persistent attempts to feed will be necessary for the duration of the illness.[43]

○ Secondly, families need to know the early symptoms of an acute lower respiratory infection so that they can, if at all possible, get the child to a health worker or a clinic before life itself is threatened. The most revealing of these symptoms, in almost all cases, is the suddenly rapid rate

Thailand: PHC in practice

With the help of nearly half a million village volunteers, Thailand has brought health services to 95% of its 56,000 villages and their population of about 40 million. The figure was due to reach 100% by the end of 1985 – making Thailand one of the few countries to introduce primary health care (PHC) on a national scale.

Thailand's primary health care policy, adopted in 1977, calls on villagers themselves to join in improving their health and living standards. Teams of villagers, trained for five days as village health communicators (VHCs), pass on knowledge about health, nutrition and hygiene to their neighbours in 10-15 households. One of every ten VHCs is then chosen by the others for a further 15 days' training as a village health volunteer (VHV). Backed by a comprehensive network of health centres and hospitals, VHVs weigh children to monitor their growth, supply first aid and basic drug treatment, provide family planning services and distribute supplementary foods for children and women in need. In mid-1985, 419,300 VHCs were at work alongside 43,000 VHVs.

Thailand's national immunization programme, also launched in 1977, depends on the volunteers to explain to parents the value of immunization and to organize immunization drives. The proportion of children who drop out from three-dose vaccinations has been reduced: the number of children under two fully vaccinated against diphtheria, whooping cough and tetanus has more than doubled, from 21% in 1982 to 53% in 1984, and vaccination against polio, started in 1982, has also reached 53%. Measles vaccination was added to the programme in 1984. In 1977 only 4% of pregnant women received two tetanus shots to protect their unborn child; in 1984 the figure was 40%.

A national oral rehydration programme went into action in 1980, and the government now manufactures 3 million packets of oral rehydration salts a year. VHVs and VHCs alike play a key role in promoting the new therapy to combat diarrhoeal dehydration. Leaflets, posters, and radio and television spots complement their work. A 1983 review found that the programme had already surpassed its interim target: oral rehydration is available to well over 50% of all village children under five.

The VHVs are currently weighing more than 60% of Thailand's pre-school children to monitor their growth and advise mothers on nutrition. Of a million children weighed between 1972 and 1982, only 49% could be considered well nourished; but between October and December 1984, of 1.5 million children weighed, 70% were well nourished. Mild malnutrition had fallen to a third and serious malnutrition to an eighth of the earlier levels. Growth monitoring has also been introduced in Thailand's 31,000 primary schools and every schoolchild now has a growth chart, to complement the lessons in health care which are being introduced into the curriculum.

In over 20,000 villages VHVs operate village drug banks to ensure that essential drugs are available to villagers at a fair price. If 70% of village households buy shares (costing less than a dollar) in a drug bank, the government donates a supply of drugs to start a revolving fund. Drugs are then bought from the government at a discount and sold to villagers at a small profit. The proceeds go to renewing supplies, paying the shareholders and subsidizing medicines for the poorest villagers.

Nutrition co-operatives, active in 6,325 villages, work on the same principle. Villagers use the initial share money and a matching donation by the government and UNICEF to prepare low-cost, high-protein foods for their own use or for sale; VHVs distribute the food packets free to severely malnourished children.

Thailand's voluntary health workers have laid a base for a better future for Thai children. The country is entering 1986 – Mother and Child Health Year in Thailand – with a new emphasis on improving pre-natal care and lowering still further the nation's infant mortality rate, already one of the lowest in Asia.

of the child's breathing, along with fever, obvious breathing distress, a flaring of the child's nostrils, and a drawing in of the spaces between the ribs.[44]

In the home of the community health worker, or at a clinic, the majority of acute respiratory infections can be effectively treated by injections of penicillin or by tablets of antibiotics. And so common and so dangerous are the respiratory illnesses, that there is now the strongest possible case for making antibiotics available not only via doctors but also via much larger numbers of community health workers (see Lifelines: Acute respiratory infections).[45]

The cost is negligible – less than 10 cents per dose. But the effect can be dramatic – almost a 50% reduction in the pneumonia death rate in one major trial so far.[46]

The lives and the growth of children can therefore be sheltered, if not completely protected, against respiratory infections by empowering parents with basic knowledge on both prevention and treatment and by empowering community health workers to use antibiotics (see Lifelines: Acute respiratory infections).

Finally, malarial illness must be included among the most important threats to the life and growth of children in several regions of the developing world.[47] In Africa alone, malaria is now estimated to be responsible for the deaths of almost a million children a year. By the end of the decade, it is quite possible that a low-cost antimalarial vaccine will have taken its place alongside the other vaccines in national immunization programmes. But in the meantime, a degree of basic protection is possible at relatively low cost. Community health workers, or village volunteers, can distribute chloroquine to all mothers-to-be in order to prevent malaria in pregnancy (which is closely associated with both low birth-weight and maternal mortality) and to all young children who show signs of hay-fever – the major symptom of malaria. (Routine chloroquine prophylaxis is no longer recommended for young children as it can interfere with the development of the child's own immunity.[*48])

---

* Routine use of anti-malarial drugs is still necessary for travellers to endemic areas and their families.[50]

Feeding in illness

Just as important as the parents' response to any of these specific illnesses is the knowledge that all illnesses threaten the child's nutritional health and normal growth. And the practical significance of that knowledge, to parents, is that there are two basic things which a family can do to minimize the nutritional impact of illness.

The first has already been mentioned – the importance of persisting with food and fluids, frequently and in small amounts, even when the sick child's appetite is low.

The second is special attention to feeding in the few days *after* an illness. It is now known that, in the brief few days following a bout of diarrhoea or a respiratory illness, a child can gain weight at three, four or even five times its normal rate – if particular attention is paid to feeding. Nature itself has therefore provided an opportunity for catching up on the nutritional losses suffered in times of illness – if parents know that the opportunity exists:-

"No therapeutic goal is as important as the rapid recovery of pre-illness weight after acute infection. Food supplements during this three to five days in convalescence may be one of the most effective means of reducing the nutritional effect of infections and assuring the continued nutritional health of the child. This requires feeding with readily digested foods, administered throughout the day almost as if on prescription. But the opportunity is a brief and fleeting one which remains to be widely exploited".[49]

Growth checking

In all of these ways, parents and families can provide basic protection for the lives and normal growth of their children – not just against malnutrition or specific individual illnesses, but against the synergistic combination of the two.

And it is against this background of possible protection strategies that the importance of regular growth checking is thrown into clear relief.

Regular monthly weighing, and the recording of the results, makes visible the subtle, vital process of the child's growth – drawing a line

Iodine: protecting the mind

22

The low-cost strategies discussed in this report are of almost universal relevance. But similarly effective and inexpensive solutions also exist for other problems which affect children in specific parts of the world. A quarter of the world's children, for example, are at risk from iodine deficiency, the world's leading cause of preventable mental retardation. Yet iodizing salt – the simplest remedy – costs only 2 or 3 extra cents per kilo. And where iodizing salt is not feasible, iodized oil injections cost as little as 40 cents and give protection for up to five years.

Wherever iodine leaches from the soil, in mountainous regions and flood-prone areas, whole populations are low in iodine. Severe deficiency carries the risk of increased neonatal mortality and visible handicaps for the survivors: stunted growth, poor physical co-ordination, goitre (swelling of the thyroid gland at the base of the throat), deafness, muteness, and cretinism. But the damage done by lesser degrees of iodine deficiency is increasingly being recognized. Even mild iodine deficiency undermines children's physical and mental growth, sapping their energy and slowing the progress of both individuals and communities.

Iodine deficiency is prevalent in the Andes; in much of Africa, especially south of the Sahara; in a wide arc extending from the Middle East through the Himalayas to south-east Asia and into Indonesia, China and Papua New Guinea; and in pockets of Western Europe. In Bolivia 65% of schoolchildren have goitres and in some villages 20% of villagers may be cretins, the result of their mother's iodine deficiency during pregnancy. In highland villages of Ecuador, 60% had goitres before an iodization programme. All of Bhutan's inhabitants are at risk, and in some villages 30% are cretins. In large areas of India, Zaire and the Central African Republic, 5% of infants are born mentally retarded.

Iodization programmes in such countries as Argentina, Colombia, China, Brazil, Ecuador and Zaire have helped to increase birth-weights, lower infant mortality, and improve schoolchildren's intelligence scores. In central Java, cretinism disappeared after a programme combining iodized salt and oil injections; 7% of children born before the programme were cretins. Papua New Guinea achieved similar results with mass injections of iodized oil, followed by legislation for the iodizing of salt.

Though bread, water supplies and even sugar have been iodized, salt is cheaper and technically simpler to treat. Even so, the costs may be high for a poor country, and the collaboration of salt producers difficult to obtain. Organizing the injection teams and transport for iodized injection programmes can prove equally complex.

But as the full impact of iodine deficiency disorders has become clear, more and more countries are returning to the attack. Several Andean governments have launched salt iodizing programmes. Nepal is nearing the end of a five-year drive to inject 2 million of its population of 16 million. Bhutan, which imports its salt from India, has installed an iodizing plant at a border crossing, where all the country's salt is now treated. In India, where 50 million have goitres and 200 million are at risk from iodine deficiency, several hundred new iodizing plants are planned, since only a third of the country's salt is currently iodized; in the meantime iodized oil injections are due to be given to 15 million people in the north, especially young women.

An International Council for the Control of Iodine Deficiency Disorders was established this year (1985), with UNICEF support, to assist governments in tackling the problem. Given political will, community awareness, and backing from salt producers, children could be freed from the burden of iodine deficiency within ten years.

which is the child's 'lifeline', the single most important indicator of its well-being.

The basic aim of regular growth checking is therefore to give parents early warning if a child's growth is beginning to falter. At that early stage, most children can be put back on course by the range of parent-based actions just discussed. Both the technique of detecting the problem – and the practical steps which can be taken to remedy it – are cheap and simple enough to be put at the disposal of the vast majority of parents. That is why the growth checking technique is potentially the greatest breakthrough of all against the malnutrition and infection complex which holds back the normal development of so many of the developing world's children.

At the monthly growth check, health workers can discuss with the parents any and all of the low-cost actions now available – whether it be the timing and spacing of births, the need for extra food and rest in pregnancy, the importance of a full course of vaccination, the method of coping with diarrhoeal illnesses, the importance of continuing to breast-feed, knowledge of when and how to wean a child properly, the reasons for frequent handwashing with soap, or the value of paying particular attention to persistent feeding during and immediately after a child's illness.

And because it is a regular activity, bringing mothers and children into monthly and predictable contact with community health workers, growth checking provides the ideal opportunity for beginning to build community-based primary health care. It can provide, for example, a practical focus for the demonstration of how and when to make and use an oral rehydration solution. It can provide a forum for the visit of an immunization team or for the distribution of vitamin A supplements. It can be the activity through which to supply parents with chloroquine tablets or anti-parasitic drugs. It can be the opportunity for parents themselves to discuss their own concerns and priorities.

Not least, regular growth checking provides a filter for finding those children who are at special risk and who need special help. Even if parents do all that is now possible to protect a child's growth, there will still be a minority of children who will fail to put on weight over a two- or three-month period. Special help is then needed – as it is then clear that the child is simply not getting enough of the right kind of food to eat or that there is a specific health problem such as a heavy parasitic load, or chronic otitis media, or silent tuberculosis. In this way, the regular growth checking of all children also allows other resources, whether it be food supplements or more specialized health care, to be used more efficiently by being targeted to those most in need.

But in the majority of cases, the value of growth checking lies not in the screening of children for treatment but in the education of parents for prevention. That is why there is very little to be gained from the growth checking technique if it merely means that a mother queues up for an hour to have her baby weighed by a health worker who then draws meaningless marks on a meaningless card before calling for the next mother in the line.

To fulfil its potential for drastically improving the nutritional health of children, growth checking needs to be organized on a monthly basis for small groups of women, preferably at a neighbourhood gathering. And if the idea is well understood and the weighing itself is well organized, then growth checking is something which should be looked forward to as a time for mothers to discuss how their children are doing, to meet and exchange experiences with friends, to spend a relaxed and informative few minutes talking with the health worker, to have the chance to ask questions and raise worries, to pick up important practical tips, to reassure themselves and be complimented on the fact that their child is growing well, or to get an early warning and some realistic advice if things are not.

In such a setting, the idea and importance of growth checking can be understood by mothers who may never have been to school. At its simplest, understanding the growth checking idea means understanding that a normal healthy child should be gaining weight every month. On the chart, it means understanding that a rising line means a child is growing well, a level line means that there are things to be done to get the line moving upwards next month, and a falling line shows that there is a definite problem which has to be acted on straight away and which a mother needs help with. And in explaining this, it is not the mother's literacy or numeracy that matters, but the time taken, the sensitivity shown, and the realism of the advice given.

For all the difficulties – and there are many – the concept of growth checking could therefore stand at the centre of the web of support which it is now possible for parents to spread under their children's health and normal growth.

At the moment, different kinds of growth charts are being introduced in different countries. Several nations, including Brazil, China, Ethiopia, Haiti, and Indonesia have all recently drawn up national growth charts and are in the process of issuing them to parents of all young children. In most cases, the growth chart also carries information about immunization and ORT, about breast-feeding and child spacing, and about other low-cost actions which the parents of a particular nation or region can take to protect their own children in their own circumstances.

But more important than the mechanics of the growth chart itself is the principle of parental involvement in the continuing promotion of the child's health and growth. And in that sense the child's growth chart – in the hands of the mother – is a symbol of a change in the concept of health care which could bring more benefits to the developing world's children than any technological advance.

First, the growth chart is a practical symbol of health care as the continuing protection and promotion of health rather than as the periodic response to illness.

Second, the growth chart is a practical symbol of the change from the idea of health care as passive recipience of services to a concept of health care which sees parents as active participants in the promotion of their own and their family's health.

Children and world development

Growth checking can therefore draw together and unify the range of low-cost parent-based actions now available for protecting the life and the normal development of a child growing up in a poor community. In combination, those actions now have the potential to save the lives of at least half of the 40,000 young children who are now dying each day in the developing world. Just as important, they could help to protect the growth of many millions of the developing world's infants and children.

That is why the present opportunity for the protection of children is also central to the process of development.

Clearly, high death rates, prevalent malnutrition, and frequent illness are closely linked to poverty (Fig. 13). And in that sense, using a packet of oral rehydration salts to prevent a child from dying of diarrhoeal dehydration could be said to be merely attacking symptoms. Except for the fact that the symptom also happens to be a child's life. And except for the fact that there is an obvious and profound connection between the mental and physical development of children and the social and economic development of nations.

Any action – like the use of oral rehydration salts or immunization or improved weaning – which protects not only the child's life but its normal growth, is therefore simultaneously attacking both a symptom of poverty and a cause.

The aim – and the potential – of the revolution in child well-being which is now possible, is therefore not only the saving of lives but the protecting of growth. And on that basis, there is also a powerful economic case to be made for an all-out effort to put what is now known at the disposal of all parents.

To cite one specific example:-

"The long-term effects of malnutrition in infancy and childhood are only recently being established. Thus in a 17-year follow-up study of Indian children under five, those who had suffered second or third-degree malnutrition were found to have a 30% deficit in work capacity, as young adults, when compared with the work performance of control subjects from the same social class and villages."[1]

Similarly, it is also known that mental development can also be held back by poor nutritional health.

By the age of three or four years, 90% of a person's brain cells are already linked and physical development is advanced to the point where the pattern is set for the rest of a person's life. Those early years therefore cry out for protection – both to defend the child's right to life and its right to develop to its full mental and physical potential – and to invest in the development of people so that they can more fully contribute to, and benefit from, the well-being of their families and nations.

In many parts of the world, it is clear that economic development will not lift the majority out of poverty within the next few years. With this in mind, a recent report prepared for the WHO/UNICEF Joint Nutrition Support Programme has concluded:-

"... perhaps the most important goal to strive towards is to protect the health and development of the next generation of young children in the world's poorest regions. It is these children who must eventually lead their countries out of economic stagnation and into an era of rapid development."[2]

Human capital

In this sense, the protection afforded to the mental and the physical development of children is an investment in human capital. And in the last two decades, there has been a growing realization that human capital formation has perhaps been

the neglected factor in the struggle for economic development. As Nobel Prize-winning economist Theo Schultz has commented: *"Increases in the acquired abilities of people throughout the world, and advances in useful knowledge, hold the key to future economic productivity and to contributions to human well-being".*[3]

Similarly, the World Bank, in its annual report on the progress of world development, has concluded: *"Few would dispute that the health, education and well-being of the majority of the people in industrialized countries are a cause, as well as a result, of national prosperity. Similarly, people who are unskilled and sick make little contribution to a country's economic growth".*[4]

From here it is but a short step to the conclusion that spending on such services as health and education – and especially on the protection of children's normal growth – should not automatically be listed on the 'consumption' side of the national economic equation. For they are the most basic of investments in human capital. And if it can be shown, as the World Bank has shown in several specific instances, that health care increases work capacity or that primary education increases the productivity of farmers, then why should spending on health or education be classified as 'consumption' rather than 'investment'?[5]

Equally clearly, a renewed stress on the importance of human capital leads naturally to a concern for the special problems of the young child. As Hans Singer, Professor of Development Economics at Britain's Institute for Development Studies, said at a UNICEF symposium held earlier this year: *"Any long-term policy of human investment or human capital formation must start with today's children... malnutrition amongst children has more devastating and more irreversible and more long-term effects on the future productivity of children than is the case with adults."*[6]

But in the real world of recent years, the logic of investing in children has made little progress against the head wind of economic recession. UNICEF's 1984 study of *The impact of world recession on children* documents the cut-backs in government spending on such services as health and education in the early 1980s. And this year's special report on Africa (see box in Preface) describes how the adjustment to recession has meant that the main burden has again been passed on to those who are least able to sustain it – the poorest families and their children.

Summing up this declining investment in today's children – and tomorrow's world – World Bank figures show that the 43 countries with the highest infant mortality rates (over 100 deaths per 1,000 live births) are currently spending three times as much on defence as on health. Meanwhile, aid from the industrialized nations (OECD countries) has fallen from 0.51% of their combined GNP in 1960 to 0.37 in 1982. And of that less than one-half of 1% of GNP, less than one-tenth is allocated to health.

Meanwhile, arms spending has continued to increase in both industrialized and developing nations (Fig. 19) to the point where the industrialized world is now spending more than 20 times as much on the military as on development assistance and the developing world itself is spending twice as much on arms as on the health of its children.

In total, world-wide spending on armaments now exceeds the combined incomes of the poorest half of humanity. It is a statistic which casts a shadow of shame on our generation. For as Dwight Eisenhower said almost a generation ago:-

"This world in arms is not spending money alone. It is spending the sweat of its laborers, the genius of its scientists, the hopes of its children... This is not a way of life at all in any true sense. Under the cloud of threatening war, it is humanity hanging from a cross of iron."

The halt of progress

Through economic recession and falling prices for the labours and raw materials of the developing world, through rising debts and interest rates, through falling levels of aid and concessional loans, through increased arms spending and the distortion of development to the benefit of the few, investments in 'human capital', and particularly in the protection of children, are therefore now declining in many of the poorest nations of the world.

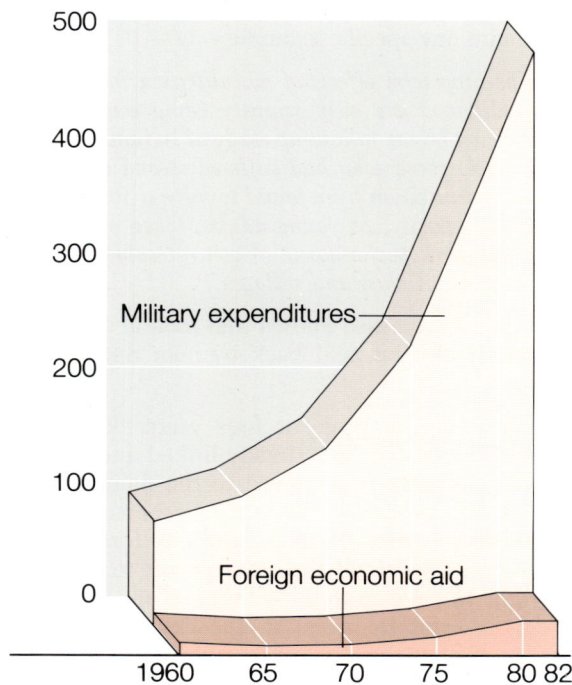

Fig. 19 Military and aid expenditures, industrialized nations, 1960–1982

Source: *World Development Report 1984, The World Bank, Washington DC, 1984.*

Progress against absolute poverty is therefore coming to a halt. And the achievements of recent decades are coming under threat in our times.

With the issuing of this report, UNICEF itself begins its fortieth year. And in general, those four decades have been a period of unprecedented progress. In the developing world as a whole:-

◯ Infant and child death rates have been almost halved.

◯ Average life expectancy has increased by approximately 40%.

◯ The proportion of children who enter school has been lifted from less than 30% to more than 80%.

◯ Food production has been trebled while population has doubled – and the rate of population growth has been slowed down in every region of the world except Africa south of the Sahara (Fig. 20).

◯ Average real incomes have been almost doubled.

By any historical standards, these are remarkable achievements. But it is equally clear that over large parts of the earth's surface this progress has been shuddering to a halt in the late 1970s and early 1980s:-

In Latin America, where average real incomes have fallen by as much as 25% in many nations, there is fragmentary but alarming evidence of a rise in the incidence of malnutrition and illness, in the number of low birth-weight babies being born (Fig. 21), in the rate of infant and child deaths, and in the numbers of children who are being abandoned on the streets of the cities.

Only in Asia, where several of the most populous nations have been able to insulate themselves from the worst effects of the industrialized world's recession, has progress in child health and nutrition been maintained and even

accelerated. In particular, countries like China, India, Pakistan, Indonesia, and Thailand, countries which together are home to nearly half the world, have achieved or are moving towards new levels of protection for the lives and growth of the next generation (see panel 21).

But in sub-Saharan Africa, as all the world now knows, development has not only come to a halt but begun to slide, carrying millions of families back towards the edge of subsistence and beyond.

This year, a special UNICEF report on Africa's complex problems has already been issued. The human consequences of those problems have been seen on virtually every television screen and in virtually every newspaper in the world. But they have never been more movingly expressed than in the unaccompanied words of one of Africa's foremost novelists, Chinua Achebe:-

"No madonna and child could touch that picture of a mother's tenderness for a son she would soon have to forget...

"She held a ghost smile between her teeth, and in her eye the ghost of a mother's pride as she combed the rust-coloured hair left on his skull and then – singing in her eyes – began carefully to part it.

"In another life this must have been a little daily act of no consequence before his breakfast and school; now she did it like putting flowers on a tiny grave."

A safety net of protection

Even in nations where there has been no visible famine, the adjustment to economic crisis has meant a cutting back of the kind of services which are essential for the protection of both life and long-term development. Thousands of school-teachers have been dismissed and tens of thousands of children are not being educated as a result. Food subsidies for pregnant mothers and children are being cut back and malnutrition is measurably on the increase (Fig. 22). Clinics are being closed and immunization programmes are being brought to a halt for the lack of fuel and spare parts for vehicles. Spending on essential social services has fallen even in countries with the most praiseworthy track records of commitment to the protection of the poor.

Fig. 20 Food production per person, Africa, Asia, and Latin America, 1961–1983

Index of per capita food production, based on the average figure for 1961–65 (= 100).

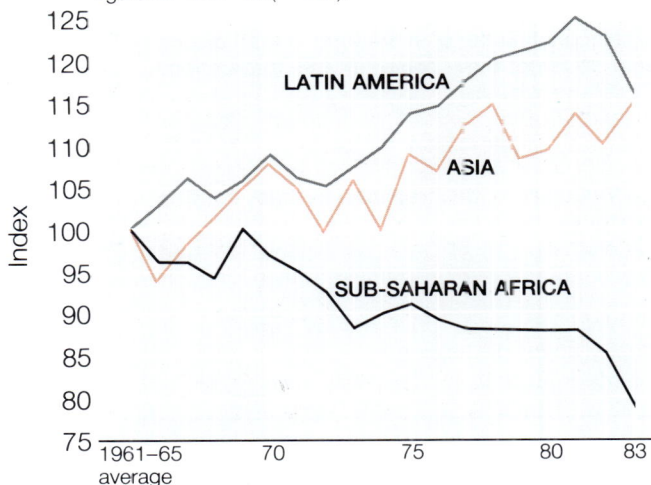

Source: "Towards sustained development in Sub-Saharan Africa", The World Bank, Washington DC, 1984 (based on data provided by the United States Department of Agriculture).

The Code: a progress report

In a poor community of the developing world, bottle-fed babies have been found to be two or three times more likely to die in infancy than babies who are exclusively breast-fed for the first few months.

But bottle-feeding is on the rise in many towns and cities of the developing world. And the inevitable result has been poor nutritional health, and often death, for many thousands of infants.

In May 1981, after a ten-year campaign by health professionals, non-governmental organizations, and international agencies, the World Health Assembly adopted the International Code of Marketing of Breast-milk Substitutes. The Code asks all governments, in developed and developing countries alike, to protect and encourage breastfeeding. More specifically, it calls on commercial baby-food companies to end the promoting of infant formula directly to the public or through health centres.

Most infant-formula manufacturers have accepted the Code's main provisions, in principle. Yet the Code can only become fully effective if it is backed up by national governments. In the four and a half years since the Code was adopted, the following countries have taken action:-

○ **Code in effect as actual law**
Argentina, Kenya, Peru, Sri Lanka

○ **Some of the Code in effect as law**
Belgium, Botswana, Brazil, Colombia, Denmark, Egypt, Ethiopia, Finland, France, Guinea, Haiti, Indonesia, Israel, Italy, Mozambique, Nicaragua, Papua New Guinea, Tunisia, Venezuela, Zaire, Zambia, Zimbabwe

○ **Government controls distribution**
Algeria, Bulgaria, China, Cuba, Czechoslovakia, Democratic Yemen, Hungary, Libya, Mongolia, Mozambique, Romania, Soviet Union, Togo, Viet Nam

○ **Code recommended by government committee and awaiting legislation**
Bolivia, Cameroon, Central African Republic, Congo, Costa Rica, Ecuador, Ethiopia, Fiji, Guatemala, India, Israel, Jordan, Lesotho, Libya, Mexico, Mozambique, Nepal, Pakistan, Rwanda, Samoa, Sierra Leone, Swaziland, Tunisia, Uganda, Zambia, Zimbabwe

○ **Code in effect as a voluntary measure**
New Zealand, Portugal, Sweden, Syria, Trinidad and Tobago, Yugoslavia

○ **Some of the Code's provisions in effect as a voluntary measure**
Australia, Canada, Chile, Cook Islands, El Salvador, Finland, France, Gabon, German Democratic Republic, Hong Kong, Ivory Coast, Japan, Netherlands, Norway, Panama, Philippines, Thailand

○ **Code being studied by working party**
Afghanistan, Bahrain, Bangladesh, Burkina Faso (Upper Volta), Denmark, Dominica, Grenada, Honduras, Iran, Italy, Kuwait, Malawi, Mali, Morocco, Panama, Paraguay, Saudi Arabia, Senegal, Saint Vincent, Tanzania, Turks and Caicos Islands

○ **National code of marketing under discussion incorporating some of the International Code's provisions**
Austria, Brazil, Denmark, Dominican Republic, Malaysia, Sudan, Turkey, Yemen

○ **Voluntary code prepared by baby-food industry in effect**
Federal Republic of Germany, Ireland, Malaysia, Nigeria, Singapore, Switzerland, United Kingdom

○ **Voluntary code prepared by baby-food industry under discussion**
European Economic Community, Ivory Coast

Note: some countries may appear under more than one heading since, for example, a voluntary code may be in effect while legislation is pending.

As UNICEF has argued in its special report on Africa, adjustment to economic crisis need not and should not involve increasing the poverty and deprivation of a nation's poorest families. Specifically, it should not be allowed to threaten the lives and the normal growth of the most vulnerable section of any community – the children of the poor. Passing on the burdens of recession to those who have the least political muscle to resist the blow, and the least economic fat to absorb it, is not only unjust and inhuman – it also undermines the health and growth of the poorest children and so copes with the crisis of today only by guaranteeing more crises tomorrow.

A better way has to be found. And since Africa's crisis is as much of the world's making as of Africa's own, both justice and humanity now demand that the international community should share in the challenge of protecting the progress that has been made and of constructing a safety net of basic protection below which the poorest families and children will not be allowed to fall. As the United Nations Committee for Development Planning has argued:-

"*Many African governments have begun to implement major structural reforms. Others would be ready to begin if they were assured of the necessary extra resources and technical support. We urge the governments of the industrialized countries to commit themselves now to their share of the responsibility for assuring at least a minimally tolerable future for Africa over the next decade.*"[7]

The first strands in that safety net of protection are the strategies for protecting the lives and the growth of the poorest children (see panel 14). Breast-feeding, improved weaning (including supplementary food for those most at risk), immunization, oral rehydration therapy and growth monitoring, are among the most vital of all available techniques for meeting the needs of both immediate survival and the long-term need for the protection of growth. And because all of them can be put into action at relatively low cost, they are therefore practical symbols, in the field of child well-being, of the possibility of coping with economic crises at the same time as investing in, rather than mortgaging, the future.

The silent emergency

UNICEF and many other organizations are now working with governments to put these ideas into action in both the well-publicized emergencies of Africa and in the quieter crises diffused throughout the developing world (Fig. 9).

And to conclude this year's report, it is appropriate to turn to just one example of that quieter crisis, to just one village, and to just one of the many millions of mothers with whom UNICEF has made contact over the last forty years.

That mother's name is Maria Auxilia Paja. Her home is in an ordinary rural area of South America. Not long before the arrival of a trained health worker in her village, two of her children

Fig. 21 Increase in low birth-weight, Recife, Brazil, 1977–1984

127,948 births, poor urban areas of Recife, Northeast Brazil (low birth-weight = less than 2500 grammes)

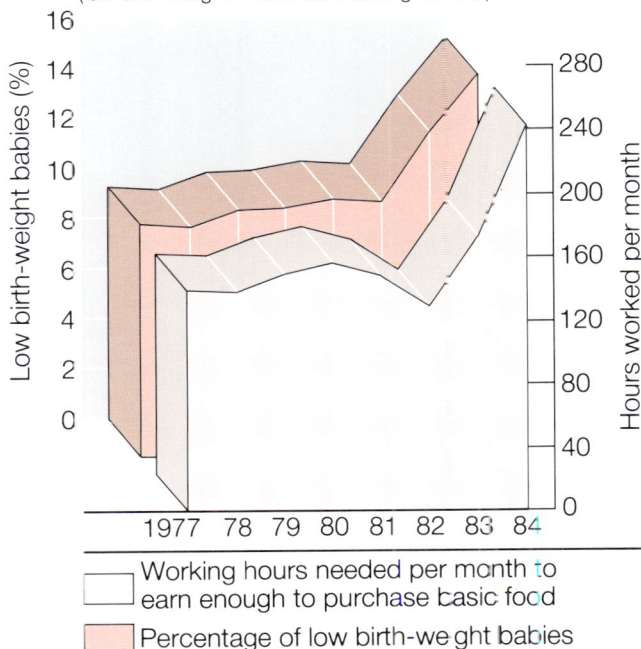

Working hours needed per month to earn enough to purchase basic food

Percentage of low birth-weight babies

Source: L. Dias, M. R. Camarano, A. Lechtig, "Drought, Recession, and Prevalence of Low Birth-weight Babies in Poor Urban Populations of the Northeast of Brazil", report from UNICEF Brasilia, 1985.

Parasites:
the damage to growth

24

The low-cost child survival measures discussed in this report can also have a significant impact on the problem of intestinal worms and parasites that sap children's growth wherever poverty, overcrowding and lack of hygiene co-exist. Breastfeeding, for example, protects young children against the dangers of contaminated water in feeding-bottles. Human breast-milk also contains a factor which kills the organisms of giardiasis and amoebiasis, two major causes of diarrhoea in children; and oral rehydration therapy can stave off the worst effects of diarrhoea. When parasitic infections cannot be prevented they can be reduced at little cost: a drug treatment for worms can cost less than 5 US cents.

Large parasite loads eat at their host's supply of nutrients, doing their greatest damage to the growing bodies of young children:-

○ The intestinal roundworm *Ascaris* infects 1,000 million people, or a quarter of the world's population. Twenty roundworms – by no means an unusual load – consume 2.8 grammes of carbohydrate a day and can eat up nearly 10% of a child's total energy intake.

○ Hookworm infects some 900 million people and often causes severe anaemia. Among pregnant women, anaemia increases the risk of low birth-weight and its attendant high mortality.

○ Giardiasis and amoebiasis, infecting 600 million between them, cause diarrhoea and poor absorption of nutrients.

○ The debilitating blood fluke of schistosomiasis, carried by a freshwater snail, is endemic in 74 countries. Ironically, irrigation projects have encouraged its spread. Some 200 million people are infected and a further 400 million at risk.

Children are both the principal victims and the main agents of transmission, excreting parasite eggs and cysts into the soil and water where they play and where they can repeatedly pick up the infection. As well as draining children's nutritional reserves, multiple worm burdens can cause oral polio vaccine to lose its effectiveness.

In the long run, parasite control entails breaking the cycle of infection and reinfection. In the industrialized world and some developing countries, improved standards of living – and especially of water supply and sanitation – have steeply reduced infection rates. In Costa Rica, for example, the last twenty years have seen a steady increase in clean water supply, latrines, and the wearing of shoes (which prevent hookworm from entering through the skin); parasite infections have fallen to a tenth of their earlier level.

But for many countries clean water and sewerage systems carry a high price tag. So most efforts to control parasitic infections centre on mass deworming campaigns, which can also be a starting-point for community health education. Successful deworming campaigns produce immediate and highly visible results, and encourage communities to reduce parasitic infections by knowing more and doing more about hand washing, hygienic food handling, avoiding contaminated water, and sanitary waste disposal.

The Japanese Organization for International Cooperation in Family Planning, active in several Asian and Latin American countries, uses parasite control to spark community interest in improved nutrition and in family planning. In two counties of the Republic of Korea, a project which motivated communities by training their leaders and conducting outdoor campaigns on market-days brought parasite infection rates down from 50.6% in 1977 to 5.3% in mid-1983. At the start of another project in north-east Brazil in 1980, 46.3% of rural schoolchildren and 42.8% of urban schoolchildren had roundworm and hookworm: after three deworming treatments over two years, the children's infection rates were 14.1% in the rural areas and 6.1% in the towns.

had died – one from a respiratory infection and one from measles. Or in Maria Auxilia's exact words:-

"*For the baby boy, I tried to get help. But as I was carrying him for help, he just died in my arms.*

"*My daughter was older. I had got used to playing with her, being with her. It's difficult... it's sad to remember those times with my children. She was alright when she went to bed. By midnight she was sick. She died just as day broke.*

"*I am not alone. It's happened to a lot of women.*"

Maria Auxilia Paja is indeed not alone. In the last twelve months, approximately 15 million mothers like her have been forced to watch their children die.

The vast majority of those 40,000 children never looked into a television camera and were never seen by anyone outside their own community. They did not die in any particular place or at any one particular time or from any one particular cause. They were therefore not news. But they nonetheless suffered, and they are nonetheless dead.

Theirs was the 'silent emergency'.

In the last year, the 'loud emergency' of Africa has been met with private generosity and public concern on an unprecedented scale. In almost all nations of the world, many millions of men, women and children have made it clear that they do not find such suffering acceptable in a world which so clearly has the financial and technical resources to prevent it.

That response is, in itself, an important milestone on the road to a more genuinely civilized world community. Forty years ago, when UNICEF was founded, there was no such international response to the great 1943-1944 famine in Bengal, in which even greater numbers of men, women and children lost their lives.

The international response to Africa's desperate need therefore marks the development, in our lifetime, of a different degree of global consciousness and concern. But if it is to match the scale and urgency of the problem itself then, in the remaining years of this century, that concern will have to be translated into new dimensions.

First, the concern for poverty and the concern for justice need to be translated into a concern for the quiet emergencies as well as for the loud. For just as the *seen* suffering of Africa has been regarded as unacceptable by so many citizens in 1985, so the unseen and unnecessary sufferings of much larger numbers of children in poor communities throughout the world must also become unacceptable, to both people and governments, if we are to continue making progress towards a more genuinely civilized – and peaceful – world.

Second, it needs the dimension of political and economic action by governments. The world-wide private generosity of millions of individuals in response to the African emergency has amounted to perhaps $300 million. The amount pledged by governments in extra aid for Africa in 1985 has amounted to approximately $3,000 million. And

Fig. 22 Increase in child malnutrition, Ghana, 1980–1983

Percentage of pre-school children (aged 7 to 44 months) severely and moderately malnourished (below 3rd percentile of weight-for-age, Harvard standard).

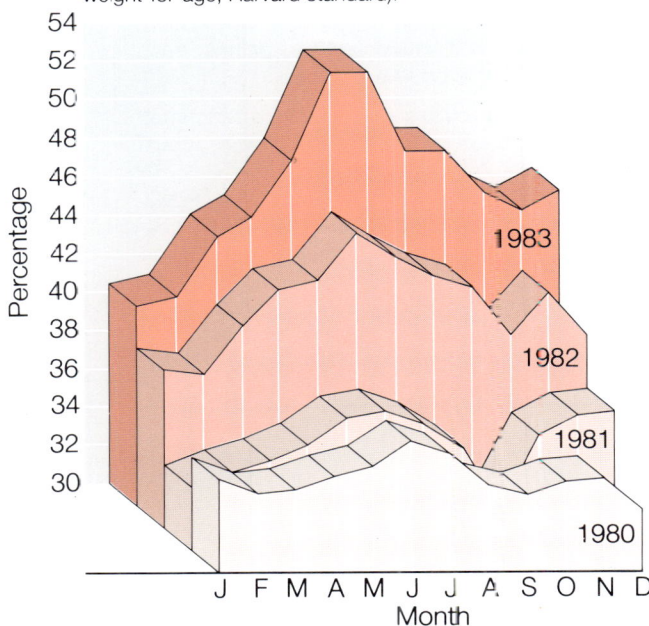

Source: Catholic Relief Services – Ghana.

Population:
less deaths – less births

25

For the last three years, the *State of the World's Children* report has described the breakthroughs which now make it possible to save the lives of several million children each year. But the most commonly asked question about this potential for a revolution in child survival is 'won't it lead to even more rapid population growth?'

Paradoxically, the answer is 'no'. A sharp reduction in child deaths would lead to an eventual reduction in population growth:-

○ Many parents 'insure' against child deaths by having more children. If parents become confident that their existing children will survive, they tend to have only the number of children they actually want. As the late Indira Gandhi said in 1983, *"parents are more likely to restrict their families if they have reasonable assurance of the healthy survival of their two children"*.*

○ Several of the key low-cost strategies for reducing child deaths are also key strategies for reducing births:-

Family spacing. In poor communities, infant mortality is typically twice as high when the interval between births is less than two years. Birth spacing is therefore a key strategy for child survival and reducing birth rates.

Female literacy is another powerful determinant of child survival. And as the World Fertility Survey has shown, rising female literacy also brings steadily falling birth rates.

Breast-feeding is also a key to child survival. And a mother who is breast-feeding is also protected, to a significant degree, against becoming pregnant.

○ If an infant dies, breast-feeding obviously stops and its effect in inhibiting conception is lost. In this way too, saving a child's life can help to postpone the next birth.

As important as any of these individual links between falling deaths and falling births is the overall fact that the 'child survival revolution' increases parents' sense of control over their lives. Probably the most important prerequisite for the acceptance of family planning is the growing confidence of parents that they can improve their lives by their own informed decisions and actions. Anything which helps to increase that confidence, as all parent-based child survival strategies do, is therefore also likely to lower birth rates.

These arguments are borne out by those countries which have already achieved a revolution in child survival. Nations such as China, Sri Lanka, the Republic of Korea, Costa Rica, and Singapore now have the lowest infant death rates – and the lowest birth rates – in the developing world. Taking their experience as a guide, it has been estimated that a country which has halved its infant mortality over the last two decades can now expect its population to stabilize at a level 30% to 40% smaller than would otherwise have been the case. Put another way, if all of India had the same low infant mortality and the same low birth rates as Kerala state, the nation as a whole would have approximately 4.4 million fewer deaths each year – and 7.5 million fewer births.

A revolution in child survival, far from exacerbating the problem of population growth, could therefore contribute to fertility decline. That is why the 1984 World Population Conference in Mexico included in its final declaration this statement:-

"Through breast-feeding, adequate nutrition, clean water, immunization programmes, oral rehydration therapy, and birth spacing, a virtual revolution in child survival could be achieved. The impact would be dramatic in humanitarian and fertility terms."

* The same point has been made by the President of the World Bank: *"Poor parents worry about who will take care of them in their old age or when they are ill, and for many the need for support in old age outweighs the immediate cost of children. Since many children die young ... the incentive to have many babies, to ensure that a few survive, is very great."*

in the meantime, the amount which Africa has paid back to the industrialized world in debt and interest repayments during 1985 has amounted to over $7,000 million. Those figures do not lessen the importance of the generosity of millions or the results it has achieved. But they brutally demonstrate that economic and political action – by governments in both developing and industrialized nations – is a prerequisite of any solution which matches the scale of the problem.

A choice for the 1980s

Present knowledge holds out the opportunity to provide, for the first time, a basic minimum protection for the lives and growth of all the world's children and to do so at a very low cost and in a very short time.

Several nations are already beginning to take up that opportunity – and with some remarkable early results.

To fulfil that potential, it is clear that – above all else – parents need to be empowered with infor-

mation and support from all sides. They need the support of their own political leaders and of the international community, of the health services and of all branches of government, of the community health workers and the mass media, of the schoolteachers and the religious leaders, of the community organizations and the women's movements, of the employers and the trade unions, and of people's movements in both developing and industrialized nations.

If this opportunity is taken, then the years ahead could see the achievement of one of the greatest goals which mankind has ever set for itself – basic protection for the lives and the health and the normal development of all its children. If that opportunity is not taken, then the 1980s and 1990s will be rightly stigmatized as the generation which failed to protect and maintain the hard-won progress of the post-war years and which presided over the co-existence of unprecedented financial and technical capacity with the continued malnutrition, stunting, and death of millions of its most vulnerable citizens.

The choice is ours.

——— II ———
LIFELINES

Extracts and summaries from recent
research and writing on strategies for
protecting the lives and normal
development of the world's children

Growth monitoring

Oral rehydration therapy

Breast-feeding

Immunization

Iron, iodine and vitamin A

Acute respiratory infections

Combating malaria

Female education

Food supplements

Family spacing

Introduction to Lifelines

The central theme of the last three reports on the *State of the World's Children* is that recent advances in knowledge make it possible for parents themselves to be so effective as front-line health workers that they could bring about a drastic improvement in their children's chances of survival and healthy, normal growth. At the same time, the spread of the primary health care idea, and the growth of communications and organizational capacity in most nations of the developing world, means that it is now possible to put such knowledge at the disposal of the vast majority of parents and to support them in using it.

The combinations of child protection techniques to be promoted will differ according to national and local circumstance. But the principal 'lifeline' techniques discussed in this part of the report are chosen because they are relevant to most nations, because they can be implemented at low cost, because they can achieve rapid results against some of the major problems, and because they promote the essence of primary health care by involving people in knowing more, demanding more, and doing more about their own and their families' health. In combination with each other, these actions also offer a considerable degree of protection against the synergistic alliance of malnutrition and infection which is the central problem of child survival and child development in the world today.

This year, sections on 'Respiratory infections', 'Malaria', and 'Iron, iodine and vitamin A' have been added because, in these fields too, recent advances in knowledge now offer practical low-cost ways of protecting the lives and normal development of children.

In addition, it has been repeatedly shown that three other factors – female education, family spacing, and food supplementation – are also among the most powerful levers for raising the level of child health. Although more costly and more difficult to achieve, these changes are of such potential significance – for the lives and health of both women and children – that they must also now be counted among the breakthroughs in knowledge which could change the ratio between the health and wealth of nations.

LIFELINES INDEX

□ This symbol indicates a new entry for 1986. Lifelines is updated annually.

Growth Monitoring

In the developing world, about 40% of children under five suffer from protein-energy malnutrition, which can permanently affect mental and physical development. The root of malnutrition is poverty and its long-term solution depends on economic growth and social justice. In the meantime, however, low-cost methods are available to significantly reduce the incidence and severity of malnutrition – and its impact on child health and development.

Malnutrition has many causes – of which frequent infection is one of the most important. The invisible slowing down of normal growth happens long before a child becomes malnourished. Regular monthly weighing and the use of a child growth chart can make visible this faltering growth and so provide an early warning to mothers and health workers. At this stage, malnutrition can be relatively easily and cheaply prevented. With basic advice, growth monitoring can therefore help mothers themselves to prevent most child malnutrition. More than 200 different growth charts are now coming into use in over 80 countries.

Malnutrition and Infection

Lack of food is only one of malnutrition's many causes. Probably the most important cause of all is repeated infection:

Recent research shows that repeated infections – especially respiratory and diarrhoeal infections – play a much greater role in causing malnutrition than was previously supposed. Studies in a Gambian village have shown that frequent bouts of diarrhoea are a common and almost constant illness before a child develops malnutrition. During diarrhoea 500-600 calories may be lost each day in the stools. This cyclical relationship of cause and effect needs to be broken.

Summarized from: David Morley and Margaret Woodland, See how they grow: monitoring child growth for appropriate health care in developing countries, Macmillan, 1979.

"All infections have a nutritional impact. They can depress the appetite. They can decrease the body's absorption of nutrients. They can induce rejection of food by vomiting. They can drain away nutrients through diarrhoea. They can induce mothers to stop feeding whilst the diarrhoea lasts. And by any or all of these methods, infections become a major cause, perhaps the major cause, of malnutrition among the world's children."

The state of the world's children 1984, Oxford University Press, 1983.

A study of 716 rural Guatemalan children under seven years showed that those suffering from frequent diarrhoeal infections gained less weight and height than those affected by other illnesses. Apart from impairing the functioning of the gastro-intestinal tract, diarrhoea almost always induces a loss of appetite and a drop in calorie and nutrient intake of 20-30%.

Summarized from: R. Martorell, "Acute morbidity and physical growth in Guatemalan children", American Journal of Diseases of Children, no. 129, 1975.

The Narangwal project in the Punjab region of north India found that young children bore a heavy burden of infection:

□"At the time of this project, malaria had not yet reappeared, there were relatively few intestinal parasitic infections, and levels of child and adult nutrition were among the best in India. Yet our prevalence figures indicate that children were ill 11% of the time with respiratory tract infections, 6% of the time with diarrheal diseases, 6% of the time with eye infections, and 4% of the time with fever. Prevalence of infectious diseases tended to be highest when the child was nutritionally most vulnerable – between 7 to 15 months of age, during the period when breast-feeding alone is insufficient."

Arnfried A. Kielmann and others, Child and maternal health services in rural India: the Narangwal experiment. Volume 1: integrated nutrition and health care, Johns Hopkins University Press, 1983.

"With weaning on contaminated foods and loss of passive immunity, the incidence of infectious diseases, particularly diarrhoea, attained rates of the order of seven to eight episodes per child per year in Cauque (Guatemala) children, during the first three years of life. Acute infections, mainly of the upper respiratory tract, were the most common, followed by diarrhoea, but the latter was more important in view of its adverse effect on host nutrition... The implications of diarrhoea and other infectious diseases are: reduced food consumption, nutrient losses, metabolic alterations, hormonal imbalance, and alterations in immune function; they manifest themselves as wasting, stunting, reduced activity, impaired learning and creativity, and acute malnutrition and death...

"It is then evident that infection and infectious diseases are the main determinants of acute and chronic malnutrition and death among children in societies not suffering from persistent food shortages or famines."

Leonardo Mata, "The evolution of diarrhoeal diseases and malnutrition in Costa Rica", Assignment Children, vol. 61/62, 1983.

Malnutrition and Weaning

Not knowing when and how to begin introducing other foods, in addition to breast-milk, is a major cause of child malnutrition in many parts of the world:

WEANING – WHEN

"... Between the age of four and six months, the child needs semi-solids and solid foods (though breast-feeding should also be continued for as long as possible). To avoid faltering growth, it is essential that parents know that this is the right age for weaning to begin. In some parts of India, only about 2% of infants in villages are receiving semi-solids even at the age of six to eight months."

Kusum P. Shah, "Food supplements", in The state of the world's children 1984, Oxford University Press, 1983.

"Both the early and late introduction of foods have been linked with child health problems. Introducing foods before 4 months leads to an increased incidence of diarrhea and may lead to increased mortality. On the other hand, the introduction of foods too late may mean nutrition requirements are not met, beginning the malnutrition process and leaving the child more vulnerable to other common childhood diseases."

Program activities for improved weaning practices, World Federation of Public Health Associations, 1984.

"The exact time that weaning should begin is determined by the lactation performance of the mother and the rate of growth and maturation of the infant; it does not therefore depend strictly on age, but for most infants it is between the ages of 4 and 6 months... The late initiation of weaning may lead to malnutrition. This is apparent in data from the WHO Collaborative Study, which show that with low rates of supplementation after the age of 6 months, e.g. among the urban poor and the rural population of India, the rate of growth of infants slowed down to well below the norm for this age.

"The late initiation of weaning was particularly noticeable among the urban poor in India and Ethiopia, where 40% and 15% of infants respectively were still exclusively breast-fed at 12 and 13 months; in rural India the proportion was 36%. At 18 months, among the urban poor, 12% of infants in Ethiopia and 20% of infants in India were still not being weaned. Among the urban well-to-do, almost all infants everywhere were receiving regular supplementation at 6 to 7 months of age."

WHO/UNICEF, Infant and young child feeding: current issues, WHO, 1981

WEANING – HOW

A child needs a higher concentration of protein and calories in food than an adult. But a child's stomach is small and the staple foods of the poor are often bulky and low in both calories and proteins. The result may be that a child's hunger is satisfied – but not his nutritional needs. The solution is more frequent feeding of smaller amounts of more calorie-dense foods. But this can be very demanding of a mother's time, energy, and available food:

"Good weaning practices are a major factor in avoiding faltering growth. The amount of extra local food required is small. Lack of income is not, therefore, the only constraint. There may also be important social and organizational constraints, e.g. lack of knowledge about how to prepare appropriate local foods, mother's time required, lack of community production facilities, e.g. grinders, absence of mothers out working during long hours, too long periods between meals, difficulties of keeping prepared food, shortage of fuel, etc. These problems need to be addressed by various local arrangements, strengthened by appropriate health education."

James P. Grant, "New hope in dark times. UNICEF's assessment of past experience with a child survival package: its effectiveness and its social and economic feasibility", paper prepared for International Conference on Population, Mexico City, May–June 1983.

☐"The normal healthy infant doubles his birth weight by the age of 4 to 6 months on mother's milk alone.

"The faltering of growth noticed at age 4 to 6 months requires the addition of a food equivalent to the energy density of breast milk and not the cessation of breast-feeding as thought in classical paediatric texts. When diets of rural Ugandan children in the second year of life were studied it was found that those who were still being breast-fed and offered solid food received up to 25 per cent more energy compared to those who had been completely weaned even though the latter consumed 60 per cent more solids.

"All traditional weaning foods tend to be in the form of a gruel made from the local staple. Because of the natural property of the starch granule which swells on boiling in water and gets gelatinized on cooling, the gruel increases in viscosity. The state of development of the structures of the mouth in the young child is such that only a gruel of fluid consistency can be swallowed without choking. Hence there is a limit to which the gruel can be thickened and consequently most traditional weaning gruels do not contain more than 10-12 per cent flour. The rest is water. Addition of edible fat or oil during cooking has two effects. It increases the energy density and at the same time makes the gruel less viscous. Similarly the use of edible oil and fats can help to increase the energy density of other foods, especially of convalescent diets."

G.J. Ebrahim, "Energy content of weaning foods", Journal of Tropical Pediatrics, vol. 29, August 1983.

CONTAMINATED WEANING FOODS

A mother who is already overworked may not have the time to feed a weanling child frequently enough. In the rainy season when work in the fields is usually at its heaviest, the mother may prepare food in the morning for the whole day. Inadequate storage facilities combined with tropical temperatures mean that such food easily becomes contaminated. A sample survey of infant food in the Gambia showed that even with freshly prepared food, up to one-third would be condemned as microbiologically unfit for human consumption by international standards, and particularly during the rainy months (see table 1):

☐"Kwashiorkor, which is prevalent in the tropical Third World, has been considered as a symptom of extreme protein deficiency, and the treatment up until now has been the administration of protein.

"It is now believed, however, that kwashiorkor is a specific disease caused by a fungus known as aflatoxin which forms in badly stored crops in hot damp conditions. This theory solves many puzzles associated with the complaint, notably that not all sufferers from malnutrition suffer from kwashiorkor, and that its victims are never found in temperate areas.

"The discovery was made by Professor Hendrickse of the Liverpool School of Tropical Medicine, and studied further in Khartoum University with the support of Oxfam. Samples from several hundred children have confirmed the presence of aflatoxin in kwashiorkor sufferers and their food... Researchers now say that the incidence of kwashiorkor could be reduced by better storage of crops, and by improving the quality of oil used for cooking."

Jitendra Pal, "Rethinking on tropical disease", Development Forum, September 1984.

(For further information on weaning, see Lifeline on Breast-feeding.)

Table 1: Percentage of food samples containing unacceptable levels of one or more pathogens according to season.

Time after preparation (in hours)	Wet season June–October	Dry season November–May
0–1	34.9 (43)	6.3 (73)
1–2	52.6 (19)	30.8 (13)
4–6	57.8 (38)	46.3 (41)
8	96.2 (26)	70.7 (41)

Figures in parentheses are the actual numbers of samples studied.

R. G. Whitehead, "Infant Feeding Practices and the Development of Malnutrition in Rural Gambia", Food and Nutrition Bulletin, vol. 1, No. 4.

Malnutrition – other causes

PARASITES

Parasites affect hundreds of millions of people the world over, especially children, feeding on their host's nutrients. Twenty Ascaris roundworms (not a heavy load – some 20 million people in the Philippines alone are estimated to harbour about 20) will steal 2.8 grammes of carbohydrate a day from their host.

Summarized from: Benjamin D. Cabrera, "Ascaris: most 'popular' worm", World Health, March 1984.

"Intestinal parasites compete for nutrients while damaging the intestinal structure and decreasing nutrient absorption. Roundworms, the most common of the helminths, can lead to nutrient wastage: about 3% of calories for light infections, up to 25% for heavy, plus increased nitrogen losses... Hookworm infection also reduces absorption, and results in caloric losses estimated at one calorie per worm per day, or as much as 5% of a person's daily consumption. Combined with its effect on women's iron supply, this parasite can have especially serious impact on pregnant women."

James E. Austin and others, Nutrition intervention in developing countries: assessment and guidelines, Oelgeschlager, Gunn and Hain, 1981.

LOW BIRTH-WEIGHT

Maternal malnutrition can lead to poor foetal growth and low birth-weight, which is, in turn, associated with poor growth in infancy and childhood (see Lifeline on Food supplements).

BOTTLE-FEEDING

The trend from breast-feeding to bottle-feeding in many of the developing world's towns and cities is also an important cause of malnutrition (see Lifeline on Breast-feeding).

HUNGER AND POVERTY

"For those who simply do not have enough to eat, the long-term solution lies in having either the land with which to grow food or the jobs and the incomes with which to buy it. But as many as one-third of the Third World's labour force is now unemployed or under-employed.

"Land reforms and economic growth to give the poor access to land, jobs, increased productivity, higher incomes, are an essential part of the long-term solution to the poverty from which malnutrition and ill-health are born...

"The answer to hunger is ... not ultimately technological. The problem is rather one of what crops are grown by whom on whose lands and for whose benefit. And the solution lies in political and economic change to allow the poor to both participate in, and benefit from, the increases in production which can most certainly be achieved."

The state of the world's children 1982-83, Oxford University Press, 1982.

Monitoring Child Growth

Most child malnutrition is invisible until it reaches an advanced stage. Growth monitoring – by means of regular monthly weighing and entering the results on a child growth chart – makes faltering growth visible long before malnutrition begins. At that stage, prevention is relatively inexpen- sive and relatively simple. The growth monitoring technique – and some basic advice – can therefore help mothers to prevent much of the child malnutrition in the developing world, even within existing resources:

IMPORTANCE OF GROWTH

"The most useful indicator of nutrition in a young child is whether growth is proceeding normally, i.e. it is the rate of weight gain that is important rather than the nutritional status measured in relation to a norm, at a particular point in time."

"Promotion of nutrition and growth monitoring", programme manual prepared for UNICEF workshop, Bangkok, July 1984.

"A child who grows well is probably healthy and adequately nourished. If a child is not growing well there must be some reason: usually some illness or lack of adequate nourishment. A child's growth will slow down or even stop months before there are obvious signs of malnutrition."

"Training in recording the child's growth", WHO, 1983 (EPI/FHW/83/TM.1/Rev.1).

INVISIBLE MALNUTRITION

"The average moderately malnourished child in the 6-24-month age range looks entirely normal but is too small for his or her age, has lowered resistance to infection, and therefore easily succumbs to illness. The child receiving only 60 percent of caloric requirement may give no outward sign of hunger beyond a frequent desire to breast-feed. In a Philippines study, 58 percent of the mothers of ... malnourished children said they thought their babies were growing and developing well."

James E. Austin and others, Nutrition intervention in developing countries: assessment and guidelines, Oelgeschlager, Gunn and Hain, 1981.

"The concept of growth as such is not necessarily known to everybody. However, growth seen as change in body size is well known to all parents. Any mother in a typical village of developing countries knows that her child will have to grow bigger and taller over time. What is very important is that she does not easily and quickly recognize slowed growth in her child. In other words, by pure observation and without some form of visual aid she cannot see early enough if the child is small or light-for-age and does not gain steadily, or understand the relationship between the child's growth, diet and health."

H. Ghassemi, "Growth charts: one good means for better child health and growth", paper prepared for UNICEF, November 1982.

The Child Growth Chart

"Regular monthly weighing, and the entering of the results on a child growth chart, can make faltering growth visible long before malnutrition sets in. Once the mother can see the problem, she will normally take action to correct it. With some basic advice on child feeding, growth monitoring can therefore help mothers themselves to prevent the majority of child malnutrition even within existing resources."

Jon E. Rohde, "Community-based nutrition programs", Management Sciences for Health, July 1982.

"... In several parts of the world, it is now being shown that even within existing health budgets – or for very little extra in the way of resources – the growth of children can be significantly improved.

"The piece of 'technology' which makes this possible is a simple cardboard or thin plastic growth chart, kept by the mother, and costing between two and ten cents. Through the regular monthly weighing of all young children and the entering up of the results on a growth chart, children at risk of malnutrition can be identified. With the appropriate help and advice from health workers, parents can then protect the development of their children. And in so doing, they can protect and improve the economic and social development of their nations.''

David Morley, "Growth monitoring" in The state of the world's children 1984, Oxford University Press, 1983.

Education of Mothers

Growth monitoring programmes are usually based on an educational strategy enabling individual mothers to become more responsible for the health, nutrition and welfare of their children:

''In the Hanover project (in Jamaica) workers felt growth monitoring itself was an intervention. Mothers learned so much about the relation between diet and health by watching their child's growth pattern that this alone led to dietary improvements and substantially reduced malnutrition and mortality. These observations have led some health professionals to conclude that ... in communities where social or cultural factors play a greater role than absolute resource inadequacy in the etiology of malnutrition, nutrition monitoring appears to have the potential for a significant impact on mortality even in the absence of more expensive and more difficult to implement components such as nutrition supplementation or education.''

Growth monitoring, Primary Health Care Issues, series I, no. 3, American Public Health Association, October 1981.

The researchers of the Narangwal project in India, one of the largest study projects ever undertaken in the developing world, came to a similar conclusion:

''World-wide experience with road-to-health cards for recording weight gain has been reinforced by experience at Narangwal showing that it is possible to help mothers learn that a child with faltering growth is a sick child. Growth monitoring therefore served both as an educational device and as the principal entry point for active nutritional supplementation.

''At the start of the project we decided against trying to provide supplementation to all children in the villages. It was obvious that mere provision of food was not needed because we were in a food surplus area. However, up to a third of children were malnourished...

''It is our belief that the most important long-term impact from our nutrition program was in the education of mothers. The nutrition problems in the Punjab result mainly from inappropriate feeding practices and the heavy load of infections. Our results showed that it is a fallacy to assume that if food supplies are sufficient in a village, people will solve their own nutrition problems. In most developing countries, just as important as improving food supplies, is the need for a major effort to help mothers learn how to make better use of food. Much of the childhood malnutrition could be ameliorated by nutrients that are already available in the village.''

Arnfried A. Kielmann and others, Child and maternal health services in rural India: the Narangwal experiment. Volume 1: integrated nutrition and health care, Johns Hopkins University Press, 1983.

Lack of food within the home is not the only factor in how a child is weaned:

''Despite national socio-economic gains in the seventies, protein calorie malnutrition (PCM) afflicts more than one-third of Indonesian children under five and is a major cause of infant mortality... A nationwide study however found no significant difference in the numbers of children with PCM in households that were classified as 'food adequate' and those classified as 'food deficient'. The study concluded that poor infant feeding practices rather than lack of food was the major cause of PCM...''

Program activities for improved weaning practices, World Federation of Public Health Associations, 1984.

The aims of growth monitoring in the Indonesian nutrition improvement programme have been described as follows:

''Emphasis is entirely on behavioural change leading to the goal 'every child should gain weight every month'. Mothers can easily understand, appreciate, and achieve this goal monthly. By contrast, improved nutritional status (or maintenance of 'normality') has less psychological attraction, is relatively static, and often leads to complacency or resignation on the part of mothers who see their children classified in a single, broad, nutritional category. Monthly growth is a self-motivating goal with recurring rewards.''

Jon Rohde and Lukas Hendrata, "Development from below: transformation from village-based nutrition projects to a national family nutrition programme in Indonesia", in David Morley, Jon Rohde and Glen Williams (eds.), Practising health for all, Oxford University Press, 1983.

BACK-UP SERVICES

When a child's growth is seriously faltering, it is essential for the mother to have access to competent medical back-up:

''It is important in village-based growth monitoring for a mother to know that repeated non-growth for two or three months is a sign that she should seek health care, even though her child may still seem well-nourished, energetic and not obviously sick. Here the important back-up of the nearest dispensary or clinic is essential to assure her that, although her child appears to be well, a complete physical exam will be given. A qualified health worker checks the common causes of faltering growth in the young, such as chronic otitis media (ear infection), intestinal worms, silent primary tuberculosis, or other important infections.

''Should the child's examination prove normal, the system will often provide food supplements for a short period with the hope that this additional input to the diet will result in a resumption of growth and demonstrate to the mother that feeding alone can restore her child's health. The timing and place of such supplementary food activities are critical to the entire success of the programme. Food supplements provided during the monthly weighing activities will destroy the entire thrust of mother-to-mother interaction and the learning and evaluative process inherent in the growth monitoring activity.''

Jon E. Rohde, "Growth monitoring", World Health, October 1984.

ENTRY POINT FOR PHC

''... Growth monitoring can form the basis of village operated primary health care (PHC) activities leading to a sustained PHC program that provides useful data on the nutritional health of a population as well as for individualized health and nutrition cases.''

USAID, "Recommendations for improved health, population and nutrition program implementation within the Bureau for Asia", report prepared for Asia Bureau health, population and nutrition officers conference, May 1984.

''Growth monitoring programmes provide an ideal opportunity for the provision of other primary health care (PHC) services. It is the only recurring activity in primary health care

II LIFELINES: GROWTH MONITORING

that serves to bring mother and child into contact with health services on a predictable and frequent basis. Children can be effectively vaccinated by a visiting health worker, while demonstrations of oral rehydration and, in some cases, distribution of oral rehydration salts can ensure mothers' prompt response to diarrhoea. Family planning can be discussed and contraceptive materials distributed and re-supplied. Periodic deworming, administration of high-dose vitamin A, and provision of chloroquine in malarious areas all contribute to the success of a growth monitoring activity at the village level.''

Jon E. Rohde, "Growth monitoring", World Health, October 1984.

COSTS OF MONITORING

Costs are minimal, though it should be remembered that growth monitoring represents only a starting-point for teaching mothers about their child's health and nutrition:

"The cost of growth monitoring is extremely low, usually ranging between U.S. $0.02-$0.10 per child per year, depending on equipment, charts, and training needs. The tools are relatively inexpensive to buy or can even be locally made at little or no cost. Moreover, the most expensive equipment should last for many years. This makes the cost per child negligible when divided by the under-five population that will use the equipment over the years. Growth charts range in cost from U.S. $0.03 to $0.33. Since ideally one chart is used per child over a five-year period, the expenditure per child per year is minimal.''

Growth monitoring, Primary Health Care Issues, series I, no. 3, American Public Health Association, October 1981.

"Of all the measurements that can be made on children in the developing countries, weighing is most likely to be useful, and its cost-benefit value is very high. For example, the cost of weighing consists mainly of the salaries of health workers. Other costs are small. Weighing scales have a long life, rarely requiring repair or replacement – at least 100,000 weighings may be possible over their normal life. The time spent by staff on weighing is available simultaneously for other purposes, such as discussion with the mother and general observation of the child.''

David Morley and Margaret Woodland, See how they grow: monitoring child growth for appropriate health care in developing countries, Macmillan, 1979.

ALTERNATIVE METHODS

Measuring the circumference of the upper arm is also a method of monitoring growth:

"The first armband for measuring malnutrition in children (Morley-Shakir) was a single thin band used to measure all children from birth to six years of age. Concerned that a single measuring tape might not be sensitive enough to detect the subtle but important differences in the various growth periods of a child, researchers in Colombia designed and are now using two tapes instead. The two tapes ... divide the first six years of growth into seven stages... When the appropriate age tape is wrapped around the upper left arm of a child, the end of the tape falls into a stripe of color which indicates the child's nutritional status: green – well nourished; yellow – early stages of malnutrition; and red – moderate to severe malnutrition.''

LIFE Newsletter (League for International Food Education), September 1982.

"Arm circumference is ... not sensitive enough to monitor an individual child's growth over short periods of time like the weight chart. It is useful, however, in situations where it is not feasible to weigh children, particularly to screen children to identify early, and established, malnutrition...''

"Promotion of nutrition and growth monitoring", programme manual prepared for UNICEF workshop, Bangkok, July 1984.

Other ways of assessing growth include measuring weight for height, and height for age. It is often impossible for health workers to see children regularly. In such instances, assessment of a child's health and nutritional status must be based on measurements taken on a single occasion:

□ "On its own, weight for age does not distinguish 'stunted' children, who are underweight because of long-standing undernutrition, from 'wasted' children whose weight deficit is due to more recent weight loss. Stunted children are identified with the height for age index, wasted children by using the weight for height index...

"Weight for height chart: ... After being weighed, the child stands against the wall chart directly in front of the vertical column marked with his weight. The upper end of this column has three differently coloured zones (red for less than 80%, yellow for 80-90% and green for over 90% of the expected weight for height). A weight for length chart has been designed for children less than 2 years who cannot stand...

"Height for age chart: A similar chart has been developed to identify children whose heights are less than expected at a given age. Charts of length for age have also been developed.''

David Nabarro, "Assessment of nutritional status in infants and children", Medical Forum, no. 2, 1982.

Challenges

Child growth charts, despite their enormous potential, are not easy to understand and use effectively. Reports from a number of countries indicate problem areas and challenges to be overcome in the design, management and evaluation of growth monitoring programmes:

□ "A major problem is that in areas or families with absolute lack of food the mothers and health workers see no benefits in growth monitoring, and it may indeed provide a barrier to mothers seeking advice or treatment. Health workers report mothers avoiding the clinic when their children are 'under the line'. Health workers may blame mothers for failing to feed their children and in some areas many better-off women and probably most men think that women whose children don't grow should be scolded and blamed for not caring for them properly...

"A study of the literature indicates four problem areas in effective monitoring of growth and development:
1. Senior health personnel are not committed to the monitoring of children's growth and development.
2. Health workers do not understand the function of monitoring growth and development. Often they do not have the skills to do it adequately or do not know what action to take.
3. Mothers and others in the community are not involved in the monitoring of growth and development of their children. This lack of involvement is most evident among those most in need. Participation is usually passive.
4. Inappropriate design of equipment (scales and growth charts).''

Gill Tremlett, "Making growth monitoring more effective", unpublished paper, March 1985.

These and other problems have led some observers to propose a flexible approach:

☐"Growth monitoring using weighing and growth charts has been successfully carried out in some small-scale projects with dedicated leadership and supervision. But these models may not be capable of replication in large-scale governmental health systems. The health systems of developing countries are at various levels of 'development'. A rigid uniform pattern of growth monitoring should not be advocated for all countries. The pattern must be adapted to suit local capabilities. Elaborate weighing and charting on Road-to-Health cards may not be possible in all situations. Indeed they may not even be necessary. Less complicated, less cumbersome, and less time-consuming technologies could be adopted in situations where the health infrastructure is relatively weak."

C. Gopalan, "Growth charts as a tool for improving nutritional status of children: a review of global experience", paper prepared for WHO, 1985.

Mothers' Involvement

There has been considerable debate about the ability of mothers – and health workers – to understand the process of plotting a child's growth on a chart:

"Often health workers think that mothers cannot understand the significance of the growth chart, since it is sometimes difficult for the health workers themselves to understand. However, projects that have measured mothers' understanding of the chart after orientation have concluded that mothers have little or no difficulty understanding the chart.

"Data gathered in Ghana indicate that .. many virtually illiterate mothers had little trouble understanding the chart. Even though only 53 percent of the mothers had more than two years of schooling, after six months in the program, 66 percent of all mothers were able to interpret ... charts correctly.

"The experience of Project Poshak in India confirms that mothers can interpret the charts. In this project mothers received weight charts and instructions about their use. By the time of the project evaluation, all mothers interviewed knew that a downward slope in the child's growth line meant illness. Seventy-six percent ... were able to mark their own child's position and to identify the child's health status correctly."

Growth monitoring, Primary Health Care Issues, series I, no. 3, American Public Health Association, October 1981.

"In Indonesia, where UNICEF has supplied 15 million growth charts and 58,700 weighing scales, studies have shown that 95 per cent of the village volunteers can use the growth charts and a survey of 2,500 mothers indicated 67 per cent understood about child health and growth and the need to weigh children monthly. The national reporting system for the nutritional programme in Indonesia shows that 7.45 million children or 35 per cent of the under-fives are enrolled, 55 per cent of those enrolled attend regular weighing sessions and at least 48 per cent are gaining weight."

The children's revolution: the Asian picture, UNICEF (Bangkok), 1984.

"It has been reported that the mothers' enthusiasm and participation in a program increases when they are given the growth cards. Possession of the card is a clear indication to the mother that she shares in the responsibility for her child's

health. Other advantages include decreasing the amount of time mothers wait for workers to find and refile records."

Growth monitoring, Primary Health Care Issues, series I, no. 3, American Public Health Association, October 1981.

"Some health workers are concerned that records kept by a mother may be lost, or left at home when she visits the clinic. Indeed, there is some evidence that, when a home-based system first starts, losses may be as high as 5 per cent and failures to bring cards to clinics even higher. But this is only a temporary phenomenon, until the new system becomes familiar. Various careful studies have shown that loss rates soon fall below 1 per cent. Even more important, the loss rates by mothers are likely to be lower than by clinic staff."

David Morley and Margaret Woodland, See how they grow: monitoring child growth for appropriate health care in developing countries, Macmillan, 1979.

"In the Dr. Efrain C. Montemayor Medical Centre in Baguio (in the Philippines), which gives mothers their copies of growth charts, only 1.05% of its more than 2,000 regular mothers in the Under Six Clinic Program forget to bring their charts. This is attributed to the education campaign given mothers at each visit to the clinic. Because mothers understand and realize its importance, they remember to bring the chart as well as come regularly for their child's weighing."

"A situation analysis of growth charts in the Philippines", UNICEF (Manila), October 1983.

The Growth Debate

Growth charts are usually based on average child growth rates in the industrialized world. But is it appropriate to judge the nutritional standing of children in developing countries by the international standards based on North American or European children?

"Monitoring the growth of a child requires comparing changes in the same measure taken at regular intervals. A single measurement only indicates the child's size at the moment; it offers little information about whether the child's size is increasing, entering a period of stability, or declining. Because most children will continue to grow – even if only slightly – unless they are extremely ill, it is easy to mistake some growth for adequate growth unless the child's measurement is compared to a reference population. Which population to use for comparison purposes is a controversial question. The debate continues about whether children from different areas of the world have the same genetic potential for growth."

Growth monitoring, Primary Health Care Issues, series I, no. 3, American Public Health Association, October 1981.

"The controversy over whether or not growth standards for children developed in Europe and North America are universally applicable appears now to be settled in favour of those who maintain that they are. Recent evidence suggests that the growth of privileged groups of children in developing countries does not differ importantly from these standards and that the poorer growth so commonly observed in the underprivileged is due to social factors – among which the malnutrition-infection complex is of primary importance – rather than to ethnic or geographical differences..."

"A measure of agreement on growth standards" Lancet, editorial, 21 January 1984.

"There has been a continuing debate as to whether small size in itself is in any way disadvantageous. Where scarcity of food is the norm, might not the nutritional savings realized from being small be decisive for survival? These questions are difficult to answer because it is difficult to isolate the nutrition factor among the deprivations suffered by affected populations. Many studies have shown, however, that the decrease in growth, in both height and weight, associated with various degrees of malnutrition is accompanied by decreases in the circumference of the head, the size of the brain – amounts of important enzymes and neurotransmitters are decreased – and, even in less-than-severe cases, a lowering of scores on tests of cognitive and sensory ability."

Alan Berg, Malnourished people: a policy view, World Bank, June 1981.

Oral Rehydration Therapy

Diarrhoeal disease is the greatest single killer of children in the developing world – and often the chief cause of childhood malnutrition.

The prevention of diarrhoea depends upon improvements in water supply, sanitation, and hygiene. But in the meantime, the majority of deaths from diarrhoeal dehydration can be cheaply prevented by oral rehydration therapy (ORT).

Diarrhoeal infections cause the body to lose salts and water faster than they can be replaced – leading to dehydration. ORT is based on the discovery that glucose greatly increases the body's capacity to absorb salts and water. Drinking a solution of salts, glucose and water can therefore prevent and treat dehydration.

Pre-packaged oral rehydration salts (ORS) cost only about 10 cents. But making the packets available to every household is not always feasible. So many ORT campaigns are also concentrating on teaching mothers to forestall dehydration by using household remedies – such as sugar and salt solutions, rice water and soups.

The common reaction of parents the world over is to withhold food and fluids during a diarrhoeal attack. The scientific rationale for ORT, and for continued feeding during – and after – diarrhoea, has been established beyond doubt: the challenge now is to place that knowledge in the hands of parents so that they themselves can protect their children against the dehydration and malnutrition caused by childhood's most common disease.

Diarrhoea Deaths

☐ "The diarrhoeal diseases today remain an enormous public health problem. Further information gathered by the Programme during the biennium indicates that they continue to be associated with about one-third of all deaths in children under 5 years of age in the developing countries, and that such children may spend up to 15-20% of the first two years of life suffering from diarrhoeal diseases. Cholera – the most severe of the diarrhoeal diseases – again took its toll, and was in fact more widespread in some areas (especially West Africa) in 1983 and 1984 than in the previous biennium."

WHO Programme for Control of Diarrhoeal Diseases, "Fourth Programme report 1983-1984", 1985 (WHO/CDD/85.13).

DEHYDRATION
Most diarrhoea deaths stem from dehydration, caused by abnormally large losses of water and salts from the body:
☐ "The body normally takes in the water and salts it needs (input) from drinks and food. The body normally loses water and salts (output) through stools, urine, and sweat.

"When the bowel is healthy, water and salts pass from the bowel into the blood. When a person has diarrhoea, the bowel is not working normally, and more than the normal amount of water and salts is passed in the stool and less than the normal amount passes into the blood.

"This larger-than-normal loss of water and salts from the body results in dehydration. Dehydration occurs when the output of water and salts is greater than the input. The more diarrhoea stools a patient passes, the more water and salts he loses. Dehydration can also be caused by vomiting, which often accompanies diarrhoea.

"Dehydration occurs faster in infants and younger children, in hot climates, and when the person has a fever."

Treatment and prevention of acute diarrhoea: guidelines for the trainers of health workers, WHO, 1985.

"About 10 percent of diarrhea episodes lead to dehydration and, if untreated, one or two percent become life-threatening."

"Oral rehydration therapy (ORT) for childhood diarrhea", Population Reports, series L, no. 2, reprinted April 1982.

Malnutrition

Diarrhoeal diseases are a frequent cause of malnutrition; and malnutrition in its turn makes children more vulnerable to sickness and death from diarrhoea:

"Diarrhoea is ... a major factor in the causation or aggravation of malnutrition. This is because the diarrhoea patient loses his appetite and is unable to absorb food properly, and because it is a common practice to withhold fluids and food (including breast-milk) from him. Such malnutrition is itself a contributing cause to the high number of deaths associated with diarrhoea in childhood."

The management of diarrhoea and use of oral rehydration therapy: a joint WHO/UNICEF statement, WHO, 1983.

"Other studies have recorded a relationship between poor nutritional status and increased duration of diarrhoea... In a prospective study in San Jose, Costa Rica, the average duration of diarrhoea episodes in children aged 12-59 months was significantly longer among those with low weight-for-age than among others.

"If poor nutritional status predisposes to more severe diarrhoea ... then it would be expected that poor nutritional status would predispose to diarrhoea mortality. Chen et al. measured the heights and weights of 2,019 children aged 12-23 months in rural Bangladesh and then recorded mortality among these children over the following 2 years. A striking association between nutritional status (weight-for-age) and subsequent diarrhoea mortality was recorded, with children below 65% weight-for-age having a diarrhoea mortality rate 3.8 times higher than children over 65% weight for age..."

R.G. Feachem, "Interventions for the control of diarrhoeal diseases among young children: supplementary feeding programmes", Bulletin of the WHO, vol. 61, no. 6, 1983.

Causes of Diarrhoea

Many pathogens give rise to diarrhoea. They are both more prevalent and more harmful in an unhygienic environment:

THE PATHOGENS

"Diarrhoeal disease is associated with poverty and with the environmental and education conditions that accompany poverty. In wealthy communities throughout the world diarrhoeal disease has become a minor public health problem. If we look at Europe and North America, for instance, some infections have become very rare (*Vibrio cholerae, Shigella* species other than *sonnei, Salmonella typhi* and *paratyphi* and *Entamoeba histolytica*) while other infections continue to occur but cause little disease compared to their status in developing countries (rotaviruses, enterotoxigenic *Escherichia coli*, salmonellae, *Campylobacter* and *Shigella sonnei*)."

Richard Feachem, "Water, excreta, behaviour and diarrhoea", Diarrhoea Dialogue, no. 4, February 1981.

TRANSMISSION

"Water-borne transmission is but one special case of faecal-oral transmission and most authorities would agree that a great deal of the transmission of rotaviruses, shigellae, enterotoxigenic *E. coli* and *Entamoeba histolytica* is by non-water-borne routes. There is less agreement on the transmission of cholera...

"Many people drink heavily contaminated water (containing up to 10,000 *E. coli* per 100 millilitres) from open wells, ponds or streams. Replacing these sources by piped water or protected wells will dramatically improve water quality... However, some studies ... have found that such improvements failed to have a marked effect on diarrhoea disease incidence. One possible explanation ... is that diarrhoeal diseases in the communities studied were mainly non-water-borne."

Richard Feachem, "Water, excreta, behaviour and diarrhoea", Diarrhoea Dialogue, no. 4, February 1981.

THE LINK WITH MEASLES

"A prospective detailed study, in which 5,775 children in 12 villages in Bangladesh were observed for a year, showed that measles and diarrhoea appeared to interact synergistically to increase mortality and the irreversible effects of nutritional deprivation. Thirty-four per cent of diarrhoeal deaths were measles-associated. Measles was the single most important cause of death during the period and diarrhoea or dysentery was the most common complication of fatal measles cases...

"It has been estimated that between 6.4 and 25.6 per cent of diarrhoea deaths could be prevented by measles immunization."

M. and V.I. Mathan, "Measles immunization: priority intervention?", Diarrhoea Dialogue, no. 16, February 1984.

Oral Rehydration

Deaths from dehydration can be cheaply prevented by oral rehydration therapy (ORT), using either pre-packed sachets of oral rehydration salts (ORS) or home-made solution. The severely dehydrated require intravenous rehydration:

"A rational response to diarrhoea is as follows:
(a) To *prevent* dehydration using solutions prepared from ingredients commonly found in the home ('home remedies'); this should be the first response;
(b) To *correct* dehydration using a balanced, more complete, glucose-salt solution; ORS is the universal solution of this type recommended by WHO and UNICEF;
(c) To correct severe dehydration (usually defined as loss of 10% or more of body weight) by intravenous therapy; this method should also be used in patients who are unconscious or unable to drink."

The management of diarrhoea and use of oral rehydration therapy: a joint WHO/UNICEF statement, WHO, 1983.

"About 90-95% of all patients with acute watery diarrhoea, including infants, can be treated with ORS alone; in the remainder, most of whom have severe dehydration or are unable to take fluids orally, intravenous therapy is required to replace the deficits rapidly."

The management of diarrhoea and use of oral rehydration therapy: a joint WHO/UNICEF statement, WHO, 1983.

II LIFELINES: ORAL REHYDRATION THERAPY

ORAL REHYDRATION SALTS

Oral rehydration salts are formulated to replace the nutrients lost during diarrhoea:

☐ "... The formula for ORS recommended by WHO and UNICEF contains:–
3.5 gms sodium chloride
2.9 gms trisodium citrate dihydrate (or 2.5 gms sodium bicarbonate)
1.5 gms potassium chloride
20 gms glucose (anhydrous)
"The above ingredients are dissolved in one litre of clean water. WHO has recently recommended a change in the complete formula, replacing 2.5 gms of sodium bicarbonate with 2.9 gms of trisodium citrate dihydrate. The new formula gives the packets a longer shelf life and is at least as effective in correcting acidosis and reducing stool volume. Packets containing sodium bicarbonate are still safe and effective."

Diarrhoea Dialogue, no. 19, insert, December 1984.

☐ "Countries should have no hesitation in continuing to use ORS-bicarbonate, which is highly effective in the treatment of dehydration. However, because of its better stability and even greater efficacy, WHO and the United Nations Children's Fund (UNICEF) now recommend that countries use and produce ORS-citrate where feasible. As in the case of any new drug, countries electing to use ORS-citrate should carefully monitor its performance during the first new months of its routine use."

"News from WHO's Diarrhoeal Diseases Control Programme", WHO Chronicle, vol. 38, no. 5, 1984.

"Glucose is included in the solution principally to help the absorption of sodium and not as a source of energy. Ordinary sugar (sucrose) can be substituted for glucose with near equal efficacy, though twice the amount of sugar is needed. Increasing the amount of sugar in the formula as a means of improving palatability or increasing its nutritive value is potentially dangerous as it can worsen the diarrhoea."

The management of diarrhoea and use of oral rehydration therapy: a joint WHO/UNICEF statement, WHO, 1983.

"The presence of potassium in ORS is particularly important for the treatment of dehydrated children, in whom potassium losses in diarrhoea are relatively high. Studies have shown that undernourished children who have suffered repeated bouts of diarrhoea are especially likely to develop a blood level of potassium below normal if the potassium is not replaced during rehydration."

The management of diarrhoea and use of oral rehydration therapy: a joint WHO/UNICEF statement, WHO, 1983.

The World Health Organization has developed a semi-automatic measuring and packing machine for the production of smaller quantities of ORS or for use where facilities are not suitable for automatic production:

☐ "This machine has been designed for easy handling, a minimum of maintenance, and for use under difficult climatic and operating conditions. A prototype of this machine is now operating satisfactorily in the ORS production facility at the State Pharmaceutical Corporation in Colombo, Sri Lanka."

WHO Programme for Control of Diarrhoeal Diseases, "Fourth Programme report 1983-1984", 1985 (WHO/CDD/85.13).

EFFECTIVENESS OF ORT

"A review of 22,559 pediatric records at the State University Hospital, Port-au-Prince, Haiti, indicated a mortality of 35% among 9,434 patients hospitalized with diarrhea and dehydration during the period 1969-1979. A program for the management of infantile diarrhea (based on ORT) was established at the University Hospital in 1980. Mortality fell to 14% during the first year, was 1.9% during the second year, and has been less than 1% since January 1982."

Jean W. Pape and others, "Management of diarrhea in Haiti: mortality reduction in 8,443 hospitalized children", in Richard A. Cash and Judith McLaughlin (eds.), Proceedings of the International Conference on Oral Rehydration Therapy, USAID, 1984.

"In a number of research studies the use of ORS for treating dehydrated children at the community level has decreased the number of deaths from diarrhoea as much as 50-60% over a one-year period."

The management of diarrhoea and use of oral rehydration therapy: a joint WHO/UNICEF statement, WHO, 1983.

Preliminary research in 1980 for the national diarrhoeal disease control programme in Egypt found that early rehydration by mothers with a salt and sugar mix made at home, backed up by ORS from health care providers, reduced pre-school child mortality by 40% and diarrhoea-specific mortality by 50%.

Summarized from: A.B. Mobarak and others, "Diarrheal disease control study: May through October 1980", Strengthening Rural Health Delivery Project, Ministry of Health, Egypt, 1981.

"A programme of distribution of oral rehydration packets was established by the government in 1980 in 20 of the 80 Costa Rican municipalities... The sachets were distributed free of charge to mothers with preschool children in the 20 experimental municipalities. The result, after one year of operation, was a 50% reduction of infant diarrhoea deaths in the 20 municipalities; no significant change was detected in the remaining municipalities where the intervention was not effected."

Leonardo Mata, "The evolution of diarrhoeal diseases and malnutrition in Costa Rica", Assignment Children, vol. 61/62, 1983.

☐ "Another outcome that may be 'expected' is that ORT protects a child's nutrition. In third world children diarrhea alone accounts for 25-75% retardation of normal growth over a year. With 2-3 years of repeated growth arrests due to episodes of diarrhea, it is probable that most malnutrition we detect in surveys is related to diarrhea, a conclusion supported by longitudinal studies in Guatemala, Bangladesh, Mexico, and the Gambia..."

Norbert Hirschhorn, "Oral rehydration therapy: the program and the promise", paper prepared for UNICEF, May 1985.

'SUPER' ORS

Research continues to improve oral rehydration salts, and new forms of 'super' ORS may soon become practical. The current ORS formula remedies dehydration but does not shorten the duration of the diarrhoea or reduce the volume of diarrhoeal stools; as a result, mothers sometimes have difficulty believing that oral rehydration works. 'Super' ORS can both shorten the diarrhoea and halve the stool volume:

☐ The International Centre for Diarrhoeal Disease Research in Dhaka, Bangladesh, has developed a rice powder-based ORS with distinct advantages over the current glucose-based formula. Because of chemical reactions within the human body, rice-based ORS reduces diarrhoea volume by 50% – thus effectively treating the diarrhoea as well as preventing dehydration.

Summarized from: W.B. Greenough and A.M. Molla, "Cereal-based oral rehydration solutions", Lancet, 2 October 1982; and A.M. Molla and others, "Rice-based ORS decreases stool volume in acute diarrhoea", Bulletin of the WHO, in press.

Another advantage of rice-based ORS is that in many developing countries rice is cheaper and more easily available than sugar. Furthermore, rice is often already used traditionally to treat diarrhoea:

☐ "Soaked rice in some form, with added salt or sugar, has been a traditional dietary therapy for diarrhoea in Bangladesh and many other developing countries for centuries, but little attention is paid to the correct concentrations of salts and water. Rice is cheaper and more readily available than glucose or sucrose and, as a familiar component of treatment for diarrhoea, it may be more acceptable."

> *A.M. Molla and others, "Rice-powder electrolyte solution as oral therapy in diarrhoea due to Vibrio cholerae and Escherichia coli", Lancet, 12 June 1982.*

Another promising – though more costly – approach involves adding the amino acid glycine to glucose-based ORS:

☐ Scientists at the Calcutta Medical Research Institute used three different forms of ORS to treat infants and children who were moderately and severely dehydrated from diarrhoea. The first group was given the standard glucose-based formula; the second group was given the same solution with glycine added; and the third group received ORS with popped-rice powder substituted for glucose. The duration of the diarrhoea was 30% shorter for the second and third groups; the amount of diarrhoeal stool output was 50% and 49% smaller; and the volume of ORS solution needed to treat them was 43% less (glycine) and 36% less (popped-rice powder).

> *Summarized from: Dilip Mahalanabis and Fakir C. Patra, "In search of a super oral rehydration solution: can optimum use of organic solute-mediated sodium absorption lead to the development of an absorption promoting drug?", Journal of Diarrhoeal Diseases Research, vol. 1, no. 2, June 1983.*

ORT AND MALNUTRITION

As well as reducing deaths from dehydration, ORT also reduces the impact of diarrhoea on the child's nutritional status:

"Field studies in the Philippines, Turkey, Egypt and Iran have demonstrated not only a reduction in deaths and hospitalization, but also a positive nutritional impact based on the provision of early rehydration either in a nearby centre or in the home by the mothers. Children receiving ORS showed from 0.25 to 0.5 kg better weight gain over one year in comparison to control groups who received only the nutrition advice. The impact was greater on children experiencing multiple episodes, further supporting the importance of ORS in the improved growth. Coupled with detailed advice to continue feeding the child and provide extra food in the recovery period, the provision of early rehydration may be one of the most effective and pragmatic means of avoiding the occurrence of malnutrition."

> *Jon Eliot Rohde and Lukas Hendrata, "Oral rehydration: technology and implementation", in D.B. Jelliffe and E.F.P. Jelliffe (eds.), Advances in international maternal and child health, vol. 1, Oxford University Press, 1981.*

Home Remedies

When ORS sachets are not available home remedies can perform a valuable function in forestalling dehydration:

"ORT can be provided in the form of prepackaged salts or as home-prepared solutions; both have important roles to play in the management of diarrhoea... There is an urgent need to accelerate the production of ORS and to disseminate more information about the early treatment of diarrhoea in the home."

> *The management of diarrhoea and use of oral rehydration therapy: a joint WHO/UNICEF statement, WHO, 1983.*

"... There is a strong rationale for beginning ORT early, before obvious signs of dehydration develop. First, within a few hours after diarrhea starts, dehydration amounting to three or four percent of body weight can occur without symptoms. Early use of ORT helps to compensate for this undetected loss as it takes place. Second, early ORT minimizes the symptoms associated with increasing water and electrolyte loss, such as vomiting, lack of appetite, and lethargy. Thus feeding can continue and nutritional damage can be avoided. Third, teaching a family to start treatment as soon as diarrhea begins may be easier than trying to explain the difference between diarrhea with and without dehydration."

> *"Oral rehydration therapy (ORT) for childhood diarrhea", Population Reports, series L, no. 2, reprinted April 1982.*

"In February 1981, only 2.3% of 500 consecutive hospitalized patients (in the State University Hospital, Port-au-Prince, Haiti) had received ORS at home and 24% were severely dehydrated. One year later, 48% of 500 hospitalized children had initiated fluid therapy at home; 3% of these patients were severely dehydrated, as opposed to 23% of children not receiving this early therapy."

> *Jean W. Pape and others, "Management of diarrhea in Haiti: mortality reduction in 8,443 hospitalized children", in Richard A. Cash and Judith McLaughlin (eds.), Proceedings of the International Conference on Oral Rehydration Therapy, USAID, 1984.*

"There are two groups of home remedies:
"(a) Household food solutions – fluids or liquids that are normally available in the home and are appropriate for the early home treatment of acute diarrhoea. Such solutions are often prepared from boiled water, thus ensuring safety for drinking, and contain sodium, sometimes potassium, and a source of glucose – such as starches – that can facilitate the absorption of salts in the intestine; they also may contain other sources of energy. Two examples are rice water, often found in homes in Asia, and various soups – e.g., carrot soup, often found in homes in North Africa; other less robust examples include juices, coconut water, and weak tea...

"(b) Salt and sugar solutions – consisting of white sugar (sucrose) and cooking salt (sodium chloride). In a few countries molasses or unrefined sugar is used in place of white sugar; it has the advantage of containing also potassium chloride and sodium bicarbonate... Costs, seasonal shortages, and varying quality of sugar or salt have made it difficult to promote and implement the use of 'salt and sugar' solutions in the home in some areas; in such cases the use of 'household food' solutions should be considered.

"As these home remedies may have a varied composition and usually lack or have insufficient amounts of the ingredients in ORS (particularly potassium and bicarbonate), they are not ideal for the treatment of dehydration at any age. However, they certainly should be used at the onset of diarrhoea to prevent dehydration and in situations where the complete formula is needed but is not available."

> *The management of diarrhoea and use of oral rehydration therapy: a joint WHO/UNICEF statement, WHO, 1983.*

"Preparing a sugar and salt solution from household supplies is more difficult than mixing from a packet since not only the water but also the sugar and salt must be measured. At least three techniques have been tested... The first is the pinch-and-scoop method, using the fingers to measure a pinch of salt and a scoop of sugar. The second uses household spoons to measure dry ingredients and available bottles, pans, or glasses to measure water. The third involves distributing to each family a plastic spoon specifically designed for measuring the dry ingredients accurately...

"Results with these three approaches have been mixed. Using either the pinch-and-scoop method or using their own household containers and measuring implements, some of the women studied in Bangladesh, Honduras, Nepal and the US mixed solutions containing excessively high salt levels... With all three techniques some Nepalese women prepared solutions containing so little salt that they would be ineffective for rehydration.

"One difficulty in evaluating the findings of mixing and measurement studies is that no definition of acceptable results has been set forth. Is one dangerously salty solution in 100 acceptable in a community-based program? One in 1,000? Is one solution in 100 with an ineffectively low salt level too many?"

"Oral rehydration therapy (ORT) for childhood diarrhea", Population Reports, series L, no. 2, reprinted April 1982.

"The strongest conclusion to emerge from studies of mixing is the importance of careful, thorough, and individual instruction. In Indonesia most women who had heard of ORS but not received personal instruction did not know how to mix solutions correctly from packets... In Indonesia few of the people who said they understood the directions on the ORS packet could in fact mix the solution properly... A few more could follow verbal instructions accurately. After the technique was actually demonstrated, however, nearly all mixed the ORS solution correctly."

"Oral rehydration therapy (ORT) for childhood diarrhea", Population Reports, series L, no. 2, reprinted April 1982.

Continued Feeding

A common reaction among parents is to withhold food – and even breast-milk – during a diarrhoeal attack. But starving a child who has diarrhoea can cause malnutrition or exacerbate existing malnutrition:

"The proper management of diarrhoea in the home also includes, along with the administration of ORT, the promotion of appropriate child feeding, both during and after a diarrhoea episode, to prevent excessive and uncompensated loss of nutrients. In many societies the parent's remedial response to diarrhoea is to withhold food and fluid, including breast-milk, in the mistaken belief that this will stop the diarrhoea and ease the strain on the intestine. This 'treatment' only adds to the dehydration and malnutrition caused by the illness."

The management of diarrhoea and use of oral rehydration therapy: a joint WHO/UNICEF statement, WHO, 1983.

☐"All children of 4 months or older, who have been weaned, should be offered solid food during diarrhoea. The best foods to give are those that are easily digested (such as boiled rice, porridge, soups, milk products, eggs, fish, and well-cooked meat) and those containing potassium (such as pineapple, bananas and coconut water). Some fat or oil may also be given. Even though the absorption of nutrients from food is lessened during diarrhoea, most of the nutrients will be absorbed from these foods.

"The child should be allowed to eat as much as he wants. Food should be offered often (5-7 times a day) during diarrhoea, because the child is not likely to eat much at each

time. The child should have at least one extra feed a day for a week after the diarrhoea has stopped."

Treatment and prevention of acute diarrhoea: guidelines for the trainers of health workers, WHO, 1985.

"A recent careful study of young children in Bangladesh revealed that, on average, each child suffered 6.8 episodes of diarrhoea per year. Added up, this meant they had diarrhoea for 55 days or 15 per cent of the year. Such children will end up severely deprived of nourishment if they are starved all the time they have diarrhoea. Although digestion is less effective during diarrhoea, there is still a significant amount of absorption of nutrients."

K.M. Elliott and W.A.M. Cutting, "Carry on feeding", Diarrhoea Dialogue, no. 15, November 1983.

Safety of ORT

Concern is sometimes expressed about the dangers of using too much salt in oral rehydration solution, especially if given to the very young:

"While experts on fluid and electrolyte metabolism continue to debate the relative theoretical merits of each fluid composition, especially the sodium concentration used for young children, it is interesting to note the wide range of sodium that has given acceptable results in studies around the world... Those using higher concentrations of sodium (90-120 meq/l) for treatment of children advocate offering extra water to the child, while those reporting lower sodium (50-80 meq/l) generally admit these solutions are too dilute for effective rehydration of severe diarrhoea especially in adults... Even young children or infants require a higher sodium level during rehydration to expand extracellular fluid and improve circulation than in the later maintenance phase when more free water is required to offset obligatory water losses... The recent Scientific Working Group convened by the World Health Organization to examine the composition of oral rehydration mixtures felt the evidence heavily favoured a sodium level of 90 meq/l as optimum for a solution to be used world-wide."

Jon Eliot Rohde and Lukas Hendrata, "Oral rehydration: technology and implementation", in D.B. Jelliffe and E.F.P. Jelliffe (eds.), Advances in international maternal and child health, vol. 1, Oxford University Press, 1981.

"... Rehydration therapy can usually be achieved orally with ORS solution, except in cases with severe dehydration, uncontrollable vomiting, or another serious complication that prevents successful oral therapy. In these cases intravenous therapy is needed. ORS solution is also the fluid used for maintenance therapy. However, normal daily fluid requirements must be given as fluids of lower salt concentration: e.g., plain water, breast milk, or diluted milk feeds. This is particularly important in infants; due to their large surface area per kg of body weight and their high metabolic rate, under normal conditions they require 2.5 times more water per kg than adults."

"A manual for the treatment of acute diarrhoea", WHO, 1984 (WHO/CDD/SER/80.2/REV. 1.)

☐A recent study in Egypt found that mothers mixed ORS with greater accuracy if a standard container was provided, and recommended that, "when the pre-packaged form of ORS is distributed to patients, it would be of great value to dispense graduated measuring containers, along with verbal instructions..."

M. El-Mongi and others, "Accuracy of mixing oral rehydration solution at home by Egyptian mothers", Journal of Diarrhoeal Diseases Research, vol. 2, no. 3, 1984.

ORT AND UNCLEAN WATER

Only one study so far, in the Gambia, has assessed the risk of using ORS solution that is not bacteria-free: 97 children received ORS solution made with clean water and 87 received ORS solution made with well water. The incidence and duration of diarrhoea and the growth rate in the two groups of children were found to be similar.

Summarized from: M. Watkinson and others, "The use of oral glucose electrolyte solution prepared with untreated well water in acute, non-specific childhood diarrhoea", Transactions of the Royal Society of Tropical Medicine and Hygiene, vol. 74, no. 5, 1980.

"On the basis of the available information, the following recommendations can be made regarding the preparation of ORS solution:

"(1) ORS solution should be prepared with water made potable by recognized methods ... in containers washed with such water... There are as yet insufficient data to show that there is no risk associated with the use of 'usual' drinking water;

"(2) ORS solution, once prepared, should be protected against subsequent contamination...

"(3) If potable water cannot be guaranteed, and ORS solution needs to be administered, the best available water should be used."

"Use of locally available drinking water for preparation of oral rehydration salt (ORS) solution", WHO, 1981 (CDD/SER/81.1).

Costs of ORT

A sachet of ORS usually costs only a few cents, and remedies given early in the home even less. Hospitals, too, have reduced their expenses by switching to ORT:

"The average cost of treating one patient with intravenous therapy can be more than $5 as compared with less than $0.50 with ORS. In contrast to intravenous therapy, ORS can be given under simple conditions and does not require any special equipment or highly skilled personnel; thus there is increased access to rehydration therapy."

The management of diarrhoea and use of oral rehydration therapy: a joint WHO/UNICEF statement, WHO, 1933.

A diarrhoea treatment centre in Bangladesh found that despite staff increases, "the replacement of intravenous fluid by ORS led to savings of 33% in the total costs incurred... Use of ORS may prolong the stay of a patient in hospital to some extent, but since mothers can be responsible for this treatment, the overall cost, compared to treatment with intravenous fluid, is less."

A.R. Samadi, R. Islam and M.I. Huq, "Replacement of intravenous therapy by oral rehydration solution in a large treatment centre for diarrhoea with dehydration", Bulletin of the WHO, vol. 61, no. 3, 1983.

"While the use of ORS may initially require more health workers' time to train mothers to give ORS to their children, in the long term it frees hospital and health centre staff for other duties. Of greater importance, ORS involves parents directly in the care of their children and presents an excellent opportunity for health workers to communicate important health education messages on diarrhoea prevention and nutrition."

The management of diarrhoea and use of oral rehydration therapy: a joint WHO/UNICEF statement, WHO, 1983.

Breast-Feeding

Breast-milk is the ideal infant food. It is more nutritious, more hygienic and much more economical than any breast-milk substitute. Breast-milk also provides a degree of immunity to infectious diseases, as well as having a contraceptive effect through inhibiting ovulation.

In poor communities, the bottle-feeding of infants sharply increases the risk of malnutrition, infection and death. Yet in many parts of the developing world, the incidence and duration of breast-feeding is on the decline and sales of breast-milk substitutes are rising.

Many factors affect a mother's decision on breast-feeding: the advice and example of hospitals and the medical profession; social attitudes and levels of knowledge; difficulties encountered in breast-feeding itself; price, availability and promotion of breast-milk substitutes; employers' policies and government strategies.

For babies who are breast-fed, the weaning period is the time of greatest danger to health and life. Like breast-feeding, good weaning makes heavy demands of the mother; but knowing when and how to wean a child could drastically reduce child malnutrition in the developing world.

Breast-Milk's Advantages

Breast-milk's advantages include a perfect infant diet for the early months, some immunity from infection, and a degree of protection against conception:

☐ "Breast-fed infants can thrive even under unhygienic conditions in areas of extreme poverty. The anti-infectious properties of human milk account for the very high resistance of the nursing infant to infection in general and in particular to diarrhea. In deprived tropical environments, most infants grow adequately, even if they have experienced fetal growth retardation or were born prematurely, as long as they are kept at the breast during the first 4 to 6 months of life. Breast milk has unique immunologic, nutritional, psychosocial and economic benefits."

Leonardo Mata, "The importance of breast-feeding for optimal child health and well-being", Clinical Nutrition, vol. 3. no. 1

PROTECTION AGAINST DISEASE

"One of the great arguments in favour of breast-feeding has long been its anti-infectious action. Breast-fed infants develop fewer bacterial and viral infections of digestive and respiratory origin than bottle-fed babies. The bottle and the teat are far greater sources of infection than the breast, particularly for families living under deficient sanitary conditions. The immediate consumption of mother's milk (from the breast to the child's mouth), with no handling, avoids the proliferation of the germs present on the nipple and areola of the breast and the penetration of other germs which abound in the environment.

"Above all, mother's milk provides direct protection against infections, and gastro-intestinal infections in particular. The disease rate for infections is also lower in breast-fed newborns in the wealthier classes than in those fed artificially."

A.M. Masse-Raimbault, "How to feed young children", Children in the Tropics, no. 138-139-140, 1982.

Research in India and Canada found that artificially fed infants were three times more likely to contract diarrhoeal infections and twice as likely to suffer from respiratory infections – the two main causes of infant death – as infants who were breast-fed (see table 2).

A.M. Masse-Raimbault, "How to feed young children", Children in the Tropics, no. 138-139-140, 1982.

Table 2: Relationship between method of infant feeding and incidence of disease.

| Ailment | Number of cases of disease in 24 months | | | |
| | INDIA | | CANADA | |
	BF	AF	BF	AF
Respiratory infections	57	109	42	98
Otitis	21	52	9	86
Diarrhoea	70	211	5	16
Dehydration	3	14	0	3
Pneumonia	2	8	—	—

BF = Breast-feeding, AF = Artificial feeding

Children in the Tropics, International Children's Centre, Paris, 1982.

"Breast milk is the best food for infants, and no substitute food exactly duplicates it. Studies of breast milk and breast-feeding show that:
"Breast milk provides some immunological protection for the infant.
"Breast milk best satisfies the infant's nutritional needs.
"Breast-feeding costs less than feeding with substitutes.
"Because of the immunological and nutritional advantages of breast milk and because preparing substitutes properly is difficult in much of the developing world, breast-fed infants are less likely to develop infections or malnutrition.
"Breast-feeding protects against pregnancy, although the length of this contraceptive effect is not predictable.
"Many other advantages have been claimed for breast-feeding ranging from closer emotional ties between mother and child to greater intellectual ability in later life for the breast-fed child."

"Breast-feeding, fertility and family planning", Population Reports, series J, no. 24, November-December 1981.

☐ "Conclusions drawn from investigations of the relationship of infant feeding mode to infectious disease outcomes have generally been limited by study design problems, by unstated or imprecise definitions of feeding mode and outcome(s), and by lack of inclusion of associated – and possible confounding – factors in the analyses... Nevertheless, the weight of the evidence from less-developed countries strongly supports an inverse association between breast-feeding and overall mortality, and between breast-feeding and diarrhoeal-related mortality and morbidity in the high-risk newborn. Further studies are needed to characterize more clearly the nature and strength of these relationships."

Janine M. Jason, Phillip Nieburg and James S. Marks, "Mortality and infectious disease associated with infant-feeding practices in developing countries", Pediatrics, vol. 74, no. 4, part 2, October 1984.

CONTRACEPTIVE EFFECT

In communities where more reliable forms of contraception are either not widely available or not widely accepted, prolonged breast-feeding offers the mother a considerable degree of protection against becoming pregnant. Breast-feeding therefore has a significant effect on the average interval between births, which in turn has a significant effect on an infant's chances of survival and healthy growth:

"Breast-feeding delays menstruation inhibits ovulation, and therefore reduces the likelihood of conception. In general, the longer a woman breast-feeds, the longer she will remain infecund. Although the contraceptive effect of lactation has been recognized by various cultures for centuries – at least since the ancient Egyptians – only during the last few decades have biological scientists and demographers focused attention specifically on the length, variations, implications, and causes of lactational infecundity. The overall conclusion is that breast-feeding makes a substantial contribution to birth spacing and fertility control in many areas but that for an individual woman it is an unreliable method of family planning."

"Breast-feeding, fertility and family planning", Population Reports, series J, no. 24, November-December 1981.

☐ "Breast-feeding is associated with a delay in the return of ovulation after a birth, with longer intervals between births, and with lower fertility rates occurring in populations where this practice is prolonged."

John E. Anderson, James S. Marks and Tai-Kenn Park, "Breast-feeding, birth interval and infant health", Pediatrics, vol. 74, no. 4, part 2, October 1984.

"If women in Ghana were to stop breast-feeding, the already high fertility rate would increase by at least 40% due to the loss of the natural birth-spacing effect of breast-feeding, with widespread economic implications."

Ted Greiner, "Some economic and social implications of breast-feeding", paper prepared for UNICEF/Commonwealth Secretariat seminar on breast-feeding, Harare, January 1983.

NUTRITION

☐ "The importance of human milk for infant nutrition stems from its unique composition. Its high lactose and lipid contents favor nutrition during the first few weeks of life, and they are particularly important for premature infants or those with fetal growth retardation...

"The unique nutritional value of human milk in the first 3 to 6 months of life has been confirmed by prospective studies of infant growth throughout the tropics and subtropics. A study in the Guatemalan village of Santa Maria Cauque showed not only that normal neo-nates grow optimally during the first months of exclusive breast-feeding, but also that pre-term and small-for-gestational-age infants thrive, provided they begin at the breast from the very first days of life and are exclusively breast-fed for several months."

Leonardo Mata, "The importance of breast-feeding for optimal child health and well-being", Clinical Nutrition, vol. 3, no. 1, January/February 1984.

PSYCHOLOGICAL BENEFITS

☐ "... Breast-feeding generally is a sine qua non result of natural childbirth, where instinctive contact and interaction between mother and child are favored. The mother, on her own or with the support of midwife, attendants, or friends, initiates skin, mouth, and sight contact followed by nipple-mouth relationship and the successful establishment of breast-feeding shortly after delivery. Breast-feeding maximizes mother-infant stimulation, leading to firm bonding, long-lasting child-rearing practices, and optimal protection of the child.

"Mother-infant separation, still practiced today in many maternity hospitals throughout the world, is detrimental to successful breast-feeding and bonding. Infants separated from the mother after birth are at greater risk of acquiring infectious diseases, of being improperly nursed and of being neglected and abused."

Leonardo Mata, "The importance of breast-feeding for optimal child health and well-being", Clinical Nutrition, vol. 3, no. 1, January/February 1984.

Current Trends

☐ "WHO has carried out a collaborative study on prevalence and duration of breast-feeding in nine countries. Findings indicate that while there are signs of a decline in breast-feeding among certain groups in developing countries, there is also a marked increase in the prevalence and duration of breast-feeding elsewhere. In Sweden and Hungary, the two most industrialized of the nine countries, only 7 per cent and 3 per cent respectively of the mothers studied had never breast-fed their youngest child, a marked improvement from 25 years ago. In the Philippines and Guatemala, the situation among middle-income mothers was significantly different: 32 per cent and 23 per cent respectively had never attempted to breast-feed their last child.

"A more recent review of 200 studies suggests that a process is emerging in which higher-income groups and industrialized countries set the trend, and are then followed gradually by the urban lower-income, rural groups and less industrialized countries. Later, there is a resurgence of interest in breast-feeding among middle-income families and this, in turn, is gradually followed by other urban and rural groups.

"The information offers clear lessons for health planners and educators. A crucial fact is that breast-feeding is declining in urban areas of developing countries. At the same time, the data show that breast-feeding is quite compatible with an urban industrial environment and that appropriate breast-feeding promotion can succeed anywhere. It would therefore be ironic if, while breast-feeding rates were to increase in countries with low infant mortality and morbidity, they were allowed to diminish in countries where breast-feeding is still critical to sound infant and young child health."

Manuel Carballo, "WHO study", Diarrhoea Dialogue, no. 17, May 1984.

"In South Korea the practice of prolonged breast-feeding – for at least 18 months – declined sharply between 1950 and 1970, from over 55 to about 35 percent of first births.

"In Thailand between 1969 and 1979 the average duration of breast-feeding declined by almost five months – from 12.9 to 8.4 months in the cities and from 22.4 to 17.5 months in rural areas...

"In Taiwan also, the percentage of infants initially breast-fed fell sharply, from 93 in 1966 to 50 percent in 1980. During the same period the average duration of breast-feeding of children ever breast-fed dropped from 14.6 months to 8.8 months...

"Less than 5 percent of the women surveyed in the cities of Sao Paulo (Brazil), Panama City (Panama), and San Salvador (El Salvador) breast-fed for six months or more, and in the state of Sao Paulo, Brazil, less than 50 percent breast-fed for as long as one month."

"Breast-feeding, fertility, and family planning", Population Reports, series J, no. 24, November-December 1981.

II LIFELINES: BREAST-FEEDING

Dangers of the Bottle

In developing countries, babies who are exclusively breast-fed are more likely to survive than those who are bottle-fed:

"A study of 1,700 women in rural Chile in 1969 and 1970 found that postneonatal death rates (between the 4th and the 52nd week) were three time higher among infants who started bottle-feeding in the first three months than among those who received only breast milk during that time. Because the infants were less likely to be breast-fed, death rates were higher among children whose mothers had moderate education, higher incomes, better sanitation, and prenatal health care than among those without – a contrast with the influence of socioeconomic factors on mortality in most studies...

"A recent study in Cairo under the auspices of the International Fertility Research Program found that children who were breast-fed for 15 to 20 months had a 93 percent probability of surviving until the birth of the next child, whereas children never breast-fed or breast-fed for less than three months had a survival probability of about 64 percent. Although the educational level of the mother also influenced child survival, the influence of breast-feeding was greater, and the lower the mother's educational level, the more influence breast-feeding had. Among children whose mothers had no education, those breast-fed for 9 to 12 months had a 30 percent higher survival probability than those never breast-fed; among children whose mothers had at least seven years of schooling, the difference was 22 percent."

"Breast-feeding, fertility and family planning", Population Reports, series J, no. 24, November-December 1981.

Studies in four countries in Latin America and the Caribbean – El Salvador, Colombia, Jamaica and Brazil – have shown that infants breast-fed for less than six months (or not at all) were six to fourteen times more likely to die in the second six months of life than babies who were breast-fed for six months or more.

Summarized from: Joe D. Wray, "Maternal nutrition, breast-feeding and infant survival", in W. Henry Mosley (ed.), Nutrition and human reproduction, Plenum Press, 1978.

A study of 9,662 newborn babies delivered at the Baguio General Hospital and Medical Centre in the Philippines between 1973 and 1977 found a strong correlation between breast-feeding and decreased morbidity and mortality. (see table 3).

Summarized from: N.R. Clavano, "Mode of feeding and its effect on infant mortality and morbidity", Journal of Tropical Pediatrics, vol. 28, December 1982.

Table 3: Infant deaths resulting from diarrhoea in relation to mode of feeding, January 1973–April 1977.

| | Mode of feeding | | Diarrhoea cases | | | |
| | | | Morbidity | | Mortality | |
	No.	%	No.	%	No.	%
Breast-fed	6,408	66.60	6	4.35	0	0.00
Mixed-fed	611	6.35	8	5.80	0	0.00
Formula-fed	2,603	27.05	124	89.85	38	100.00
Total	9,622	100.00	138	100.00	38	100.00

N. R. Clavano, "Mode of Feeding and its Effect on Infant Mortality and Morbidity", Journal of Tropical Pediatrics, vol. 28, no 6, December 1982.

CONTAMINATION AND OVER-DILUTION

To be used safely, infant formula requires access to a pure water supply, as well as means of sterilization and refrigeration. Mothers must also be able to read and understand written instructions, and have sufficient income to buy adequate amounts of the product. When these conditions are not met, the resulting milk solution is either contaminated or over-diluted:

"For many people in the developing world ... the hygienic conditions necessary for the proper use of infant formula just do not exist. Their water is unclean, the bottles are dirty, the formula is diluted to make a tin of powdered milk last longer than it should. What happens? The baby is fed a contaminated mixture and soon becomes ill with diarrhoea, which leads to dehydration, malnutrition, and very often death."

Natividad Relucio-Clavano, "The results of a change in hospital practices: a paediatrician's campaign for breast-feeding in the Philippines", Assignment Children, vol. 55/56, 1982.

An Indonesian study sampled 53 milk solutions from bottles being used to feed infants in four maternal and child health clinics. The findings:

One-third were less than 50% of proper strength and only half were within 20% of recommended concentration according to the manufacturer's label.

Milk sampled from feeding bottles in the clinics was highly contaminated by faecal organisms, with only four of 53 samples having fewer than 1,000 organisms per millilitre.

Summarized from: Dani Surjono and others, "Bacterial contamination and dilution of milk in infant feeding bottles", Journal of Tropical Pediatrics, vol. 26, April 1980.

The Costs

Breast-milk has an energy cost to the mother and is therefore not 'free'. But in cash terms it represents a very considerable saving to the poor compared with the buying of infant formula (see table 4):

Table 4: Cost of complete formula-feeding for an infant 2 months of age, expressed as a percentage of salaries for selected jobs in different countries.

Country	Hospital cleaner %	Ministry clerk %	Junior staff nurse %
Burma	73	40	21
Egypt	9	10	8
Guatemala	27	12	10
Indonesia	35	51	21
Nigeria	18	16	6
Philippines (Manila)	28	24	18
Sri Lanka	63	45	43
Sweden	4	4	4
Tanzania	32	32	14
Turkey	21	21	16
UK (London)	6	5	4
Yemen	17	13	11

Summarised from: Margot Cameron and Yngve Hosvander, Manual on feeding infants and young children, draft third edition, 1981.

"Bottle-feeding requires the purchase not only of the breast-milk substitute, but also of the bottle and nipple. It requires fuel for sterilization of the equipment and ideally, refrigeration. These costs vary, but generally the cost of proper feeding with a breast-milk substitute totals at least US$200-$300 for the first year of life. Among substitutes, commercial infant formula is generally more expensive than modifying and preparing milk products in the home.

"Poor families may spend less than $200-$300 a year on bottle-feeding, but the child may suffer as a result. To save money, families may not give enough formula or may overdilute it. They may use milk from cows or other animals without modifying it. They may even mix flour and sugar with water so that it simply looks like milk. A full estimate of the expense of bottle-feeding should include the cost to the family and to society of resulting increases in infant morbidity and mortality when bottle-feeding is inadequate or improper."

> "Breast-feeding, fertility and family planning", Population Reports, series J, no. 24, November-December 1981.

Mexico: "The average monthly expenditure on milk or formula for all sample households was $7.20 or 10% of the average monthly income of all households. Households reporting the lowest average monthly income ($23) spent $8.00 or 35% of their monthly income on milk or formula. Households reporting the second lowest average monthly income ($57) spent $6.50 or 11% of their monthly income on milk or formula."

> Kimberly K. Lillig and Carolyn J. Lackey, "Economic and social factors influencing women's infant feeding decisions in a rural Mexican community", Journal of Tropical Pediatrics, vol. 28, October 1982.

☐ "While a myriad of health and nutritional considerations have proven that the mother's milk is the ideal infant food, national policy makers have failed to recognize the great value of human milk to the economy of developing countries. Today in Indonesia, mothers produce over one billion liters annually with a conservatively estimated net market value of over US$400 million. Additional monetary savings in health and fertility reduction directly attributable to lactation add a further $120 million to the economy. Mother milk is one of Indonesia's most precious natural resources, exceeding tin and coffee in gross monetary value and approaching that of rubber."

> Jon Eliot Rohde, "Mother milk and the Indonesian economy: a major national resource", Journal of Tropical Pediatrics, vol. 28, August 1982.

☐ "Human milk is synthesized shortly before and during the act of breast-feeding as a result of the stimulus of nipple-sucking by the infant. No containers, preparation, or storage are required, and this fact alone represents a significant saving in time and money in developing nations. The cost for synthesis of about 600 to 900 ml of human milk per day is less than the cost of any substitute, regardless of country, culture, or social level."

> Leonardo Mata, "The importance of breast-feeding for optimal child health and well-being", Clinical Nutrition, vol. 3, no. 1, January/February 1984.

ENERGY COST TO MOTHERS

Breast-feeding makes heavy demands on a mother's energy and nutritional resources. In developing countries the lactation period is usually longer and more costly in terms of nutritional demand on the mother than pregnancy itself:

"... The protein intake of pregnant and lactating mothers in Africa is often extremely low... Physicians frequently see the 'wreck of a woman' following frequent pregnancies on an unsatisfactory diet. She is usually thin, miserable, anemic and often apathetic, with a dry scaly skin, sometimes rather lusterless hair, often with an ulcer that is reluctant to heal, and some mouth lesions. She is labelled in the clinic as a case of 'general malnutrition', 'multiple deficiency'. There is no universally adopted term for this syndrome, nor a sure guide to its diagnosis; is it not, in fact a caloric-protein deficiency disease of adults?"

> M.C. Latham, "Maternal nutrition in East Africa", Journal of Tropical Medicine and Hygiene, vol. 67, no. 4, 1964.

"... There is clear recent evidence of a close dependence of breast-milk output on energy intake particularly when food energy intake falls to exceptionally low levels, as occurs seasonally in many developing countries. In the Gambia in the dry season, when the mean intake of lactating women was found to be about 1800 kcal/day, mean breast-milk output was estimated at approximately 790 ml/day in early lactation. At the height of the wet season (August-September) when daily energy intake was around only 1200 kcal/day, average breast-milk output had fallen to only about 630 ml/day."

> G.A. Clugston, "Lactation: its processes and outcomes and the effect of maternal nutrition", paper presented to WHO workshop on breast-feeding, Shanghai, October 1982.

Factors in the Decision

Many factors play a part in a mother's decision to breast-feed her child or not. Among the pressures tending to influence mothers in the direction of bottle-feeding are:

"In Western societies the advertising and marketing of infant formulas were probably secondary reasons for the decline in breast-feeding.

"However, in developing countries they may be primary reasons. Companies producing baby-food have long realized that promising new markets are created by the growing monetarization of the economy of Third World countries. They have launched marketing campaigns that are clearly aimed at persuading mothers to start bottle-feeding. Advertisements show smiling, beautiful mothers bottle-feeding babies who, in sharp contrast with reality for most of the people, are well-fed and complacent. This is followed by a message that this one particular product contains 'everything your baby needs' often with protein, vitamins, or iron added for good measure. This must make a mother doubt that her own, old-fashioned product is good enough for her baby, for whom she wishes the best."

> Elisabet Helsing with F. Savage King, Breast-feeding in practice, Oxford University Press, 1982.

BREAST-FEEDING DIFFICULTIES

'Lack of milk' is usually the most common reason cited by mothers who discontinue breast-feeding after a short time:

A WHO study of breast-feeding in nine countries – Hungary, Sweden, Ethiopia, Nigeria, Zaire, Chile, Guatemala, the Philippines and India – concluded:

"It is of interest that 'insufficient milk' was a reason given by rural mothers among whom prolonged breast-feeding was usual, as well as by economically advantaged urban mothers who mostly breast-fed for a much shorter time. It would seem that this response was more possibly coloured by cultural factors than by any physiological inability to produce sufficient milk."

> "WHO Collaborative Study on Breast-feeding. Methods and main results of the first phase of the Study: preliminary report", WHO, 1979 (MCH/79.3).

Mexico: "Respondents who regularly bottle-fed milk or formula cited the greatest reason for not breast-feeding was insufficient breast-milk... Other reasons reported by mothers for not breast-feeding included breast problems, inconvenience and refusal of the infant to suckle the breast."

Kimberly K. Lillig and Carolyn J. Lackey, "Economic and social factors influencing women's infant feeding decisions in a rural Mexican community", Journal of Tropical Pediatrics, vol. 28, October 1982.

"... Women are losing the art of managing a successful breast-feeding relationship with their babies. Breast-feeding becomes so unnatural that they find it difficult to cope with problems – pain or soreness of nipples, breast engorgement and sucking difficulties of babies. But these problems can be solved if mothers understand them and have the opportunity to learn how to cope. Like any other skill, breast-feeding has to be learnt. But for many women, it has become easier to give up breast-feeding than to persevere in it."

Natividad Relucio-Clavano, "The promotion of breast-feeding", in The state of the world's children 1984, Oxford University Press, 1983.

THE COLOSTRUM PROBLEM

"Breast-milk initially appears as colostrum, a concentrated yellowish fluid measuring approximately 25 ml during the first 24 hours. The small amount and strange colour of the milk at this stage misleads many health workers and mothers into feeling anxious that the mother's own milk might not be enough to feed the baby. Because of this, many women resort to prelacteal or supplemental formula. The result is less suckling and therefore less breast-milk supply. In many cases, this process ends in breast-feeding being abandoned altogether."

Natividad Relucio-Clavano, "The promotion of breast-feeding", in The state of the world's children 1984, Oxford University Press, 1983.

LACK OF KNOWLEDGE

Mexico: "Respondents were questioned as to whether they believed infants were healthier if they were breast-fed or fed a substitute for breast-milk. 52% of the sample responded that breast-milk was better for the child's health. 24% believed milk or formula made infants healthier while 23% felt that what the child was fed made no difference."

Kimberly K. Lillig and Carolyn J. Lackey, "Economic and social factors influencing women's infant feeding decisions in a rural Mexican community", Journal of Tropical Pediatrics, vol. 28, October 1982.

FAMILY SIZE

"In the case of women who formula-fed, family size may have been a determinant in the feeding decision. More formula feeding mothers had from five to 10 children than did breast-feeding mothers. The demands on the mother's time due to large family size and the convenience of allowing an older child to bottle-feed the infant may have made milk or formula-feeding a more attractive alternative to these mothers. Perhaps more importantly, the effect of a greater number of pregnancies and childbirths on these women's health may have contributed to their reported inability to nurse the most recently born child."

Kimberly K. Lillig and Carolyn J. Lackey, "Economic and social factors influencing women's infant feeding decisions in a rural Mexican community", Journal of Tropical Pediatrics, vol. 28, October 1982.

GOING OUT TO WORK

"Lactating women whose employment requires separation from their infants face obstacles in many societies. Managing lactation under such circumstances becomes a complex task requiring hand expression of milk, use of infant formula or cow's milk, or use of a wet nurse. Among the strategies developed by employed women are working at home for the first few months; working flexible hours, part time, or shorter shifts; and breastfeeding at night."

Penny van Esterik and Ted Greiner, "Breast-feeding and women's work: constraints and opportunities", Studies in Family Planning, vol. 12, no. 4, April 1981.

"Working women reiterate that breast milk is the best for their children, but have not yet been able to muster the support of society in obtaining a longer maternity leave. Such leave can be viewed not as a privilege accorded to a working mother as an individual, but as an expression of the full responsibility of the entire community to uphold the need for mothers to breast-feed their babies – and that because of the many advantages that human milk can offer society. A well-fed, well-nourished, healthy child is an asset to any society. Maternity leave must be considered a social responsibility that is assumed in the aim of producing a healthy young generation."

Priyani E. Soysa, "The advantages of breast-feeding: a developing country point of view", Assignment Children, vol. 55/56, 1981.

CULTURAL ATTITUDES

"Unfortunately, the West's exaggerated concern with breasts as sexual objects is often forced upon and adopted by other societies. When perceived primarily as sex symbols, the breasts must be 'decently hidden' – which of course makes breast-feeding in public places difficult."

Elisabet Helsing with F. Savage King, Breast-feeding in practice, Oxford University Press, 1982.

Supporting Mothers

If mothers are to be encouraged to practise breast-feeding, there must be a supportive psychological climate, starting with health workers during and after pregnancy, and extending into the family and the mother's work-place:

☐ "Examples of legislation and policies that support breast-feeding are: maternity leave, breastfeeding 'breaks' at the worksite, allowances – either cash or commodities – for pregnant women and new mothers, flexible work schedules for new mothers, rooming-in at hospitals/maternity wards, child care at the worksite, and a national code of marketing of breastmilk substitutes. As the number of women working outside the home increases, implementation of these types of policies ensures that women receive support for breastfeeding from their health care providers and employers."

Gayle Gibbons, "Legislation, women and breastfeeding", Mothers and Children, vol. 4, no. 3, 1985.

ADVERTISING INFANT FORMULA

The International Code of Marketing of Breast-milk Substitutes, adopted by the World Health Assembly in 1981, aims to protect and promote breast-feeding and to reduce the pressures of advertising on mothers to bottle-feed their babies:

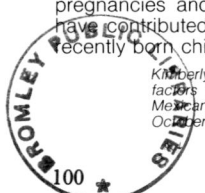

HEALTH WORKERS

"Physicians, midwives, and other health workers can actively encourage breast-feeding not only by providing information to their clients but also by altering hospital and health center policies that discourage breast-feeding. Since many women in urban areas deliver in hospitals, these policies have wide impact. Studies in Thailand and Malaysia found that women who had delivered in medical facilities were less likely to breast-feed than women who delivered at home even after taking into account the influence of socioeconomic status. This suggests that hospitals may have discouraged breast-feeding, and could be one reason that urban women breast-feed less...

"Restricting the availability and promotion of infant formula in hospitals also may encourage breast-feeding. In some countries representatives of infant formula manufacturers have visited hospitals and given free samples of formula to newly delivered mothers. Representatives often wore nursing uniforms. In addition, maternal and child health centers and 'maternity wards' have displayed posters advertising infant formula. Eliminating these practices should help avoid giving mothers the impression that health workers favor bottle-feeding...

"Family planning and other health workers should know about breast-feeding techniques so that they can teach the 'art of breast-feeding' to women. Several surveys have shown, however, that health professionals are often misinformed about breast-feeding. All health workers should be taught that frequent suckling – the pattern of breast-feeding in many traditional societies – is necessary to maintain a high level of milk production. Frequent suckling is especially critical in the first weeks after childbirth, when lactation is being established. If there are long intervals between feedings or rigid schedules, the reduced suckling causes shortages of milk. A woman may then have to supplement breast-feeding or turn entirely to bottle-feeding. Early supplementation with cow's milk or other foods further limits the production of breast-milk as an infant who is not hungry may be less inclined to suckle. Traditional practices such as delaying breast-feeding for two to four days after birth or nursing with only one breast may also reduce the milk supply."

"Breast-feeding, fertility, and family planning", Population Reports, series J, no. 24, November-December 1981

"School teachers and extension agents in contact with the community should also be informed about breast-feeding and weaning, and be able to offer information and advice that is consistent with that provided by the health services.

"This is particularly important for primary and secondary school teachers and for literacy teachers, as many girls enter motherhood within a few years after leaving school. It is thus important to introduce training modules into teacher training colleges, and into the material used in literacy campaigns."

Priyani E. Soysa, "The advantages of breast-feeding: a developing country point of view", Assignment Children, vol. 55/56, 1981.

EMPLOYMENT

□ "The International Labour Organisation (ILO) has played a major role in setting the international standards to protect women working and as mothers. Recognizing the protection of maternity as a basic human right and a social duty, the ILO objectives have focussed on extending the right to maternity protection where it doesn't exist; improving the scope and standards of maternity protection where it does exist; and insuring that maternity protection (particularly related to breastfeeding) does not allow employers to discriminate against hiring women... In 1979, only 2 percent of the employers in a large state in Brazil were complying with the law requiring nurseries (creches) at the worksite. (This law was based on the number of women employees.) The Ministry of Labor and local governments began a program to turn this around. Two regulations were instituted: 1) All companies required to provide nurseries had to register with the federal department of labor. 2) Worksite creches were inspected by the local government. In one year, 85 percent of all the companies had established nurseries, and 60 percent of the women breastfeeding were using the nurseries."

Gayle Gibbons, "Legislation, women and breastfeeding", Mothers and Children, vol. 4, no. 3, 1985.

Weaning

From the age of four or six months, breast-milk alone is no longer sufficient to meet the needs of a growing child. If supplementary feeding is not now introduced, then weight gain falters and resistance to infection is lowered:

Researchers in north India have shown that breast-fed babies were more likely to survive the early months of life, but between the ages of 9 and 24 months mortality was higher among exclusively breast-fed infants and toddlers than among those receiving food supplements as well:

"Thus, in poor countries as elsewhere, breast-feeding is advantageous early, but is not sufficient as the only source of nutrients beyond the sixth month of life."

Joe D. Wray, "Maternal nutrition, breast-feeding and infant survival", in W. Henry Mosley (ed.), Nutrition and human reproduction, Plenum Press, 1978.

(For further information on weaning, see Lifeline on Growth Monitoring.)

Immunization

For as little as $5, a child can be fully immunized against six of the most common and dangerous diseases of childhood. But at present, even though many countries have stepped up their vaccination coverage, fewer than 40% of the 100 million children born each year in the developing world are fully immunized against all or most of these diseases. As a result, almost 4 million children die and a similar number are mentally or physically disabled each year.

Many developing countries face serious supply problems with immunization services. Technological developments are helping to overcome some of these but management capacities need further strengthening.

Immunization is as much a question of demand as supply. Recent evaluations have shown that coverage rates could be doubled and in many cases trebled if parents took advantage of existing immunization services and if those bringing their children for the first vaccination were also to return for the second and third.

Demand for immunization can be increased in two principal ways. First, empowering parents with information about immunization can increase the distance which they are prepared to travel for immunization services. Second, making services available at more convenient times, closer to people's homes, can reduce the distance parents need to travel for immunization.

These strategies combined would enable immunization to bring about a reduction of up to one-third in the rate of death and disability among the developing world's children.

The Six Diseases

Each year almost 4 million children in the developing world die and an equivalent number are mentally or physically disabled through six vaccine-preventable diseases: diphtheria, pertussis (whooping cough), tetanus, measles, polio and tuberculosis. Fewer than 40% of infants in developing countries are fully immunized against all – or even most – of these diseases. Furthermore, only about 13% of mothers are fully vaccinated with tetanus toxoid, which also protects the new-born against neonatal tetanus – the main killer disease in the first month of life:

☐ "Of every 1000 children born into the world, 5 will grow up crippled by poliomyelitis, 10 die of neonatal tetanus, 20 die of whooping-cough, and 30 or more die of measles or its complications. These diseases, along with diphtheria and tuberculosis, are the targets of the World Health Organization's Expanded Programme on Immunization (EPI), and

between a quarter and a third of the world's children are now protected against them."

"Expanded immunisation", Lancet, editorial, 23 February 1985.

MEASLES

☐ "Without immunization, virtually 100% of the children in the developing world will contract measles between the ages of six months and three years – the youngest infants being protected by maternal antibodies. The age at which a child becomes infected varies with social and economic conditions: where there is overcrowding and poor housing, this may occur before one year of age; in better conditions the disease may not strike until some time in the second year or even later. Complications occur in about 30% of all cases, the most important of which may lead to pneumonia, blindness and deafness. These are more frequent and more severe in malnourished children who may have case-fatality rates of 10% or more. In the developing world, measles is also a significant cause of malnutrition and diarrhoea. Overall, it is estimated that some 3% of children in developing countries who acquire measles will die from it or from its complications."

R.H. Henderson, "Vaccine preventable diseases of children: the problem", in Protecting the world's children: vaccines and immunization, Rockefeller Foundation, 1984.

PERTUSSIS (WHOOPING COUGH)

"An acute bacterial infection affecting the respiratory tract, whooping cough is very contagious in the first week or two of infection. The spasmodic coughing or 'whooping' that characterizes the disease is readily recognized and lasts one to two months. Pertussis is most severe in children under five months of age and may lead to death through pneumonia or other conditions. In very young children, there is no characteristic whoop so the disease may be difficult to recognize."

Immunizations, World Federation of Public Health Associations, 1984.

TETANUS

☐ "Tetanus is caused by a toxin of the tetanus bacillus and causes painful muscular contractions and generalized spasms which in severe cases may reach the larynx and respiratory system. The disease can occur at any age, but is particularly dangerous during the neonatal period. Neonatal tetanus results from the contamination of the umbilical stump by unsterile methods of cutting the cord or by application to the stump of matter such as cow dung or mud. The infected newborn will first be unable to suck and then be unable to swallow or breathe. Some 85% of untreated cases die in the first few weeks of life."

R.H. Henderson, "Vaccine preventable diseases of children: the problem", in Protecting the world's children: vaccines and immunization, Rockefeller Foundation, 1984.

POLIOMYELITIS

Polio is a viral disease spread by contact with objects, food, or water contaminated with excreta. In a small minority of cases, polio leads to varying degrees of paralysis and, sometimes, death. The older the child at the time of infection, the more likely the infection will lead to severe consequences. The use of polio vaccines in the last twenty years in developed countries has markedly reduced the incidence of polio; however, its relative infrequency has led to laxity and occasional outbreaks among the unimmunized.

Summarized from: Immunizations, World Federation of Public Health Associations, 1984.

TUBERCULOSIS (TB)

☐ "Tuberculosis is most commonly a disease of adolescents and adults. The total number of tuberculosis deaths in children under the age of five years is not known with precision, but it is thought to be some 30,000 annually. Two-thirds of these deaths are attributable to TB meningitis, to which young children are particularly susceptible. Although the protective effect of immunization against TB in older persons is presently an unresolved question, its efficacy in young children has not been put in doubt."

R.H. Henderson, "Vaccine preventable diseases of children: the problem", in Protecting the world's children: vaccines and immunization, Rockefeller Foundation, 1984

DIPHTHERIA

"A major child killer of the past in temperate countries, the mortality and morbidity of diphtheria are the least well documented of the six diseases in developing countries today. Although typically manifested as an acute infection of the throat, diphtheria can affect the heart or brain of infants and young children."

Immunizations, World Federation of Public Health Associations, 1984.

The Vaccines

Vaccines differ according to schedules, number of doses, and the length of time and temperature at which they must be kept to retain their potency (see table 5):

SCHEDULES

"Immunization scheduling is affected by two biomedical factors: the age at which the infant can develop active antibodies and the number of vaccine doses which must be given. It is also greatly affected by the capabilities of the health delivery system.

"... The most critical time in the life of an infant occurs after the loss of maternal antibodies and before the acquisition of natural immunity. If an immunization is given too soon, the infant will still have passive immunity and will not develop antibodies. If the immunization is delayed, the infant is vulnerable and may fall victim to disease

"The productivity or coverage capability of a mobile team or an outreach unit of a health center depends upon how soon the unit must return to its starting point to begin a second, third, or fourth cycle of immunizations to follow up immunization of children and mothers reached during the previous rounds.

"In a fixed facility where immunizations are given on a frequent and regular basis, a short immunization cycle is

Table 5: Vaccines – number and timing of doses, administration method, and stability

Vaccine	Number of doses	Timing of doses	Route of administration	Stability at 37°C (freeze dried)
Measles	1	From 9 months where measles remains a problem for infants; from 12–15 months elsewhere.	Subcutaneous injection	Approximately 1 week
BCG	1	From birth.	Intradermal injection	Approximately 1 week
DPT	3	From 6 weeks of age, at intervals of 4 weeks. Two doses may suffice if a high potency vaccine is given at 4–6 month intervals. An additional dose is frequently given during the second year of life.	Intramuscular injection	Approximately 1 week
Oral polio	3	From 6 weeks of age, at intervals of 4 weeks. An additional dose is frequently given during the second year of life. The impact of immunization at birth needs further evaluation.	Oral	Approximately 1 day
Inactivated polio	2	From 3 months of age, at intervals of 4–6 months. The effects of a single dose, an earlier starting age and shorter intervals between doses are being evaluated.	Subcutaneous injection. May be combined with DPT	Approximately 1 week
Tetanus toxoid	2	For use in prevention of neonatal tetanus, first dose at first contact with susceptible woman, second dose 4 weeks later. In previously immunized women, 1 additional dose during pregnancy is sufficient.	Intramuscular injection	Approximately 2 months

Note: Freeze dried measles vaccines which remain stable for 3–4 weeks at 37°C are now available but are not yet in widespread use.

Source: World Health Organization, 1984.

possible. Ideally, children should be immunized as soon as they attain the minimum ages (see table 5) and should receive successive doses at the intervals shown. However, delays will be inevitable if immunizations cannot be made available on at least a monthly basis, and planners will need to use schedules which best meet their own circumstances.

''Immunization of women of childbearing age is an effective measure in controlling neonatal tetanus. In areas where most pregnant women seek prenatal care early enough to be given two doses of tetanus toxoid, these should be spaced at least four weeks apart, with the second dose at least two weeks before delivery. A third dose should be given at the next pregnancy, and any children born during the following five years will be protected.''

Immunizations, World Federation of Public Health Associations, 1984.

THE COLD CHAIN

The 'cold chain' is the name given to the system used for storing and distributing vaccines in a potent state from the manufacturer to the person being immunized. It is a supply system which is particularly critical because vaccines are spoiled by heat.

The Expanded Programme on Immunization has five vaccines. These are: 1) polio, 2) measles, 3) diphtheria, pertussis and tetanus (DPT), 4) tuberculosis (BCG), and 5) tetanus toxoid (TT) for women.

SIDE-EFFECTS

As with most drugs, vaccines occasionally have undesirable side-effects. According to the World Health Organization, however, the benefits of immunization far outweigh the risks of adverse reactions:

''Despite the safety of the vaccines used in the EPI, complications do occur. Although their rates are difficult to estimate precisely, it is known that they are far less frequent than the complications caused by the diseases themselves...

''The decision to withhold immunization should be taken only after serious consideration of the potential consequences for the individual child and the community.

''It is particularly important to immunize children suffering from malnutrition. Low-grade fever, mild respiratory infections or diarrhoea, and other minor illnesses should not be considered as contraindications to immunization.''

''Indications and contraindications for vaccines used in the EPI'', Weekly Epidemiological Record, vol. 59, no. 3, January 1984.

''Parents should be warned of the common side effects of immunizations; otherwise they may suspect that immunizations cause rather than protect against illness. In some cases, measles vaccination produces a mild fever easily controlled by aspirin and a rash which may occur 8 to 12 days after vaccination. Reactions to oral polio vaccine, including a paralysis similar to poliomyelitis, are very rare – perhaps one in every million doses. BCG vaccination will cause a small sore to develop at the vaccination site – the sore usually disappears after one to two months. Rarely, this sore will become a chronic ulcer.

''In the case of DPT vaccinations, the most frequent reactions are fever and redness, swelling, and pain at the site of injection. The pertussis component, in rare cases, can cause several neurologic reactions, some of which are severe. These severe reactions, greatly publicized recently, occur far less frequently than serious side effects from the disease itself in unimmunized children.

''More common than side effects of vaccines are infections and abscesses caused by contaminated needles and sy-ringes. While more frequently resulting from injections given by local injectionists or folk healers, this problem can also occur in organized health programs. Program personnel should be urged to report all serious side effects.''

Immunizations, World Federation of Public Health Associations, 1984.

COSTS

Compared with the cost of treatment of childhood communicable diseases, the cost of immunization is small:

''Several studies have calculated the costs per child protected or death averted. These studies generally show that measles, DPT, polio, and BCG immunizations are highly cost-effective. Immunizations are substantially more cost-effective than such other public health measures as providing curative care or safe water.

''Using EPI costing guidelines, analyses were made of program costs per completely protected child (DPT, BCG) in Indonesia, the Philippines, and Thailand. Costs ranged from US $2.86 to $10.73 and seemed most dependent on program organization, health care input costs and population accessibility.

''EPI planners estimate that development costs in starting up broad coverage immunization programs together with operating costs once they are underway will total $5-15 per fully immunized child in the 1980s. More than half this amount will consist of personnel costs, facilities, and operating expenses. The rest of this amount will be needed for vaccines, cold chain equipment, and transportation. EPI planners believe that many developing countries can supply personnel, facilities and operating expenses, but that external resources will be needed to pay for the latter items in the poorest countries; that is, vaccines, cold chain equipment, and transport will need to come from external donors.''

Immunizations, World Federation of Public Health Associations, 1984.

☐ ''Immunization is one of the most cost-effective measures to reduce childhood mortality. This in itself provides a powerful justification to provide the necessary financial resources. Furthermore, the resources required are not large. WHO estimates that it costs US$5.00 to $15.00 to fully immunize a child, and as infants generally comprise 4% or less of the population, a national immunization programme could be fully implemented for an investment of approximately US$0.20-0.60 per capita.''

R.H. Henderson, ''Vaccine preventable diseases of children: the problem'', in Protecting the world's children: vaccines and immunization, Rockefeller Foundation, 1984.

Ensuring Supply

The technical and managerial difficulties in placing immunization at the disposal of parents and children are formidable:

''To organize, on a continuous basis, the immunization of several million children during their first year of life whether they be in city slums or desert camps or mountain villages is a management problem of formidable dimensions. Add to it widespread illiteracy, inadequate roads and transport systems, rising fuel prices, budgetary cutbacks, lack of electricity for cold storage of vaccines, and over-stretched health services often reaching only 25% of the population, and we begin to see the true scale of the difficulties facing those involved in expanding immunization.''

R.H. Henderson, "Expanded immunization", in The state of the world's children 1984, Oxford University Press, 1983.

A great deal of recent research has concentrated on technologies for making vaccines more widely available. Progress on this front has been considerable and includes:

STABILITY OF VACCINES

''The stability of vaccines has been considerably improved. Efforts were first concentrated on stabilizing BCG, which is a live vaccine, sensitive to light as well as to heat. Present vaccines can last one month at 37°C and are packaged in coloured glass vials to avoid the harmful effects of ultraviolet rays.

''Since 1980, most laboratories manufacture a measles vaccine which may be stored at 37°C for one week. This improvement will probably considerably increase the effectiveness of measles vaccination... The vaccine is more resistant to heat, and while strict vigilance is still required in maintaining a low temperature, a refrigerator breakdown is no longer a catastrophe if it is of short duration.''

Nicole Guerin, "Recent progress in immunization", Assignment Children, vol. 61/62, 1983.

□ ''In recent years, the stability of measles vaccine has been improved, and vaccines now being provided to the EPI by WHO and UNICEF meet the WHO standard of being able to withstand up to 1 week's exposure at 37°C in their freeze-dried state. After reconstitution, they should be kept cool and used within a working day. Measles is mentioned particularly, as some of the newer vaccines have been erroneously termed 'heat stable', and they are certainly not! Even the highly stable tetanus toxoid can be destroyed within minutes when exposed to temperatures of 60°C, easily obtained inside of a closed vehicle parked in the sun. So all vaccines should be handled with care.''

R.H. Henderson, "Immunization update: recent recommendations from the WHO Expanded Programme on Immunization", Contact, no. 82, December 1984.

EQUIPMENT

''The quality of the cold boxes has been improved, and their cost reduced; there now exist cold boxes in which vaccines may be stored at 4°C for one week, with an outside temperature of 42°C. The same type of research has been carried out on refrigerators: their qualities have been tested, their faults inventoried, their performance improved, the conditions for greatest effectiveness studied. In many countries, workers have been trained to repair simple breakdowns. New sources of energy are being studied and evaluated as substitutes for petroleum or gas, which are costly and not available everywhere...

''The maintenance and checking of equipment does not suffice, however, to guarantee the quality of the vaccine administered. The most recent research deals with indicators of the vaccines' potency. These indicators change colour when exposed to temperatures higher or lower than those recommended for storage over a period of time long enough to alter the vaccine.''

Nicole Guerin, "Recent progress in immunization", Assignment Children, vol. 61/62, 1983.

NEW VACCINES

''Improved forms of present vaccines, as well as vaccines against additional diseases, including malaria, are on the way. New developments will also provide the opportunity to reduce the number of doses required to protect children against the six current EPI diseases.''

R.H. Henderson, "Expanded immunization", in The state of the world's children 1984, Oxford University Press, 1983.

HUMAN RESOURCES

Lack of adequate management capacities is one of the most serious constraints faced by the EPI:

''Current inadequacies are reflected in the frequent failures experienced in national cold-chain and logistics systems and in the low immunization within national programmes. The low rates reflect the fact that appropriate numbers of staff have not been identified in many programmes, and that those who have been identified have often not been given the responsibility or the authority to complete the tasks essential to the programme's success. Supervisory systems remain weak so that such staff are not held accountable for their performance.''

"Expanded Programme on Immunization: progress and evaluation report by the Director-General", WHO, 1982 (A35/9).

The main training needs are for middle- and lower-level health workers:

''The training of 12,000 national and international staff by the EPI is an important start. But few national programmes have so far developed the ways and means to pass on the necessary technical and supervisory skills to hundreds and thousands of middle- and lower-level health workers who must ultimately carry out the immunization programmes on the ground. That is why the World Health Assembly, reviewing the overall progress of the EPI in 1982, identified the lack of human resources in general and management skills in particular as the main programme constraints.''

R.H. Henderson, "Expanded immunization", in The state of the world's children 1984, Oxford University Press, 1983.

Creating the Demand

Immunization is at least as much a question of demand as of supply. A WHO survey of 81 immunization programmes in 31 countries between 1978 and 1983 found that the drop-out rate between the first and third DPT 'shots' was almost 40%, ranging from 12% in Senegal to 60% or over in nine other countries.

Summarized from: R.H. Henderson, "Results of EPI sample surveys of immunization coverage performed during review of national programmes by year, 1978-1983", paper prepared for UNICEF, April 1984.

MOTIVATION

''The high drop-out rates between the first and third doses of DPT and poliomyelitis vaccines bear witness to the fact that the mother has not understood the importance of returning and/or has been discouraged by the long waiting times or other inconveniences experienced during her first visit.''

R.H. Henderson, "Vaccine preventable diseases of children: the problem", in Protecting the world's children: vaccines and immunization, Rockefeller Foundation, 1984.

''For almost every intervention of this type, the benefit-cost ratios are high, often extraordinarily so; the cost of the illness or the death or disability caused by vaccine-preventable disease, diarrhoea or the unwanted pregnancy being far greater than the cost of prevention. Delivering these services, however, poses special problems. Healthy individuals in a community are not strongly motivated to seek such services. In rural areas, for

II LIFELINES: IRON, IODINE AND VITAMIN A

example, few will travel more than a few kilometers to a health clinic in order to obtain vaccination...''

Donald Henderson, ''Childhood immunization as an impetus to primary health care'', in Protecting the world's children: vaccines and immunization, Rockefeller Foundation, 1984.

TAKING UP THE SLACK

Taking up the 'slack' between available immunization services and the proportion of children actually immunized can be done in two ways:

''(1) Provision of the services at a convenient location near the residence of recipients and at a convenient time; and (2) active promotion of the service being offered. When immunization, for example, is brought to the residence at a time of day when villagers are not in the fields or at the market, acceptance by 90% or more is common. Comparable results are obtained if immunization is offered at convenient assembly points which are not too distant provided that the program is well-organized and promoted... Remarkably high levels of acceptance have been achieved when educational and promotional methods have been imaginative.''

Donald Henderson, ''Childhood immunization as an impetus to primary health care'', in Protecting the world's children: vaccines and immunization, Rockefeller Foundation, 1984.

Parents need two types of information in order to be able to utilize immunization services:

''General information regarding immunizable diseases, the benefits and possible side effects of inoculations, and the need for repeat doses; and

''Specific dates, times, and locations and clear directions on who should come for each immunization session.

''Parents and others who bring children to be immunized should know the following:
* which diseases the immunizations protect against, that immunizations will not protect against all diseases;
* which age groups are to be immunized and why other age groups are excluded;
* the need for repeat doses;
* that immunizations are safe and that side effects, such as fever, are signs that the vaccines are working to build their child's protection; and
* that vaccines do little or no good once a child has contracted the disease.''

Immunizations, World Federation of Public Health Associations, 1984.

Implementation

Immunization coverage is most effective when offered along with other, mutually reinforcing primary health care (PHC) services:

''While immunization services can be delivered alone, they are best delivered along with other services needed by children in their first year of life, and by pregnant women: the persons who constitute the priority groups for primary health care services in the developing world. In addition to the monitoring of the growth of the child, the use of oral rehydration to treat diarrhoea and the promotion of breast-feeding, these services

may include malaria treatment and prophylaxis, and counselling with respect to child spacing, nutrition during pregnancy, weaning, clean water and sanitation.''

R.H. Henderson, ''Expanded immunization'', in The state of the world's children 1984, Oxford University Press, 1983.

INTENSIFIED STRATEGIES

☐Intensified strategies have been developed in several countries in an effort to raise immunization levels more rapidly. These include:
1. Accelerated implementation of existing plans.
2. Use of periodic rounds of intensified activity.
3. Designation of one or more days each year as 'National Immunization Days', on which children in the target age group are immunized.

Some efforts have been extremely successful, while others have had less impact than desired. Political commitment from the highest levels has been an essential characteristic of successful implementation. However, political commitment by itself is insufficient without concomitant managerial, technical and logistical support. To have lasting impact, immunization programmes must be part of the general health structure.

Summarized from: ''Report of the Expanded Programme on Immunization global advisory meeting, 21-25 October 1984, Alexandria'', WHO, 1985 (EPI/GEN/85/1).

SURVEILLANCE

☐''Important increases in immunization coverage have occurred in most developing countries during the past decade, and those increases are now being accelerated in several of them. Although many countries have surveillance data adequate to reflect disease incidence trends, few developing countries have surveillance data adequate for programme management. Surveillance data, drawn either from the country as a whole or from selected areas, are needed for use by EPI managers at all levels.''

''Report of the Expanded Programme on Immunization global advisory meeting, 21-25 October 1984, Alexandria'', WHO, 1985 (EPI/GEN/85/1).

THE COMMUNITY

☐''The participation of communities as active partners in planning, implementation and evaluation is crucial for the success of immunization programmes, and is a fundamental strategy for the development of primary health care as a whole. Yet community involvement at the local level, and the success of 'social marketing' approaches at national level, require that the health services have the capacity to make an adequate response to the demands which these actions generate. Unless the logistic support has been well planned, users may respond to appeals through community leaders or the mass media only to find long waiting lines and no vaccines at the clinics which are supposed to be providing services. School teachers, religious leaders and other opinion leaders of the community need to be involved so as to encourage a full utilization of immunization and other primary health care services. Investments in these areas, however, will need to go hand in hand with investments in training and supervision of the health staff.''

R.H. Henderson, ''Providing immunization: the state of the art'', in Protecting the world's children: vaccines and immunization, Rockefeller Foundation, 1984.

Iron, Iodine and Vitamin A

Deficiencies in key micronutrients contribute to high rates of death and disability among children in the developing world.

Improving mothers' and children's diets with specific vitamin and mineral supplements can be a highly cost-effective means of protecting children's lives and healthy growth.

For example: iron supplements can prevent anaemia; iodine supplements can prevent goitre and cretinism; and vitamin A supplements can prevent blindness, and reduce both diarrhoeal and respiratory infections – the two main causes of death among the children of the developing world.

Iron-Deficiency Anaemia

Women in their child-bearing years and young children are especially vulnerable to iron-deficiency anaemia:

A recent study of 500 million women in developing countries other than China found that 46% – around 230 million – had haemoglobin concentrations below those specified by the World Health Organization as indicative of anaemia. Among pregnant women, nearly two-thirds could be described as 'anaemic':

"Women in the reproductive ages form one of the two main vulnerable groups with regard to anaemia, the second group being very young children. They are vulnerable primarily because of their great nutritional needs, and in the case of young children also because of their complete dependence on the support of others...

"The daily requirement for iron, as well as folate, is six times greater for a woman in the last trimester of pregnancy than for a non-pregnant woman. This need cannot be met by diet alone, but is derived at least partly from maternal reserves. In a well-nourished woman about half the total requirement of iron may come from iron stores. When these reserves are already low – from malnutrition and/or frequent pregnancies – anaemia results."

E. Royston, "The prevalence of nutritional anaemia in women in developing countries: a critical review of available information", World Health Statistics Quarterly, vol. 35, no. 2, 1982.

□"Although the characteristic sign of iron deficiency is anaemia, a state of deficiency exists well before the anaemia becomes apparent. Those affected are mainly children below school age, adult women of childbearing age, and pregnant women: all three are groups with a particularly high iron requirement. It has recently been estimated that some 200-250 million women suffer from iron deficiency anaemia; the number of children affected is probably about the same, which means that at any time there are about 500 million people with anaemia due to iron deficiency. Folic acid deficiency is an associated condition frequently found in pregnant women."

Edouard M. DeMaeyer, "Vitamin and mineral deficiencies", World Health, October 1984.

"(In infants) a supply of iron is necessary to ... cope with needs imposed by rapid growth... During the first four months, stored iron is used to help meet needs... Even in the most favourable cases, iron stores are exhausted around the fourth or fifth month, whence the evident risk of deficiency in case of exclusive and prolonged milk or milk and starch diet."

S. Hercberg and C. Rouaud, "Nutritional anemia", Children in the Tropics, no. 133, 1981.

EFFECTS OF IRON DEFICIENCY

"Anaemia in its severest form can lead to death, but this is rare. It does, however, have a profound effect on the psychological and physical behaviour of the individual. The mild and moderate degrees of anaemia which are much more frequent are, under normal circumstances, more or less well tolerated. Nevertheless they lessen the resistance to fatigue and affect work capacity under conditions of stress. Even very mild forms influence the sense of wellbeing. In pregnancy, anaemia has been shown to be associated with an increased risk of maternal and fetal morbidity and mortality."

E. Royston, "The prevalence of nutritional anaemia in women in developing countries: a critical review of available information", World Health Statistics Quarterly, vol. 35 no. 2, 1982.

□"Anaemia impairs work capacity, learning ability, immunological function and obstetric outcome. Severe anaemia is one of the commonest causes of maternal deaths in developing countries."

Kamala Krishnaswamy, "Nutrition in the third world", Pharmacy International, vol. 5, no. 11, November 1984.

□Two recent studies in Indonesia and Egypt clearly demonstrated that iron deficiency impairs the learning and problem-solving capacity of school-age children.

Summarized from: E. Pollitt and others, 'Cognitive effects of iron-deficiency anaemia", Lancet, 19 January 1985.

"Data from two recent experimental studies indicate that, in pre-school children, particular process features of cognition, such as selective attention, vigilance, or rehearsal strategies for memory function, may be altered by iron deficiency..."

Ernesto Pollitt and Nita Lewis, "Nutrition and educational achievement. Part I: malnutrition and behavioural test indicators", Food and Nutrition Bulletin, vol. 35, no. 2, 1982.

Causes of Iron Loss

Infections contribute to iron loss in both women and children. Frequent pregnancies further deplete women's iron stores:

INFECTIONS AND PARASITES

"Measles is a severe debilitating illness in malnourished children and is associated with an enteropathy responsible for the loss of about 20 per cent of the dietary protein intake. It is, therefore, usual to detect anaemia in children suffering from measles in the tropics...

"Diarrhoeal diseases due to bacteria and viruses are frequent in infants and young children, and interfere with nutrition. Bacillary dysentery is accompanied by intestinal bleeding which may contribute to iron loss."

Michael C.K. Chan, "Childhood anaemias in the tropics", in R.G. Hendrickse (ed.), Paediatrics in the tropics: current review, Oxford University Press, 1981.

"In the infected area studied in Venezuela, one-third of anaemias were deemed to be directly attributable to hookworm infection... There is also a strong association between anaemia and malaria.''

E. Royston, "The prevalence of nutritional anaemia in women in developing countries: a critical review of available information", World Health Statistics Quarterly, vol. 35, no. 2, 1982.

FREQUENT PREGNANCIES

"In Bangkok, the prevalence of anaemia in pregnant women doubled after the third pregnancy and increased fivefold after the fifth pregnancy.''

E. Royston, "The prevalence of nutritional anaemia in women in developing countries: a critical review of available information", World Health Statistics Quarterly, vol. 35, no. 2, 1982.

Preventing Iron Deficiency

Iron-deficiency anaemia results from poor absorption of iron in the intestine as well as inadequate iron intake. Preventive measures may take several forms:

□ ''... Absorption can be increased by changing the diet, but this approach is difficult in practice owing to eating habits and cost. There are other methods of prevention; the regular administration of an iron supplement as a medicine, and the addition of iron to a foodstuff... Research is being carried out in developing countries on the possibility of adding iron to commonly used spices and flavourings such as salt, fish sauce or sugar, but it is still too early to say whether or not this approach will be successful. In many developing countries it is impossible to fortify food with iron; consequently, health authorities distribute iron supplements in the form of tablets or syrup to the groups most at risk, i.e. children and pregnant women.''

Edouard M. DeMaeyer, "Vitamin and mineral deficiencies", World Health, October 1984.

Besides measures in supplementing and enriching foods (fortification), it is indispensable to develop general measures aimed at ensuring a nutritional iron supply, such as:
* augmenting the availability of proteins of animal origin;
* increasing the consumption of vegetable foods rich in iron, such as green leafy vegetables and beans;
* improving the nutrition education of the population and, above all, learning to make better use of available resources;
* improving the distribution of food in the family group so that high-risk subjects (particularly pregnant women) gain access to animal proteins with a high iron content.

Summarized from: S. Hercberg and C. Rouaud, "Nutritional anaemia", Children in the Tropics, no. 133, 1981.

Recording the results of a pilot project in rural India, the authors observed:
□ ''Prior to the use of community health workers for anaemia screening and iron and folic acid distribution, anaemia was very common in pregnancy, being present in 66% of 641 women delivering between August 1977 and January 1978. Following the introduction of screening and treatment by the community health workers, the prevalence of anaemia fell dramatically, being present in only 20% of women delivering between March and August 1978.
''Thus, the results of using community health workers for screening and treatment were highly satisfactory. The cost of each screening test worked out at less than one US cent (0.08 rupees).

''In summary, our experience suggests that, with adequate training and using appropriate technology, community health workers can screen for anaemia in pregnant women and give simple treatment, provide advice on nutrition, and make referrals for more intensive treatment as indicated. Moreover, they appreciate being given an opportunity to play such an important role in maternal and child health care, particularly since it enhances their credibility and prestige in the community.''

Usha Shah and others, "Using community health workers to screen for anaemia", World Health Forum, vol. 5, no. 1, 1984.

Iodine Deficiency Disorders

Thyroxine, the hormone produced by the thyroid gland, is essential for the physical and mental development of children, and dependent on iodine intake. Iodine deficiency disorders (IDD) include goitre and cretinism:

"In many areas of the world, mainly in mountainous regions, the soil and water are very poor in iodine; if the populations in these areas are dependent primarily on the foods produced locally, they may not have enough iodine in their diet.
"In an effort to compensate for this deficiency, the thyroid gland enlarges so that it can utilize the available iodine more efficiently and produce enough thyroxine. This pathological enlargement of the thyroid gland is known as goiter, which presents as a swelling on the front of the neck.''

"Endemic goiter: a brief for policy makers", Sub-committee on Nutrition, United Nations Administrative Committee on Co-ordination, 1979 (ACC/SCN-NS1).

''... The fully developed syndrome (of IDD) is only the most obvious manifestation in a whole range of developmental disorders prevalent in goitrous communities – expressed as combinations of retarded mental development, hearing disabilities, speech disorders, neuromuscular abnormalities, coordination defects, and poor physical growth. The more severe the iodine deficiency, the more frequent is endemic cretinism.''

"From endemic goitre to iodine deficiency disorders", Lancet, editorial, 12 November 1983.

''It seems that in severely iodine-deficient areas the iodine stores of the mother's thyroid become more depleted with each successive pregnancy and lactation, and her thyroid accumulates iodine more avidly. It is an old experience that the successive children are usually more retarded and finally only cretins are born.''

Josip Matovinovic, "Endemic goiter and cretinism at the dawn of the third millennium", Annual Review of Nutrition, vol. 3, 1983.

PREVALENCE OF IDD
Though mostly limited to mountainous regions, iodine deficiency affects large numbers of people:

''In 1960, Kelly and Snedden estimated that there were 200 million goitrous persons worldwide. Twenty years later Matovinovic's figure for the less developed regions of the world was 329 million, and this is probably an underestimate. As for endemic cretinism, it is impossible to make even an intelligent guess. There are said to be 1-2 million cretins in China alone. In some South-East Asian localities, up to a third of the population may be hypothyroid.''

"From endemic goitre to iodine deficiency disorders", Lancet, editorial, 12 November 1983.

CONTROLLING IDD

Iodine deficiency disorders can be prevented at low cost:

"A single dose of iodised oil can correct severe iodine deficiency for 3-5 years. Iodised oil offers a satisfactory immediate measure for primary care services until an iodised salt programme can be implemented. The complete eradication of iodine deficiency is therefore feasible within 5-10 years."

Basil S. Hetzel, "Iodine deficiency disorders (IDD) and their eradication", Lancet, 12 November 1983.

□"Iodine deficiency is relatively easy to control by administering sufficient iodine – between 100 and 400 mcg per person per day – in any of various ways. Periodic distribution of a potassium iodide supplement to groups most at risk, i.e. children and women of childbearing age, has been organized in some countries with good results, but it is a difficult technique to apply over a long period and is relatively costly in terms of staff. Another method is to add iodine to a food: in some countries this has been done with bread. Cooking salt, however, has been the vehicle most widely fortified with excellent results, and the method has the advantage of being cheap. Another approach used successfully now for several years is the intramuscular injection of iodised oil (1-2 ml), which provides protection for three to four years: although more expensive than adding iodine to salt, it has the advantage that it can be done rapidly and in places where iodisation of salt is not feasible or would not really be justified because of the scattered nature and the small size of the pockets of endemic goitre. Intramuscular injection of iodised oil has been used successfully in New Guinea and Indonesia, and on a large scale in Zaire."

Edouard M. DeMaeyer, "Vitamin and mineral deficiencies", World Health, October 1984.

"(In Papua New Guinea) a recent evaluation in 1982 revealed an absence of goitre and the disappearance of cretinism under the age of 9 years since iodisation, initially with oil injection and then with salt, became widespread from 1972...

"In northern India, goitre has been controlled over a 16-year period with iodised salt...

"A recent report from Bolivia describes improvement in intelligence tests in goitrous school children following the oral administration of a single dose of iodised oil (374 mg iodine) when followed up for a period of 22 months."

Basil S. Hetzel, "The control of iodine deficiency in South East Asia", paper presented at the Pacific Science Congress, Dunedin, New Zealand, February 1983.

Vitamin A Deficiency

Vitamin A deficiency – often the result of lack of knowledge about nutrition – is a leading cause of blindness:

PREVALENCE

"Xerophthalmia – from the Greek for 'dry eye' – is nutritional blindness caused by a lack of Vitamin A in the diet. It is the leading cause of preventable blindness among young children in developing countries, who are at greatest risk in the first two or three years of life. In general the disease is linked to protein-calorie malnutrition – failure to consume Vitamin A-rich foods such as green and yellow vegetables and fish, liver, eggs and milk. Often, however, the unavailability of these foods is less responsible than cultural practices with regard to child feeding. For example, while breast-feeding usually provides a baby with adequate Vitamin A, diluted substitute milk or early weaning food is often lacking in this substance and therefore puts the child at risk..."

"Xerophthalmia", Impact fact sheet no. 2 (Rehabilitation International), 1981.

□"Vitamin A deficiency is prevalent in many developing countries. As many as 5 million Asian children may develop xerophthalmia every year. One-tenth of children with xerophthalmia have severe corneal involvement, and half of them become blind."

Alfred Sommer and others, "Increased mortality in children with mild vitamin A deficiency", Lancet, 10 September 1983.

"Children are born with limited vitamin A reserves and are dependent for the first 6-12 months of life on vitamin A provided in the breast milk. When the mother is deficient in vitamin A the newborn child's reserves are even smaller, and the amount of vitamin A provided in the breast milk is reduced. Bottle-fed children are often at an even greater disadvantage, receiving skimmed milk (already low in vitamin A) that has been overdiluted with water (frequently contaminated). After 6 months of life the child requires supplementary feedings with foods rich in vitamin or provitamin A."

Alfred Sommer, Field guide to the detection and control of xerophthalmia, second edition, WHO, 1982.

INCREASED MORTALITY RISK

Recent research demonstrates that even mild xerophthalmia is associated with greatly increased rates of infectious disease and mortality among children:

□A study of 3,481 pre-school-age children in Indonesia concluded: "The mortality rate among children with mild xerophthalmia ... was on average 4 times the rate, and in some age groups 8 to 12 times the rate, among children without xerophthalmia. Mortality increased, almost linearly, with the severity of mild xerophthalmia... Mild vitamin A deficiency was directly associated with at least 16% of all deaths in children aged from 1 to 6 years."

Alfred Sommer and others, "Increased mortality in children with mild vitamin A deficiency", Lancet, 10 September 1983.

□The same Indonesian study also found that children with mild xerophthalmia developed respiratory infections and diarrhoea at twice and three times the rate, respectively, of children with normal eyes.

Summarized from: Alfred Sommer and others, "Increased risk of respiratory disease and diarrhea in children with pre-existing mild vitamin A deficiency", American Journal of Clinical Nutrition, no. 40, November 1984.

"There is a close connection between vitamin A deficiency and protein-calorie malnutrition. Seriously malnourished children cannot utilize the vitamin A stored in the body... Moreover, vitamin A deficiency leads to other infections (diarrhea, respiratory ailments) that affect nutritional status."

James E. Austin and others, Nutrition intervention in developing countries, Oelgeschlager, Gunn and Hain, 1981.

PREVENTION

Effective remedies for vitamin A deficiency lie in fortifying common foods, distributing vitamin A capsules to pre-school children, and nutrition education – all relatively inexpensive solutions:

"Vitamin A fortification has begun more recently in Guatemala (sugar), India (tea), and the Philippines (monosodium glutamate). Previously, several countries were fortifying cereal products, e.g., bread in India and corn flour in Guatemala. Margarine is fortified in most developed countries and in several developing nations, including Brazil, Colombia, Chile, Mexico, Peru, the Philippines, and Turkey."

James E. Austin and others, Nutrition intervention in developing countries, Oelgeschlager, Gunn and Hain, 1981.

"A year's supply of vitamin A in capsule form costs only US$ 0.15. However, the cost of delivering capsules and of any required information support must also be taken into consideration. In programmes in Bangladesh and Indonesia, total costs of delivering vitamin concentrates to children at risk are less than $0.20 a year for each protected child.

"Even less expensive, in areas with favourable growing conditions, is the addition of dark green leafy vegetables and other foods containing vitamin A to the child's diet. This can easily be accomplished at minimal extra cost..."

"Xerophthalmia," Impact fact sheet no. 2 (Rehabilitation International), 1981.

Acute Respiratory Infections

Children in the developing world get coughs, colds, influenza and bronchitis as often as children in industrialized countries – but their chances of dying from the infection are up to 70 times greater. The deadly alliance of malnutrition and acute respiratory infections (ARI) underlies a third of all child deaths, and weakens the survivors' chances of healthy growth and development.

Few developing countries can provide sophisticated diagnosis and care for the 300 or so different infections that make up ARI. Yet the toll of deaths can be brought down, and at very low cost. Immunization protects against diphtheria, whooping cough, tuberculosis and the respiratory complications of measles. Most ARI can be treated at home provided the child's mother understands the need to continue giving liquids and food, and especially the need to continue breast-feeding. And both mothers and community workers can learn to recognize the warning signs that the child needs antibiotics or more specialized care.

about 20 per cent of infants born in developing countries fail to survive their fifth birthday, and that one-fourth to one-third of the child mortality is attributed to ARI as an underlying or a contributing cause."

Basic principles for control of acute respiratory infections in children in developing countries: a joint UNICEF/WHO statement, WHO, 1985.

Children under five account for most of the deaths from ARI (the elderly are also vulnerable):

☐ A review of data from 88 countries on five continents concluded that about 2.2 million deaths are caused by ARI every year.

The mortality rates in babies under a year old are highest in Middle America (nearly 1,500 per 100,000 population), followed by Africa (1,454), the developing countries of Asia (1,242), and South America (1,110). In children between one and four years old, mortality is highest in Africa (467 per 100,000) and the developing countries of Asia (204), followed by Middle America (149) and South America (113). Mortality rates are lowest in North America (8 per 100,000).

In America, Europe and Oceania the relative importance of ARI as a cause of death declines as children reach school age; but this is not true of one-to-four-year-olds in Africa and Asia, where ARI continues to cause 30% of deaths. This is consistent with the fact that malnutrition in tropical countries is most common around the age of two.

Summarized from: A. Bulla and K.L. Hitze, "Acute respiratory infections: a review", Bulletin of the WHO, vol. 56, no. 3, 1978.

ARI: The Problem

ARI is one of the leading causes of child death in the modern world:

☐ "Acute respiratory infections (ARI), diarrhoeal diseases and malnutrition are the principal causes of illness and death in children in developing countries...

"Mortality from ARI in developing countries is 30-70 times higher than in developed countries. It has been estimated that

Child Sickness

Children in developed countries contract ARI as often as children in developing countries:

☐ "Accurate data on the incidence of ARI are limited, but community-based longitudinal studies indicate that it is very high everywhere. On the average, a child in an urban area has from five to eight attacks of ARI annually, with a mean duration of 7-9 days. Most of these are the less serious upper respiratory infections. In rural areas the ncicence seems to be lower...

"The magnitude of the problem is also well represented by health services' statistics. ARI are the eading reason for the use of health services; they constitute 30 to 50% of pediatric outpatient attendances, and 10 to 30% of child admissions to hospitals."

Basic principles for control of acute respiratory infections in children in developing countries: a joint UNICEF/WHO statement, WHO, 1985.

□"In studies of respiratory diseases seen by general physicians in the United Kingdom, it was found that these diseases accounted for about one-quarter of all consultations, and one-half of all patients... Upper-respiratory-tract infections decreased with age, whereas lower-respiratory-tract infections such as pneumonia and bronchitis were particularly frequent in both the young and the old..."

Viral respiratory diseases, WHO technical reports, no. 642, WHO, 1980.

□Children under five in two Bangladesh villages were visited every other day for a year to assess how often they were ill. They had one or more illnesses on 75% of all the observation days. Upper respiratory infections were the most common illness – 60% of the observation days – followed by diarrhoea. Respiratory illnesses were more common during the cool dry months, while diarrhoea was more frequent in the hot rainy season.

Summarized from: Robert E. Black and others, "Longitudinal studies of infectious diseases and physical growth of children in rural Bangladesh. I: patterns of morbidity", American Journal of Epidemiology, vol. 115, no. 3, March 1982.

□"Mata has reported on the incidence of various illnesses in a cohort of 45 children in the Santa Maria Cauque Valley in Guatemala who were followed from birth to three years of age. Diarrheal disease accounted for 43 per cent of recognized cases of illness followed by acute respiratory infections at 35 per cent. Over a three-year period, children had 853 episodes of respiratory infections, with 6.44 attacks per child per year. The upper respiratory infections predominated, and severe bronchopneumonia had maximal attack rates at the end of the second year...

"The duration of symptoms in children with bronchopneumonia did not vary with age, averaging approximately 7.5 days. If children have approximately six attacks per year and each episode lasts about seven to eight days, this provides some indication of the amount of time children are ill and thus some idea of the burden of illness to the community as a whole."

Acute respiratory infections in children, Pan American Health Organization, 1983 (RD/21/3).

Child Deaths

Children are at far greater risk of dying from ARI in developing countries:

□"The national data of registered deaths from influenza and pneumonia in children show striking differences between the developing and the developed countries... (In one study) in the Philippines the mortality rates in infants and in children 1-4 years old were 24 and 73 times higher, respectively, than those in Australia.

"... Comparison can be made with data from special surveys such as the study on childhood mortality conducted by the Pan American Health Organization in the Americas in

the late 1960s and early 1970s... In Bolivia and in Recife, Brazil, mortality was 11-14 times higher among infants and 48-51 times higher among children 1-4 years old than in Quebec, Canada, and California, USA... Respiratory diseases either as underlying or as associated causes constituted 50-60% of all deaths in children below 5 years old in developing countries. This proportion was only 18-21% in the developed areas...

"While a tiny proportion of children suffering from pneumonia or bronchopneumonia die in developed countries, this ratio ranges from 5 to 10% in hospitals of large towns (reports from Brazil, Thailand and Zambia). In rural areas without adequate diagnosis and treatment facilities the case fatality has been estimated to be above 10%. In the WHO research project of Goroka, Papua New Guinea, the case fatality for untreated acute respiratory infections classified as moderate and severe was 25%, but with treatment (essentially antimicrobial treatment) at an aid post, a health centre or the hospital, the case fatality dropped to less than 4%."

A. Pio, J. Leowski and H.G. ten Dam, "The problem of acute respiratory infections in children in developing countries", WHO, 1983 (WHO/RSD/83.11).

Causes of ARI

Over 300 organisms cause ARI:

□"... The acute respiratory infections now involve over 300 antigenic types of viruses and bacteria. These infections can be divided into two main groups: upper respiratory infections and lower respiratory infections. The upper and lower respiratory tracts are often affected simultaneously or consecutively and there are also diffuse forms such as the influenza syndrome... Suffice to say that the group includes influenza, measles, diphtheria, pertussis, sinusitis, acute otitis media, nasopharyngitis, tonsillitis, epiglottitis, laryngitis, tracheitis, acute bronchitis and pneumonia."

"A programme for controlling acute respiratory infections in children: memorandum from a WHO meeting", Bulletin of the WHO, vol. 62, no. 1, 1984.

□"Lung infection (pneumonia) is the most frequent cause of respiratory death among children under five years old. Bronchiolitis, acute laryngitis (croup) and epiglottitis also often have a fatal outcome."

Basic principles for control of acute respiratory infections in children in developing countries: a joint UNICEF/WHO statement, WHO, 1985.

Risk Factors

Infants are automatically vulnerable to ARI because their lungs are not yet fully developed. But the greatest threat to children's lives and growth stems from the vicious cycle of malnutrition and frequent attacks of ARI:

MALNUTRITION

□"The incidence of severe lower respiratory infections, which accounts for most of the mortality for ARI, is of particular importance in developing countries; low birth weight and malnutrition are associated with a very high mortality risk."

Basic principles for control of acute respiratory infections in children in developing countries: a joint UNICEF/WHO statement, WHO, 1985.

□"The malnourished child is prone to many types of infection, particularly diarrhea and respiratory infection, and the basis for this is multifactorial. In some studies malnutrition did not increase the incidence of ARI, but its severity and the likelihood of serious outcome were greater in the malnourished child.

"... There is also a converse relationship, and respiratory infections undoubtedly contribute to the development of malnutrition. In most cases only the result of the vicious cycle of infection-malnutrition-infection is seen. It is difficult to know where it started.

"... The loss of body protein which may be caused by severe respiratory infections in malnourished children can be as high as 12 per cent...

"Iron absorption is decreased by any febrile illness, and respiratory infections could be only one of the factors contributing to the development of anemia in these children.

"The development of clinical malnutrition may be linked not so much to the severity of the infection as to the frequency with which the child suffers from infection. It is normal after infections in children to have a period of 'catch-up growth'. If infections recur in rapid succession, and food, especially energy intake, is marginal, then there will never be 'catch-up growth'. There will be steady nutritional deterioration, itself contributing to the recurrence of new infections."

Acute respiratory infections in children, Pan American Health Organization, 1983 (RD/21/3).

LOW BIRTH-WEIGHT
Low birth-weight adds to the child's vulnerability:

□"Studies of Maya children in Guatemala showed that low birth weight is a major determinant of death in infancy. Therefore it seems that improving the weight of newborns in the community will enhance the resistance of infants and probably reduce mortality from ARI at this critical age. In Costa Rica, an important effort was made in order to decrease the proportion of children with low birth weight; a 28% reduction was achieved and it is possible that indirectly this fact contributed to the 74% reduction in ARI mortality from 1970 to 1980."

Edgar Mohs, "Acute respiratory infections in children: possible control technologies", WHO (WHO/RSD/83.10).

(For further information on low birth-weight, see Lifeline on Food Supplements.)

Preventing ARI

Immunization and breast-feeding can go a long way towards reducing the impact of ARI:

IMMUNIZATION
Several of the most important respiratory diseases – diphtheria, pertussis (whooping cough) and tuberculosis – are easily and cheaply prevented by immunization (see Lifeline on Immunization).

MEASLES VACCINATION
Measles, which is also preventable by immunization, carries the danger of severe respiratory complications:

□"... Respiratory complications, whether viral or bacterial in origin, that occur during measles, for instance, are more frequently fatal in developing countries where malnutrition is prevalent. In such instances, respiratory complications may account for about half the deaths associated with measles. In a hospital sample in Uganda, as much as 50.6% of deaths occurring during measles were attributed to bronchopneumonia and 9.6% to severe laryngotracheobronchitis. In contrast, in Britain, fatal respiratory complications are extremely rare; the overall mortality rate in measles is only 2 per 1,000."

A. Bulla and K.L. Hitze, "Acute respiratory infections: a review", Bulletin of the WHO, vol. 56, no. 3, 1978.

□"In a hospital in South Africa, it was reported that pneumonia occurred in 31 per cent of 879 autopsies in children and was the chief cause of death. Twenty-eight per cent of these children with pneumonia died within 28 days of an attack of measles..."

Acute respiratory infections in children, Pan American Health Organization, 1983 (RD/21/3).

OTHER VACCINES
□"Two vaccines which must be considered in the future, but which cannot at this stage be advocated as primary care interventions, are pneumococcus and influenza. In the case of pneumococcus, the vaccine is effective in adults, but efficacy in young children needs further evaluation, and its expense makes it as yet unfeasible for use in developing countries. In the case of influenza vaccine, antigenic shift and its short-term efficacy put it generally beyond the resources of developing countries."

R.M. Douglas, "Identification of acute respiratory infections control technologies that can be applied at the primary health care level of developing countries", WHO, 1983 (WHO/RSD/83.9).

BREAST-FEEDING
□"Children who are breastfed have fewer infections, including those of the respiratory tract... A recent study in London has reexamined this association and reports that fewer episodes of acute bronchitis and pneumonia occur in children who are breastfed compared with those who are bottle fed."

Acute respiratory infections in children, Pan American Health Organization, 1983 (RD/21/3).

Research in India and Canada found that artificially fed infants were twice as likely to suffer from ARI as those who were breast-fed – see table 2, in Lifeline on Breast-feeding.

Treating ARI

Severe ARI infections need specialized treatment, including oxygen, at a health centre or hospital. But in the vast majority of cases, families and health workers can provide adequate care:

HOME CARE
□"Supportive treatment has an important role in the management of ARI. Most sick children can well be managed at home provided that the community health workers and families are able to give them appropriate supportive treatment.

"Children with ARI may suffer anorexia and breastfeeding infants might have difficulties in sucking due to blocked airways and troublesome breathing... If the child suffers from repeated attacks of ARI, severe malnutrition may ensue and increase the risk of a fatal outcome. During ARI breastfeeding must be continued and the quantity of liquids increased.''

Basic principles for control of acute respiratory infections in children in developing countries: a joint UNICEF/WHO statement, WHO, 1985.

☐ "... Especially in situations in which food intake is marginal at best, special care must be taken to persuade the child to feed.''

Acute respiratory infections in children, Pan American Health Organization, 1983 (RD/21/3).

☐ "It is recognized that many families bring ill children into the health care system far too late, thus the families must be given some information about the critical symptoms indicating when attention must be sought. Thus, family health education becomes the first important aspect of the management of ARI..."

Acute respiratory infections in children, Pan American Health Organization, 1983 (RD/21/3).

☐ "Effectiveness of case management depends on getting the community informed and involved through health education, which aims at:
(a) Increasing the capability of families to differentiate moderate and serious respiratory illness from mild disease and to decide when to seek help;
(b) Educating the community regarding simple supportive therapy;
(c) Promoting timely immunization against measles, pertussis, diphtheria and childhood tuberculosis;
(d) Promoting breastfeeding;
(e) Reducing parental smoking and other domestic air pollution to prevent ARI.''

Basic principles for control of acute respiratory infections in children in developing countries: a joint UNICEF/WHO statement, WHO, 1985.

HEALTH WORKERS

In various countries simplified management schemes have been drawn up which use key symptoms of ARI to guide community health workers in knowing what level of care a child needs:

☐ "In health services when semiprofessional personnel are the first contact with the supposedly ill child, less attention has to be given to the nature of the clinical diagnosis than the severity of illness. It is of little interest at the primary care level whether the child has bronchiolitis or lobar pneumonia..."

Acute respiratory infections in children, Pan American Health Organization, 1983 (RD/21/3).

☐ "The most difficult part (of an ARI control programme) will be the development of a management system that can be used by semi-literate parents and community health workers. Yet it is the easy access to effective therapy which will be the major determinant for the reduction of mortality. This, in turn, means availability of appropriate antimicrobial treatment at the community level and a functioning referral system for more severe cases.''

Basic principles for control of acute respiratory infections in children in developing countries: a joint UNICEF/WHO statement, WHO, 1985.

Antibiotics

Penicillin, especially when combined with immunization, has proven an effective remedy for ARI (see table 6):

☐ "... The implementation of well-known technologies in Costa Rica caused a reduction in ARI mortality among infants of about 70% between 1970 and 1980. Immunization (especially against measles, diphtheria, and whooping cough) and the prompt use of certain antibiotics (such as penicillin), prevented illness and suppurative and non-suppurative bacterial complications.''

Edgar Mohs, "Acute respiratory infections in children: possible control technologies", WHO, 1983 (WHO/RSD/83.10).

☐ "Parenteral penicillin is generally the drug of choice for the initial treatment because of its high effectiveness and its low cost. The selection of the best initial drug treatment is more difficult when the community health worker is unable or is not allowed to give injections. In such a case oral ampicillin (or amoxicillin) or cotrimoxazole can be considered as possible first choice.''

Basic principles for control of acute respiratory infections in children in developing countries: a joint UNICEF/WHO statement, WHO, 1985.

HEALTH WORKERS AND PENICILLIN

Community health workers are rarely allowed to give penicillin injections for fear that they might misjudge the dosage or need. Experience in the Narangwal project in India has shown that with training, they can be relied on:

☐ "... Detailed discussion of the pneumonia problem led to a special training program to help family health workers diagnose pneumonia. A presumptive diagnosis was made if there was a combination of fever and respiratory distress with drawing in of the spaces between the ribs and flaring of the nasal openings. Family health workers became expert in making appropriate clinical judgements and were remarkably conservative and accurate in their diagnoses. On the basis of these signs, they were authorized to give a penicillin injection and then to refer the patient to a project pediatrician...

"(The) changes in services procedures ... led in one year ... to a 45 percent reduction in the death rate from pneumonia, despite the fact that severe weather conditions seemed to have increased the incidence...''

Arnfried A. Kielmann and others, Child and maternal health services in rural India: the Narangwal experiment. Volume 1: integrated nutrition and health care, Johns Hopkins University Press, 1983.

PENICILLIN RESISTANCE

☐ "In recent years infections with bacterial strains with decreased susceptibility to antibiotics belonging to the penicillin group have been increasingly encountered. Most reports, however, relate to developed countries, and in many cases the drug resistance is relative... However, monitoring of the therapeutic efficacy and surveillance of microbial drug sensitivity is an essential part of strategies anywhere in view of the threat of increasing drug resistance...''

Basic principles for control of acute respiratory infections in children in developing countries: a joint UNICEF/WHO statement, WHO, 1985.

TREATMENT COSTS

☐ "The drug cost of treating a child with ARI with injectable penicillin or oral ampicillin or cotrimoxazole is very low (20 cents, 40 cents and 8 cents, respectively, for a five-day course of treatment at 1984 UNICEF list prices). It has been estimated that in developing countries, in any year, 5 to 10% of children less than 5 years old will require such treatment.''

Basic principles for control of acute respiratory infections in children in developing countries: a joint UNICEF/WHO statement, WHO, 1985.

Combating Malaria

Malaria, transmitted by the Anopheles mosquito, is one of the oldest and most debilitating diseases known to mankind. In many developing countries, especially in tropical Africa, it is one of the five main causes of infant and child mortality. Pregnant women are also especially vulnerable, particularly if already malnourished.

During the late 1950s hopes ran high that malaria would soon be completely eradicated. But the disease has since made a spectacular come-back, largely because of the expense of maintaining control programmes indefinitely, growing resistance to insecticides among the mosquitoes which carry the disease, and increasing drug resistance in the most important of the malaria parasites.

Long-term control of malaria depends on the selective use of insecticides, eliminating the mosquito's breeding grounds, and using mosquito nets, screens and repellents to protect humans from contact with mosquitoes.

These measures are either expensive, technically difficult, or both. In the meantime, though, mothers and children can be protected against malaria, at low cost, if they are given preventive drug treatment as part of community-based primary health care activities.

Resurgence of Malaria

Since the early 1960s malaria has re-emerged as a major public health problem in many developing countries, especially in tropical Africa:

☐ Nearly 2,400 million people – just over half the world's population – now live in countries or areas where malaria constitutes a health risk. In many countries in the developing world, malaria is one of the top five causes of infant and child mortality. The World Health Organization estimates that, in Africa south of the Sahara, of the order of 750,000 malaria deaths occur annually, mostly among young children.

Summarized from: Basic principles for the control of malaria: a joint UNICEF/WHO statement, WHO, 1985.

☐ "Many decision-makers in Western countries do not realize the enormous public health importance of malaria. Informed guesses put the number of cases at 200 million per year, and in some parts of the world, 50 of every 1,000 children below the age of 5 die from malaria."

G.J.V. Nossal, "The biotechnology revolution and new vaccines", in Protecting the world's children: vaccines and immunization, Rockefeller Foundation, 1984.

Impact of Malaria

Malaria is particularly severe in infants and children, who have not yet developed immunity, and in pregnant women, who lose their immunity during pregnancy. Malnutrition adds to the burden of infection:

☐ "Malaria in humans is normally transmitted by the bite of a female Anopheles mosquito that is infected with one of four species of the genus Plasmodium – *P. falciparum, P. malariae, P. ovale,* or *P. vivax...* Malaria is an acute disease, clinically typified by chills, fever, and heavy sweating. The clinical features of malaria vary from mild to severe, according to the species of parasite present, the patient's state of immunity, the intensity of the infection, and the presence of concomitant conditions such as malnutrition or other diseases."

Manual on malaria control in primary health care in Africa, USAID, 1982.

☐ "One likely consequence of the resurgence of malaria is deterioration in maternal and infant health in areas where the disease is endemic. Pregnant women ... apparently lose antimalarial immunity, since they contract acute falciparum malaria at rates 4 to 12 times their nonpregnant counterparts. Such women can become severely anaemic, especially from the 16th to 24th weeks of pregnancy – a complication that can be prevented with antimalarial therapy... Low birth weight is characteristic of babies born to infected mothers, and successful malaria eradication campaigns have resulted in dramatic increases in recorded mean birth weights."

David J. Wyler, "Malaria: resurgence, resistance, and research", New England Journal of Medicine, vol. 308, no. 15, 1982.

☐ "Like many other tropical diseases, malaria interacts with other diseases and with malnutrition. Someone suffering from malaria is much more susceptible to other infections and vice versa. With each malaria attack, a person loses the equivalent of 3 days of food for an adult. The effect of this kind of interaction between malaria and nutrition is particularly dangerous for malnourished groups with few reserves and low resistance, such as babies, small children and pregnant women."

"Malaria and tetanus: turning back the tide", Contact, no. 74, August 1983.

DEVELOPMENT OF IMMUNITY

☐ "In areas where malaria is endemic, indigenous people who have lived there from infancy are able to develop a partial immunity to the local varieties of the Anopheles mosquito and the malaria parasites. This amount of protective immunity requires, it seems, repeated infections over several years. When immunity begins to develop, the human can tolerate malaria parasites in the blood without becoming clinically ill... Children under the age of 5 will not, as a rule, have enough immunity to protect them against clinical infection. The greatest toll of morbidity and mortality is found in this age-group. In hyperendemic areas, children over the age of 5 and adults will demonstrate clinical disease relatively seldom. Pregnant women, especially late in their pregnancy, have a tendency to become susceptible to clinical attacks to a variable degree and, like children under 5, are a population at special risk."

"Malaria and tetanus: turning back the tide", Contact, no. 74, August 1983.

Treatment of Malaria

With elementary training, mothers and community health workers can be taught to diagnose fevers and administer chloroquine treatment:

☐ "Where and when malaria is a recognized health problem, the first responsibility of the health services is to provide accessibility to appropriate diagnosis and to make treatment available to the whole population at risk...

"An anti-malarial activity should be organized as a spearhead of health promotion and as a possible port of entry for primary health care in every situation where malaria is an overwhelming priority and where it is feasible to maintain the specific antimalaria activity and to develop it into a system for provision of essential health care."

J.A. Najera, "Operational and epidemiological field research activities for the implementation of malaria control through primary health care in Africa", Bulletin of the WHO, vol. 62 supplement, 1984.

☐ "Mortality from malaria may be very high during the first years of life... The priority is therefore to provide prompt, adequate treatment for fevers where malaria is suspected – thus preventing mortality, reducing disease severity, and allowing development of natural immunity. This can be taught to mothers using the opportunities provided through antenatal services. She can be taught both to protect herself during pregnancy, and at the same time learn early detection and treatment of malaria episodes for her child. This will involve keeping supplies of chloroquine readily available from a community health worker or village pharmacy...

"It is feasible to train lay persons in the recognition and management of fever and in the treatment of clinical malaria. If supported by adequate information and drug distribution, it is possible to develop a community-based programme for the early detection and treatment of malaria cases, as part of the development of a comprehensive primary health care system. Diagnosis and treatment with appropriate antimalarials by community-based workers, including volunteers, could be carried out together with oral rehydration salts and contraceptives."

Basic principles for the control of malaria: a joint UNICEF/WHO statement, WHO, 1985.

PREVENTIVE CARE

☐ "A high-risk priority group for preventive treatment is pregnant women who should receive full prophylactic protection throughout pregnancy. This not only protects the mother but also reduces the risk of low birth-weight and perinatal death. The drug of choice is chloroquine, 300 mg base weekly. There are no contra-indications to utilizing this drug in this dosage during pregnancy. This can most effectively be done through a community-based primary health care (PHC) network using community health workers and traditional birth attendants (TBAs), backed up by the maternal and child health services.

"The widescale use of prophylactics for 'underfives' is not recommended any more. Originally it was thought that the infant living in an endemic area should be completely protected by full prophylactic therapy. However, this is considered to have four disadvantages. Firstly, the risk of toxicity through the accumulation of chloroquine in tissues since it is the total life accumulation that is the cause of retinal damage, and five years of chemo-prophylaxis is sufficient. Secondly, in practice, it has not been found feasible to ensure full prophylaxis on a wide scale, for a long period of time. Thirdly, full prophylaxis may prevent the development of a child's natural immunity from exposure to infection, thereby rendering the child vulnerable and susceptible to severe forms of malaria at a later age. Fourthly, this group is highly infective (i.e., it is a major carrier of the parasite), and long-term prophylaxis with low dosages of drugs normally used for treatment may accelerate the selection of drug-resistant parasites."

Basic principles for the control of malaria: a joint UNICEF/WHO statement, WHO, 1985.

CHOICE OF DRUG

☐ "Chloroquine should be the first choice in antimalaria drugs at the community level, but referral facilities should provide alternative drugs. In endemic areas all young children with fever from any cause should be immediately treated for malaria... Early treatment is critically important especially in infants: this implies readily accessible chloroquine."

Basic principles for the control of malaria: a joint UNICEF/WHO statement, WHO, 1985.

☐ "Selection of the drug of choice should be based on the following criteria: safety and freedom from serious side effects, simplicity in administration, effectiveness, acceptability to patients, availability and low cost... Chloroquine is the antimalarial drug of choice in Africa because it best satisfies the above criteria. The PHC worker should have chloroquine in two forms – tablets and syrup for children."

Manual on malaria control in primary health care in Africa, USAID, 1982.

Control of Malaria

Long-term control entails reducing the contact between humans and mosquitoes, insecticide spraying, and eliminating the mosquito's breeding grounds in stagnant water:

☐ Reduction of man-mosquito contact involves the use of mosquito nets, screening windows, and using mosquito repellents of various kinds, combined with health education.

The spraying of houses with residual (long-lasting) insecticides is complex, expensive and demands a high level of technical support and supervision. Action of this kind should be considered only when the health care system already has the capacity to deal effectively with the first priority of malaria control – the prevention of mortality through prompt, appropriate treatment.

Mosquito breeding can be controlled by the selective use of larvicides, biological control methods (e.g. fish), or cleaning of ponds, ditches, drains and water-collection containers. This method, however, is useful and effective only in certain well-defined instances such as urban areas and irrigation schemes, since it requires precise technical information about where the Anopheles mosquito breeds and when.

Summarized from: Basic principles for the control of malaria: a joint UNICEF/WHO statement, WHO, 1985.

THE PROBLEMS

☐ "One set of reasons for the resurgence of malaria are factors like increased cost of materials and equipment; lack of adequate administrative and general services and structures to support anti-malaria activities; shortage of trained personnel and difficulties in attracting and keeping experienced personnel; and limits to the involvement of rural health services in anti-malaria activities. Another reason is uncontrolled development of irrigation, deforestation and human settlement in malarious areas, resulting in increased breeding of the vector.

"Two of the most critical causes of malaria resurgence are, firstly, the Anopheles mosquito's growing resistance to the insecticides used to control it and, secondly, the development of resistance in malaria parasites, particularly *P. falciparum*, to drugs used in malaria treatment and prevention."

"Malaria and tetanus: turning back the tide", Contact, no. 74, August 1983.

RESISTANCE TO DRUGS

The most important of the malaria parasites has become increasingly resistant to chloroquine:

☐ "Since it was first detected in one part of Indochina and South America at the end of the 1950s and beginning of the 1960s, *P. falciparum* resistance to chloroquine has, up until early 1985, been detected in 38 countries. Resistance, however, is not an all or none phenomenon. Within each parasite species, and in particular *P. falciparum*, natural infections often consist of a mixture of individual parasites, some of which are fully sensitive and other which have different degrees of resistance. Chloroquine, therefore, can still be effective and give a clinical cure, especially if there is some immunity. The presence of resistant parasites in a country does not necessarily mean that it is a widespread phenomenon, although it can quite rapidly become so. Furthermore, *P. falciparum* is the only human malaria parasite that has been shown to be resistant to chloroquine at the present time... The presence of resistance should not be equated with abandonment of the drug but a signal for the establishment of a back-up treatment capability to deal adequately with those cases not responding."

Basic principles for the control of malaria: a joint UNICEF/WHO statement, WHO, 1985.

RESISTANCE TO INSECTICIDES

The widespread use of insecticides in agriculture has created resistance in many species of mosquito:

☐ "... Since 1975, this resistance has continued to spread and to affect malaria control programmes in many countries. The most significant development has been the appearance of multi-resistance. Altogether, 51 species of Anopheline mosquito have been reported to be resistant to one or more insecticides: 34 are resistant to DDT, 47 to dieldrin and 30 to both. Resistance to another, more expensive group of insecticides, the organophosphates, has been recorded in 10 species, and resistance to a third class, the carbamates, in 4 species."

"Malaria and tetanus: turning back the tide", Contact, no. 74, August 1983.

Alternative insecticides should not be adopted, though, without thorough research:

☐ "The decision to change a particular insecticide in use must be based on sound epidemiological information, including not only entomological but parasitological, ecological, socio-economic and other factors... A clear evaluation of the degree and geographical extent of resistance and its impact on the malaria control effort is essential for programme planning and revision."

Basic principles for the control of malaria: a joint UNICEF/WHO statement, WHO, 1985.

THE FUTURE

Vaccination against malaria may prove possible in a few years' time:

☐ "... The recently reported success in the development of an antimalarial vaccine can be taken as a real highlight in current medicinal research. A joint research project ... has now developed a method for the production of sufficient amounts of vaccine against *Plasmodium falciparum* sporozoites, which are responsible for 85% of human malaria infections...

"The development of an experimental vaccine for clinical trials could be achieved within 12-18 months, and vaccinations on a large scale could be expected within 5 years. According to current estimates, the number of new infections during this period could have doubled."

Heinrich Koch, "New antimalarial vaccine", Pharmacy International February 1985.

Costs

Antimalarial drugs cost relatively little, especially if distributed through a primary health care (PHC) network. The costs of control are much higher:

TREATMENT COSTS

☐ "... For complete suppression of malaria of a pregnant woman with chloroquine the cost in 1985 of the drug would be US$ 0.49... Similarly the cost of full treatment of an episode of malaria in a two-year-old child with chloroquine ... is US$ 0.02 (two cents). It is estimated that the number of episodes of fever per child per year in tropical Africa is about four. Thus the total drug cost for the treatment of a child using chloroquine would be US$ 0.08 (eight cents) per year, considerably less than most other drugs in common use at the primary care level. As with immunization and oral rehydration therapy, the major cost is not the drug, but the delivery system. But the addition of antimalarials and training to an existing PHC programme will not require excessive costs.

"Antimalarial drugs should be included in the first core group of essential drugs in countries where malaria is endemic. In some countries, second-line antimalarial drugs will need to be provided ... and these increase the cost slightly."

Basic principles for the control of malaria: a joint UNICEF/WHO statement, WHO, 1985.

PREVENTION COSTS

☐ "In some programmes, where the objective is a reduction of malaria transmission, residual insecticide spraying operations are a major cost item... As an example, assume a hypothetical population of one million, receiving two rounds of spraying per year with DDT 75% water-dispersible powder to the houses, with an average surface area of 50m² per capita, and spraying operations completed in 40 working days. The total cost for such an operation has been estimated at about US$ 1,460,000, that is US$ 1.5 per capita. This estimate includes the cost of DDT, spraying equipment, transport and vehicle operating costs, and personnel salaries."

Basic principles for the control of malaria: a joint UNICEF/WHO statement, WHO, 1985.

Female Education

Research in many countries shows a clear correlation between high levels of female literacy and low levels of infant and child mortality.

It has usually been assumed, however, that female literacy is merely an indicator of general living standards rather than a factor, in its own right, in determining infant and child health.

Recent research suggests that this assumption is generally untrue. Far from being merely a reflection of living standards, maternal education acts as a powerful independent force in reducing the numbers of infant and child deaths.

The mechanisms linking maternal education with improved child survival have not yet been illuminated by detailed research. But it is already clear that the education of girls is one of the best health investments which a developing country can make.

Education and Survival

Many studies during the past three decades have established that low levels of infant and child mortality are almost invariably associated with high levels of female education. A leading authority in this field, Professor John Caldwell of the Australian National University, has summarized the results of these studies as follows:

''Figures from the 1960 Census of Ghana show very large differences in child survivorship by education of mother. The proportion of children dead was almost twice as high for mothers with no education as for mothers with elementary education, and over four times as high for mothers with no education as for mothers with secondary education...

''Figures from a 1966 survey of Greater Bombay, carried out by the International Institute for Population Studies, showed that the infant mortality rate among mothers with no education was almost double that among mothers who had completed elementary education and almost three times that among mothers with education beyond elementary levels...

''In a United Nations study of 115 countries correlation between literacy and expectation of life at birth was higher than between any other specific factor considered and expectation of life; indeed, the correlation with literacy was only marginally lower than that with the General Development Index.

''It might also be noted that very low infant and child mortality levels have been achieved in some societies where levels of female education are high, health inputs moderate and incomes per head low to moderate: Kerala is a prime example, but Sri Lanka probably also fits the description.''

J.C. Caldwell, ''Education as a factor in mortality decline: an examination of Nigerian data'', Population Studies, vol. 33, no. 3, 1979.

☐''Recent studies have clearly established that the more educated the mother, the greater the probability that her child will survive to age five... In Haiti, for example, while nearly one-quarter of children born to women with no education die by

age five, fewer than 10% born to women with seven or more years of schooling die. Even in relatively low mortality countries maternal schooling has a considerable effect. Child mortality among the uneducated in Korea is nearly twice that of the most educated. In fact the variation in child mortality by the mother's education is independent of the overall level of mortality. The ratio of the lowest educational group to the highest is virtually the same in Nepal where 26% of children do not survive to age five as it is in Sri Lanka where approximately only 8% do not survive. Irrespective of the level of development, then, programmes to expand women's education have the potential to yield a considerable payoff.''

Barbara Mensch, ''Child mortality differentials within countries'', paper prepared for UNICEF, 1984.

A study in Bangladesh by the International Centre for Diarrhoeal Disease Research concluded that '... the single most important correlate of child survival is not, as might be expected, the family's wealth or the availability of medical facilities, but the mother's educational level. Thus, during very tough times in Bangladesh – the 1974-77 post-revolution and famine period – under-three children of mothers with no education were five times more likely to die than were children of mothers with seven or more years' education. Why this is so is unknown – and is the subject of on-going research.''

Annual report 1983, International Centre for Diarrhoeal Disease Research, Bangladesh, 1984.

☐The World Fertility Survey concluded that in virtually all 42 countries surveyed between 1972 and 1984. ''both infant and child mortality decrease consistently with increasing education. In Cameroon, for example, mothers with no education had twice as many of their infants (under a year) die as women with secondary education.

''Similar to its effect on infant mortality, education has a great impact on the level of mortality at ages one to four. For example, at these ages in Cameroon, 109 per 1000 children of uneducated mothers died as against 55 of secondary educated mothers.''

''World Fertility Survey: major findings and implications'', International Statistical Institute, 1984.

☐In a comparative study of 25 countries, giving all mothers seven or more years of education was estimated to lower infant and child mortality by an average of 41%. In two further studies, in which the effects of many more socioeconomic variables were controlled, the implied reduction averaged 25% for Indonesia, Pakistan, the Philippines and Sri Lanka.

Summarized from: James Trussell and Anne R. Pebley, ''The potential impact of changes in fertility on infant, child, and maternal mortality'', Studies in Family Planning, vol. 15, no. 6, November/December 1984.

An Independent Force

It has frequently been assumed that the level of female education is simply a reflection of general living standards, rather than a prime factor, in its own right, in reducing levels of infant and child mortality. Recent research, however, proves this assumption to be generally unfounded. A survey of 24 studies in 15 countries showed that, in three-quarters of the cases analysed, infant and child mortality declined unequivocally as educational levels increased.

Summarized from: Susan Hill-Cochrane, Fertility and education: what do we really know?, Johns Hopkins University Press, 1979.

II LIFELINES: FOOD SUPPLEMENTS

Further evidence is provided by studies in West Africa and Latin America:

"Two surveys carried out in Nigeria as part of the Changing African Family Project have shed considerable light on the relationship between child mortality and education of the mother. They confirm that maternal education is the single most significant determinant of child mortality; moreover, they make it clear that maternal education cannot be employed as a proxy for general social and economic change but must be examined as an important force in its own right."

J.C. Caldwell, "Maternal education as a factor in child mortality", World Health Forum, vol. 2, no. 1, 1981.

"There are now several studies from different parts of the world that demonstrate conclusively the link between a mother's education and her children's chances of survival. One of the pioneering investigations of the connection was carried out by Hugo Behm and his colleagues at the Latin American Demographic Center (CELADE). In studies of the socioeconomic context of infant and child mortality, the researchers found that maternal education showed the strongest correlation of any variable observed... It outweighed rural-urban variations, income differentials, and ethnic origin. In 11 countries studied, the mortality rate of children whose mothers had ten or more years of schooling was only one-third to one-fifth the rate of children whose mothers were illiterate."

Kathleen Newland, "Infant mortality and the health of societies", Worldwatch Papers, no. 47, Worldwatch Institute, December 1981.

A study in Kenya attributed 86% of the decline in infant mortality between 1967 and 1979 to maternal education:

"Nationally, the data indicated that fully 86% of the child mortality decline between 1962 and 1979 may be 'explained' by the increase in maternal education. The remaining 14% can reasonably be attributed to improvement in the household economic situation."

W. Henry Mosley, "Will primary health care reduce infant and child mortality?", paper presented at IUSSP seminar, 1983.

Possible Explanations

The exact nature of the link between female education and child health has been little illuminated by detailed research. Professor Caldwell proposes three possible explanations:

"The first explanation is usually the only reason given: that educated mothers break with tradition, or become less 'fatalistic' about illness, and adopt many of the alternatives in child care and treatment of illness becoming available in a rapidly changing society, thus profoundly influencing their children's chances of survival.

"A second explanation is that an educated mother is more capable of manipulating the modern world. She is more likely to be listened to by doctors and nurses; she can demand their attention even when their reluctance to do anything more would completely rebuff an illiterate. She is more likely to know where the proper facilities are and to regard them as part of her world, and their use as a right, not a boon.

"There is a third explanation that may be more important than the other two combined. It has apparently been almost totally ignored in spite of the fact that it can be seen operating in any West African household that includes educated women. This explanation is that the education of women greatly changes the traditional balance of familial relationships, with profound effects on child care.

"As traditional society becomes transitional society, and as educated people appear within it, those without schooling no longer expect the same adherence to traditional roles from the educated that they do from the illiterate. Everywhere in West Africa the impact of schooling is so decisive because it changes not only the educated but the attitudes of others toward them.

"A woman with schooling is more apt to challenge her mother-in-law, and the mother-in-law is much less inclined to fight the challenge. The younger woman will assert the wisdom of the school against the wisdom of the old. She is more likely to attempt to communicate with her husband, and her husband is less likely to reject the attempt...

"Ultimately, the family may even move toward child-centredness, with all that such a development means for reducing child mortality. More of the family resources will be devoted to the children; they may work less hard; they may take fewer risks; they will almost certainly live a healthier life."

J.C. Caldwell, "Maternal education as a factor in child mortality", World Health Forum, vol. 2, no. 1, 1981.

□ "Numerous reasons have been suggested for the dominant effect of maternal education in accounting for child mortality differentials. Initially it was thought that the level of education was just a reflection of the household's standard of living. The more educated the woman, the more likely she is to have an educated husband and a higher income. Improved purchasing power results in better housing, sanitation, nutrition and health care. Increasingly, these arguments have been superseded by others demonstrating an important independent role for education. It is now believed that schooling enhances a woman's ability to provide adequate child care not simply because she is wealthier, but because she is less fatalistic, more knowledgeable about health, hygiene and nutrition, and better equipped to deal with modern ideas and institutions. Education is said to increase the mother's status and power within the family, encouraging her to abandon such customs as providing food for male adults at the expense of children... The strong influence of the mother's schooling is all the more noteworthy when one considers that educated women are increasingly giving up breast-feeding in developing countries. Since breast-feeding dramatically reduces infant mortality in societies where water and sanitation facilities are inadequate, it might have been expected that the mother's education would not confer as great an advantage. The fact that it does suggests that if women can be educated and at the same time persuaded to continue breast-feeding, a very considerable reduction in mortality could be achieved."

Barbara Mensch, "Child mortality differentials within countries", paper prepared for UNICEF, 1984.

Girls in School

Empowering women through education has enormous potential for raising the levels of maternal, infant and child health. During the past quarter of a decade, the developing countries as a whole have succeeded in more than doubling the proportion of girls who at least start school: in 1960 only 35% of girls aged 6-11 began school; by 1979 the figure was over 80% – an enormous achievement.

Summarized from: The state of the world's children 1984, Oxford University Press, 1983.

But discrimination against girls still persists:

"Currently in the low-income countries, 90 per cent of the boys aged 6 to 11 are in primary school, but only 64 per cent of the girls are. In another ten years or so, these girls will enter the child-bearing years – and one in three of them will be desperately ill-equipped to keep her children alive and well...

"Discrimination against women in educational systems is a recipe for higher infant mortality – as are most other forms of discrimination against women. The relationship between maternal malnutrition and low birth weight has been established, and yet women, even when they are pregnant, continue to be underfed more commonly than men. Research has shown that it is not only malnutrition during pregnancy that impairs a woman's ability to deliver healthy babies. Chronic undernourishment in childhood leads to growth deficiencies that have an impact on reproductive health in later life."

Kathleen Newland, "Infant mortality and the health of societies", Worldwatch Papers, no. 47, Worldwatch Institute, December 1981.

☐ "Since 1960, school enrolment rates for children aged 6 to 11 in the developing regions have increased markedly. Just twenty years ago, they were about 20 to 30 percentage points below their current levels. From 1960 to 1980, however, enrolment rates for girls have lagged consistently behind the rates for boys. As of 1980 in Asia, for example, girls aged 6 to 11 had not yet attained the levels of enrolment that boys in this age group attained in 1960. In the Arab region, the enrolment level of girls is approximately where the levels for boys were in 1965 and in Africa, the level for girls is approximately where the African boys' level was in 1975. Latin America is the only region where girls' and boys' enrolment rates have been virtually identical, at least since 1960... One of the most significant factors discouraging girls' school attendance at the primary level is that girls in general have greater and earlier responsibilities than boys in productive labor in the home and outside the home. Girls spend significantly more hours doing productive household labor than boys. Time budget studies conducted in rural areas of Yemen, Bangladesh, Botswana, Nepal and Java repeatedly found that young girls spend more time in household and child care tasks than do boys. In rural Nepal, for example, girls between the ages of six and eight spent over eight times more hours doing child care tasks than did six to eight-year-old boys. They also spent one-fifth the number of hours in school than did boys. A rural study of dropouts in Ghana found that eight out of ten female dropouts from primary school were occupied in learning trades, either by helping their mothers or guardians, or on their own. Their trading activities undoubtedly conflicted with their school attendance."

International Center for Research on Women, "Factors affecting young girls' school attendance in developing societies", paper prepared for USAID, February 1983.

Food Supplements

One of the prime causes of infant death is low birth-weight (LBW). Babies weighing less than 2.5 kilos at birth are three times more likely to die in infancy. Over 90% of the 20 million LBW babies born each year are in the developing world.

The chief contributing factor to LBW is the mother's own level of nutrition. Food supplements for 'at-risk' pregnant women have been shown to be effective in helping to prevent LBW in many countries.

As LBW is associated with 30-40% of infant deaths in the developing world, food supplements in pregnancy could be a powerful lever for raising levels of child health and survival.

Supplementary feeding programmes for infants and children have the potential to reduce malnutrition, but their effectiveness is still a matter of debate.

A 1983 review by the World Health Organization, based on information from 90 countries, concluded that of the 127 million infants born in 1982, 16% – some 20 million – were born weighing less than 2,500 grammes. The majority were born in developing countries. By region, the proportion of infants with low birth-weight was 31.1% in Middle and South Asia (Bangladesh, India, Iran, Pakistan and Sri Lanka) and 19.7% in Asia as a whole, 14.0% in Africa, 10.1% in Latin America, 6.8% in North America, and 6.5% in Europe.

Summarized from: "The incidence of low birth weight: an update", Weekly Epidemiological Record, vol. 59, no. 27, July 1984.

"The birth weight of an infant, simple as it is to measure, is highly significant in two important respects. In the first place it is strongly conditioned by the health and nutritional status of the mother, in the sense that maternal malnutrition, ill-health and other deprivations are the most common causes of retarded fetal growth and/or prematurity, as manifested in low birth weight (LBW). In the second place, low birth weight is, universally and in all population groups, the single most important determinant of the chances of the newborn to survive and to experience healthy growth and development."

"The incidence of low birth weight: a critical review of available information", World Health Statistics Quarterly, vol. 33, no. 3, 1980.

"Low-birth-weight babies are less likely to survive during the first year of life than babies with a higher birth weight. This human wastage places considerable stress on poor societies, both emotionally and economically. At a rural health unit in India, peri-natal deaths were five times more common in low-

Low Birth-Weight

In some areas nearly one in three babies is born underweight. Mortality is high for low birth-weight babies, and even if they survive their chances of healthy growth and development are reduced:

birth-weight infants than in the new-borns with normal birth weight, and 70.6% of the neo-nates who died were low-birth-weight babies.''

Kusum P. Shah, "Maternal nutrition in deprived populations", Assignment Children, vol. 55/56, 1981.

''... No child in Santa Maria Cauque (a Guatemalan village) died in the first year of life if his birth weight was at least 2750 grams and he was breast-fed, despite an environment of crowding, poverty, poor sanitation, rampant infection, and lack of governmental effort to prevent diseases by vaccination. A better definition of the variable 'birth weight' revealed that about 7% of all births in Cauque were preterm, and an additional 34% were term-small-for-gestational-age (TSGA). If most of the TSGA births had been prevented, the infant mortality would have been reduced by 30%.''

Leonardo Mata, "Diarrhoeal diseases and malnutrition in Costa Rica", Assignment Children, vol. 61/62, 1983.

''The effects of malnutrition are most serious in early life and especially during foetal life. Inadequate nutrition in foetal life is a common cause of low birth weight... We know that there is a higher incidence (four to six times normal) of physical and mental handicap in infants of low birth weight. Mortality in the newborn period is also eight to ten times that in infants of adequate weight, and this increased likelihood of death is present up to the age of one year.''

G.J. Ebrahim, "Maternity and child health services (MCH) and the prevention of disability", Journal of Tropical Pediatrics, vol. 28, August 1982.

''Neurological studies have shown that about two-thirds of five-year-old children with LBW had normal motor development and neurological status. The rest suffered from cerebral palsy (3.6 percent), minimal brain dysfunction (3.4 percent) and delayed motor development (27.3 percent). All of them had lower IQs than babies with normal birth-weight. The majority of reports on this subject show similar figures...''

A. Lechtig and others, "Birth-weight and society: the societal cost of low birth-weight", in Goran Sterky and Lotta Mellander (eds.), Birth-weight distribution: an indicator of social development, Swedish Agency for Research Cooperation with Developing Countries, 1978.

Causes of Low Birth-Weight

The mother's malnutrition, both before and during pregnancy, is the primary cause of low birth-weight. Infection, anaemia and too-frequent pregnancies add to the risk:

MATERNAL MALNUTRITION

''There is great variation in the proportion of LBW infants and there are various reasons for low birth weight, but the available evidence suggests that wherever LBW rates are higher than 10 or 15 per cent it can be assumed that significant undernutrition among mothers is widespread.''

Joe D. Wray, "Supplementary feeding of pregnant and lactating women", paper prepared for FAO, 1983.

□''Quite simply, if the mother does not have enough food in pregnancy, then the growing foetus will not receive the nourishment it needs. During pregnancy and breast-feeding, a woman needs to receive approximately 2,500 calories a day. In practice, many women in the poorer communities of the developing world receive nothing like this amount. One study by the Indian National Institute of Nutrition in Hyderabad, for example, showed that pregnant women were receiving, on average, only about 1,400 calories a day, or just 60% of their needs...

''The result of too little food in pregnancy – often compounded by too much hard physical work – is that the mother-to-be does not gain enough weight during the nine months of gestation... The consequence of insufficient weight increase during pregnancy is likely to be low birth-weight.''

Kusum P. Shah, "Food supplements", in The state of the world's children 1984, Oxford University Press, 1983.

INFECTIONS

''In deprived populations in developing countries, pregnant women suffer frequently from upper respiratory tract infections, malaria, dysentery, diarrhoea, parasitic infestations, pneumonia, and hepatitis... It has been reported that pregnant women suffering from malaria deliver a higher number of low-birth-weight infants than those who do not have malaria. Robinson noticed a reduction of the mean birth weight of between 100 and 300 g when placental parasitism was confirmed.''

Kusum P. Shah, "Maternal nutrition in deprived populations", Assignment Children, vol. 55/56, 1981.

ANAEMIA

''It has also been shown that the frequency of low-birth-weight infants is higher among anaemic women. Menon reported an average birth weight of 2.4 kg in infants of mothers whose haemoglobin level was 6.5 g, as compared to 2.8 kg in the infants whose mothers had a haemoglobin level of 10.5 g. In addition, the infants of low-income mothers have been found to have liver stores of iron, folic acid, vitamin B12, and vitamin A representing only 50 to 60% of what is considered to be the required amount.''

Kusum P. Shah, "Maternal nutrition in deprived populations", Assignment Children, vol. 55/56, 1981.

FREQUENT PREGNANCIES

''Spacing of less than two years between births is especially hazardous because it means lower birth weights and poorer nutrition, possibly including a shorter period of breast-feeding or more competition for family resources and care.''

"Healthier mothers and children through family planning", Population Reports, series J, no. 27, May-June 1984.

''There is no doubt that cycles of pregnancy and lactation deplete the low-income mother nutritionally and result in a high proportion of low-birth-weight babies and in quantities of breast milk considerably below those of well nourished mothers in more privileged circumstances. Low-birth-weight babies show poorer growth and higher morbidity and mortality during the first year of life, and the combination of low nutrient reserves at birth and reduced quantity of breast milk means a need to introduce complementary feeding at an earlier age. This, in turn, adds to the risk of infection with enteric organisms and increases the likelihood of malnutrition beginning relatively early in the first year. Presumably, this adverse sequence of events could be prevented by improving the nutritional status of the mother.''

Nevin S. Scrimshaw, "Programs of supplemental feeding and weaning food development", in Nevin S. Scrimshaw and Mitchel B. Wallerstein (eds.), Nutrition policy implementation, Plenum Press, 1982.

Food in Pregnancy

Extra food during pregnancy significantly reduces the risk of low birth-weight for the baby:

The participants at an international workshop reviewed eight studies from both developed and developing countries of the effect of food supplements during pregnancy:

"All of the studies ... show that in malnourished populations nutritional supplementation during pregnancy increased birth weight. The fact that each of the studies individually provide data in the same direction is very impressive, particularly given the variety of cultural and socioeconomic situations represented...

"These studies show that supplementation provided during the third trimester of pregnancy will increase birth weight, a finding which is consistent with the rapid increase in fetal weight observed during this period. Several studies reveal benefits from supplementation initiated during earlier periods in gestation."

> Aaron Lechtig and others, "Effects of maternal nutrition on infant health: implications for action", Journal of Tropical Pediatrics, vol. 28, December 1982.

"Field studies have shown that supplementation during the last three months of pregnancy is sufficient to increase birth weight, and that 500 calories a day is enough under most conditions."

> Joe D. Wray, "Supplementary feeding of pregnant and lactating women", paper prepared for FAO, 1983.

In a study in India in which poor women were fed an additional 500 calories and 10 grammes of protein, raising their total daily intake to 2,500 calories and 60 grammes of protein during the last month of pregnancy, they gained an extra 1.5 kilos compared with a control group of women. Their infants' birth-weight was on average 300 grammes more than the weight of those born to the control group.

> Summarized from: L. Iyangar, "Influence of the diet on the outcome of pregnancy in Indian women", Proceedings of the Ninth International Congress of Nutrition, Karger, 1975.

A classic study of nutrition supplements for pregnant women in four Guatemalan villages found that the percentage of babies with low birth-weight was 21% in the group receiving low supplementation (less than 5,000 calories during the pregnancy) but fell to 4% in the group receiving a high level of supplementation (40,000 calories and over). The researchers also assessed the effects of supplements when the mothers were under 1.47 metres tall, or weighed less than 48 kilos at the start of the pregnancy: in both cases, the percentage of low birth-weight babies born to the mothers in the low-supplement group was three to four times greater than in the high-supplement group.

> Summarized from: A. Lechtig and others, "Influence of food supplementation during pregnancy on birth weight in rural populations of Guatemala", Proceedings of the Ninth International Congress of Nutrition, Karger, 1975.

WOMEN AT RISK

"... The most economical and effective way to use supplementary food is to identify those among the pregnant or lactating women who are malnourished and target the program to them... These women may be identified in several ways:

"... Generally speaking, a woman whose weight is 90 per cent of standard (weight for height) should be considered a candidate for supplementation.

"Where weights and heights cannot be measured, women whose mid-upper arm circumference is less than 22.5 centimeters may be targeted.

"... When a woman becomes pregnant she should be weighed at regular intervals to see that she is gaining sufficient weight – about 1.5 kg per month during the last six months of pregnancy. If she fails to do so, she should be considered for food supplementation.

"... The measures required ... are simple to obtain and not too difficult to apply."

> Joe D. Wray, "Supplementary feeding of pregnant and lactating women", paper prepared for FAO, 1983.

"Field studies have provided us with tools and methods to identify nutritionally 'at-risk' women. Simplified techniques, such as weight or arm circumference measured with tri-coloured arm tapes, are the most practical for assessing nutritional status... A simple mother's care, similar to a child's growth chart, can constitute a comprehensive, informative, and simple tool for surveillance. Such a card has been used by community health workers and nurses in some countries with rewarding results."

> Kusum P. Shah, "Maternal nutrition in deprived populations", Assignment Children, vol. 55/56, 1981.

COST OF PREVENTION

"Much of the maternal malnutrition could be combated through the training of elderly women and traditional birth attendants to provide nutrition information and to promote beliefs and customs favourable to pregnant and lactating women, as well as to young children, particularly girls. It has been estimated, for example, that rural women in Guatemala could satisfy their needs for additional nutrients during pregnancy through locally available food products. The additional investment required would come to about $0.09 per day, compared to the $1.00 required to use the foods traditionally mentioned in the nutrition education schemes of developed countries."

> Kusum P. Shah, "Maternal nutrition in deprived populations", Assignment Children, vol. 55/56, 1981.

"There is extensive evidence of an association between malnutrition of pregnant women and low birth weight of their infants. Supplementation of caloric intake during pregnancy does increase the weight of the infant at birth. This suggests that measures to improve nutrition of the fetus, and thus birth weight, might be more effective in reducing infant mortality and less costly than providing intensive medical care for the mass of underweight and premature babies born to undernourished women."

> Alan Berg, Malnourished people: a policy view, World Bank, June 1981.

☐ "Supplementary feeding of pregnant and lactating women is an intervention that can produce direct, specific benefits to infants and their mothers. As a component of prenatal care programs, it is rivaled in effectiveness by only one other measure, namely the provision of tetanus immunization to women in populations where neonatal tetanus is common. Otherwise, nothing approaches it and ... it has been shown to be the single most cost-effective way of reducing mortality in the peri-natal period.

"... The intervention is relatively simple and inexpensive. Where it can be incorporated in an on-going, effective maternal and child health or nutrition program, it requires commitment and effort, but cannot be considered excessively difficult compared with many other activities, and it will be far more effective."

> Joe D. Wray, "Supplementary feeding of pregnant and lactating women", paper prepared for FAO, 1983.

Feeding Children

High-protein food supplements for malnourished children are a major – and costly – component of many health care programmes. That malnutrition impairs children's chances of healthy growth and development has been established beyond a doubt. But demonstrating the value of supplementary feeding programmes has proved difficult:

□ "Supplementary feeding programs are generally of two types: central feeding, where the beneficiaries are assembled at a single place and fed; and the 'take-home' distribution system where the rations are distributed at regular intervals with the expectation that the food will be eaten by the beneficiary at home. The former type of feeding has the disadvantage of beneficiaries having to travel to the feeding center every day and in the case of children, carries the risk of cross-infections. The 'take-home' system, on the other hand, offers scope for more frequent feedings and probably a better intake of the supplement."

"How useful are supplementary feeding programs?", Nutrition Reviews, vol. 36, no. 9, September 1978.

IMPACT OF FOOD SUPPLEMENTS ON CHILDREN

□ "Some on-site and take-home programs have reduced second- and third-degree (moderate and severe) malnutrition by about 50%. The greatest improvement appears to be in the most malnourished children... The permanency of improvement ... is not known...

"Clear evidence on the reduction of morbidity and mortality due to supplementation is not abundant. Nonetheless, positive impact appears likely, especially when integrated with health care services...

"Maternal education is a critical component of most feeding programs where there are correctable nutritionally deleterious feeding and health habits. Unfortunately, this component has often not been given adequate attention and results have not been dramatic. Nonetheless, some improvements have been noted, including positive effects on the nutritional status of siblings."

Mary Ann Anderson and others, Nutrition intervention in developing countries. Study I: supplementary feeding, Oelgeschlager, Gunn and Hain, 1981.

□ "Increased physical activity has been demonstrated as a response of young children and adults to additional food intake. This is a very important observation in view of the fact that increased voluntary activity among children may affect cognitive development. The available information suggests that the observed growth response accounts for only a small part of the net increase in energy intake derived from supplementary foods.

"The 'missing energy' may be producing unmeasured benefits such as physical activity ... and changes in body composition. Some of these benefits may have greater significance than growth per se."

Current views on nutrition strategies, UNICEF, 1983.

FOOD SUPPLEMENTS AND HEALTH CARE

Food supplements are generally most effective when combined with health care:

□ A study of 10 projects combining health and nutrition measures found that "under some circumstances, the health interventions employed appear to have been more effective than the particular nutrition components used. At Narangwal, for example, the cost of preventing an infant or child death was lower in the medical care area than in the nutrition care area for all but the very youngest age groups. And the leaders of the Rural Guatemala II project attributed 70 per cent of the observed mortality decline to their health interventions, only 30 per cent to their nutrition efforts. Such experiences illustrate the difficulty, even in carefully managed programs, of reaching enough needy children with enough additional food at the right time to realize fully the inherent potential of a nutrition supplement program."

Davidson R. Gwatkin, Janet R. Wilcox and Joe D. Wray, Can health and nutrition interventions make a difference?, monograph no. 13, Overseas Development Council, February 1980.

COSTS

Cost-effectiveness is a major issue in the debate about supplementary feeding programmes:

□ "The annual costs per child fed in take-home and on-site programs generally are in the range of $10 to $30, with food constituting about 50 to 90% of program costs...

"Experience has shown that not all of the supplement results in an increment to the child's diet. Some supplement replaces food the child received previously (substitution) and some (in take-home programs) goes to other individuals (sharing). These leakages can be sizable, ranging from 40 percent to 70 percent of the rations; therefore, increased ration size and special education efforts become necessary. The on-site programs tend to have higher facility operating costs and substitution rates than take-home programs, and they are less able to feed large numbers of recipients: on the positive side, however, on-site programs encounter smaller leakages due to sharing of rations. Although leakages increase the cost per target group and may prevent sufficient quantities from reaching the most needy, they do represent an economic contribution to the family and thus have social utility."

James E. Austin and others, Nutrition intervention in developing countries: an overview, Oelgeschlager, Gunn and Hain, 1981.

□ "... The efficacy of direct intervention efforts has increasingly come into question. It has been found, for example that when a child's diet is inadequate in calories, high-protein supplements intended to aid the child's growth are instead utilized by its body for energy – which can be equally well obtained through much less expensive foods. Also, when other members of the family are hungry too, as is almost always the case, the extra food provided is likely to be shared by all rather than allocated to the intended beneficiaries...

"Of equally serious concern is the possibility that direct interventions may even be counterproductive. Significant and lasting improvements in health and nutritional conditions require social and economic changes that can be brought about only when the poorest perceive opportunities for changing their lives and have greater access to the productive resources necessary for them to do so. Intervention programs that increase the dependence of villagers on local power structures or on outside assistance – instead of increasing their potential productivity or contributing to a more equitable distribution of resources – work against the establishment of the capability and the sense of self-reliance that are vital for change.

Family Spacing

Family planning is often regarded as simply a means of population control. Yet even if there were no such thing as a world 'population explosion', there would still be a powerful and urgent case for family planning as a method of improving mother and child health and reducing infant mortality rates.

The more numerous and closely spaced the pregnancies in a woman's child-bearing cycle, the more her nutritional reserves become depleted – and the greater the risks to the health of both mother and child. In poor communities, the infant mortality rate for babies born within one year of a previous birth is usually between two and four times as high as for babies born after an interval of two years or more.

In practice, however, many women do not have either the means or the freedom to decide on the number or the spacing of their children.

Empowering women with the means to control their own fertility could therefore have a dramatic impact on both the health of mothers and the growth and survival chances of their children. At the same time, it could also contribute to a reduction in population growth rates.

The Risks

The spacing, timing and number of births a woman has are crucial determinants of her own health and of her children's chances of survival:

The risks to the health of mothers and infants are greatest in four types of pregnancy: before the age of 18; after the age of 35; after four births; less than two years apart.

In other words, pregnancies can be considered high-risk if they are 'too young, too old, too many, or too close'.

Summarized from: "Healthier mothers and children through family planning", Population Reports, series J, no. 27, May-June 1984.

INFANT AND CHILD DEATHS

"Children born to very young mothers are more likely to die than those born to women aged 20 to 30. Data from the World Fertility Survey (WFS) relating to three Asian countries show that mothers aged under 16 are twice as likely to lose their babies than are those over 20... Children born to mothers over 35 run a greater risk of having birth defects than those born to younger mothers. In addition, the world over, fetal and neonatal mortality rates increase with high maternal age."

Angele Petros-Barvazian, "Family planning: a preventive health measure", World Health, June 1984.

"The harmful effects of rapid childbearing on the survival of children have been studied for at least the past 60 years. The analysis of WFS data has now contributed to a better understanding of this relationship and has provided policy-relevant findings. In general, children born less than two years after the preceding birth are much less likely to live until their fifth birthday than those born within two to three years. Equally, children born after long intervals (four or more years) have a better chance of living up to their fifth birthday. In some countries, babies born after short intervals are two-and-a-half times more likely to die within the first five years of life than those born after four-year intervals... The harmful nature of closely spaced births affects both the younger and older children."

"World Fertility Survey: major findings and implications", International Statistical Institute, 1984.

"... From a study of 26 countries it emerges that the occurrence of a birth less than two years after the previous birth increased the mortality rate in the first month of life by at least 50 per cent in 24 countries, and more than doubled it in 14 of them. The effects of rapid childbearing were equally apparent in the 2nd to 12th month of life, where the mortality risk was raised by at least 50 per cent in 22 countries and actually doubled in 12..."

"World Fertility Survey: major findings and implications", International Statistical Institute, 1984.

123

II LIFELINES: FAMILY SPACING

"... Irrespective of the age of the mother or birth order, a child with a pre- or post-birth interval of less than 18 months was about three times more likely to die in the first five years than a child with intervals of 42 months or more."

Raymond W. Charlaw and Kokila Vaidya, "Birth intervals and the survival of children to age five – some data from Nepal", Journal of Tropical Pediatrics, vol. 29, February 1983.

☐ "Even in countries where standards of nutrition and health are higher and childhood mortality is moderate, the risks of deaths are still 30 to 50 per cent higher for closely spaced babies than for widely spaced births."

John Cleland, "New WFS findings prove spacing benefits", People, vol. 10, no. 2, 1983.

MATERNAL DEATHS

"Maternal deaths increase with birth order because many complications of pregnancy and childbirth rise sharply among third and later births. An estimated 25 million women in developing countries have such complications every year...

"Deaths from hemorrhage (uncontrolled bleeding) and from pulmonary embolism (blood clots in the lungs) are especially common among fourth and higher order births...

"Other complications that increase with birth order are problems with the placenta and umbilical cord, collapse and tearing of the uterus, abnormal birth position of the fetus, and anemia."

Deborah Maine, Family planning: its impact on the health of women and children, Center for Population and Family Health, Columbia University, 1981.

"Not only age and parity, but also the interval between births has an effect on maternal death rates. In Bangladesh and Indonesia, for example, some of the highest death rates are found in women under age 20 with three or more children. When women under 20 have several children, birth intervals must be short. Thus, while differences in living conditions and health care may also be involved, these studies suggest that short birth intervals lead to high maternal death rates."

"Healthier mothers and children through family planning", Population Reports, series J, no. 27, May-June 1984.

☐ "Women, too, are the victims of unregulated fertility. Maternal mortality rates – the risk of dying from pregnancy-related causes – vary greatly in different parts of the world. In Europe today, the rates are as low as 5 per 100,000 live births compared to rates up to 1,000 reported in parts of Africa and Asia.

"Not only do women in the world's poorest countries undergo the highest risk of dying from a given pregnancy – due to their own poor health and to the lack of appropriate care – but they also undergo this risk more frequently and over a longer period of their lives than do women in developed countries. A woman in countries where the average number of live births is eight – as it is in many African countries – will probably experience at least ten pregnancies. Typically a poor woman in such countries will spend almost her whole adult life either pregnant or breast-feeding. Often she will begin this cycle when she is sexually mature, but before she herself is fully grown."

Angele Petros-Barvazian, "Family planning: a preventive health measure", World Health, June 1984.

LOW BIRTH-WEIGHT

Results from the World Fertility Survey point to a link between insufficient birth spacing and low birth-weight:

"The nutritional drain on the mother of a rapid succession of pregnancies and periods of nursing may affect the survival

chances of infants and children through an initial low birth-weight and perhaps through breast-milk of inferior composition."

John Cleland, "New WFS findings prove spacing benefits", People, vol. 10, no. 2, 1983.

"Spacing of less than two years between births is especially hazardous because it means lower birth weights and poorer nutrition, possibly including a shorter period of breast-feeding or more competition for family resources and care. From infancy to adolescence, children born into large or closely spaced families experience more sickness, slower growth, and lower levels of academic achievement. Lower socioeconomic status has similar effects, but birth patterns also are important."

"Healthier mothers and children through family planning", Population Reports, series J, no. 27, May-June 1984.

MENTAL DEVELOPMENT

"Childbearing patterns may influence later intelligence through low birth weight. Low birth weight infants have lower test scores than other children. The difference is marked among children from poor families."

"Healthier mothers and children through family planning", Population Reports, series J, no. 27, May-June 1984.

"As might be expected, the same factors that affect children's health also seem to affect their development. Children in large families and children born close together grow less well, both physically and intellectually, than other children. The decline in intelligence test scores as family size increases has been vividly demonstrated in studies of large numbers of children in Scotland, England, France, and the United States."

Deborah Maine, Family planning: its impact on the health of women and children, Center for Population and Family Health, Columbia University, 1981.

"A study in the US matched births within 1 year of the previous full-term pregnancy to those that were over 1 year. The variables used were hospital of birth, sex, race, and socioeconomic status. The study found a significantly larger mean birth weight in infants born after longer intervals. In the study, short spacing was a result of biological factors, not socioeconomic differences between the two groups. An interesting finding was that intelligence scores for children at four years of age were significantly lower in the short birth interval group..."

Sandra L. Huffman, "Child spacing: for maternal and child health", Mothers and Children, vol. 4, no. 1, March-April 1984.

BIRTH DEFECTS

"Concerning spacing, in a study of US birth certificates, birth defects of all kinds were more common among children born within a year of the previous birth. Birth defects were least common when birth intervals were one to five years."

"Healthier mothers and children through family planning", Population Reports, series J, no. 27, May-June 1984.

MALNUTRITION

"Short birth intervals contribute to malnutrition in young infants by putting an early end to breast-feeding. Field studies in a number of countries have found higher death rates among children weaned early, especially those weaned because the mother was pregnant or had just given birth to another infant. In Senegal children weaned after their mothers had conceived were more likely to die within the following six months than children weaned at the same age but whose mothers were not pregnant.''

"Healthier mothers and children through family planning", Population Reports, series J, no. 27, May-June 1984.

"Studies in Candelaria, Colombia, have shown that as the number of children in the family increases, the per capita expenditures on food decrease. When families of similar socioeconomic status with 2 adults and 2 children were compared to those families with 4 children one study found nearly a 500 kcal difference in food consumption. Where increases in family size are associated with decreases in food expenditures and food consumption, it is evident that increasing spacing between births will ensure more food availability for children.''

Sandra L. Huffman, "Child spacing: for maternal and child health", Mothers and Children, vol. 4, no. 1, March-April 1984.

EFFECTS ON OLDER SIBLING

Insufficient birth spacing affects not only the new-born but also his or her elder sibling:

☐"One of the greatest threats to infant and child health and well-being is close spacing. Both the child born before and the child born after a short birth interval suffer an increased risk of illness and death. For the older child a new pregnancy may mean early or abrupt weaning from its mother's milk which, apart from its nutritive value, can protect the infant from infection. The early introduction of breast-milk substitutes and weaning foods carries with it the risk of contamination, diarrhoea and ensuing malnutrition. Even later in life, such children are more likely to die. Recent data have shown that mortality rates for children aged between one and two years are up to four times higher if their birth was followed by another within 18 months.''

Angele Petros-Barvazian, "Family planning: a preventive health measure", World Health, June 1984.

☐"Aside from influencing general food availability, birth-spacing has an impact on breastfeeding duration. A major problem for the older child in a short interval is early weaning. One of the most common reasons for early weaning is a new pregnancy. In a study in Senegal, one-third of all children were weaned because of a new pregnancy. Mortality was much higher among those weaned too early, and the probability of death within one year following weaning increased by 50-150 percent... A similar finding emerged in Thailand, where the percentage of children malnourished was 70 percent for children younger than 2 years when siblings were born, 53 percent for those over two years, and 37 percent if there was no subsequent child born.''

Sandra L. Huffman, "Child spacing: for maternal and child health", Mothers and Children, vol. 4, no. 1, March-April 1984.

MATERNAL DEPLETION

"Births too close together can produce what is often termed the 'maternal depletion syndrome' resulting from the lack of time for the mother's body to recover adequately from the last pregnancy. This is likely to be particularly important when women who are malnourished breast-feed their children, and perform the heavy physical work typical of life in the Third World.''

Davidson R. Gwatkin, "Birth spacing", paper prepared for UNICEF, December 1982.

☐"The harmful effects of short birth intervals on childhood mortality are sometimes explained by the 'maternal depletion syndrome', whereby one pregnancy coming too soon after the previous confinement leaves the mother little time to recover

her health, especially if the child is breasted for a long time or is still unweaned at the time of the next conception. Moreover, a continuous cycle of pregnancy and lactation leads to a progressively higher risk of low birth-weight babies with decreased chances of survival in the early years.''

"World Fertility Survey: major findings and implications", International Statistical Institute, 1984.

Benefits of Spacing

The timing and spacing of births through family planning enables women to have children when they are best prepared – with clear health benefits for both mother and child:

☐"Recent technological advances enable families to choose the timing and spacing of their children and to complement the traditionally and culturally accepted means of child spacing, such as breast-feeding. Admittedly, none of the currently available methods of family planning is 100 per cent perfect, but there is a wide range of choice between various effective and safe methods. When considering the risks inherent in certain methods, it is important to remember the health risks of not practising family planning – which particularly in developing countries are much higher. In some parts of the world infertility, as against high fertility, affects a large number of couples; family planning, as part of maternal and child health, has a role to play in enabling such couples to become parents.

"By reducing the number of short birth intervals and by preventing births to very young women as well as to women of high parity, family planning can prevent many unnecessary deaths and much ill-health among women and children. Few preventive health measures can have so great an effect in a relatively short time as the implementation of a family planning programme providing easy access to effective methods of contraception. That is why appropriate maternal and child health care must include family planning, which is crucial not only for health but also as a means of breaking the vicious circle of high mortality and high fertility.''

Angele Petros-Barvazian, "Family planning: a preventive health measure", World Health, June 1984.

CHILD SURVIVAL

"It is estimated that, if women chose to use family planning to avoid the four types of high-risk pregnancy identified earlier, in 1984 about 5.6 million infant deaths and 200,000 maternal deaths could be avoided. This estimate is based on the work of James Trussell and Anne R. Pebley, who, using data from 25 developing countries, calculated that infant mortality rates would be reduced by about 5 percent if childbearing occurred entirely within ages 20 to 34, by another 3 percent if all births after the third were avoided, and by about 10 percent if all births were spaced at least two years apart. This is a total reduction of 18 percent.''

"Healthier mothers and children through family planning", Population Reports, series J, no. 27, May-June 1984.

"Recent analyses conducted at Princeton University using data from 25 developing countries illustrate a substantial impact of spacing on child mortality. If all births were spaced at least 2 years apart, infant mortality can be reduced by 10% and child mortality (ages 1-4 years) by 16%.''

Sandra L. Huffman, "Child spacing: for maternal and child health", Mothers and Children, vol. 4, no. 1, March-April 1984.

"The impact of declines in high-risk pregnancies on infant mortality has been analyzed in a number of countries. In Costa Rica, for example, birth rates have declined rapidly in recent years (in large part due to the widespread availability of contraceptives). Between 1960 and 1977, births of fifth and higher order and births among older women decreased sharply. During the same period, the infant mortality rate fell by almost 60 percent. An estimated one-fifth of this decline is due to the changes in child-bearing patterns. In the United States, one-half of the decline in infant mortality during 1960-1970 is attributed to the increasing concentration of births among women of more favorable age and family size."

Deborah Maine, Family planning: its impact on the health of women and children, Center for Population and Family Health, Columbia University, 1981.

MOTHERS' LIVES

"In developing countries today, about 5.6 million infant deaths and 200,000 maternal deaths could be avoided if women chose to have their children within the safest years with adequate spacing between births and completed families of moderate size. This amounts to about half of the estimated 10.5 million infant deaths and 450,000 maternal deaths now occurring and represents the combined effect of fewer births and lower death rates."

"Healthier mothers and children through family planning", Population Reports, series J, no. 27, May-June 1984.

FAMILY BENEFITS

"Increasing spacing between births is an important way to promote the health of young children and mothers, although many of the benefits of birth spacing may be indirect. The mother has more time for each child to breast-feed, to prepare weaning foods, or to care for a sick child. Her other work responsibilities are less of a physical strain if she has fewer young children to care for. Increased birth spacing may also mean that there is more food available for the family, and illness and disease may be reduced because of less crowding in the home."

Sandra L. Huffman, "Child spacing: for maternal and child health", Mothers and Children, vol. 4, no. 1, March-April 1984.

POPULATION GROWTH

"In addition to averting infant and child deaths, of course, a lengthening of the birth interval would result in fewer births. The exact number is difficult to determine, but it would almost certainly be several million. Since this number of averted births could be expected to exceed the number of deaths prevented, an extension of birth intervals would also produce a reduction in population growth."

Davidson R. Gwatkin, "Birth spacing", paper prepared for UNICEF, December 1982.

Unmet Demand

It is often assumed that women in developing countries have large families because they choose to. In many developing countries, however, large proportions of women want no more children:

"World Fertility Survey data disprove the common assumption that poor, uneducated women in developing countries generally want as many children as they can have or 'as many

as God sends'... For example, among women with three living children the proportions who said that they want no more children were 24% in Jordan, 35% in Nepal, 50-60% in Costa Rica and Mexico, and 60-70% in Bangladesh and Thailand."

Deborah Maine and Joe Wray, "Family spacing", in The state of the world's children 1984, Oxford University Press, 1983.

☐ "Approximately half of the women surveyed in 31 countries (excluding sub-Saharan Africa) do not want any more children. An analysis in 18 countries has shown that the prevention of all births reported as unwanted would reduce the population growth rate from 2.2 to 1.3 per cent, increasing the time it takes populations to double from 32 years to 53 years. In sub-Saharan Africa, only 10-15 per cent of women do not want any more children.

"The average number of children desired by women ranges from 3-5 in some Asian countries to 7-8 in parts of Africa."

"World Fertility Survey: major findings and implications", International Statistical Institute, 1984.

☐ "In sub-Saharan Africa, family planning programmes cannot be framed on the assumption of a massive latent demand for smaller sizes of family. There appear to be two main feasible policies – to attempt to change people's views about the desirability of large families or to stress the benefits of birthspacing through contraception. The former course of action presents a formidable challenge. There are few instances where government action alone has been effective in changing family size ideals. The second course of action is perhaps more likely to succeed. There are already in most African societies strong beliefs in the benefits of birthspacing, and a rapid succession of births is considered undesirable or even shameful. As traditional means of birthspacing, that is prolonged lactation and post-natal abstinence, are weakening, a process which may be difficult to arrest, a strong demand for contraception as a substitute may emerge. Once the habit of contraception is established, the prospects for decline in the perceived desirability of large families may be enhanced. This scenario underlines the importance, particularly in Africa, of integrating family planning with maternal and child health services."

"World Fertility Survey: major findings and implications", International Statistical Institute, 1984.

☐ "About 95% of the people in the developing world live in countries which provide some form of public support to family planning programmes, generally as part of maternal and child health programmes. Despite this, it has been estimated that there are about 300 million couples who do not want any more children but who are not using any method of family planning, chiefly due to inadequate access to services in the developing world, especially in rural areas and urban slums..."

"Health and family planning", In Point of Fact, WHO, no. 23/1984.

☐ "If women the world over were able to have the children they say they want, the crude birth rate would range between 16 and 28 per 1,000 population rather than the present range of 28 and 40. In many countries, couples use no method of contraception at all or resort to traditional methods and illegal abortion..."

"Health and family planning", In Point of Fact, WHO, no. 23/1984.

"Women all over the world know the dangers of ill-timed pregnancies and having many children. In India, Iran, Lebanon, the Philippines, and Turkey, 21,000 women were interviewed in a WHO study. More than nine in ten women said the health of the child and the mother are better if the child is born three years after the previous birth, rather than after an interval of only one year. About nine in ten said that they believe that the health of mother and child are better if the family is small. More than nine in ten know that contraception improves the health of women and children."

Deborah Maine, Family planning: its impact on the health of women and children, Center for Population and Family Health, Columbia University, 1981.

"In developed and developing countries, as contraceptive use increases, women have smaller families and fewer births at unfavorable ages... Given a chance, women can and do avoid high-risk pregnancies."

Deborah Maine, Family planning: its impact on the health of women and children, Center for Population and Family Health, Columbia University, 1981.

———III———
STATISTICS

Economic and social statistics on the nations of the world, with particular reference to children's well-being.

Note on the new index of infant and child mortality.

New Index of Infant and Child Mortality

As a result of collaboration between the United Nations Population Division and UNICEF it is now possible to present a new and considerably improved index of infant and child mortality.

At the beginning of the 1980s there was no internationally comparable set of infant mortality estimates, and UNICEF decided to support the United Nations Population Division in preparing the first internationally standardized set of infant mortality estimates and projections. These were completed in 1982 and were first presented in *The State of the World's Children* report for 1983. A second phase of the collaboration between the two agencies involved the preparation of a comparable set of child mortality estimates and projections while at the same time revising the infant mortality data.

In international publications, child mortality has hitherto been expressed statistically as deaths per 1,000 children aged 1-4 years inclusive. This is a different denominator from that used for the infant mortality rate (deaths per 1,000 live births). This meant that the two estimates could not be easily combined and analysed. In addition, because the denominator used for the child death rate is so large, the rate quickly falls below 1 as the country improves its health conditions. Standardized and consistent sets of both infant and child mortality estimates and projections have now been completed and are presented here in these tables for the first time. It is now quite simple, as a result, for the reader to combine, compare and analyse these two sets of mortality estimates.

It is hoped that this new index of infant and child mortality will be adopted by countries for national and subnational analyses and presentation over the next few years so that it quickly becomes the standard form used when discussing child mortality. For many countries there are also national estimates of internal differentials in infant and child mortality, and at the end of the statistical section these internal disparities are presented for a number of countries. It is hoped that next year's report will present data on internal differentials within countries for both infant and child mortality.

As a result of the rigorous review of child mortality data undertaken in the course of this work, it now appears that of the 15 million infants and children in the world currently dying each year, as many as 5 million are above the age of 1 – a higher proportion than was previously estimated. It would seem that rather than 1 child death for every 2.5 infant deaths in the developing countries, as previously thought, there is in fact 1 child death for every 2 infant deaths. It is interesting to note that in the developed countries there is now only 1 child death for every 5 infant deaths.

Another very significant conclusion of these new estimates is the projection that the total number of annual infant and child deaths will fall from its current level of 15 million to around 10 million by the end of the century. Of course, one of the purposes of UNICEF supporting country activities in the area of child survival and development is to accelerate this projected rate of progress and to ensure that the consequences of current global economic difficulties are averted. The aim is to achieve a world-wide reduction in infant and child mortality by the end of the century considerably over and above that projected on the basis of past and current trends. However, one very disturbing projection is that the number of infant and child deaths in Africa will be no less at the end of this century than it is today – about 4.3 million a year. Thus Africa, which now accounts for less than 30% of all infant and child deaths, is projected, by the end of the century, to account for over 40% of all infant and child deaths and will even overtake South Asia in absolute numbers. Above all, in Africa, the greatest efforts have to be made to reduce the tragedy of avoidable infant and child deaths.

Index to countries

In the following tables, countries are listed in descending order of infant mortality rounded to the nearest 5 in the case of countries with a rate of 50 deaths or more per 1,000 live births. Countries with the same rates are listed alphabetically. The reference numbers indicating that order are shown in the alphabetical list of countries below.

131

TABLE 1: BASIC INDICATORS

#		Infant mortality rate (under 1) 1983	(under 1) 1960	Total population (millions) 1983	Annual no. of births/infant and child deaths (0–4) (thousands) 1983	GNP per capita (US $) 1983	Life expectancy at birth (years) 1983	% adults literate male/female 1980–1983	% of age group enrolled in primary school male/female 1980–1983	% share of household income 1970–1982 lowest 40%	highest 20%
	Very high IMR countries (over 100) Median	**135**	**190**	**1,346T**	**51,041T/9,876T**	**270**	**46**	**39/16**	**74/42**	**. .**	**. .**
1	Afghanistan	195	220	14.2	725/246	170[x]	37	30[x]/5[x]	19/9	. .	. .
2	Mali	180	210	7.6	378/118	160	42	14[x]/6[x]	35[x]/20[x]		
3	Sierra Leone	180	225	3.5	164/51	330	34	31/17	46[y]/32[y]	15[x]	53[x]
4	Malawi	165	210	6.6	339/97	210	45	48/25	72/51	22[x]	51[x]
5	Guinea	160	215	5.2	240/65	300	40	35/14	44/21		
6	Kampuchea	160	150	6.9	314/75	70[x]	43	78/39	. ./. .		
7	Ethiopia	155	180	34.5	1,683/440	120	43	. ./. .	58/34		
8	Mozambique	155	175	13.3	578/151	230[x]	49	44/12	91/68		
9	Somalia	155	180	5.3	236/62	250	43	11/3	33/18		
10	Angola	150	215	8.3	389/98	470[x]	42	36/19	. ./. .		
11	Burkina Faso	150	230	6.6	314/80	180	42	15[x]/3[x]	31/18		
12	Niger	145	195	5.8	292/72	240	43	14/6	34/19		
13	Bhutan	140	190	1.4	52/11	80[x]	46	. ./. .	31/16		
14	Central African Rep.	140	190	2.4	108/26	280	43	48/19	98/51		
15	Chad	140	200	4.8	210/51	80[x]	43	35/8	51[x]/19[x]		
16	Guinea-Bissau	140	195	0.9	35/8	180	43	33[x]/9[x]	88/40		
17	Nepal	140	190	15.7	649/140	160	46	32/9	93/39	13	59
18	Senegal	140	185	6.2	292/70	440	43	31/14	61/41		
19	Mauritania	135	195	1.8	88/20	480	44	. ./. .	45/29		
20	Yemen	135	220	6.2	300/67	550	44	18/2	99/17		
21	Yemen, Dem.	135	220	2.0	95/21	520	46	48[x]/8[x]	94/34		
22	Bangladesh	130	160	95.8	4,240/867	130	48	40/18	74/46	17	47
23	Haiti	130	205	6.3	256/48	300	53	37/33	74/64	6	48*
24	Liberia	130	185	2.1	99/22	480	49	30[x]/12[x]	95/57	11	73
25	Rwanda	130	150	5.7	288/64	270	50	51[x]/27[x]	65/60		
26	Bolivia	125	170	6.0	263/52	510	51	76[x]/51[x]	94/81	13	59
27	Burundi	125	160	4.4	207/43	240	44	39/15	41/25		
28	Benin	120	195	3.8	191/38	290	43	25[x]/10[x]	92/43		
29	Lao People's Dem. Rep.	120	160	4.2	169/30	80[x]	50	51/36	97/82		
30	Pakistan	120	170	96.0	4,018/733	390	50	36/15	57/31	20	42
31	Sudan	120	175	20.4	923/182	400	48	38/14	59/42	13[x]	50[x]
32	Iran (Islamic Rep. of)	115	175	42.5	1,700/286	2,160[x]	60	48[x]/24[x]	111/81	13[x]	54[x]
33	Nigeria	115	195	89.0	4,431/846	770	49	46/23	. ./. .		
34	Oman	115	220	1.1	52/10	6,250	50	. ./. .	89/63		
35	Tanzania, U. Rep. of	115	150	21.0	1,043/200	240	51	62[x]/31[x]	94/85	16[x]	50[x]
36	India	110	175	732.3	24,095/4028	260	53	55/26	100/68	16	49
37	Ivory Coast	110	210	9.2	415/68	710	47	45/24	91[x]/58[x]	20	50
38	Lesotho	110	150	1.4	60/9	460	49	58/81	94/126		
39	Uganda	110	140	14.6	720/134	220	52	65/41	65/49	17	47
40	Zaire	105	150	31.2	1,390/247	170	50	74/37	103[x]/74[x]	. .	. .
	High IMR countries (55–100) Median	**75**	**150**	**802T**	**28,404T/3,286T**	**900**	**58**	**68/47**	**105/99**	**12**	**58**
41	Cameroon, U. Rep. of	100	170	9.2	394/67	820	48	55[x]/25[x]	119/99		
42	Egypt	100	185	44.5	1,692/251	700	57	54[x]/22[x]	101/76	17	48
43	Peru	100	150	18.7	679/97	1,040	59	90/75	120/112	7	61
44	Togo	100	195	2.8	124/21	280	49	46/20	137/90		
45	Ghana	95	135	12.6	587/94	310	52	59/37	85/66		
46	Libyan Arab Jamahiriya	95	170	3.3	150/21	8,480	58	67[x]/30[x]	. ./. .		
47	Morocco	95	170	22.1	961/136	760	58	41/18	100/62	12	49
48	Algeria	90	175	20.6	916/117	2,320	58	57/32	106/82		
49	Turkey	90	205	47.7	1,536/177	1240	63	81/50	105/95	12	57
50	Zambia	90	140	6.2	296/42	580	51	79/58	100/89	11	61
51	Indonesia	85	145	159.4	4,841/655	560	53	78/58	116/109	14	49
52	South Africa	85	140	30.8	1,181/132	2,490	53	. ./. .	. ./. .		
53	Tunisia	85	165	6.9	232/28	1,290	61	61/32	126/100	15	42
54	Congo	80	155	1.7	73/9	1,230	47	70/44	. ./. .		
55	Honduras	80	150	4.1	177/22	670	60	59[x]/55[x]	102/100	7[x]	68[x]
56	Kenya	80	130	19.0	1,029/132	340	53	60/35	109/91	9	60
57	Zimbabwe	80	115	8.2	381/49	740	56	77/61	135/126		
58	Botswana	75	120	1.0	50/5	920	54	61/61	89/102	8	60
59	Dominican Rep.	75	130	6.0	195/18	1370	63	. ./. .	104/115	15	54
60	Iraq	75	150	14.7	648/69	3,020[x]	59	68/32	113/99	. .	. .
61	Nicaragua	75	150	3.1	134/15	880	60	. ./. .	101/107	9[x]	65[x]
62	Papua New Guinea	75	175	3.5	140/14	760	53	48/30	68/55		
63	Viet Nam	75	165	57.2	1,766/186	170[x]	59	91[x]/78[x]	120/105		
64	Brazil	70	120	129.8	3,929/377	1,880	63	76/73	106/99	7	67

		Infant mortality rate (under 1)		Total population (millions)	Annual no. of births/infant and child deaths (0–4) (thousands)	GNP per capita (US $)	Life expectancy at birth (years)	% adults literate male/female	% of age group enrolled in primary school male/female	% share of household income 1970–1982	
		1983	1960	1983	1983	1983	1983	1980–1983	1980–1983	lowest 40%	highest 20%
65	Burma	70	165	37.6	1,406/136	180	55	86/70	75*/70*	21	40
66	Ecuador	70	130	8.8	353/34	1420	63	84/76	117/114	..	..
67	El Salvador	70	155	5.2	208/20	710	65	73×/67×	68/68	16	47
68	Guatemala	70	130	7.9	301/36	1,120	61	54×/39×	78/67	13	60
69	Madagascar	65	115	9.5	415/43	310	50	68/55	78*/71*	..	..
70	Saudi Arabia	65	180	10.4	440/40	12,230	56	35/12	81/56	..	..
71	Syrian Arab Rep.	60	145	9.8	450/36	1,760	67	72/35	113/92	..	..
72	Jordan	55	145	3.2	144/10	1,640	64	80×/51×	105/100	..	..
73	Mexico	55	100	75.1	2,516/193	2,240	66	86/80	120/117	10	58
74	Mongolia	55	120	1.8	60/4	780×	65	93/86	105/107	..	..
	Middle IMR countries (25–50) Median	**36**	**85**	**1,641T**	**32,931T/1,688T**	**1,430**	**68**	**89/84**	**107/104**	**..**	**..**
75	Colombia	50	100	27.5	845/63	1,430	64	86/84	129/132	10	60
76	Philippines	50	85	52.1	1,663/138	760	65	84/83	115/113	14	54
77	Lebanon	48	75	2.6	78/5	1070×	65	83/64	115/105	..	..
78	Thailand	48	110	49.6	1,399/86	820	63	92/84	98/94	15	50
79	Albania	45	125	2.9	80/4	840×	71	../..	105/99	..	..
80	Paraguay	45	90	3.5	123/8	1,410	65	90/85	107/99	..	..
81	China	39	180	1,039.7	19,096/1041	300	67	79/51	128/103	18	39
82	Sri Lanka	39	75	15.7	422/22	330	67	91/81	104/99	19	43
83	Venezuela	39	90	17.3	598/28	3,840	68	87/83	106/104	10	54
84	United Arab Emirates	38	160	1.2	31/1	22,870	71	58×/38×	93/93	..	..
85	Argentina	36	60	29.6	722/31	2,070	70	94/94	107/107	14	50
86	Guyana	36	75	0.9	26/1	520	68	96/93	99/99	..	..
87	Yugoslavia	32	105	22.9	372/13	2,570	71	96/84	101/100	19	39
88	Korea, Dem. Rep. of	30	100	19.2	578/22	1,130×	65	../..	118×/114×	..	..
89	Korea, Rep. of	30	100	39.8	829/32	2,010	68	96/88	106/106	17	45
90	Malaysia	30	80	14.9	430/17	1,860	67	80/60	100/98	11	56
91	Uruguay	30	55	3.0	58/2	2,490	70	93×/94×	110/107	16×	46×
92	Mauritius	28	80	1.0	26/1	1,160	67	86/72	114/113	14	55
93	Romania	28	80	22.7	393/13	2,560	71	97/94	101/100	..	..
94	Panama	26	75	2.1	58/2	2,120	71	86/85	112/108	7	62
95	USSR	25	44	273.2	5,104/158	4,550×	71	../..	../..	..	..
	Low IMR countries (Under 25) Median	**11**	**37**	**876T**	**12,734T/183T**	**7,180**	**73**	**../..**	**101/101**	**18**	**40**
96	Trinidad and Tobago	24	65	1.1	27/1	6,850	70	96/93	107/108	13	50
97	Chile	23	115	11.7	287/8	1,870	67	94/91	112/110	13×	51×
98	Kuwait	23	100	1.6	58/2	17,880	71	73/59	99/97	..	..
99	Jamaica	21	70	2.3	64/2	1,300	70	../..	105/108	..	..
100	Portugal	20	85	9.9	176/4	2,230	71	85/75	122/123	15	49
101	Costa Rica	19	85	2.5	74/2	1,020	73	89×/88×	104/102	12	55
102	Hungary	19	60	10.8	154/3	2,150	71	99/99	100/100	21	36
103	Poland	19	70	36.9	680/15	3,900×	72	99/98	100/100	..	..
104	Bulgaria	17	60	9.1	140/3	4,150×	72	96/93	100/100	..	..
105	Cuba	17	70	9.9	167/3	1,410×	73	96×/96×	112/105	..	..
106	Czechoslovakia	16	30	15.5	250/5	5,820×	72	../..	88/90	..	..
107	Greece	15	55	9.8	155/3	3,920	74	96/85	102/102	..	..
108	Israel	14	36	4.1	97/2	5,370	74	96/91	96/97	8	40
109	New Zealand	13	24	3.2	51/1	7,730	73	../..	104/103	6	45
110	Austria	12	42	7.5	91/1	9,250	73	../..	99/98	..	..
111	Italy	12	48	56.6	726/10	6,400	74	96/95	101/101	18	44
112	Belgium	11	35	9.9	119/2	9,150	73	../..	97/98	22	36
113	German Dem. Rep.	11	44	16.7	209/3	7,180×	73	../..	94/96	..	..
114	USA	11	26	233.7	3,717/50	14,110	74	../..	../..	17	40
115	Australia	10	21	15.3	246/3	11,490	74	../..	105/104	15	47
116	Germany, Fed. Rep. of	10	37	61.3	625/8	11,430	73	../..	../..	20	40
117	Hong Kong	10	55	5.4	95/1	6,000	74	94/77	107/105	16	47
118	Ireland	10	34	3.5	73/1	5,000	73	../..	97/97	20	39
119	Spain	10	50	38.4	648/8	4,780	74	96/90	112/110	19	40
120	United Kingdom	10	24	55.6	714/9	9,200	74	../..	101/102	19	40
121	Canada	9	30	25.0	403/4	12,310	75	../..	107/104	17	40
122	France	9	33	54.3	746/9	10,500	75	../..	111/109	16	46
123	Singapore	9	41	2.5	45/1	6,620	72	92/74	112/107	..	..
124	Denmark	8	23	5.1	57/1	11,570	75	../..	100/101	17	39
125	Netherlands	8	19	14.4	167/2	9,890	76	../..	96/98	22	36
126	Norway	8	20	4.1	51/1	14,020	76	../..	99/100	19	38
127	Switzerland	8	23	6.3	51/(.)	16,290	76	../..	../..	20	38
128	Sweden	7	17	8.3	37/1	12,470	76	../..	98/99	21	42
129	Finland	6	25	4.8	51/(.)	10,740	73	../..	100/100	18	38
130	Japan	6	37	118.9	1,473/13	10,120	77	../..	100/100	22	38

TABLE 2: NUTRITION

		% of infants with low birth-weight 1979–83	% of mothers breast-feeding 1975–1983			% of children under five suffering from mild-moderate/severe malnutrition 1975–1983	Prevalence of wasting aged 12–23 months (% of age group) 1975–1983	Average index of food production per capita (1974–76=100) 1981–1983	Daily per capita calorie supply as % of requirements 1982
			3 months	6 months	12 months				
	Very high IMR countries (over 100) Median	15	96	94	85	32/7	21	98	95
1	Afghanistan	20	..	..	..	../..		105	94
2	Mali	13				../..	26	106	74
3	Sierra Leone	17	98*	94	83	24*/3*	36	98	85
4	Malawi	12	..	..	95*	../..	28	101	97
5	Guinea	18	..	..		../..	..	85	86
6	Kampuchea	..	100*	100*	93*	../..		98	81
7	Ethiopia	13	..	97*	95*	60*/10*	41	106	93
8	Mozambique	16	..	..		../..	..	68	79
9	Somalia	..	100*	100*	..	16y/..	62	72	91
10	Angola	19	96x	..	..	../..	..	82	87
11	Burkina Faso	21	..	..	..	../40*	17	100	79
12	Niger	15	65*	30*	15*	17*/9*	21	122	105
13	Bhutan	..	..	..	..	../..	..	104	
14	Central African Rep.	23	..	..	..	../..	..	94	97
15	Chad	11	..	..	..	../..	..	101	68
16	Guinea-Bissau	13	..	..	..	../..			86
17	Nepal	..	99	99	97	50*/7*	27	91	
18	Senegal	10	94	94	82		20	71	101
19	Mauritania	..				30*/10*	..	102	97
20	Yemen	..	80*	76*	55*	54*/4*	17	80	97
21	Yemen, Dem.		85x	73x	58x	../..	36	84	97
22	Bangladesh	50	98	97	89	63*/21*	21	101	83
23	Haiti	..	93	85	72	70*/3*	18	90	84
24	Liberia	..	96	92	64	17*/2*	7	92	98
25	Rwanda	20	..	..	..	29*/8*	23	114	95
26	Bolivia	10	93	91	..	49*/3*	1	87	90
27	Burundi	14	..	95*	90*	30*/3*	36	97	95
28	Benin	10	95*	90*	75*	../..	14	95	101
29	Lao People's Dem. Rep.	18	90*	90*	90*	../..	..	125	90
30	Pakistan	27	98	96	90	62*/10*	14	105	99
31	Sudan	17	91	86	72	50*/5*	..	94	96
32	Iran (Islamic Rep. of)	14	..	..	..	../..	..	103	119
33	Nigeria	18	98*	94*	90*	24*/16*	..	98	104
34	Oman	16	..	..	..	../..	..		
35	Tanzania, U. Rep. of	14	..	..	..	43*/7*	16	103	101
36	India	30	..	..	..	33*/5*	37	108	93
37	Ivory Coast	14	93*	90*	50*	23*/28*	21*	108	115
38	Lesotho	8	99	98	90	../..	7	76	100
39	Uganda	10	85*	70*	20*	15y/4y	..	91	78
40	Zaire	16	100	100	85	../..	11	93	98
	High IMR countries (55–100) Median	12	90	84	71	../..	..	93	110
41	Cameroon, U. Rep. of	13	..	98	97	../..	2	84	91
42	Egypt	7	..	91*	84*	46y/1y	3	92	128
43	Peru	9	78	72	55	42y/2y	1	82	90
44	Togo	17	..	99	90	../..	9	99	94
45	Ghana	15*	100*	70*	25*	../..	28	65	68
46	Libyan Arab Jamahiriya	..	..	..	..	../..	..	84	152
47	Morocco	9	93*	93*	93*	40y/5y	..	89	110
48	Algeria	12	..	..	..	../..	..	83	110
49	Turkey	8	99*	91*	51*	../..	..	104	122
50	Zambia	14	..	..	93*	../..	47	74	89
51	Indonesia	14	98*	97*	83*	27*/3*	17	121	111
52	South Africa	12	..	..	..	../..	3	93	116
53	Tunisia	7	95*	92*	71*	60y/4y	3x	87	111
54	Congo	15	97*	97*	85*	../..	..	99	113
55	Honduras	..	48*	28*	24*	29*/2*	..	107	95
56	Kenya	13	89	84	44	30*/2*	8	86	88
57	Zimbabwe	15	..	..	88*	../..	..	79	89
58	Botswana	12	..	..	97*	31y/1y	19		
59	Dominican Rep.	15	66	47	26	../..	4	95	96
60	Iraq	6	..	..	..	../..	..	110	118
61	Nicaragua	..	..	..	71*	65*/3*	0	74	101
62	Papua New Guinea	25	..	..	..	38y/..	52	95	79
63	Viet Nam	10	..	..	..	../..	..	111	93
64	Brazil	9	59*	19*	5*	../..	6x	113	110

		% of infants with low birth-weight 1979–83	% of mothers breast-feeding 1975–1983			% of children under five suffering from mild-moderate/severe malnutrition 1975–1983	Prevalence of wasting aged 12–23 months (% of age group) 1975–1983	Average index of food production per capita (1974–76=100) 1981–1983	Daily per capita calorie supply as % of requirements 1982
			3 months	6 months	12 months				
65	Burma	20	90*	90*	90*	50[y]/1[y]	48	121	115
66	Ecuador	..	..	..	57*	40[y]/..	..	92	91
67	El Salvador	13	..	77	55	52*/6*	1	91	90
68	Guatemala	18	..	84	74	../..	..	102	97
69	Madagascar	10	95*	95*	85*	../..	..	90	114
70	Saudi Arabia	..	..	..	..	../..	9	34	129
71	Syrian Arab Rep.	..	88	72	41	../..	..	129	123
72	Jordan	7	79	70	41	../..	9	107	117
73	Mexico	12	62	48	27	../..	..	106	128
74	Mongolia	10	..	..	..	../..	..	88	115
	Middle IMR countries (25–50) Median	8	..	..	..	../..	..	110	121
75	Colombia	10	78	63	44	43[y]/8[y]	10	106	110
76	Philippines	20	68	58	28	40[y]/3[y]	16	113	106
77	Lebanon	12	..	..	..	../	..	124	121
78	Thailand	38	48	47	20	34*/1*	18	112	103
79	Albania	..	..	..	..	../..	..	105	121
80	Paraguay	..	80	77	49	../..	..	109	122
81	China	6	..	..	..	../..	..	119	109
82	Sri Lanka	27	83	74	48	../..	22	127	107
83	Venezuela	9	50	40	30	../..	..	91	104
84	United Arab Emirates	7	..	..	..	../..	..	..	..
85	Argentina	6	..	..	..	../..	..	112	127
86	Guyana	..	77	60	35	../..	..	108	143
87	Yugoslavia	7	..	..	..	../..	1	111	130
88	Korea, Dem. Rep. of	..	..	..	..	../..	..		
89	Korea, Rep. of	9	94[x]	93[x]	84[x]	../..	..	109	125
90	Malaysia	11	47[x]	34[x]	19[x]	../..	6	113	120
91	Uruguay	8	51*	21*	13*	../..	..	106	103
92	Mauritius	11	..	..	..	../..	..		
93	Romania	..	..	..	..	../..	..	114	126
94	Panama	10	62	48	30	48[y]/3[y]	8	102	108
95	USSR	8	..	..	..	../..	..	98	132
	Low IMR countries (under 25) Median	6	..	..	..	../..	..	108	130
96	Trinidad and Tobago	..	59	50	14	../	..	70	127
97	Chile	9	..	..	..	10[y]/(.)[y]	11	102	109
98	Kuwait	7*	..	..	..	../..	3	..	111
99	Jamaica	12	57	40	16	../..	14	95	111
100	Portugal	8	..	..	..	../..	..	82	130
101	Costa Rica	9	38	20	9	46*/(.)*	..	88	118
102	Hungary	12	45	21	4	../..	..	119	134
103	Poland	8	42	32	..	../..	..	91	126
104	Bulgaria	..	..	..	..	../..	..	117	148
105	Cuba	9	..	..	..	../..	..	127	130
106	Czechoslovakia	6	..	..	..	../..	..	110	146
107	Greece	6	..	..	..	../..	..	102	142
108	Israel	7	..	..	..	../..	..	93	119
109	New Zealand	5	..	..	..	../..	..	110	134
110	Austria	6	..	..	..	../..	..	111	134
111	Italy	7	..	..	..	../..	1	112	140
112	Belgium	6	..	..	..	../..	..	103	142
113	German Dem. Rep.	6	..	..	..	../..	..	108	145
114	USA	7	33	25	8	../..	2	108	137
115	Australia	5	..	..	..	../..	..	103	120
116	Germany, Fed. Rep. of	6	..	..	..	../..	..	113	127
117	Hong Kong	8	..	8[x]	..	../..	..	101	121
118	Ireland	5	..	..	..	../..	..	97	162
119	Spain	..	..	..	..	../..	..	101	136
120	United Kingdom	7	..	..	..	../..	..	119	128
121	Canada	6	26	3	..	../..	..	121	129
122	France	5	9	..	..	../..	(.)	112	142
123	Singapore	7	..	..	..	../..	9	107	128
124	Denmark	6	..	..	..	../..	..	117	150
125	Netherlands	4	17	..	..	../..	..	112	133
126	Norway	4	..	..	..	../..	..	114	119
127	Switzerland	5	..	..	..	../..	..	112	128
128	Sweden	4	35[x]	14[x]	..	../..	..	108	120
129	Finland	4	..	..	..	../..	..	101	114
130	Japan	5	56[x]	..	..	../..	4	91	124

TABLE 3: HEALTH

#		% of population with access to drinking water 1975–1983			% of one-year-old children fully immunized 1981–1983				% of pregnant women fully immunized against tetanus 1981–1983	Life expectancy at birth (years)	
		Total	Urban	Rural	TB	DPT	Polio	Measles		1960	1983
	Very high IMR countries (over 100) Median	21	50	15	30	40	13	23	11	37	46
1	Afghanistan	10	28	8	10	5	5	8	1	33	37
2	Mali	6	37	(.)	19	..	10	..	1	34	42
3	Sierra Leone	16	50	2	30	12	10	23	..	29	34
4	Malawi	41	77	37	72*	66*	68*	64*	..	36	45
5	Guinea	17	69	2	..	..	..	77*	..	32	40
6	Kampuchea	..	..	..	..	..	..	..	..	41	43
7	Ethiopia	..	..	..	16	9	9	16	3	35	43
8	Mozambique	13*	50*	7*	40	14	16	22	40	39	49
9	Somalia	32*	60*	20*	10	5	5	12*	8*	35	43
10	Angola	21	85	10	67*	13*	7y	17y	21*	32	42
11	Burkina Faso	30	27	31	21*	13*	13*	71*	11	32	42
12	Niger	33	41	32	70*	5*	5*	16*	9*	35	43
13	Bhutan	7	50	5	9	4	4	18	..	38	46
14	Central African Rep.	16	..	..	25	14	14	16	16	34	43
15	Chad	26	..	..	..	..	..	..	..	34	43
16	Guinea-Bissau	10	18	8	38*	16*	3*	27*	..	35	43
17	Nepal	12	83	7	49*	17*	2*	10*	7*	38	46
18	Senegal	42	77	25	56*	22*	22*	38*	..	36	43
19	Mauritania	16*	..	..	74*	21*	21*	55*	1	35	44
20	Yemen	20*	50*	17*	29*	39*	39*	48*	(.)	35	44
21	Yemen, Dem	44	85	25	12x	8x	8x	9x	3	35	46
22	Bangladesh	38	26	40	2	1	1	1	1	43	48
23	Haiti	14*	40*	5*	65*	13*	13*	8*	67*	41	53
24	Liberia	20	..	..	87	39	26	..	60	39	49
25	Rwanda	54	48	55	60*	36*	25*	53*	19*	42	50
26	Bolivia	37	69	10	30	19x	64*	56x	..	42	51
27	Burundi	24	90	20	65	37*	29*	38*	17*	37	44
28	Benin	20	26	15	7*	6*	5*	15*	35*	34	43
29	Lao People's Dem. Rep.	5*	20*	3*	6*	5*	5*	4*	4*	43	50
30	Pakistan	35	72	20	68*	49*	60*	47*	8*	42	50
31	Sudan	40*	..	..	8x	4x	4x	3x	8	38	48
32	Iran (Islamic Rep. of)	..	..	..	10	33	34	38	4	48	60
33	Nigeria	28*	68*	18*	23	24*	24*	20*	11	39	49
34	Oman	..	..	..	89	10	10	37	16	37	50
35	Tanzania, U. Rep. of	47*	85*	41*	84	58	56	82	35	39	51
36	India	41	77	31	20	40	18	(.)	31	41	53
37	Ivory Coast	20*	30*	10*	16x	11x	11x	31x	32*	37	47
38	Lesotho	14	37	11	87*	66*	64*	63*	..	39	49
39	Uganda	..	..	..	18	9	8	22	20	42	52
40	Zaire	..	..	..	65*	63*	66*	53*	47*	40	50
	High IMR countries (55–100) Median	49	80	31	56	47	52	54	17	45	58
41	Cameroon, U. Rep. of	26	..	..	8	5	5	16	..	38	48
42	Egypt	75	88	64	53*	57*	67*	41*	20*	45	57
43	Peru	42*	67*	15*	58	20	21*	27	8*	46	59
44	Togo	34*	52*	30*	44	9	9	47	57	38	49
45	Ghana	47	72	33	41*	14*	11*	10*	2*	42	52
46	Libyan Arab Jamahiriya	98	100	90	60	60	60	62	7	45	58
47	Morocco	..	..	..	28*	52*	66*	68*	..	45	58
48	Algeria	77	..	..	59	33	30	17	..	46	58
49	Turkey	63*	63*	63*	47	50*	61	64	..	49	63
50	Zambia	46*	..	..	87*	49*	47*	56*	38*	40	51
51	Indonesia	..	..	..	61	30x	4	5*	20	40	53
52	South Africa	..	..	..	..	..	..	..	..	43	53
53	Tunisia	58*	86*	27*	98*	59*	54*	56*	8*	47	61
54	Congo	20*	40*	8*	97*	53*	53*	67*	..	38	47
55	Honduras	44	50	40	74	70	68	66x	11*	45	60
56	Kenya	26	85	15	76*	58*	57*	55*	..	41	53
57	Zimbabwe	52*	..	..	87*	66*	61*	53*	30*	44	56
58	Botswana	76*	98*	72*	81*	82*	77*	75*	24*	44	54
59	Dominican Rep.	59	85	33	41	24	84y	23y	26*	49	63
60	Iraq	73*	97*	22*	62	16	16	5	2	47	59
61	Nicaragua	38*	70*	7*	89	33*	82*	41*	31*	45	60
62	Papua New Guinea	16	55	10	49	43x	45	..	..	39	53
63	Viet Nam	..	..	32	..	..	..	..	..	43	59
64	Brazil	71	80	51	79*	67*	92x	80x	..	53	63

		% of population with access to drinking water 1975–1983			% of one-year-old children fully immunized 1981–1983				% of pregnant women fully immunized against tetanus 1981–1983	Life expectancy at birth (years)	
		Total	Urban	Rural	TB	DPT	Polio	Measles		1960	1983
65	Burma	21	38	5	34 *	13 *	5 *	..	17 *	43	55
66	Ecuador	45	82	16	64	48 *	47 *	54 *	11 *	50	63
67	El Salvador	51	67	40	49	45 *	41 ˣ	47 ˣ	26 ˣ	49	65
68	Guatemala	45	89	18	25	44	44	12	..	45	61
69	Madagascar	22	80	7	13	35	3	..	..	40	50
70	Saudi Arabia	..	98	..	88 *	81 *	81 *	79 *	..	42	56
71	Syrian Arab Rep.	71	98	54	49 *	23 *	23 *	21 *	2	49	67
72	Jordan	89	100	65	2	80 *	80 *	76 *	7	46	64
73	Mexico	72 *	..	..	25 *	30	85	85 ˣ	..	55	66
74	Mongolia	..	..	..	52	79	50	89	..	50	65
	Middle IMR countries (25–50) Median	..	..	..	80	65	67	62	..	59	68
75	Colombia	92	100	79	68 *	60 *	61 *	53 *	6 *	54	64
76	Philippines	40 *	55 *	33 *	76 *	68 *	54 *	65 *	21 *	51	65
77	Lebanon	92 *	95 *	85 *	..	4	9	1	40 *	59	65
78	Thailand	42 *	50 *	41 *	76 *	53 *	53 *	..	40 *	51	63
79	Albania	..	..	..	93	94	92	90	..	59	71
80	Paraguay	21	39	10	80 *	67 *	47	62 *	44 *	55	65
81	China	..	85 *	..	..	..	..	..	..	34	67
82	Sri Lanka	19 *	49 *	10 *	63	64	66	..	42	61	67
83	Venezuela	81	91	50	48	49	67	42	..	56	68
84	United Arab Emirates	93	95	81	31 *	47 *	47 *	24 *	..	50	71
85	Argentina	57	65	17	64	65	94	62	..	65	70
86	Guyana	72	100	60	78 *	56	73 *	68 *	..	59	68
87	Yugoslavia	..	..	..	99	90	95	95 ˣ	..	61	71
88	Korea, Dem. Rep. of	..	..	..	..	..	..	..	..	53	65
89	Korea, Rep. of	78	86	61	99	80 *	81 *	55	..	53	68
90	Malaysia	63	90	49	96	60	61	..	..	52	67
91	Uruguay	..	..	..	93 *	76 *	74 ˣ	82 ˣ	13 *	67	70
92	Mauritius	95 *	95 *	95 *	98	97	97	..	1	58	67
93	Romania	..	..	..	..	..	..	..	..	64	71
94	Panama	82	100	65	81	61	60	60	16 ˣ	59	71
95	USSR	..	..	..	..	95	95	95 ˣ	..	68	71
	Low IMR countries (under 25) Median	..	..	..	90	86	91	71	..	69	73
96	Trinidad and Tobago	98	100	93	..	60	61	..	..	62	70
97	Chile	84	100	17	96 *	94 *	96 *	100 *	..	56	67
98	Kuwait	89	..	..	0	82	89	14	24	58	71
99	Jamaica	86	..	..	56	51	47	15	..	61	70
100	Portugal	..	..	..	..	90	85	70 ˣ	..	62	71
101	Costa Rica	79 *	100 *	63 *	56	56	54 *	73	..	60	73
102	Hungary	..	..	..	99	99	98	99 ˣ	..	67	71
103	Poland	..	..	..	95	95	95	65 ˣ	..	66	72
104	Bulgaria	..	..	..	97	97	98	98 ˣ	98	67	72
105	Cuba	..	..	..	91	91	93 ʸ	71	..	62	73
106	Czechoslovakia	..	..	..	95	95	95	95 ˣ	..	70	72
107	Greece	..	..	..	12	31	95	..	..	68	74
108	Israel	..	..	..	68	86	92	69	..	68	74
109	New Zealand	..	..	..	..	73 ˣ	..	80 ˣ	..	71	73
110	Austria	..	..	..	90	90	90	90 ˣ	..	68	73
111	Italy	..	..	..	..	..	..	..	..	69	74
112	Belgium	..	..	..	..	95	99	50 ˣ	..	70	73
113	German Dem. Rep.	..	..	..	95	80	90	95 ˣ	..	69	73
114	USA	..	..	..	..	..	..	96 ˣ	..	70	74
115	Australia	..	..	..	..	33 ˣ	17 ˣ	..	..	70	74
116	Germany, Fed. Rep. of	..	..	..	40	50	80	35 ˣ	..	69	73
117	Hong Kong	100	100	95	100 *	80	90	74 ˣ	..	63	74
118	Ireland	..	..	..	..	33	65	..	..	69	73
119	Spain	..	..	..	..	..	..	..	..	68	74
120	United Kingdom	..	..	..	..	35	79	50 ˣ	..	70	74
121	Canada	..	..	..	..	..	..	..	..	71	75
122	France	..	..	..	81	90	92	15 ˣ	..	70	75
123	Singapore	100	..	..	85 *	86	88	92	..	63	72
124	Denmark	..	..	..	..	85	97	..	..	72	75
125	Netherlands	..	..	..	..	97	97	93 ˣ	..	73	76
126	Norway	..	..	..	..	..	..	..	..	73	76
127	Switzerland	..	..	..	..	..	..	..	..	71	76
128	Sweden	..	..	..	..	99 ˣ	99	56 ˣ	..	73	76
129	Finland	..	..	..	90	92	90	70 ˣ	..	68	73
130	Japan	..	..	..	96	81	95 ˣ	66 ˣ	..	67	77

TABLE 4: EDUCATION

		Adult literacy rate		No. of radio receivers per 1,000 population 1982	Primary-school enrolment ratio			% of grade 1 enrolment completing primary school 1975–1983	Secondary-school enrolment ratio 1980–1983 male/female
		1970 male/female	1980–83 male/female		1960 (gross) male/female	1980–83 (gross) male/female	1980–83 (net) male/female		
	Very high IMR countries (over 100) Median	**27/10**	**39/16**	**51**	**36/16**	**74/42**	**../..**	**49**	**19/8**
1	Afghanistan	13/2	30^x/5^x	80	15/2	19/9	16/8	54	11/5
2	Mali	11/4	14^x/6^x	16	14/6	35^x/20^x	../..	61	13^x/5^x
3	Sierra Leone	18/8	31/17	177	30/15	46^y/32^y	37^y/26^y	48	23^y/10^y
4	Malawi	42/18	48/25	46	81/45	72/51	47/39	28	6/2
5	Guinea	21/7	35/14	29	44/16	44/21		...	21/8
6	Kampuchea	71/23	78/39	115	../..	../..			../..
7	Ethiopia	8/(.)	../..	92	11/3	58/34	../..	49*	17/9
8	Mozambique	29/14	44/12	25	60/36	91/68	51/41	26	8/4
9	Somalia	5/1	11/3	25	13/5	33/18	24/13	33*	19/8
10	Angola	16/7	36/19	20	../..	../..	../..	24	../..
11	Burkina Faso	13/3	15^x/3^x	19	12/5	31/18	26/15	75	5/2
12	Niger	6/2	14/6	48	7/3	34/19	../..	67	5^x/2^x
13	Bhutan	../..	../..	8	5/..	31/16	../..	25	6/1
14	Central African Rep.	26/6	48/19	56	53/12	98/51	80/42	53	24/8
15	Chad	20/2	35/8	26	29/4	51^x/19^x	37^x/14^x	29	6^x/1^x
16	Guinea-Bissau	13/6	33^x/9^x	45	35/15	88/40	76/35	18	17/4
17	Nepal	23/3	32/9	23	19/1	93/39	../..	27*	32/9
18	Senegal	18/5	31/14	62	36/17	61/41	49/33	86	17/8
19	Mauritania	../..	../..	98	13/3	45/29	../..	80	19/6
20	Yemen	9/1	18/2	20	14/..	99/17	../..	15*	12/2
21	Yemen, Dem.	31/9	48^x/8^x	55	20/5	94/34	../..		24/11
22	Bangladesh	36/12	40/18	8	66/26	74/46	63/39	20	25/10
23	Haiti	26/17	37/33	21	50/42	74/64	42/38	45	13/12
24	Liberia	27/8	30^x/12^x	173	45/18	95/57	../..		33/13
25	Rwanda	43/21	51^x/27^x	30	68/30	65/60	61/58	47	3/2
26	Bolivia	68/46	76^x/51^x	571	78/50	94/81	82/72	32*	38/32
27	Burundi	29/10	39/15	37	27/9	41/25	27/17	94	4/2
28	Benin	23/8	25^x/10^x	75	38/15	92/43	../..	63	32/12
29	Lao People's Dem. Rep.	37/28	51/36	100	34/16	97/82	../..		20/13
30	Pakistan	30/11	36/15	75	46/13	57/31	../..	45*	20/8
31	Sudan	28/6	38/14	75	35/14	59/42	../..	69	21/15
32	Iran (Islamic Rep. of)	40/17	48^x/24^x	179	56/27	111/81	../..	70^x	47/32
33	Nigeria	35/14	46/23	80	46/27	../..	../..		../..
34	Oman	../..	../..	185	../..	89/63	75/56	60	34/15
35	Tanzania, U. Rep. of	48/18	62^x/31^x	28	33/18	94/85	73/72	76	4/2
36	India	47/20	55/26	56	80/40	100/68	../..	38^x	44/24
37	Ivory Coast	26/10	45/24	128	68/24	91^x/58^x	../..	89	25^x/11^x
38	Lesotho	49/74	58/81	28	63/102	94/126	60/82	38	16/23
39	Uganda	52/30	65/41	22	65/32	65/49	43/37	58	10/5
40	Zaire	61/22	74/37	53^x	88/32	103^x/74^x	../..	65	33^x/13^x
	High IMR countries (55–100) Median	**57/36**	**68/50**	**157**	**81/50**	**105/99**	**83/79**	**68**	**39/26**
41	Cameroon, U. Rep. of	47/19	55^x/25^x	90	87/43	119/99	81^x/69^x	67	26/15
42	Egypt	50/20	54^x/22^x	157	80/52	101/76	67/43	64	67/45
43	Peru	81/60	90/75	161	95/71	120/112	94/89	70	64/57
44	Togo	27/7	46/20	209	63/24	137/90	91/64	43	43/14
45	Ghana	43/18	59/37	172	52/25	85/66	../..	75	42/26
46	Libyan Arab Jamahiriya	60/13	67^x/30^x	50	92/24	../..	../..	82	../..
47	Morocco	34/10	41/18	157	67/27	100/62	67/43	80	34/22
48	Algeria	39/11	57/32	207	55/37	106/82	89/71	77	49/35
49	Turkey	69/35	81/50	119	90/58	105/95	../..	85*	45/26
50	Zambia	66/37	79/58	26	51/34	100/89	85/79	85	21/12
51	Indonesia	66/42	78/58	131	86/58	116/109	100/95	68	39/28
52	South Africa	../..	../..	274	94/85	../..	../..		../..
53	Tunisia	44/17	61/32	164	88/43	126/100	97/81	78	41/26
54	Congo	50/19	70/44	63	103/53	../..	../..	74	../..
55	Honduras	55/50	59^x/55^x	48	68/67	102/100	81/79	27*	28/36
56	Kenya	44/19	60/35	34	64/30	109/91	73/70	62	21/14
57	Zimbabwe	63/47	77/61	40	../..	135/126	100/100		36/25
58	Botswana	37/44	61/61	116	35/48	89/102	71/81	73	19/23
59	Dominican Rep.	69/65	../..	44	99/98	104/115	../..	29^x	../..
60	Iraq	50/18	68/32	179	94/36	113/99	98/90	87	67/37
61	Nicaragua	58/57	../..	274	65/66	101/107	74/76	27	38/45
62	Papua New Guinea	39/24	48/30	68	59/7	68/55	../..	67*	15/8
63	Viet Nam	../..	91^x/78^x	..	../..	120/105	../..	47	53/43
64	Brazil	69/63	76/73	355	97/93	106/99	76^x/76^x	27	29^x/35^x

		Adult literacy rate		No. of radio receivers per 1,000 population 1982	Primary-school enrolment ratio			% of grade 1 enrolment completing primary school 1975–1983	Secondary-school enrolment ratio 1980–1983 male/female
		1970 male/female	1980–83 male/female		1960 (gross) male/female	1980–83 (gross) male/female	1980–83 (net) male/female		
65	Burma	85/57	86/70	22	61/52	75*/70*	66×/64×	32×	22×/18×
66	Ecuador	75/68	84/76	319	87/79	117/114	88×/86×	62	53/54
67	El Salvador	61/53	73×/67×	336	82/77	68/68	56/57	68*	22/23
68	Guatemala	51/37	54×/39×	43	50/39	78/67	63/56	38	16/15
69	Madagascar	56/43	68/55	206	58/45	78*/71*	../..	50	../..
70	Saudi Arabia	15/2	35/12	312	22/2	81/56	64/40	79	38/25
71	Syrian Arab Rep.	60/20	72/35	192	89/39	113/92	100/83	87	63/40
72	Jordan	64/29	80×/51×	156	94/59	105/100	95/90	97	79/76
73	Mexico	78/69	86/80	292	82/77	120/117	../..	66	54/49
74	Mongolia	87/74	93/86	99	79/78	105/107	../..	95	82/90
	Middle IMR countries (25–50) Median	85/76	89/84	214	101/94	106/104	../..	73	58/61
75	Colombia	79/76	86/84	122	77/77	129/132	../..	37×	45/51
76	Philippines	83/80	84/83	43	98/93	115/113	97/98	72	61/66
77	Lebanon	79/58	83/64	748	105/99	115/105	../..		61/63
78	Thailand	86/72	92/84	149	88/79	98/94	../..	43	30/28
79	Albania	../..	../..	75	102/86	105/99	../..		72/61
80	Paraguay	84/75	90/85	74	105/90	107/99	92/89	48	37/35
81	China	../..	79/51	64	../..	128/103	../..	66*	49/32
82	Sri Lanka	85/69	91/81	112	100/90	104/99	../..	91	52/56
83	Venezuela	79/71	87/83	408	100/100	106/104	../..	68	37/46
84	United Arab Emirates	24/7	58×/38×	342	../..	93/93	73/74	97	48/59
85	Argentina	94/92	94/94	727	98/99	107/107	../..	66	57/62
86	Guyana	94/89	96/93	352	107/106	99/99	89/91	84	58/62
87	Yugoslavia	92/76	96/84	219	113/108	101/100	../..	98	85/79
88	Korea, Dem. Rep. of	../..	../..		../..	118×/114×	../..		../..
89	Korea, Rep. of	94/81	96/88	432	99/89	106/106	100/100	94	89/82
90	Malaysia	71/48	80/60	429×	108/83	100/98	../..	97	50/49
91	Uruguay	93/93	93×/94×	577	111/111	110/107	../..	88	59/60
92	Mauritius	77/59	86/72	209	103/93	114/113	99/99		51/47
93	Romania	96/91	97/94	146	101/95	101/100	../..		69/74
94	Panama	81/81	86/85	159	98/94	112/108	92/92	73	59/68
95	USSR	98/97	../..	504	100/100	../..	../..		../..
	Low IMR countries (under 25) Median	../..	../..	352	104/102	100/101	96/96	94	80/82
96	Trinidad and Tobago	95/89	96/93	291	89/87	107/108	76×/78×	78	69/72
97	Chile	90/88	94/91	300	111/107	112/110	90*/89*	59	62/68
98	Kuwait	65/42	73/59	286	131/102	99/97	85/79	98	85/78
99	Jamaica	96/97	96/97	386	92/93	105/108	97/100	80	72/80
100	Portugal	78/65	85/75	164	132/129	122/123	82/81	88×	41/46
101	Costa Rica	88/87	89×/88×	84	97/95	104/102	88/89	75	43/49
102	Hungary	98/98	99/99	262	103/100	100/100	98/98	93	74/72
103	Poland	98/98	99/98	246	110/107	100/100	99/99	94	73/78
104	Bulgaria	94/89	96/93	229	94/92	100/100	98/97	87	83/82
105	Cuba	86/87	96×/96×	317	109/109	112/105	99/98	86	70/75
106	Czechoslovakia	../..	../..	308	93/93	88/90	../..	94	34/59
107	Greece	93/76	96/85	352	104/101	102/102	95/96	93	85/76
108	Israel	93/83	96/91	286	99/97	96/97	../..		72/82
109	New Zealand	../..	../..	893	110/106	104/103	99/99		83/86
110	Austria	../..	../..	475	106/104	99/98	86/87	95	72/76
111	Italy	95/93	96/95	247	112/109	101/101	../..	100	73/72
112	Belgium	99/99	../..	507	111/108	97/98	93/95	75	93/94
113	German Dem. Rep.	../..	../..	385	111/113	94/96	../..		91/86
114	USA	99/99	../..	2133	../..	../..	../..		../..
115	Australia	../..	../..	1159	103/103	105/104	96/96		91/93
116	Germany, Fed. Rep. of	../..	../..	392	../..	../..	79/81	96	47/53
117	Hong Kong	90/64	94/77	506	93/79	107/105	96/95	98	64/70
118	Ireland	../..	../..	445	107/112	97/97	87/87		88/98
119	Spain	93/87	96/90	274	106/116	112/110	100/100	95	88/93
120	United Kingdom	../..	../..	986	92/92	101/102	94/95		83/85
121	Canada	../..	../..	758	108/105	107/104	97/96		98/97
122	France	99/98	../..	854	144/143	111/109	100×/100×	95	77/93
123	Singapore	82/55	92/74	201	121/101	112/107	98/98	90	64/65
124	Denmark	../..	../..	384	103/103	100/101	../..	99	106/104
125	Netherlands	../..	../..	318	105/104	96/98	88/91	95	99/96
126	Norway	../..	../..	365	100/100	99/100	98/99	100	92/98
127	Switzerland	../..	../..	370	118/118	../..	../..	99	../..
128	Sweden	../..	../..	853	95/96	98/99	97/97	98	80/90
129	Finland	../..	../..	933	100/95	100/100	../..		95/107
130	Japan	99/99	../..	696	103/102	100/100	100/100	100	92/93

TABLE 5: DEMOGRAPHIC INDICATORS

		Total population/ child population (ages 0–4) (millions) 1983	Population annual growth rate (%) 1973–1983	Infant mortality rate under 1		Infant and child mortality rate under 5		Crude death rate		Crude birth rate		Total fertility rate 1983	% population urbanized 1983	Average annual growth rate of urban population (%) 1973–83
				1960	1983	1960	1983	1960	1983	1960	1983			
	Very high IMR countries (over 100) Median	1,346T/212T	2.6	190	135	310	220	26	19	48	47	6.4	21	5.1
1	Afghanistan	14.2/2.5	2.6	220	195	390	340	31	27	50	50	6.9	17	6.2
2	Mali	7.6/1.4	2.5	210	180	370	310	30	22	50	50	6.7	20	4.4
3	Sierra Leone	3.5/0.6	2.1	225	180	400	310	36	30	48	47	6.1	27	3.3
4	Malawi	6.6/1.3	3.0	210	165	370	285	29	20	53	52	7.0	11	7.3
5	Guinea	5.2/0.9	2.0	215	160	355	270	34	24	48	47	6.2	21	6.3
6	Kampuchea	6.9/0.8	. .	150	160	225	240	22	20	45	45	5.1	15	. .
7	Ethiopia	34.5/6.5	2.7	180	155	300	260	29	21	51	49	6.7	16	6.0
8	Mozambique	13.3/2.4	2.6	175	155	305	260	24	16	45	44	6.1	17	10.2
9	Somalia	5.3/0.9	2.8	180	155	300	260	29	21	47	46	6.1	33	5.5
10	Angola	8.3/1.5	2.6	215	150	360	250	32	22	50	47	6.4	23	6.0
11	Burkina Faso	6.6/1.2	1.9	230	150	410	255	32	22	50	48	6.5	8	4.8
12	Niger	5.8/1.1	3.0	195	145	330	245	33	23	46	51	7.1	15	7.0
13	Bhutan	1.4/0.2	1.9	190	140	305	215	26	18	43	38	5.5	4	4.6
14	Central African Rep.	2.4/0.4	2.3	190	140	315	240	31	22	44	45	5.9	44	4.6
15	Chad	4.8/0.8	2.1	200	140	335	240	30	21	46	44	5.9	20	6.6
16	Guinea-Bissau	0.9/0.1	. .	195	140	325	240	28	22	41	41	5.4	26	. .
17	Nepal	15.7/2.6	2.6	190	140	305	215	26	18	46	42	6.3	5	8.2
18	Senegal	6.2/1.1	2.8	185	140	320	240	28	21	48	48	6.5	41	3.8
19	Mauritania	1.8/0.3	2.2	195	135	325	230	29	21	51	50	6.9	32	4.6
20	Yemen	6.2/1.1	2.9	220	135	390	225	30	22	50	48	6.8	18	8.8
21	Yemen, Dem.	2.0/0.4	2.2	220	135	390	225	30	19	51	48	6.9	39	3.5
22	Bangladesh	95.8/17.2	2.4	160	130	275	205	23	17	47	45	6.1	11	7.6
23	Haiti	6.3/1.1	1.8	205	130	305	190	24	14	45	41	5.7	27	4.2
24	Liberia	2.1/0.4	3.3	185	130	310	225	25	17	46	49	6.9	38	6.1
25	Rwanda	5.7/1.2	3.4	150	130	255	225	23	17	51	51	7.3	5	6.6
26	Bolivia	6.0/1.0	2.6	170	125	290	195	23	16	47	44	6.3	43	3.3
27	Burundi	4.4/0.8	2.2	160	125	270	210	26	21	43	48	6.4	2	3.2
28	Benin	3.8/0.7	2.8	195	120	325	200	34	22	46	51	7.0	35	4.7
29	Lao People's Dem. Rep.	4.2/0.7	2.2	160	120	240	180	20	16	42	41	5.8	15	5.7
30	Pakistan	96.0/16.6	3.0	170	120	295	180	25	15	49	43	5.8	29	4.3
31	Sudan	20.4/3.7	3.2	175	120	305	200	26	17	47	46	6.6	28	5.5
32	Iran (Islamic Rep. of)	42.5/7.1	3.1	175	115	265	170	20	10	55	41	5.6	53	5.1
33	Nigeria	89.0/17.7	2.7	195	115	325	190	25	17	52	50	7.1	22	5.1
34	Oman	1.1/0.2	4.8	220	115	390	185	30	16	51	47	7.1	8	17.6
35	Tanzania, U. Rep. of	21.0/4.2	3.3	150	115	255	190	25	15	51	50	7.1	14	8.6
36	India	732.3/101.1	2.3	175	110	300	165	26	13	48	33	4.4	25	4.2
37	Ivory Coast	9.2/1.7	4.6	210	110	340	165	28	18	44	46	6.7	40	8.5
38	Lesotho	1.4/0.2	2.5	150	110	215	150	25	16	43	42	5.8	5	21.4
39	Uganda	14.6/2.9	2.8	140	110	235	185	22	15	50	50	6.9	13	0.3
40	Zaire	31.2/5.7	2.5	150	105	255	180	25	16	48	45	6.1	42	6.9
	High IMR countries (55–100) Median	802T/124T	2.8	150	75	240	115	21	11	47	43	6.0	46	4.8
41	Cameroon, U. Rep. of	9.2/1.6	3.1	170	100	290	170	26	18	45	43	5.8	39	8.4
42	Egypt	44.5/7.1	2.5	185	100	310	150	21	13	46	38	5.2	46	2.9
43	Peru	18.7/2.9	2.4	150	100	245	145	20	11	47	37	5.0	66	3.6
44	Togo	2.8/0.5	2.6	195	100	325	170	27	17	47	45	6.1	19	6.6
45	Ghana	12.6/2.4	3.1	135	95	230	160	21	15	46	47	6.5	38	5.3
46	Libyan Arab Jamahiriya	3.3/0.6	4.3	170	95	290	140	20	11	49	46	7.2	61	8.1
47	Morocco	22.1/4.0	2.6	170	95	280	140	23	11	50	44	6.4	43	4.2
48	Algeria	20.6/3.8	3.1	175	90	285	130	21	12	51	45	7.0	64	5.4
49	Turkey	47.7/6.5	2.2	205	90	275	115	16	9	45	33	4.4	47	3.7
50	Zambia	6.2/1.2	3.2	140	90	235	140	24	15	50	48	6.8	47	6.5
51	Indonesia	159.4/21.6	2.3	145	85	245	135	24	13	45	31	3.9	24	4.8
52	South Africa	30.8/4.9	2.4	140	85	200	110	22	14	41	39	5.1	55	3.9
53	Tunisia	6.9/1.0	2.5	165	85	265	120	20	10	47	34	4.9	55	3.7
54	Congo	1.7/0.3	3.1	155	80	260	130	26	19	45	44	6.0	39	5.5
55	Honduras	4.1/0.8	3.5	150	80	245	125	20	10	51	44	6.5	38	5.8
56	Kenya	19.0/4.2	4.0	130	80	220	130	25	14	57	55	8.1	16	8.0
57	Zimbabwe	8.2/1.6	3.2	115	80	190	130	20	12	47	47	6.6	23	6.0
58	Botswana	1.0/0.2	. .	120	75	180	105	21	13	51	50	6.5	18	. .
59	Dominican Rep.	6.0/0.9	2.4	130	75	215	95	18	8	49	33	4.2	54	4.7
60	Iraq	14.7/2.7	3.6	150	75	245	105	21	11	49	45	6.7	69	5.3
61	Nicaragua	3.1/0.6	3.9	150	75	225	115	20	10	52	44	5.9	58	5.2
62	Papua New Guinea	3.5/0.6	2.1	175	75	260	105	25	14	44	40	6.0	14	5.1
63	Viet Nam	57.2/8.4	2.7	165	75	245	105	22	10	42	31	4.3	20	2.4
64	Brazil	129.8/17.5	2.3	120	70	170	95	14	8	43	31	3.8	71	4.1

		Total population/ child population (ages 0–4) (millions) 1983	Population annual growth rate (%) 1973–1983	Infant mortality rate under 1		Infant & child mortality rate under 5		Crude death rate		Crude birth rate		Total fertility rate 1983	% population urbanized 1983	Average annual growth rate of urban population (%) 1973–83
				1960	1983	1960	1983	1960	1983	1960	1983			
65	Burma	37.6/6.0	2.0	165	70	250	95	22	13	43	38	5.3	29	3.9
66	Ecuador	8.8/1.5	2.6	130	70	190	95	17	9	47	41	6.0	46	3.9
67	El Salvacor	5.2/0.9	3.0	155	70	220	100	18	8	49	40	5.6	42	3.6
68	Guatemala	7.9/1.3	3.1	130	70	240	120	20	9	49	38	5.2	40	4.1
69	Madagascar	9.5/1.7	2.6	115	65	190	105	24	16	44	44	6.1	21	5.5
70	Saudi Arabia	10.4/1.8	4.7	180	65	315	90	24	12	49	43	7.1	71	7.4
71	Syrian Arab Rep.	9.8/1.9	3.3	145	60	240	80	19	7	47	46	7.2	49	4.2
72	Jordan	3.2/0.6	2.7	145	55	240	70	21	8	47	45	7.4	63	4.8
73	Mexico	75.1/11.6	2.9	100	55	155	75	13	7	46	34	4.6	69	4.1
74	Mongolia	1.8/0.3	2.8	120	55	175	70	17	7	41	34	4.8	54	4.2
	Middle IMR countries (25–50) Median	1,641T/160T	1.9	85	36	125	45	12	7	44	28	3.5	53	3.2
75	Colombia	27.5/3.8	1.9	100	50	160	75	14	8	46	31	3.9	66	2.9
76	Philippines	52.1/7.6	2.7	85	50	140	85	16	7	47	32	4.2	39	3.8
77	Lebanon	2.6/0.3	−0.3	75	48	100	60	15	9	43	29	3.8	78	1.6
78	Thailand	49.6/6.5	2.3	110	48	160	60	16	8	44	29	3.6	15	3.6
79	Albania	2.9/0.4	2.1	125	45	185	55	12	6	42	28	3.6	38	3.2
80	Paraguay	3.5/0.6	2.5	90	45	140	65	13	7	44	36	4.9	41	3.3
81	China	1,039.7/95.0	1.5	180	39	240	55	30	7	46	18	2.3	21	...
82	Sri Lanka	15.7/2.0	1.7	75	39	125	50	10	7	37	27	3.4	21	2.9
83	Venezuela	17.3/2.7	3.5	90	39	125	47	12	6	47	35	4.3	85	4.3
84	United Arab Emirates	1.2/0.1	11.3	160	38	270	47	21	4	48	27	5.9	79	11.2
85	Argentina	29.6/3.4	1.6	60	36	80	42	9	9	24	25	3.4	84	2.1
86	Guyana	0.9/0.1	...	75	36	105	45	11	6	44	28	3.3	32	...
87	Yugoslavia	22.9/1.8	0.8	105	32	130	34	10	9	25	16	2.1	45	2.8
88	Korea, Dem. Rep. of	19.2/2.7	2.5	100	30	140	39	13	7	42	30	4.0	62	4.2
89	Korea, Rep. of	39.8/4.0	1.6	100	30	140	39	15	6	46	21	2.5	62	4.8
90	Malaysia	14.9/2.0	2.4	80	30	120	41	17	6	45	29	3.7	31	3.5
91	Uruguay	3.0/0.3	0.5	55	30	60	34	10	10	22	20	2.8	85	0.8
92	Mauritius	1.0/0.1	...	80	28	120	36	11	6	45	26	2.8	55	...
93	Romania	22.7/1.9	0.8	80	28	95	33	10	10	23	17	2.5	53	3.1
94	Panama	2.1/0.3	2.3	75	26	115	37	11	5	41	28	3.5	51	3.0
95	USSR	273.2/24.1	0.9	44	25	60	31	8	9	25	19	2.4	65	−3.4
	Low IMR countries (under 25) Median	876T/63T	0.7	37	11	48	14	9	10	21	16	1.8	75	1.3
96	Trinidad and Tobago	1.1/0.1	0.6	65	24	80	28	9	6	38	25	2.9	22	1.0
97	Chile	11.7/1.3	1.7	15	23	150	28	13	8	37	25	2.9	82	2.4
98	Kuwait	1.6/0.3	6.4	00	23	150	27	11	3	44	37	6.1	92	7.8
99	Jamaica	2.3/0.3	1.3	70	21	100	27	10	7	39	28	3.4	52	2.7
100	Portugal	9.9/0.8	1.1	85	20	120	24	7	10	24	18	2.3	30	2.5
101	Costa Rica	2.5/0.3	2.4	85	19	130	24	11	4	48	31	3.5	45	3.2
102	Hungary	10.8/0.8	0.3	60	19	65	22	10	13	18	14	2.1	56	1.4
103	Poland	36.9/3.3	0.9	70	19	80	22	9	9	27	19	2.3	58	1.9
104	Bulgaria	9.1/0.7	0.1	60	17	80	22	9	11	19	15	2.2	67	2.1
105	Cuba	9.9/0.8	0.8	70	17	95	20	10	6	28	17	2.0	70	1.9
106	Czechoslovakia	15.5/1.3	0.6	30	16	36	18	10	12	19	16	2.2	65	1.8
107	Greece	9.8/0.7	1.1	55	15	70	19	7	10	19	16	2.3	64	2.6
108	Israel	4.1/0.5	2.3	36	14	44	16	6	7	28	24	3.1	90	2.7
109	New Zealand	3.2/0.3	0.6	24	13	29	15	9	8	26	16	1.8	84	0.8
110	Austria	7.5/0.4	(.)	42	12	48	14	12	13	17	12	1.6	56	0.6
111	Italy	56.6/3.6	0.3	48	12	55	14	10	10	18	13	1.8	71	1.1
112	Belgium	9.9/0.6	0.1	35	11	39	14	12	12	17	12	1.6	89	1.3
113	German Dem. Rep.	16.7/1.0	−0.1	44	11	50	14	13	14	16	13	1.6	78	0.2
114	USA	233.7/17.7	1.0	26	11	31	13	9	9	25	16	1.8	74	1.2
115	Australia	15.3/1.2	1.3	21	10	26	12	9	8	23	16	2.0	87	1.5
116	Germany, Fed. Rep. of	61.3/3.0	−0.1	37	10	42	13	11	12	16	10	1.4	86	0.3
117	Hong Kong	5.4/0.5	2.5	55	10	80	12	7	6	36	18	2.1	91	2.7
118	Ireland	3.5/0.4	1.3	34	10	39	13	12	10	21	21	3.2	56	2.2
119	Spain	38.4/3.2	1.0	50	10	65	12	9	9	21	17	2.4	76	2.0
120	United Kingdom	55.6/3.5	(.)	24	10	28	12	12	12	16	13	1.8	91	0.3
121	Canada	25.0/2.0	1.2	30	9	35	11	8	7	28	16	1.8	75	1.2
122	France	54.3/3.7	0.4	33	9	39	11	12	11	18	14	1.8	76	1.2
123	Singapore	2.5/0.2	1.3	41	9	55	13	9	5	42	18	1.7	74	1.3
124	Denmark	5.1/0.3	0.2	23	8	27	10	9	11	17	11	1.5	85	0.2
125	Netherlands	14.4/0.8	0.7	19	8	24	10	8	9	21	12	1.4	91	−1.1
126	Norway	4.1/0.3	0.4	20	8	24	10	9	11	18	12	1.7	76	2.4
127	Switzerland	6.3/0.3	(.)	23	8	29	10	10	11	18	8	1.3	59	0.7
128	Sweden	8.3/0.5	0.2	17	7	21	8	10	12	14	11	1.5	85	0.7
129	Finland	4.8/0.3	0.4	25	6	32	8	9	10	20	13	1.6	65	1.9
130	Japan	118.9/7.8	0.9	37	6	49	9	8	7	18	12	1.7	76	1.3

141

TABLE 6: ECONOMIC INDICATORS

		GNP per capita average annual growth rate (%)		Rate of inflation (%) 1973–1983	% of population below absolute poverty level 1977–1983 urban/rural	% of central gov't. expenditure allocated to health/education/defence 1982	ODA inflow in millions US $ (1983)/ as % of recipient GNP (1982)	Debt service as a % of exports of goods and services	
	GNP per capita (US $) 1983	1965–83	1980–83					1970	1983
Very high IMR countries (over 100) Median	270	1.0	−1.5	11.2	36/65	4.5/13.6/13.9	139/9	4.9	11.2
1 Afghanistan	170[x]	0.5	−0.8[x]	. .	18/36	. ./. ./. .	14/(.)		
2 Mali	160	1.2	−1.5	10.3	27[x]/48[x]	2.8/10.4/8.4	215/21	1.3	6.1
3 Sierra Leone	330	1.1	−1.8	14.7	. ./65	. ./. ./. .	65/5	9.9	7.2
4 Malawi	210	2.2	0.0	9.8	25/85	5.2/14.3/7.7	117/9	7.1	20.3
5 Guinea	300	1.1	−2.1	4.0	. ./. .		68/4		
6 Kampuchea	70[x]	. .	. .		. ./. .	. ./. ./. .	37/5		
7 Ethiopia	120	0.5	−0.1	4.4	60[x]/65[x]	5.7[x]/14.4[x]/14.3[x]	341/8	11.4	11.5
8 Mozambique	230[x]		−5.1				211/4		
9 Somalia	250	−0.8	1.7	20.1	40/70	7.2[x]/5.5[x]/23.3[x]	327/35	2.1	13.1
10 Angola	470[x]	. .	−6.1	. .	. ./. .	. ./. ./. .	75/1		
11 Burkina Faso	180	1.4	−2.6	10.8		6.6/15.7/17.1	181/16	6.3	. .
12 Niger	240	−1.2	−3.8	11.8	. ./35[x]		175/12	3.8	. .
13 Bhutan	80[x]		2.7[x]		. ./. .	. ./. ./. .	13/9		
14 Central African Rep.	280	0.1	−3.0	14.4		5.1/17.6/9.7	93/15	4.8	11.3
15 Chad	80[x]	. .	−15.6[x]	8.3	30/56	4.4[x]/14.8[x]/24.6[x]	95/30	3.9	0.6
16 Guinea-Bissau	180		2.7	6.9	. ./. .	. ./. ./. .	64/44		
17 Nepal	160	0.1	1.0	8.1	55/61	4.5/9.9/5.4	201/8		3.0
18 Senegal	440	−0.5	3.8	8.9		3.6/15.8/9.1	321/13	2.8	. .
19 Mauritania	480	0.3	−0.4	7.8	. ./. .		171/25	3.2	10.0
20 Yemen	550	5.7	5.3	13.9	. ./. .	4.5/16.4/35.5	330/9	. .	13.9
21 Yemen, Dem.	520	. .	−1.9		. ./20		106/11	. .	25.1
22 Bangladesh	130	0.5	1.0	9.6	86/86		1071/10		14.7
23 Haiti	300	1.1	−4.1	7.8	55/78		130/8	7.7	5.0
24 Liberia	480	0.8	−5.1	7.2	23/. .	7.2/15.3/13.5	118/13		6.6
25 Rwanda	270	2.3	1.6	11.2	30/90[x]	. ./. ./. .	149/10	1.3	2.6
26 Bolivia	510	0.6	−10.7	35.2	65*/85[x]	2.0/13.6/7.4	166/3	11.3	30.5
27 Burundi	240	2.1	−1.5	12.4	55/85	. ./. ./. .	141/12		. .
28 Benin	290	1.0	−0.1	10.8	. ./65	. ./. ./. .	87/9	2.3	. .
29 Lao People's Dem. Rep.	80[x]	. .	. .		. ./. .	. ./. ./. .	30/2		
30 Pakistan	390	2.5	2.8	11.1	32/29	1.1/2.2/33.5	669/2	23.6	28.1
31 Sudan	400	1.3	−1.2	18.0	. ./85[x]	1.3/6.1/9.5	957/11	10.7	11.2
32 Iran (Islamic Rep. of)	2,160[x]	. .	. .		. ./. .	5.5/13.6/10.2	48/(.)	12.2	. .
33 Nigeria	770	3.2	−8.5	13.3	. ./. .	3.6[x]/4.5[x]/40.2[x]	48/(.)	4.2	18.6
34 Oman	6,250	6.5	−4.1	17.9	. ./. .	3.1/7.7/49.4	71/1		3.2
35 Tanzania, U. Rep. of	240	0.9	−6.5	11.5	10/60	5.5/12.1/11.2	621/12	4.9	. .
36 India	260	1.5	2.7	7.7	40/51	2.2/1.9/20.2	1,700/1	22.0	10.3
37 Ivory Coast	710	1.0	−6.6	11.9	30*/26*	. ./. ./. .	157/2	6.8	31.0
38 Lesotho	460	6.3	1.2	11.9	50/55	8.0[x]/19.5[x]/. .	102/17		2.5
39 Uganda	220	−4.4	5.8	62.7	. ./. .	5.2/14.9/19.8	137/5	2.7	. .
40 Zaire	170	−1.3	−2.4	48.2	. ./80	. ./. ./. .	317/6	4.4	. .
High IMR countries (55–100) Median	900	2.7	−1.6	12.4	21/42	6.2/16.2/12.1	184/3	6.9	20.1
41 Cameroon, U. Rep. of	820	2.7	2.9	12.6	15/40	2.7/7.5/5.1	129/2	3.1	13.9
42 Egypt	700	4.2	4.5	13.2	21[x]/25[x]	2.4/9.2/12.7	1,422/5	36.4	27.5
43 Peru	1,040	0.1	−5.1	52.3	49/. .	6.2[x]/22.7[x]/14.8[x]	294/1	11.6	19.6
44 Togo	280	1.1	−7.7	8.3	42/. .	6.1/22.9/7.1	111/14	2.9	16.8
45 Ghana	310	−2.1	−8.9	51.6	. ./. .	5.8/18.7/6.2	109/3	5.0	14.2
46 Libyan Arab Jamahiriya	8,480	−0.9	−10.5	11.6			6/(.)		
47 Morocco	760	2.9	0.2	8.4	28/45	2.8/16.2/16.5	392/3	8.4	38.2
48 Algeria	2,320	3.6	1.7	12.8	20/. .		150/(.)	3.8	33.1
49 Turkey	1,240	3.0	1.9	42.0		2.1/16.8/15.2	353/1	22.0	28.9
50 Zambia	580	−1.3	−1.8	10.3	25/. .	8.4/15.2/. .	216/6	5.9	12.6
51 Indonesia	560	5.0	2.5	18.0	26/44	2.5/8.4/13.9	749/1	6.9	12.8
52 South Africa	2,490	1.6	−3.0	13.3	. ./. .	. ./. ./. .			22.3
53 Tunisia	1,290	5.0	0.6	9.4	20/15	6.7/14.2/10.6	213/3	19.0	22.3
54 Congo	1,230	3.5	12.7	12.4	. ./. .	. ./. ./. .	108/5		20.5
55 Honduras	670	0.6	−4.0	8.6	14/55	10.2[x]/22.3[x]/12.4[x]	189/7	2.8	14.9
56 Kenya	340	2.3	−1.3	10.8	10/55	7.3/19.9/13.2	400/7	5.4	20.6
57 Zimbabwe	740	1.5	−2.9	9.7	. ./. .	6.4/21.9/17.3	208/3		31.6
58 Botswana	920	8.5	6.6	9.8	40[x]/55[x]	. ./. ./. .	104/13		. .
59 Dominican Rep.	1,370	3.9	0.4	8.5	45/43	10.7/15.9/9.8	101/1	4.7	22.7
60 Iraq	3,020[x]	. .	. .		. ./40[x]	. ./. ./. .	13/(.)	2.2	. .
61 Nicaragua	880	−1.8	−2.0	16.5	21/19	4.0[x]/16.6[x]/12.3[x]	120/4	11.1	18.3
62 Papua New Guinea	760	0.9	−1.8	6.9	10/75	9.2/17.9/3.9	333/15		11.2
63 Viet Nam	170[x]	. .	. .		. ./. .		106/1		
64 Brazil	1,880	5.0	−4.2	63.9	. ./. .	7.8/4.6/4.3	101/(.)	12.5	28.7

		GNP per capita (US $) 1983	GNP per capita average annual growth rate (%)		Rate of inflation (%) 1973-1983	% of population below absolute poverty level 1977-1983 urban/rural	% of central gov't. expenditure allocated to health/education/defence 1982	ODA inflow in millions US $ (1983)/ as % of recipient GNP (1982)	Debt service as a % of exports of goods and services	
			1965-83	1980-83					1970	1983
65	Burma	180	2.2	3.5	6.5	40/40	7.0/11.2/19.0	302/5	15.8	33.8
66	Ecuador	1,420	4.6	−2.2	16.6	40/65	7.7/26.5/10.7	63/1	9.1	32.5
67	El Salvador	710	−0.2	−7.4	11.7	20/32	7.1/16.9/11.9	290/8	3.6	6.4
68	Guatemala	1,120	2.1	−5.1	9.9	21/25	9.5×/19.4×/11.0×	74/1	7.4	11.7
69	Madagascar	310	−1.2	−6.0	13.9	50/50	4.2×/9.1×/3.6×	184/7	3.5	. .
70	Saudi Arabia	12,230	6.7	−7.3	16.5	. . /. .	. . /. . /. .	. /.		
71	Syrian Arab Rep.	1,760	4.9	1.9	12.7	. . /. .	1.1/7.1/37.7	970/6	11.0	11.2
72	Jordan	1,640	6.9	3.0	10.0	14/17	3.8/10.4/24.8	789/15	3.6	11.3
73	Mexico	2,240	3.2	−3.4	28.2	. . /. .	1.3/13.1/1.6	132/(.)	23.6	35.9
74	Mongolia	780×	. .	0.0	. .	. . /. .	. . /. . /. .	. . /. .	. .	. .
	Middle IMR countries (25–50) Median	1,430	2.9	0.0	12.7	. . /. .	. . /. . /. .	48/1	. .	. .
75	Colombia	1,430	3.2	−1.6	24.0	34/.	. /. /.	86/(.)	12.0	21.3
76	Philippines	760	2.9	−0.4	11.7	32/41	5.3/16.0/13.6	424/1	7.2	15.4
77	Lebanon	1,070×	. .	. .	. .	. /.	. /. /.	123/3		
78	Thailand	820	4.3	2.9	8.7	15/34	5.0/20.7/20.6	432/1	3.4	11.3
79	Albania	840×	. .	0.0	. .	. . /. .	. /. /.	. . /. .		
80	Paraguay	1,410	4.5	−1.2	12.6	19/50	3.7/12.0/12.5	51/1	11.9	14.9
81	China	300	4.4	5.0	1.7	. . /. .	. /. /.	670×/ (.)		
82	Sri Lanka	330	2.9	3.1	14.5	. . /. .	3.3/7.4/1.4	470/10	10.3	11.9
83	Venezuela	3,840	1.5	−4.3×	11.7	. . /. .	7.6/15.7/5.8	10/(.)	2.9	15.0
84	United Arab Emirates	22,870	. .	−11.8	12.7	. . /. .	7.1/7.5/36.4	4/(.)		
85	Argentina	2,070	0.5	−6.4	167.8	30*/35*	1.1/6.2/11.0	48/(.)	21.5	24.0
86	Guyana	520	0.5	−7.2	7.7	. . /. .	. /. /.	30/6		
87	Yugoslavia	2,570	4.7	−1.0	22.8	. . /. .	24.8×/. . /50.4	3/(.)	9.9	7.6
88	Korea, Dem. Rep. of	1,130×	. .	0.0	. .	. /.	. /. /.	. . /. .		
89	Korea, Rep. of	2,010	6.7	5.3	19.0	18/11	1.4/19.5/31.3	8/(.)	19.4	12.3
90	Malaysia	1,860	4.5	3.0	6.5	13/38	4.4/15.9/15.1	177/1	3.6	5.9
91	Uruguay	2,490	2.0	−7.2	51.0	25*/.	3.3/7.7/13.6	3/(.)	21.6	19.8
92	Mauritius	1,160	2.8	2.2	13.1	12/12	. /. /.	41/4	. .	. .
93	Romania	2,560		2.6		. . /. .	0.8/3.2/4.9			
94	Panama	2,120	2.9	0.4	7.1	21/30	13.1/11.0/. .	47/1	7.7	6.8
95	USSR	4,550×	. .	0.0	. .	. . /. .	. . /. . /. .	. . /. .		
	Low IMR countries (under 25) Median	7,180	2.8	0.0	10.4	. . /.	10.6/9.3/7.6	. . /.		
96	Trinidad and Tobago	6,850	3.4	1.2	15.6	. . /39	5.9/11.2/2.0	6/(.)	4.4	2.8
97	Chile	1,870	−0.1	−3.3	86.2	35*/45*	6.8/14.7/11.5	1/(.)	8.9	18.3
98	Kuwait	17,880	0.2	−9.3	10.2	. . /. .	5.4/8.8/10.9	5/(.)		
99	Jamaica	1,300	−0.5	−0.6	16.0	. . /80	. . /. . /. .	181/6	2.7	15.4
100	Portugal	2,230	3.7	−0.1	20.1	. . /. .	. . /. . /. .	45/(.)	. .	26.7
101	Costa Rica	1,020	2.1	−7.4	23.2	. . /. .	32.8/22.6/2.9	252/11	0.0	50.6
102	Hungary	2,150	6.4	2.1	4.1	. . /. .	. . /. . /. .	. . /. .		18.5
103	Poland	3,900×	. .	0.0	. .	. . /. .	. . /. . /. .	. . /. .		
104	Bulgaria	4,150×	. .	0.0	. .	. /.	. . /. . /. .	. . /. .		
105	Cuba	1,410×	. .	. .	. .	. . /. .	. . /. . /. .	13/(.)	. .	. .
106	Czechoslovakia	5,820×	. .	0.0	. .	. . /. .	. /. /.	. . /. .		
107	Greece	3,920	4.0	−1.3	16.8	. . /. .	10.5/9.6/10.8	13/(.)	9.3	18.3
108	Israel	5,370	2.9	0.3	73.0	. . /. .	4.3/8.3/30.3	. . /. .	2.7	19.6
109	New Zealand	7,730	1.2	0.8	14.2	. . /. .	13.5/12.7/5.3	. . /. .		
110	Austria	9,250	3.7	0.8	5.4	. . /. .	12.2/9.6/2.9	. . /. .		
111	Italy	6,400	2.8	−0.7	17.4	. . /. .	10.6/8.9/3.6	. . /. .		
112	Belgium	9,150	3.1	−0.2	6.4	. . /. .	1.5×/15.5×/6.7×	. . /. .		
113	German Dem. Rep.	7,180×		0.0		. . /. .	. /. /.	. . /. .		
114	USA	14,110	1.7	−0.4	7.5	. . /. .	10.8/2.1/23.1	. . /. .		
115	Australia	11,490	1.7	0.0	10.5	. . /. .	10.0/8.2/9.8	. . /. .		
116	Germany, Fed. Rep. of	11,430	2.8	0.0	4.3	. . /. .	19.3/0.8/9.1	. . /. .		
117	Hong Kong	6,000	6.2	3.7	9.9	. . /. .	. . /. . /. .	9/(.)	. .	. .
118	Ireland	5,000	2.3	−2.1	14.5	. . /. .	. /. /.	. . /. .		
119	Spain	4,780	3.0	0.3	16.7	. . /. .	0.6/7.1/3.9	. . /. .		
120	United Kingdom	9,200	1.7	1.5	14.3	. . /. .	12.2×/2.6×/16.7×	. . /. .		
121	Canada	12,310	2.5	−1.2	9.4	. . /. .	5.2/3.2/7.8	. . /. .		
122	France	10,500	3.1	0.3	10.8	. . /. .	14.7/8.3/7.4	. . /. .		
123	Singapore	6,620	7.8	7.6	4.5	. . /. .	6.4/19.2/22.9	15/(.)	0.6	1.3
124	Denmark	11,570	1.9	1.7	9.5	. . /. .	7.2×/15.9×/7.2×	. . /. .		
125	Netherlands	9,890	2.3	−1.3	6.2	. . /. .	11.6/11.9/5.4	. . /. .		
126	Norway	14,020	3.3	0.7	9.7	. . /. .	10.6/8.6/8.5	. . /. .		
127	Switzerland	16,290	1.4	0.1	3.9	. . /. .	12.8/3.1/10.4	. . /. .		
128	Sweden	12,470	1.9	0.1	10.3	. . /. .	2.1/10.1/7.3	. . /. .		
129	Finland	10,740	3.3	1.5	10.6	. . /. .	10.9/14.0/5.2	. . /. .		
130	Japan	10,120	4.8	2.7	4.7	. . /. .	. . /. . /. .	. . /. .		

TABLE 7: BASIC INDICATORS ON LESS POPULOUS COUNTRIES

		Infant mortality rate under 1		Total population (millions)	Annual no. of births/infant and child deaths (0–4) (thousands)	GNP per capita US $	Life expectancy at birth (years)	% adults literate male/female	% of age group enrolled in primary school male/female
		1983	1960	1983	1983	1983	1983	1980–83	1980–1983
1	Gambia	175	205	0.6	30/9	290	35	29 /12	79/45
2	Equatorial Guinea	135	195	0.4	16/4	180[x]	44	. . / . .	. . / . .
3	Djibouti	130[•]	. .	0.3	. . / . .	480[x]	. .	. . / . .	56[•]/ 44[•]
4	Swaziland	130	155	0.6	29/5	870	49	57[x]/54[x]	112/109
5	Gabon	110	180	1.1	39/7	3,950	49	63 /44	120/117
6	Comoros	90	130	0.4	20/3	340	50	56 /40	107/76
7	Vanuatu	85[y]	. .	0.1	. . / . .	350[x]	. .	57[x]/48[x]	. . / . .
8	Cape Verde	75[x]	150	0.3	7/1	320	57	54 /34	137[•]/ 149[•]
9	Maldives	75[x]	. .	0.2	. . / . .	400[x]	. .	83[x]/82[x]	. . / . .
10	Solomon Islands	75[y]	. .	0.3	. . / . .	640	. .	. . / . .	. . / . .
11	Sao Tome and Principe	70	. .	0.1	. . / . .	310	. .	73 /42	. . / . .
12	St. Christopher/Nevis	43	. .	0.1	. . / . .	950	. .	. . / . .	. . / . .
13	Qatar	38	160	0.3	8/(.)	21,210	71	51[x]/51[x]	105/101
14	Suriname	36	75	0.4	10/(.)	3,420	69	68[x]/63[x]	107[x]/100[x]
15	Bahrain	32	150	0.4	13/(.)	10,510	68	77 /59	107/93
16	Fiji	31	75	0.7	18/1	1790	73	84[x]/74[x]	111/109
17	Saint Lucia	26	. .	0.1	. . / . .	1,060	. .	. . / . .	. . / . .
18	Bahamas	22	. .	0.2	. . / . .	4,060	. .	. . / . .	. . / . .
19	Belize	21[x]	. .	0.2	. . / . .	1140	. .	. . / . .	. . / . .
20	Dominica	20	. .	0.1	. . / . .	980	. .	. . / . .	. . / . .
21	Cyprus	17	31	0.7	13/(.)	3,680	74	96[x]/83[x]	. . / . .
22	Grenada	15	. .	0.1	. . / . .	840	. .	. . / . .	. . / . .
23	Barbados	14	85	0.3	5/(.)	4,050	72	. . / . .	107/105
24	Malta	14	40	0.4	7/(.)	3,490	72	83 /80	98/92
25	Seychelles	14	. .	0.1	. . / . .	2,400	. .	. . / . .	103[•]/ 102[•]
26	Samoa	13[x]	. .	0.2	. . / . .	350[x]	. .	. . / . .	. . / . .
27	Brunei Darussalam	12	. .	0.3	. . / . .	21,140	. .	85 /69	. . / . .
28	Antigua and Barbuda	11	. .	0.1	. . / . .	1,710	. .	. . / . .	. . / . .
29	Luxembourg	11	37	0.4	4/(.)	14,650	73	. . / . .	82/85
30	Iceland	6	17	0.2	4/(.)	10,260	77	. . / . .	97/101
31	Saint Vincent	. .	. .	0.1	. . / . .	860	. .	. . / . .	. . / . .

General Note on the Data

The data provided in these tables are accompanied by definitions, sources, explanations of signs, and individual footnotes where the definition of the figure is different from the general definition being used. Tables derived from so many sources – nine major sources are listed in the explanatory material – will inevitably cover a wide range of reliability. Official government data received by the responsible United Nations agency have been used wherever possible. In the many cases where there are no reliable official figures, estimates made by the responsible United Nations agency have been used. Where such internationally standardized estimates do not exist, the tables draw on data from relevant UNICEF field offices. All such UNICEF field office sources are marked with * or Y.

The figures for infant mortality rates, life expectancy, crude birth rate, crude death rate, etc., are part of the regular work on estimates and projections undertaken by the United Nations Population Division. These and other international estimates are revised periodically, which explains why some of the data differ from those found in earlier UNICEF publications. In the case of GNP per capita and official development assistance, the data are the result of a continuous process of revising and updating by the World Bank and the Organisation for Economic Co-operation and Development respectively.

Where possible only comprehensive or sample national data have been used although, as in the table on 'wasting', there are certain exceptions. Where the figures refer to only a part of the country, this is indicated in a footnote.

In ranking countries by the main indicator used in these tables – the estimate of the infant mortality rate for 1983 – all rates have been rounded to the nearest 5 in the case of countries with a rate of 50 or more. In countries with rates below 50, where there is usually a fairly comprehensive registration system, the figures have been rounded to the nearest unit.

Signs and explanations

Unless otherwise stated, the summary measures for the four IMR (infant mortality) groups of countries are the median values for each group. The median is the middle value of a data set arranged in order of magnitude. The median is the commonly used average where there are a large number of items of data with a great range, as is the case in these tables, and has the advantage of not being distorted by the very small countries or the very large countries. In cases where the range of the data is not all that extensive, the most commonly used average is the mean, which is the sum of all the items divided by the number of the items. However, because we are dealing with countries of very different sizes of population, we immediately encounter the problem of weighting. Hence the choice of the median to give the reader some idea of the situation in a typical country of the appropriate IMR group.

..   Data not available.

*   UNICEF field office source.

(.)   Less than half the unit shown.

T   Total (as opposed to a median).

X   See footnote at the end of the tables.

Y   UNICEF field office source; see footnote at the end of the tables.

Most of the IMR figures are based on five-year estimates prepared by the United Nations Population Division on an internationally comparable basis using various sources. In some cases, these interpolated estimates may differ from the latest national figures.

Footnotes to Tables

Table 1:
Basic Indicators

Afghanistan	GNP per capita	1979
Afghanistan	Adult literacy	1979
Mali	Adult literacy	1976
Mali	Primary enrolment	1978
Sierra Leone	Primary enrolment	1979
Sierra Leone	Household income	1967–69
Malawi	Household income	1967–68
Kampuchea	GNP per capita	1974
Mozambique	GNP per capita	1980
Angola	GNP per capita	1980
Burkina Faso	Adult literacy	1975
Bhutan	GNP per capita	1981
Chad	GNP per capita	1982
Chad	Primary enrolment	1976
Guinea–Bissau	Adult literacy	1979
Yemen, Dem.	Adult literacy	1973
Liberia	Adult literacy	1974
Rwanda	Adult literacy	1978
Bolivia	Adult literacy	1976
Benin	Adult literacy	1979
Lao People's Dem. Rep.	GNP per capita	1981
Sudan	Household income	1967–68
Iran (Islamic Rep. of)	GNP per capita	1977
Iran (Islamic Rep. of)	Adult literacy	1976
Iran (Islamic Rep. of)	Household income	1968 urban only
Tanzania, U. Rep. of	Adult literacy	1978
Tanzania, U. Rep. of	Household income	1969
Ivory Coast	Primary enrolment	1979
Zaire	Primary enrolment	1978
Cameroon, U. Rep. of	Adult literacy	1976
Egypt	Adult literacy	1976
Libyan Arab Jamahiriya	Adult literacy	1973
Honduras	Adult literacy	1974
Honduras	Household income	1967
Iraq	GNP per capita	1980
Nicaragua	Household income	1969–71 rural only
Viet Nam	GNP per capita	1978
Viet Nam	Adult literacy	1979
El Salvador	Adult literacy	Age 10 +
Guatemala	Adult literacy	1973
Jordan	Adult literacy	1979
Mongolia	GNP per capita	1979
Lebanon	GNP per capita	1974
Albania	GNP per capita	1979
United Arab Emirates	Adult literacy	1975
Korea, Dem. Rep. of	GNP per capita	1979
Korea, Dem. Rep. of	Primary enrolment	1976
Uruguay	Adult literacy	1975
Uruguay	Household income	Montevideo only
USSR	GNP per capita	1980
Chile	Household income	1968
Costa Rica	Adult literacy	1973
Poland	GNP per capita	1980
Bulgaria	GNP per capita	1980
Cuba	GNP per capita	1979
Cuba	Adult literacy	Age 10 +
Czechoslovakia	GNP per capita	1980
German Dem. Rep.	GNP per capita	1980

Table 2:
Nutrition

Somalia	Malnutrition	Age 0–6
Angola	Breast-feeding	Duration not stated
Yemen, Dem.	Breast-feeding	Rural only
Uganda	Malnutrition	Between 70% and 80% standard weight/length
Zaire	Malnutrition	Less than 70% standard weight/length
Egypt	Malnutrition	Pre-school population
Peru	Malnutrition	1972
Morocco	Malnutrition	1971
Tunisia	Malnutrition	Age 0–5
Tunisia	Wasting	1974
Botswana	Malnutrition	Age 0–5
Brazil	Wasting	1974
Burma	Malnutrition	Age 0–3
Ecuador	Malnutrition	Age 0–6
Colombia	Malnutrition	Age 0–5
Thailand	Malnutrition	Age 0–6
Korea, Rep. of	Breast-feeding	1974
Malaysia	Breast-feeding	1974
Panama	Malnutrition	Age unspecified
Chile	Malnutrition	Age 0–5
Hong Kong	Breast-feeding	1974
Sweden	Breast-feeding	Fully breast-feeding
Japan	Breast-feeding	1971

Table 3:
Health

Angola	Measles		1980
Yemen, Dem.	Measles		Age 1–5
Bolivia	DPT		Age 0–3
Bolivia	Measles		Age 1–5
Sudan	Measles		Age 0–3
Ivory Coast	Measles		Age 0–3
Indonesia	DPT		2 doses only
Honduras	Measles		Age 1–5
Dominican Rep.	Polio		Age 0–3
Dominican Rep.	Measles		Age 1–5
Papua New Guinea	DPT		2 doses only
Brazil	Polio		2 doses only
Brazil	Measles		Age 1–5
El Salvador	DPT, polio		2 doses only
El Salvador	Measles		Age 1–5
El Salvador	Pregnant women immunized 1980		
Mexico	Measles		Age 1–5
Yugoslavia	Measles		Age 1–5
Uruguay	Polio		2 doses only
Uruguay	Measles		Age 1–5
Panama	Pregnant women immunized 1980		
USSR	Measles		Age 1–5
Portugal	Measles		Age 1–5
Hungary	Measles		Age 1–5
Poland	Measles		Age 1–5
Bulgaria	Measles		Age 1–5
Cuba	Polio		2 doses only
Czechoslovakia	Measles		Age 1–5
New Zealand	DPT		2 doses only
New Zealand	Measles		Age 1–5
Austria	Measles		Age 1–5
Belgium	Measles		Age 1–5
German Dem. Rep.	Measles		Age 1–5
USA	Measles		Age 1–5
Australia	DPT		1980
Australia	Polio		1980
Germany, Fed. Rep. of	Measles		Age 1–5
United Kingdom	Measles		Age 1–5
France	Measles		Age 1–5
Netherlands	Measles		Age 1–5
Sweden	DPT		DT only
Sweden	Measles		Age 1–5
Finland	Measles		Age 1–5
Japan	Polio		2 doses only
Japan	Measles		Age 1–5

Table 4:
Education

Afghanistan	Adult literacy	1979
Mali	Adult literacy	1976
Mali	Primary enrolment	1978
Mali	Secondary enrolment	1978
Sierra Leone	Primary enrolment	1979
Sierra Leone	Secondary enrolment	1979
Burkina Faso	Adult literacy	1975
Niger	Secondary enrolment	1978
Chad	Primary enrolment	1976
Chad	Secondary enrolment	1976
Guinea–Bissau	Adult literacy	1979
Yemen, Dem.	Adult literacy	1973
Liberia	Adult literacy	1974
Rwanda	Adult literacy	1978
Bolivia	Adult literacy	1976
Benin	Adult literacy	1979
Iran (Islamic Rep. of)	Adult literacy	1976
Iran (Islamic Rep. of)	Completing primary level	1969
Tanzania, U. Rep. of	Adult literacy	1978
India	Completing primary level	1972
Ivory Coast	Primary enrolment	1979
Ivory Coast	Secondary enrolment	1979
Zaire	Radio receivers	1980
Zaire	Primary enrolment	1978
Zaire	Secondary enrolment	1978
Cameroon, U. Rep. of	Adult literacy	1976
Cameroon, U. Rep. of	Primary enrolment	1979
Egypt	Adult literacy	1976
Libyan Arab Jamahiriya	Adult literacy	1973
Honduras	Adult literacy	1974
Dominican Rep.	Completing primary level	1969
Viet Nam	Adult literacy	1979
Brazil	Primary enrolment	1979
Brazil	Secondary enrolment	1978
Burma	Primary enrolment	1977
Burma	Completing primary level	1972
Burma	Secondary enrolment	1977
Ecuador	Primary enrolment	1979
El Salvador	Adult literacy	Age 10+
Guatemala	Adult literacy	1973
Jordan	Adult literacy	1979

	Colombia	Completing primary level	1973
	United Arab Emirates	Adult literacy	1975
	Korea, Dem. Rep. of	Primary enrolment	1976
	Malaysia	Radio receivers	1980
	Uruguay	Adult literacy	1975
	Trinidad and Tobago	Primary enrolment	1979
	Portugal	Completing primary level	1974
	Costa Rica	Adult literacy	1973
	Cuba	Adult literacy	Age 10+
	France	Primary enrolment	1979

Table 5:
Demographic indicators

There are no footnotes to Table 5

Table 6:
Economic Indicators

Country	Indicator	Year
Afghanistan	GNP per capita	1979
Afghanistan	GNP annual growth rate	1980–82
Mali	Poverty level	1975
Kampuchea	GNP per capita	1974
Ethiopia	Poverty level	1976
Ethiopia	Government expenditure	1972
Mozambique	GNP per capita	1980
Somalia	Government expenditure	1972
Angola	GNP per capita	1980
Niger	Poverty level	1975
Bhutan	GNP per capita	1981
Bhutan	GNP annual growth rate	1980–82
Chad	GNP per capita	1982
Chad	GNP annual growth rate	1980–82
Chad	Government expenditure	1972
Rwanda	Poverty level	1975
Bolivia	Poverty level	1975
Lao People's Dem. Rep.	GNP per capita	1981
Sudan	Poverty level	1975
Iran (Islamic Rep. of)	GNP per capita	1977
Nigeria	Government expenditure	1972
Lesotho	Government expenditure	1972
Egypt	Poverty level	1976
Peru	Government expenditure	1972
Honduras	Government expenditure	1972
Botswana	Poverty level	1971–72
Iraq	GNP per capita	1980
Iraq	Poverty level	1975
Nicaragua	Government expenditure	1972
Viet Nam	GNP per capita	1978
Guatemala	Government expenditure	1972
Madagascar	Government expenditure	1972
Mongolia	GNP per capita	1979
Lebanon	GNP per capita	1974
Albania	GNP per capita	1979
China	ODA inflow	Excludes Taiwan
Venezuela	GNP annual growth rate	1980–82
Yugoslavia	Government expenditure	1972
Korea, Dem. Rep. of	GNP per capita	1979
USSR	GNP per capita	1980
Poland	GNP per capita	1980
Bulgaria	GNP per capita	1980
Cuba	GNP per capita	1979
Czechoslovakia	GNP per capita	1980
Belgium	Government expenditure	1972
German Dem. Rep.	GNP per capita	1980
United Kingdom	Government expenditure	1972
Denmark	Government expenditure	1972

Table 7:
Basic Statistics on less populous countries

Country	Indicator	Year
Equatorial Guinea	GNP per capita	1981
Djibouti	GNP per capita	1981
Swaziland	Adult literacy	1976
Vanuatu	IMR	1979
Vanuatu	GNP per capita	1981
Vanuatu	Adult literacy	1979
Maldives	IMR	Incomplete estimate
Maldives	GNP per capita	1981
Maldives	Adult literacy	1977
Solomon Islands	IMR	1976
Qatar	Adult literacy	Age 10+
Suriname	Adult literacy	1978
Suriname	Primary enrolment	1978
Fiji	Adult literacy	1976
Belize	IMR	Incomplete estimate
Cyprus	Adult literacy	1976
Samoa	IMR	Incomplete estimate
Samoa	GNP per capita	1976

Definitions

Infant Mortality Rate: annual number of deaths of infants under 1 year of age, per 1,000 live births.

Infant and Child Mortality Rate: annual number of deaths of children under 5 years of age, per 1,000 live births.

Life Expectancy at Birth: the number of years new-born children would live if subject to the mortality risks prevailing for the cross-section of population at the time of their birth.

Crude Death Rate: annual number of deaths per 1,000 population.

Crude Birth Rate: annual number of births per 1,000 population.

Total Fertility Rate: the number of children that would be born per woman, if she were to live to the end of her child-bearing years and bear children at each age in accordance with prevailing age-specific fertility rates.

Low Birth-weight: 2,500 grammes or less.

Breast-feeding: either wholly or partly breast-feeding.

Prevalence of Wasting (acute malnutrition): the percentage of children with greater than minus two standard deviations from the 50th percentile of the weight-for-height reference population, i.e. roughly less than 77% of the median weight-for-height of the United States National Center for Health Statistics reference population.

DPT: Diphtheria, pertussis (whooping cough) and tetanus.

Adult Literacy Rate: percentage of persons aged 15 and over who can read and write.

GNP: Gross national product. Annual GNPs per capita are expressed in current United States dollars. GNP per capita growth rates are annual average growth rates that have been computed by fitting trend lines to the logarithmic values of GNP per capita at constant market prices for each year of the time period.

Absolute Poverty Level: that income level below which a minimum nutritionally adequate diet plus essential non-food requirements is not affordable.

ODA: Official development assistance.

Income Share: the percentage of private income received by the highest 20% and lowest 40% of households.

Child Malnutrition: Mild or moderate: between 60% and 80% of the desirable weight-for-age; Severe: less than 60% of the desirable weight-for-age.

Primary and Secondary Enrolment Ratios: The gross enrolment ratio is the total number of children enrolled in a schooling level – whether or not they belong in the relevant age group for that level – expressed as a percentage of the total number of children in the relevant age group for that level; The net enrolment ratio is the total number of children enrolled in a schooling level who belong in the relevant age group, expressed as a percentage of the total number of children in that age group.

Children Completing Primary School: percentage of the children entering the first grade of primary school who successfully complete that level in due course.

Main Sources

Infant and Child Mortality:	United Nations Population Division and United Nations Statistical Office
Total Population:	United Nations Statistical Office and United Nations Population Division
Child Population Aged 0-4:	United Nations Population Division
Births:	United Nations Population Division
Infant and Child Deaths:	United Nations Population Division and UNICEF
GNP per Capita:	World Bank
Life Expectancy:	United Nations Population Division
Adult Literacy:	United Nations Educational, Scientific and Cultural Organization (UNESCO)
Radio Receivers:	United Nations Educational Scientific and Cultural Organization (UNESCO)
School Enrolment and Completion:	United Nations Educational Scientific and Cultural Organization (UNESCO)
Share of Household Income:	World Bank
Immunization:	World Health Organization (WHO) and UNICEF field offices
Low Birth-weight:	World Health Organization (WHO)
Breast-feeding:	World Health Organization (WHO) and World Fertility Survey
Child Malnutrition:	UNICEF field offices
Wasting (acute malnutrition):	World Health Organization (WHO)
Food Production and Calorie Intake:	Food and Agriculture Organization of the United Nations (FAO) and World Bank
Access to Drinking Water:	World Health Organization (WHO)
Crude Death and Birth Rates:	World Bank
Population Growth Rate:	United Nations Population Division
Total Fertility Rate:	United Nations Population Division
Urban Population:	United Nations Population Division
Rate of Inflation:	World Bank
Absolute Poverty Level:	World Bank
Official Development Assistance:	Organisation for Economic Co-operation and Development (OECD)
Expenditure on Health, Education and Defence:	World Bank
Debt Service:	World Bank

Variations in infant mortality rate (IMR) within countries

Like the average GNP per capita, the average IMR for a country can give a misleading picture of the situation. In slums and poorer rural areas, the prevailing IMR is usually considerably above the national average. Conversely the IMR is usually much lower among those with higher levels of education or income. Statistics on the differences in IMR within countries are therefore useful supplements to the national averages.

The attached table presents two sets of measures of IMR variations within countries.

Measure A, columns 2 to 4, shows the estimated percentage of births per 1,000 population occurring in areas where the IMR is more than 25% above, or 25% below, the national average. This measure can be compared to measures of income distribution (or relative poverty), showing the percentage of a country's population receiving incomes some fixed percentage above or below the national average.

Measure B, columns 5 to 8, shows the estimated percentage of the country's population living in areas where the IMR is 150 per 1,000 and over, 100 to 149, 50 to 99, and less than 50. This measure can be compared to measures of absolute poverty, showing the percentage of a country's population living below various poverty lines of increasing severity.

The margin of error involved in the estimates themselves and in the estimating procedures varies widely from country to country, particularly in the case of the second measure, making it important not to draw conclusions from small differences in the figures. But, sensibly used, the data can be an important complement to data showing national IMR averages.

It is interesting to note in the case of the first measure that the degree of regional inequality does not depend on the overall mortality level. Thus Jamaica and Venezuela, with low average mortality levels, show a much greater degree of inequality than is found for example in Indonesia, Morocco or North Sudan where overall mortality levels are much higher. Other recent studies show the role of various social and economic factors in maintaining these differentials. Above all they have clearly established that the more educated the mother, the greater the probability that the child will survive, and this applies to both high and low infant mortality countries. In fact, the variation in child mortality by the mother's education is independent of the overall level of mortality.

Next year's *State of the World's Children* report will look in more detail at this subject of IMR variations within countries. In the meantime, it is hoped that countries will be encouraged to prepare more detailed estimates of internal IMR variations – as well as to monitor the progress in its reduction, especially in the relatively higher IMR states or areas.

IMR Internal differentials by country 1970–1980

In descending order of 1982 national IMR as estimated by the UN Population Division

Country	Percentage of births[1] in areas with an IMR more than 25% above or below the national average			Percentage of population in areas with an IMR of			
	More than 25% above	More than 25% below	Total	150 and over	100–149	50–99	Less than 50
Sierra Leone	—	—	—	100	0	0	0
Yemen	—	—	—	57	43	0	0
Benin	25	26	51	25	49	26	0
Nepal	—	—	—	50	50	0	0
Senegal	21	17	38	21	50	29	0
Mauritania	20	15	35	—	—	—	—
Swaziland	—	—	—	27	73	0	0
Bolivia	—	—	—	45	55	0	0
India	—	—	—	23	54	19	4
Ivory Coast	—	—	—	20	63	17	0
Sudan (North)	0	13	13	0	0	100	0
Cameroon, U. Rep. of	5	14	19	0	58	42	0
Egypt	—	—	—	0	67	33	0
Lesotho	—	—	—	0	100	0	0
Turkey	—	—	—	41	59	0	0
Haiti	—	—	—	21	60	19	0
Morocco	12	0	12	0	43	57	0
Ghana	27	10	37	0	27	63	10
Peru	—	—	—	40	27	33	0
Indonesia	0	6	6	0	62	38	0
Tunisia	15	14	29	0	15	85	0
Nicaragua	—	—	—	0	14	86	0
Kenya	30	36	66	0	44	56	0
Ecuador	—	—	—	0	14	86	0
El Salvador	—	—	—	0	0	58	42
Guatemala	—	—	—	0	5	78	17
Dominican Rep.	—	—	—	0	32	68	0
Jordan	—	—	—	0	0	100	0
Syrian Arab Rep.	0	13	13	0	0	87	13
Colombia	—	—	—	0	0	91	9
Mexico	0	2	2	0	0	100	0
Philippines	—	—	—	0	0	90	10
Thailand	—	—	—	0	0	94	6
Chile	—	—	—	0	0	11	89
Sri Lanka	0	0	0	0	0	100	0
Venezuela	21	24	45	0	0	44	56
Argentina	—	—	—	0	0	6	94
Korea, Rep. of	0	0	0	0	0	36	64
Mauritius	—	—	—	0	0	17	83
Fiji	—	—	—	0	0	42	58
Malaysia (Peninsula)	—	—	—	0	0	0	100
Jamaica	25	34	59	0	0	25	75
Panama	—	—	—	0	0	9	91
Costa Rica	—	—	—	0	0	0	100
Cuba	—	—	—	0	0	0	100

[1] Source: World Fertility Surveys.
[2] Source: Population censuses, sample registration data and World Fertility Surveys.

153

Main sources

Immunization leads the way
(pages 1 to 20)

1 "Report of the Executive Director", UNI-CEF, February 1985 (E/ICEF/1985/2).

2 "Report of the Expanded Programme on Immunization", WHO, 1985 (EPI/GEN/85/1).

3 Neal A. Halsey and Ciro A. de Quadros, *Recent advances in immunization: a bibliographic review*, Pan American Health Organization, scientific publications, no. 451, 1983. See also Robert Davis, "The future of EPI", paper prepared for Save the Children Fund (United Kingdom), February 1985.

4 "Report of the Expanded Programme on Immunization", WHO, 1985 (EPI/GEN/85/1).

5 R.H. Henderson, "Providing immunization: the state of the art", in *Protecting the world's children: vaccines and immunization within primary health care*, Rockefeller Foundation, June 1984.

6 Carlyle Guerra de Macedo, announcement on polio eradication in the Americas, Pan American Health Organization, 14 May 1985.

7 William H. Foege, statement to Subcommittee on Oversight and Investigation, Committee on Energy and Commerce, United States House of Representatives, 13 March 1985.

8 William H. Foege, "Banishing measles from the world", *World Health Forum*, vol. 5, 1984.

9 William H. Foege, "Banishing measles from the world", *World Health Forum*, vol. 5, 1984.

10 "Italy to give $100 million to save one million children following Secretary-General's call for support", UNICEF press release, 12 June 1985 (PR/10/85).

11 Ralph Henderson, "Expanded immunization", in *The state of the world's children 1984*, Oxford University Press, 1983.

12 Deborah Maine and others, "Report on financial resources for maternal/child health and family planning", WHO, 1985 (MCH/85.4).

12 Deborah Maine and others, "Report on financial resources for maternal/child health and family planning", WHO, 1985 (MCH/85.4).

14 Report of Expanded Programme on Immunization, WHO, prepared for Global Advisory Group meeting, Copenhagen, November 1985, in press.

15 Donald A. Henderson, statement to Subcommittee on International Development Institutions and Finance, Committee on Banking, Finance, and Urban Affairs, United States House of Representatives, 21 March 1984.

16 William H. Foege, statement to Subcommittee on Oversight and Investigation, Committee on Energy and Commerce, United States House of Representatives, 13 March 1985.

17 William H. Foege, statement to Subcommittee on Oversight and Investigation, Committee on Energy and Commerce, United States House of Representatives, 13 March 1985.

Reaching all children
(pages 20 to 36)

1 Roger M. Goodall, "ORS in Haiti", UNICEF internal memorandum, January 1985 (NEDP/RMG/451).

2 Alfred Sommer, Joanne Katz and Ignatius Tarwotjo, "Increased risk of respiratory disease and diarrhea in children with preexisting mild vitamin A deficiency", *American Journal of Clinical Nutrition*, vol. 40, November 1984.

3 Alfred Sommer, Joanne Katz and Ignatius Tarwotjo, "Increased risk of respiratory disease and diarrhea in children with preexisting mild vitamin A deficiency", *American Journal of Clinical Nutrition*, vol. 40, November 1984.

4 Alfred Sommer, "Vitamin A deficiency and child survival", paper prepared for UNICEF, February 1985.

5 John H. Costello, statement to Select Committee on Hunger, United States House of Representatives, May 1985.

6 Gerson da Cunha, "Telling the mothers: 'you can breastfeed'", *UNICEF News*, no. 114, 1982. See also "The national breastfeeding programme, Brazil", UNICEF (Brasilia), April 1982 (8203).

7 Juan Aguilar, "CSDR actions in the Americas 1984", UNICEF (Bogota), December 1984.

8 B.N. Tandon and others, "Management of severely malnourished children by village workers in Integrated Child Development Services in India", *Journal of Tropical Pediatrics*, vol. 30, October 1984.

9 "Country programme profile: India", UNICEF, March 1985 (E/ICEF/1985/CRP-22).

10 "Country programme profile: India", UNICEF, March 1985 (E/ICEF/1985/CRP-22).

11 "Mass communications", in *India: a reference manual, 1983*, Ministry of Information and Broadcasting, Government of India, 1983.

12 Jon Eliot Rohde and Tonny Sadjimin, "Elementary-school pupils as health educators: role of school health programmes in primary health-care", *Lancet*, 21 June 1980.

13 "Programme development in the East Asia and Pakistan region and China", UNICEF, February 1985 (E/ICEF/1985/8).

14 *Child Alive*, League of Red Cross and Red Crescent Societies, no. 1, November 1984.

15 John H. Costello, statement to Select Committee on Hunger, United States House of Representatives, May 1985.

16 John H. Costello, statement to Select Committee on Hunger, United States House of Representatives, May 1985.

17 "*People* report on primary health care", *People*, 1983.

18 Michael V.d. Bogaert, "Primary health care as rural communication", *Assignment Children*, vol. 63/64, 1983.

19 Virat Dumrongphol and Dera Sumitra, "Self-reliant health care: options for health development", UNICEF (Bangkok), 1985.

20 "Traditional midwives and family planning", *Population Reports*, series J, no. 22, May 1980.

The benefits for women
(pages 37 to 48)

1 *The state of food and agriculture*, FAO, 1983.

2 "Third World women at work", *Children in the Tropics*, no. 146, 1983.

3 E. Royston, "The prevalence of nutritional anaemia in women in developing countries: a critical review of available information", *World Health Statistics Quarterly*, vol. 35, no. 2, 1982.

4 "Third World women at work", *Children in the Tropics*, no. 146, 1983.

5 Kusum P. Shah, "Maternal nutrition in deprived populations", *Assignment Children*, vol. 55/56, 1981.

6 C. Gopalan, "Maternal nutrition: the foundation of child health", *Future*, vol. 13, winter 1984-1985.

7 Kusum P. Shah, "Maternal nutrition in deprived populations", *Assignment Children*, vol. 55/56, 1981. See also Robert Chambers and others (eds.), *Seasonal dimensions to rural poverty*, Allanheld, 1981.

8 *The school education of girls*, UNESCO, 1980.

9 Ted Greiner, Stina Almroth and Michael C. Latham, "The economic value of breast-feeding", Cornell international nutrition monographs, no. 6, 1979. See also "Breast-feeding , fertility and family planning", *Population Reports*, series J, no. 24, November-December 1981.

10 Kimberly K. Lillig and Carolyn J. Lackey, "Economic and social factors influencing women's infant feeding decisions in a rural Mexican community", *Journal of Tropical Pediatrics*, vol. 28, October 1982.

11 Margaret Cameron and Yngve Hofvander, *Manual on feeding infants and young children*, third edition, Oxford University Press, 1983.

12 "Breast-feeding , fertility and family planning", *Population Reports*, series J, no. 24, November-December 1981.

13 Ronald L. Kleinman and Pramilla Senanayake (eds.), *Breast feeding, fertility and contraception*, International Planned Parenthood Federation, 1984. See also "Breast-feeding and fertility regulation: current knowledge and programme policy implications", *Bulletin of the WHO*, vol. 61, no. 3, 1983: and "Breast-feeding , fertility and family planning", *Population Reports*, series J, no. 24, November-December 1981.

14 Ayten Egemen and Munevver Bertan, "A study of oral rehydration therapy by midwives in a rural area near Ankara", *Bulletin of the WHO*, vol. 58, no. 2, 1980. See also Norbert Hirschhorn, "Oral rehydration therapy: the program and the promise", paper prepared for UNICEF conference on child health and survival, Boston, Massachusetts, May 1985.

15 Robert E. Black and others, "Longitudinal studies of infectious diseases and physical growth of children in rural Bangladesh. Part I: patterns of morbidity", *American Journal of Epidemiology*, vol. 115, no. 3, March 1982.

16 G.A. Cornia, "The economic foundations of CSDR", paper prepared for UNICEF, June 1985.

17 "Letter from Honduras: financing health care", *Salubritas*, vol. 8, no. 1, January-March, 1985.

18 "World Fertility Survey: major findings and implications", International Statistical Institute, June 1984.

19 J.C. Caldwell, "Maternal education as a factor in child mortality", *World Health Forum*, vol. 2, no. 1, 1981.

20 "The incidence of low birth weight: a critical review of available information", *World Health Statistics Quarterly*, vol. 33, no. 3, 1980.

21 A. Girija, P. Geervani and G. Nageswara Rao, "Influence of dietary supplementation during lactation on lactation performance", *Journal of Tropical Pediatrics*, vol. 30, June 1984. See also Joe D. Wray, "Supplementary feeding of pregnant and lactating women", paper prepared for FAO, 1983.

22 Kusum P. Shah, "Maternal nutrition in deprived populations", *Assignment Children*, vol. 55/56, 1981. See also Robert Chambers and others (eds.), *Seasonal dimensions to rural poverty*, Allanheld, 1981.

23 Fred Sai, "Nutrition: the crucial links", in "*People* report on primary health care", *People*, 1983.

24 *The state of food and agriculture*, FAO, 1983.

25 "Women, food and nutrition in Africa: economic change and the outlook for nutrition", *Food and Nutrition*, vol. 10, no. 1, 1984.

26 Carol Carp, "Women and development", *Mothers and Children*, vol. 4, no. 1, March-April 1984. See also "Women's economic activities: their role in the improvement of nutrition and health", paper prepared for UNICEF/WHO Joint Nutrition Support Programme, December 1983.

27 "Programme development in the East Asia and Pakistan region and China", UNICEF, February 1985 (E/ICEF/1985/8).

28 *The state of food and agriculture*, FAO, 1983.

29 Ebun O. Ekunwe, "Expanding immunization coverage through improved clinic procedures", *World Health Forum*, vol. 5, 1984.

30 *The school education of girls*, UNESCO, 1980.

31 "Third World women at work", *Children in the Tropics*, no. 146, 1983.

32 Amartya Sen, "Food battles: conflicts in the access to food", *Food and Nutrition*, vol. 10, no. 1, 1984.

The self-health potential
(pages 48 to 70)

1 John P. Allegrante, "Potential uses and misuses of education in health promotion and disease prevention", *Teachers College Record*, Columbia University, vol. 86, no. 2, winter 1984.

2 "Report of the International Conference on Primary Health Care, Alma Ata, USSR, 6-12 September 1978", reproduced in "UNICEF/WHO joint study on primary health care", UNICEF, January 1979 (E/ICEF/L.1387).

3 "New approaches to health education in primary health care", WHO, technical reports, no. 690, 1983.

4 Spencer Rich, "Medical strides could frustrate cost control", *Washington Post*, 25 June 1984.

5 John P. Allegrante, "Potential uses and misuses of education in health promotion and disease prevention", *Teachers College Record*, Columbia University, vol. 86, no. 2, winter 1984.

6 Jurg H. Sommer, "Health care costs out of control: the experience of Switzerland", *World Health Forum*, vol. 6, 1985.

7 Stanley Brezenoff, "High infant-mortality rate in US requires national action", *New York Times*, 16 April 1985.

8 "Business is bullish on wellness", *Executive Fitness*, vol. 14, no. 24, November 1983.

9 "Business is bullish on wellness", *Executive Fitness*, vol. 14, no. 24, November 1983.

10 "Food and fitness", *School Food Service Journal*, March 1985.

11 Edward H. Kass, "Maternal infection and fetal growth retardation", paper prepared for UNICEF conference on child health and survival, Boston, Massachusetts, May 1985.

12 George F. Gitlitz, "Drop cigarette advertising", *New York Times*, 11 May 1985.

13 John P. Allegrante, "Potential uses and misuses of education in health promotion and disease prevention", *Teachers College Record*, Columbia University, vol. 86, no. 2, winter 1984.

14 "Healthier mothers and children through family planning", *Population Reports*, series J, no. 27, May-June 1984.

15 "The incidence of low birth weight: a critical review of available information", *World Health Statistics Quarterly*, vol. 33, no. 3, 1980. See also Kusum P. Shah, "Maternal nutrition in deprived populations", *Assignment Children*, vol. 55/56, 1981.

16 Aaron Lechtig and others, "Effects of maternal nutrition on infant health: implications for action", *Journal of Tropical Pediatrics*, vol. 28, December 1982.

17 Report of Expanded Programme on Immunization, WHO, prepared for Global Advisory Group meeting, Copenhagen, November 1985, in press.

18 "Maternal care for the reduction of perinatal and neonatal mortality" UNICEF-WHO Joint Committee on Health Policy, January 1985 (JC25/UNICEF-WHO/85.6(c)).

19 "Breast milk prevents disease", *Glimpse*, vol. 6, no. 2, March-April 1984.

20 Clifford B. David and Patricia Hallett David, ''Bottle-feeding and malnutrition in a developing country: the 'bottle-starved' baby'', *Journal of Tropical Pediatrics*, vol. 30, June 1984.

21 ''Breast-feeding, fertility and family planning'', *Population Reports*, series J, no. 24, November-December 1981. See also Joe D. Wray, ''Maternal nutrition, breast-feeding and infant survival'', in W. Henry Mosley (ed.), *Nutrition and human reproduction*, Plenum Press, 1978: and N. R. Clavano, ''Mode of feeding and its effect on infant mortality and morbidity'', *Journal of Tropical Pediatrics*, vol. 28, December 1982.

22 James E. Austin and others, *Nutrition intervention in developing countries: an overview*, Oelgeschlager, Gunn and Hain, 1981.

23 David Morley and Margaret Woodland, *See how they grow: monitoring child growth for appropriate health care in developing countries*, Macmillan, 1979.

24 Jon E Rohde, ''Growth monitoring'', *World Health*, October 1984.

25 Kusum P. Shah, ''Food supplements'', in *The state of the world's children 1984*, Oxford University Press, 1983: and David P. Haxton, UNICEF internal memorandum, April 1985 (185/85).

26 C. Dearden, P. Harman and D.C. Morley, ''Eating more fats and oils as a step towards overcoming malnutrition'', *Tropical Doctor*, Vol. 10, 1980.

27 Lukas Hendrata, Marcia Griffiths and Ellen Piwoz, ''Building a growth movement: a review of community-based growth monitoring in Indonesia'', paper prepared for UNICEF, March 1985.

28 Leonardo Mata, ''The evolution of diarrhoeal diseases and malnutrition in Costa Rica: the role of interventions'', *Assignment Children*, vol. 61/62, 1983.

29 Jon E. Rohde and Lukas Hendrata, ''Development from below: transformation from village-based nutrition projects to a national family nutrition programme in Indonesia'', in David Morley, Jon Rohde and Glen Williams (eds.), *Practising health for all*, Oxford University Press, 1983.

30 Norbert Hirschhorn, ''Oral rehydration therapy: the program and the promise'', paper prepared for UNICEF conference on child health and survival, Boston, Massachusetts, May 1985.

31 Hossein Ghassemi, ''Child growth and growth monitoring: a strategy for promotion and acceleration'', paper prepared for UNICEF/WHO Joint Committee on Health Policy, January 1985.

32 J. Briscoe, ''The quantitative effect of infection on the use of food by young children in poor countries'', *The American Journal of Clinical Nutrition*, 32: 648-676, 1979.

33 Gerald Keusch and others, ''Is there synergy among the interventions in the GOBI-FFF program?'', paper prepared for UNICEF conference on child health and survival, Boston, Massachusetts, May 1985.

34 Richard Feachem, ''Water, excreta, behaviour and diarrhoea'', *Diarrhoea Dialogue*, no. 4, February 1981.

35 W.A.M. Cutting, ''Oral rehydration in acute diarrhoea'', *Pharmaceutical Journal*, 26 June 1982.

36 *The management of diarrhoea and use of oral rehydration therapy: a joint WHO/UNICEF statement*, WHO, 1983.

37 Timothy J. Dondero, Jr., ''Impact of vaccine preventable diseases in developing countries'', paper prepared for conference of American Public Health Association, Dallas, Texas, November 1983.

38 Timothy J. Dondero, Jr., ''Impact of vaccine preventable diseases in developing countries'', paper prepared for conference of American Public Health Association, Dallas, November 1983.

39 A. Bulla and K.L. Hitze, ''Acute respiratory infections: a review'', *Bulletin of the WHO*, vol. 56, no. 3, 1978.

40 A. Pio, J. Leowski and H.G. ten Dam, ''The problem of acute respiratory infections in children in developing countries'', WHO, 1983 (WHO/RSD/83.11).

41 *Acute respiratory infections in children*, Pan American Health Organization, 1983 (RD/21/3).

42 A.M. Masse-Raimbault, ''How to feed young children'', *Children in the Tropics*, no. 138-139-140, 1982.

43 *Acute respiratory infections in children*, Pan American Health Organization, 1983 (RD/21/3).

44 ''Basic principles for control of acute respiratory infections in children in developing countries'', UNICEF-WHO Joint Committee on Health Policy, January 1985 (JC25/UNICEF-WHO/85.6(a)/Rev.1).

45 Arnfried A. Kielmann and others, *Child and maternal health services in rural India: the Narangwal experiment. Volume 1: integrated nutrition and health care*, Johns Hopkins University Press, 1983.

46 Arnfried A. Kielmann and others, *Child and maternal health services in rural India: the Narangwal experiment. Volume 1: integrated nutrition and health care*, Johns Hopkins University Press, 1983.

47 ''Basic principles for the control of malaria and general guidelines for UNICEF/WHO support'', UNICEF-WHO Joint Committee on Health Policy, January 1985 (JC25/UNICEF-WHO/85.6(b)).

48 ''Basic principles for the control of malaria and general guidelines for UNICEF/WHO support'', UNICEF-WHO Joint Committee on Health Policy, January 1985 (JC25/UNICEF-WHO/85.6(b)).

49 Jon E. Rohde, ''Community-based nutrition programs'', Management Sciences for Health, July 1982.

50 ''Malaria chemoprophylaxis: problems associated with the chemoprophylaxis of malaria in travellers to endemic areas'', *Weekly Epidemiological Record*, vol. 60, no. 24, 14 June 1985.

Children and world development
(pages 70 to 79)

1 ''Monitoring and action for optimal physical growth and psychosocial development'', paper prepared for UNICEF meeting on growth monitoring, April 1985.

2 Marian Zeitlin, Mohammed Mansour and Meera Boghani, ''State of the art paper on positive deviance in nutrition'', paper prepared for UNICEF, 1985.

3 Theodore W. Schultz, *Investing in people: the economics of population quality*, University of California Press, 1981.

4 World Bank, *World development report 1980*, Oxford University Press, 1980.

5 World Bank, *World development report 1980*, Oxford University Press, 1980.

6 Hans Singer, ''Economic investment in children'', paper prepared for UNICEF conference on media and children, Oxford, England, January 1985.

7 ''Action on sub-Sahara: statement of the Committee for Development Planning at the conclusion of its twenty-first session'', United Nations Committee for Development Planning, Geneva, November 1984.